PHD
PHANTASY DEGREE

Episode IX: The Gate

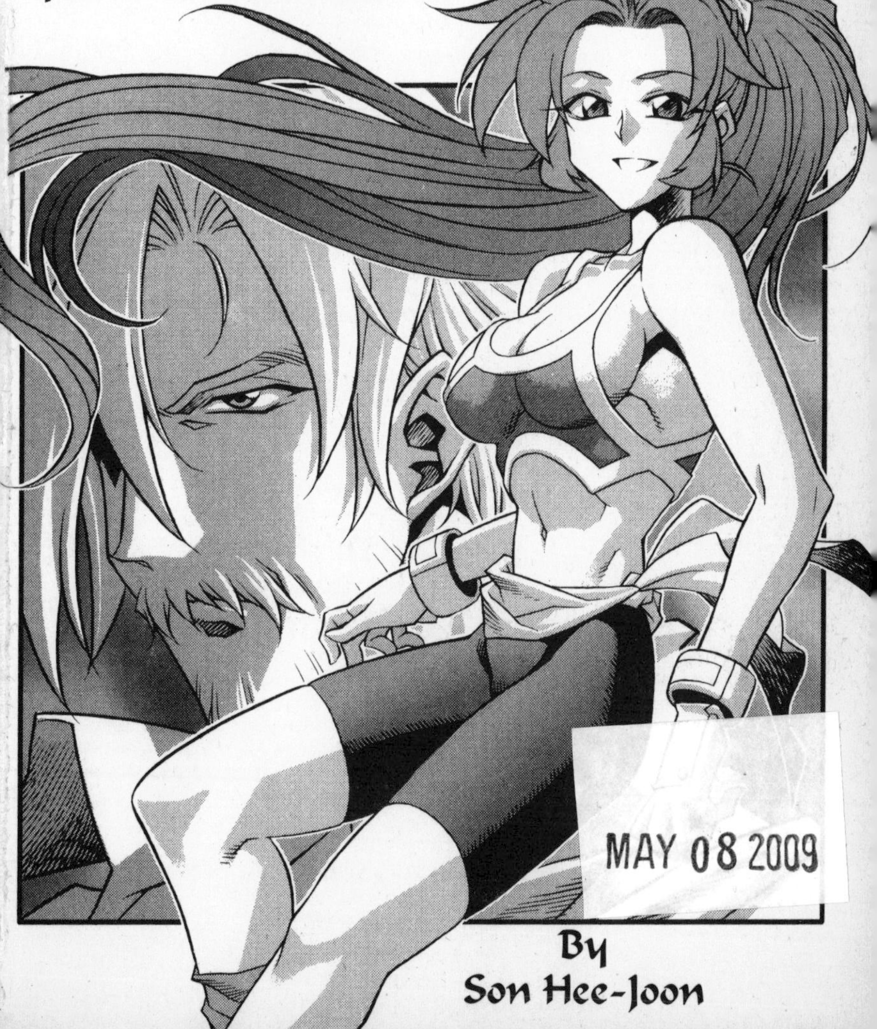

By
Son Hee-Joon

PhD: Phantasy Degree Vol. 9
Created by Son Hee-Joon

Translation - Grace Min
English Adaptation - Aaron Sparrow
Copy Editor - Stephanie Duchin
Retouch and Lettering - Star Print Brokers
Graphic Designer - Christopher Tjalsma

Editor - Hyun Joo Kim
Digital Imaging Manager - Chris Buford
Pre-Production Supervisor - Erika Terriquez
Art Director - Anne Marie Horne
Production Manager - Elisabeth Brizzi
Managing Editor - Vy Nguyen
VP of Production - Ron Klamert
Editor-in-Chief - Rob Tokar
Publisher - Mike Kiley
President and C.O.O. - John Parker
C.E.O. and Chief Creative Officer - Stuart Levy

A  Manga

TOKYOPOP Inc.
5900 Wilshire Blvd. Suite 2000
Los Angeles, CA 90036

E-mail: info@TOKYOPOP.com
Come visit us online at www.TOKYOPOP.com

ISBN: 978-1-59816-855-6

First TOKYOPOP printing: May 2007
10 9 8 7 6 5 4 3 2 1
Printed in the USA

PhD
PHANTASY DEGREE

Volume 9

By
SON HEE-JOON

TOKYOPOP®

HAMBURG // LONDON // LOS ANGELES // TOKYO

Previously in...

PhD

PHANTASY DEGREE

A spunky, ring-wearing girl named Sang searches for the Demon School Hades...and a legendary ring contained within its walls. But before Sang can snatch the ring, a group of humans from the Madosa Guild attack the school! A deadly battle ensues, and Sang fights alongside her new beastly buddy, Dev.

The Guild wants to close the doors to the Mahgae, a "lower-Earth" that is filled with monsters. During the conflict, the power of Sang's rings is revealed: Not only does her jewelry make her stronger, but they can change the gender of their wearer. In Sang's case, when she takes off her rings, she becomes a muscular and powerful man! Holy gender-bender defender! Despite a valiant effort by the denizens of the Demon School, the Madosa Guild seals the Mahgae.

While the survivors of Demon School bury their dead, Sang moves on and bumps into a girl swordmaster named Chun-Lang who also wears a ring much like Sang's. After another day of chaotic battle with yet another of the Madosa member, Sang awakens to shockingly discover that she has a bad case of amnesia! Some kindly elves take her into their home in Elftown and lovingly names her "Limbo" in hopes that she may remember her identity in peaceful surroundings.

But, what would PhD be without its share of bloodshed? The trail of blood continues as the Madosa Guild goes forth on their path of destruction, and they destroy Elftown, along with the Magical Athena Academy. Chun-Lang was training at Athena and she, with other surviving peers, clamor to Master Tower to power up for a showdown with the Guild. Those who are pursuing them, however, are no ordinary members but the top tier of the Madosa Guild called the Order Rank. Despite the new boost in power and their best efforts, Athena's remaining students are decimated and everything rests on Sang's shoulders to save everyone's hides. Chun-Lang and Dev from Hades rejoin the battle against the Order Rank but as Sang discovers her wizard lineage, she remembers everything and then some! She has inner conflicts with her other personalities, but she's not the only one suffering from multiple personality disorder.

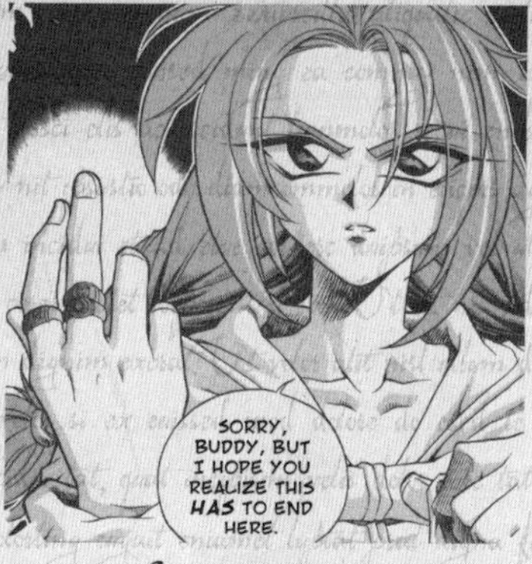
SORRY, BUDDY, BUT I HOPE YOU REALIZE THIS HAS TO END HERE.

Sang as a woman

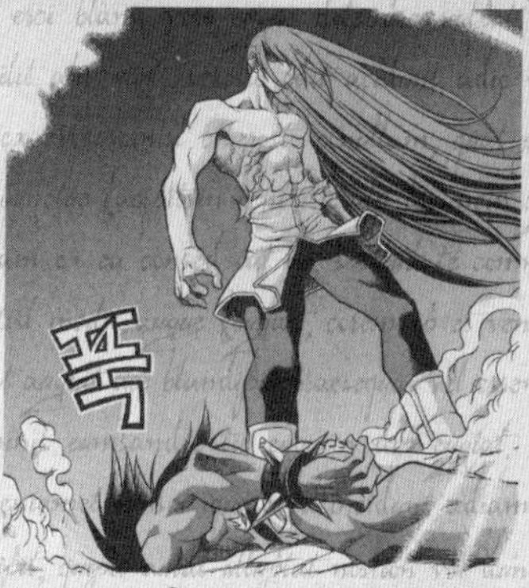

Sang as a man

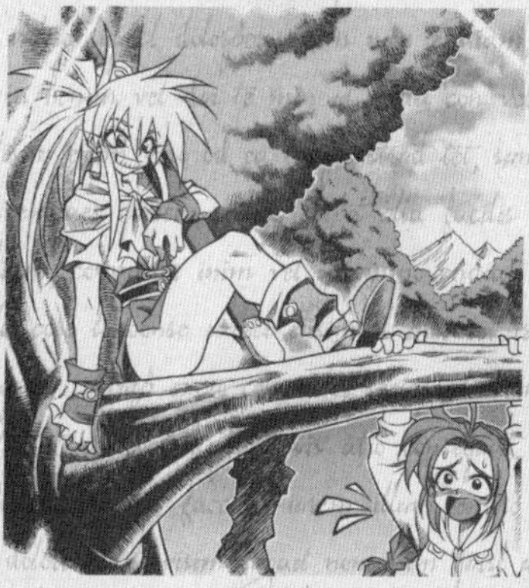

Chun-Lang & Sang

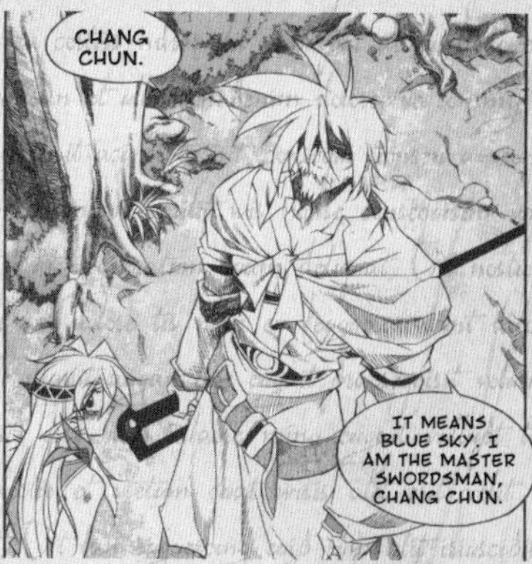
CHANG CHUN.
IT MEANS BLUE SKY. I AM THE MASTER SWORDSMAN, CHANG CHUN.

Chang Chun

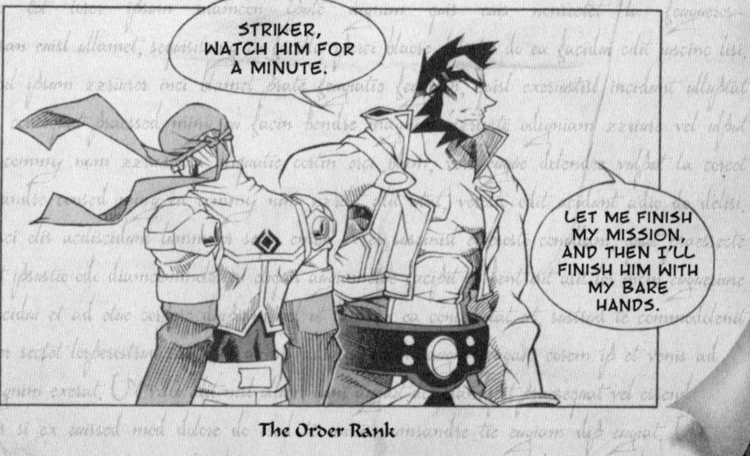
STRIKER, WATCH HIM FOR A MINUTE.
LET ME FINISH MY MISSION, AND THEN I'LL FINISH HIM WITH MY BARE HANDS.

The Order Rank

Table of Contents

The Gate

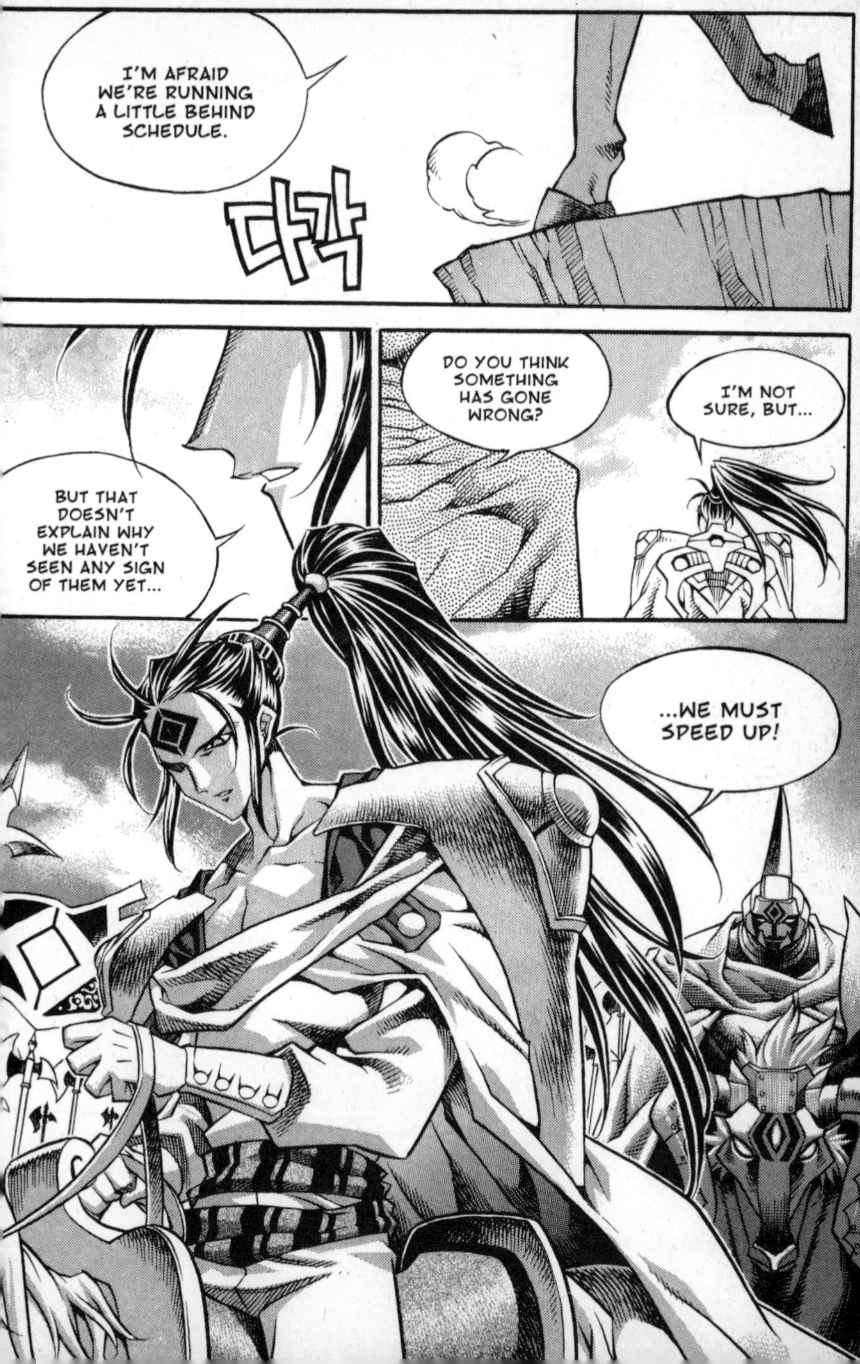
I'M AFRAID WE'RE RUNNING A LITTLE BEHIND SCHEDULE.
다각
DO YOU THINK SOMETHING HAS GONE WRONG?
I'M NOT SURE, BUT...
BUT THAT DOESN'T EXPLAIN WHY WE HAVEN'T SEEN ANY SIGN OF THEM YET...
...WE MUST SPEED UP!

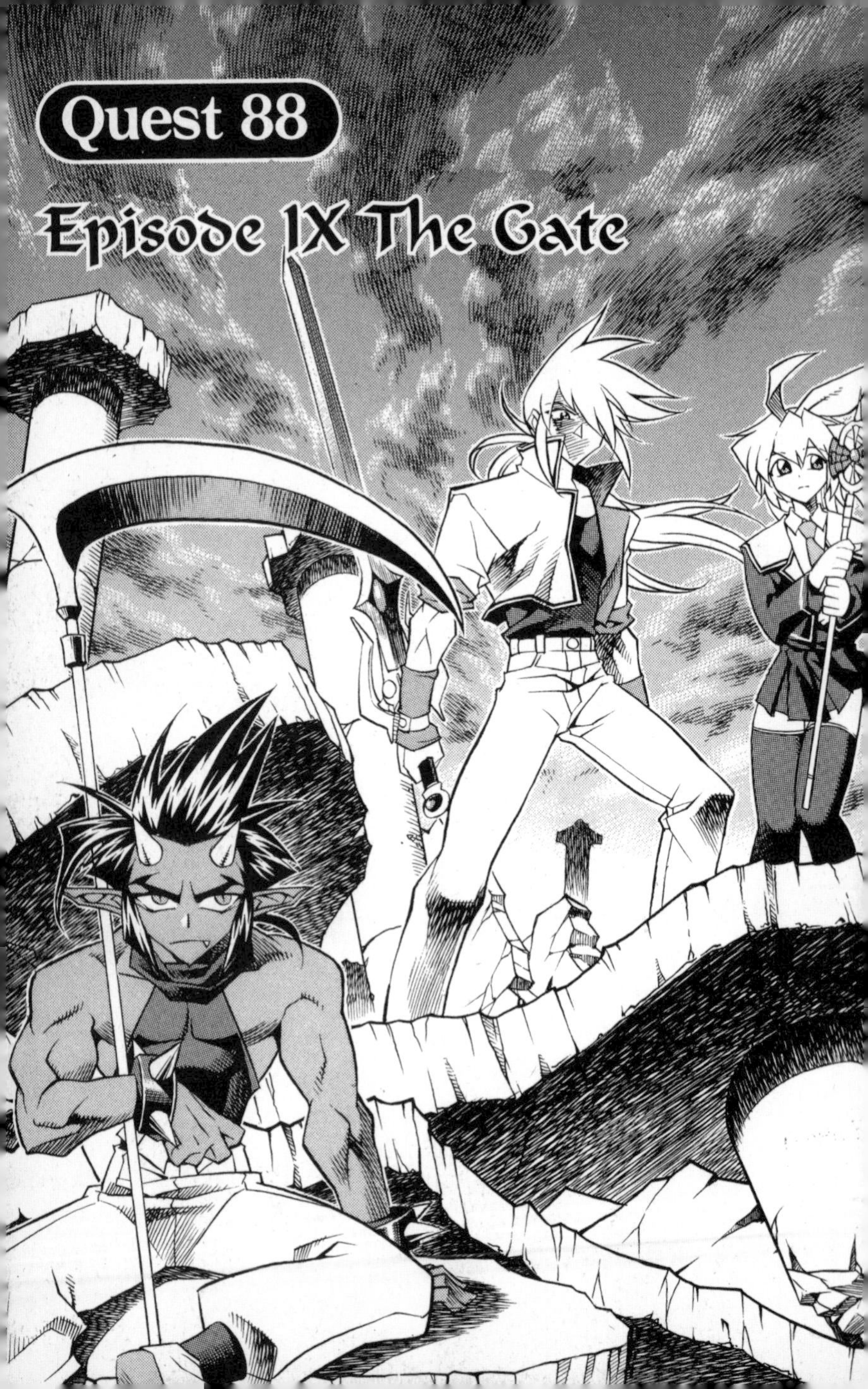
Quest 88
Episode IX The Gate

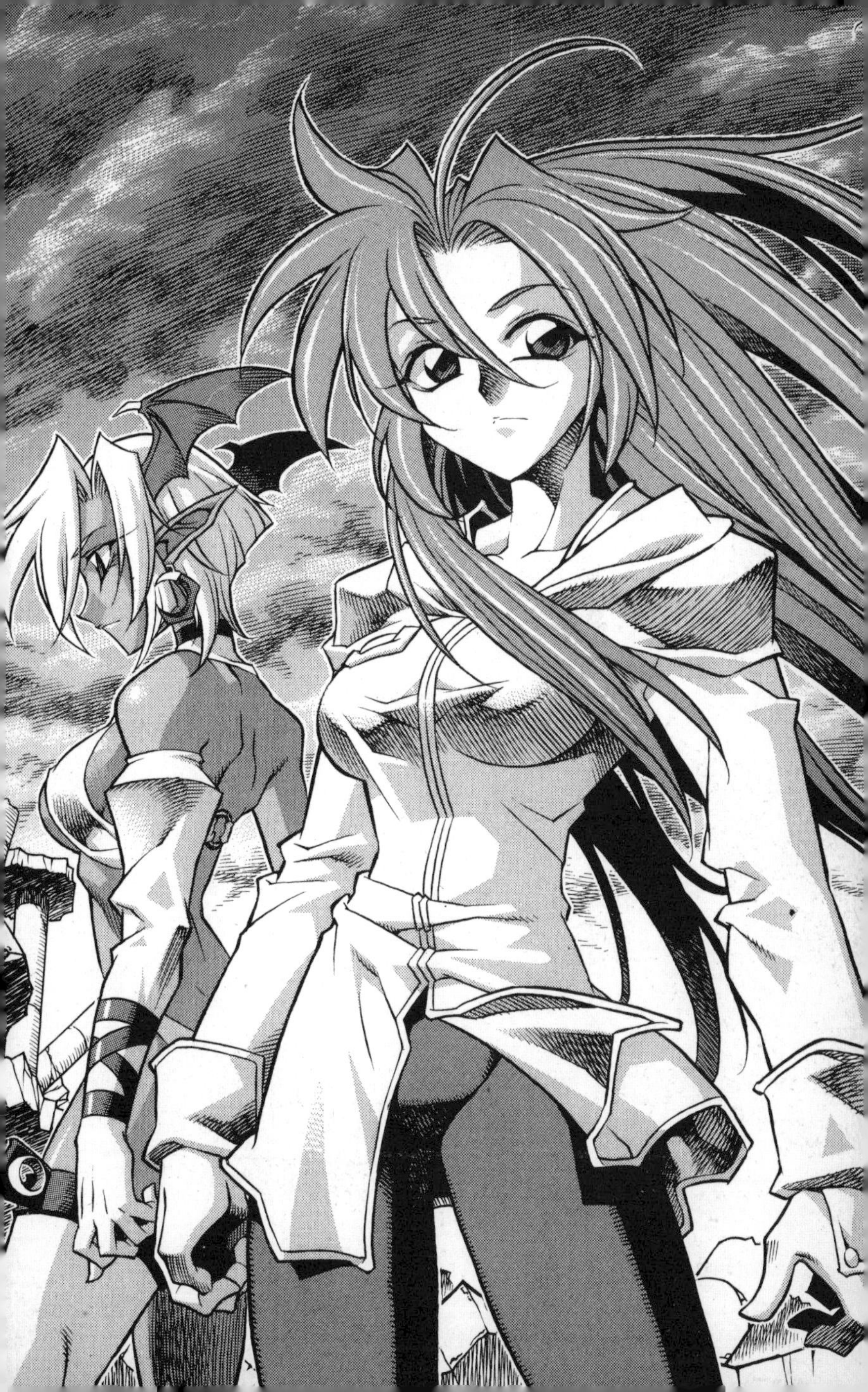

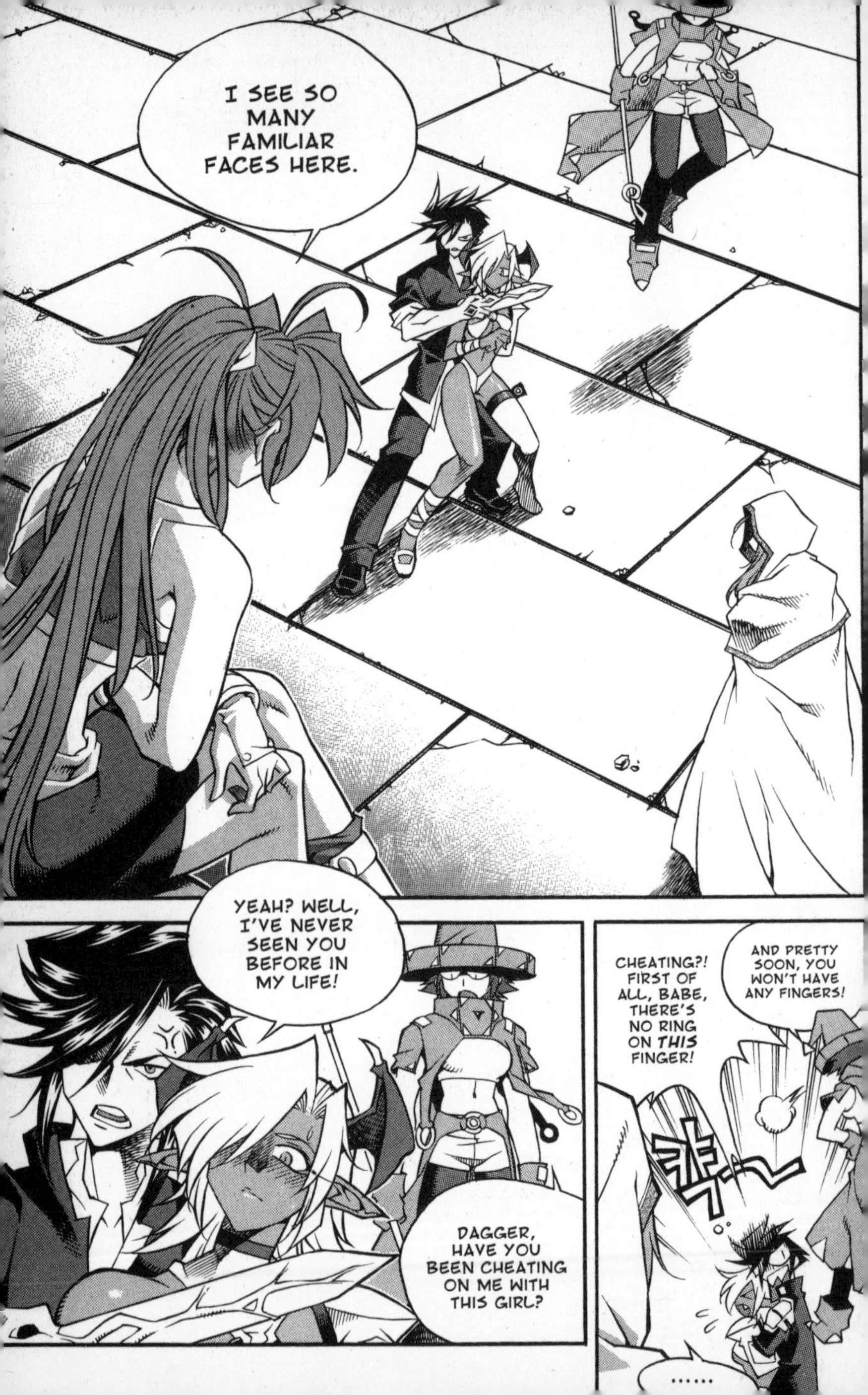
I SEE SO MANY FAMILIAR FACES HERE.
YEAH? WELL, I'VE NEVER SEEN YOU BEFORE IN MY LIFE!
DAGGER, HAVE YOU BEEN CHEATING ON ME WITH THIS GIRL?
CHEATING?! FIRST OF ALL, BABE, THERE'S NO RING ON *THIS* FINGER!
AND PRETTY SOON, YOU WON'T HAVE ANY FINGERS!
......

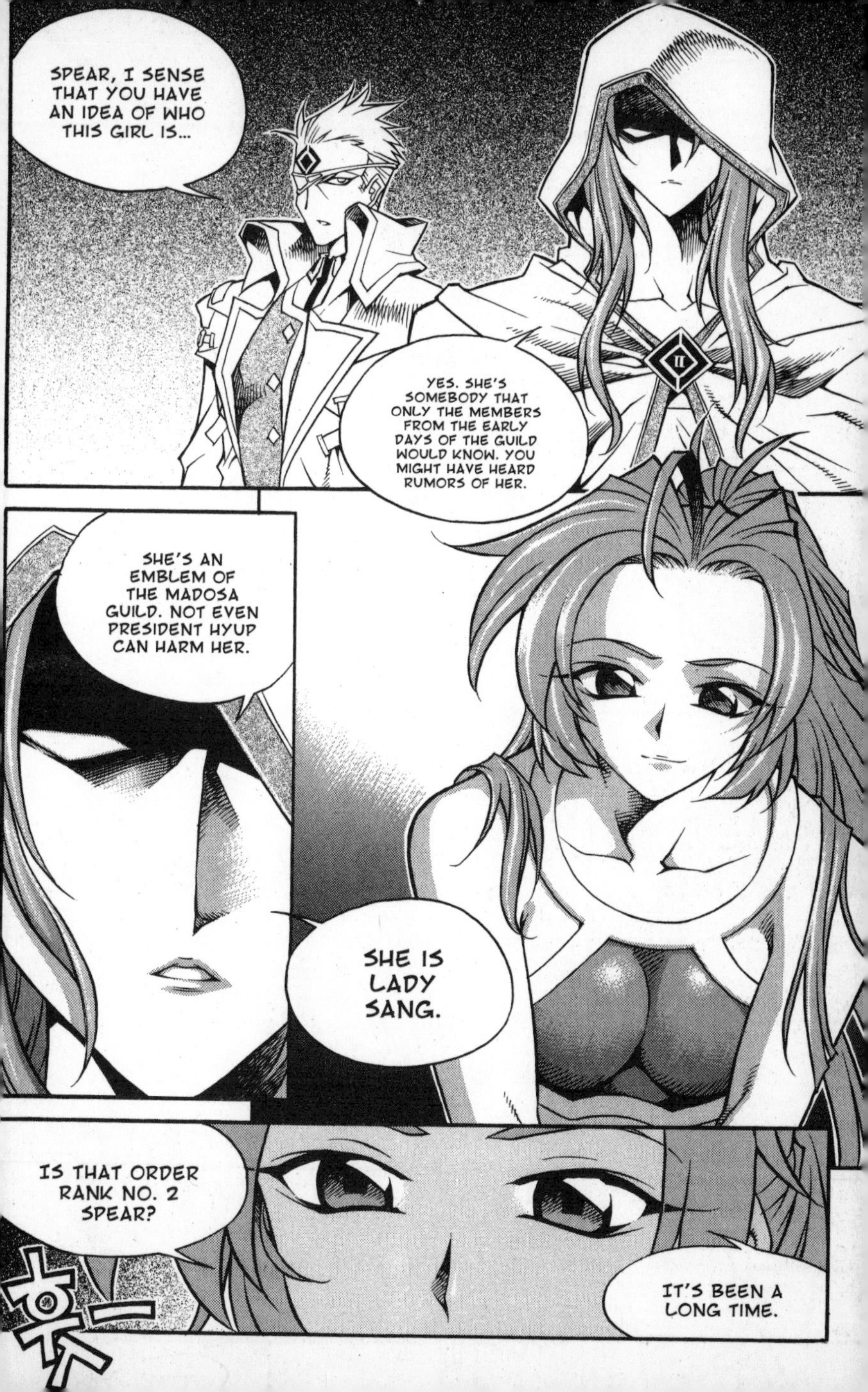
SPEAR, I SENSE THAT YOU HAVE AN IDEA OF WHO THIS GIRL IS...
YES. SHE'S SOMEBODY THAT ONLY THE MEMBERS FROM THE EARLY DAYS OF THE GUILD WOULD KNOW. YOU MIGHT HAVE HEARD RUMORS OF HER.
SHE'S AN EMBLEM OF THE MADOSA GUILD. NOT EVEN PRESIDENT HYUP CAN HARM HER.
SHE IS LADY SANG.
IS THAT ORDER RANK NO. 2 SPEAR?
IT'S BEEN A LONG TIME.

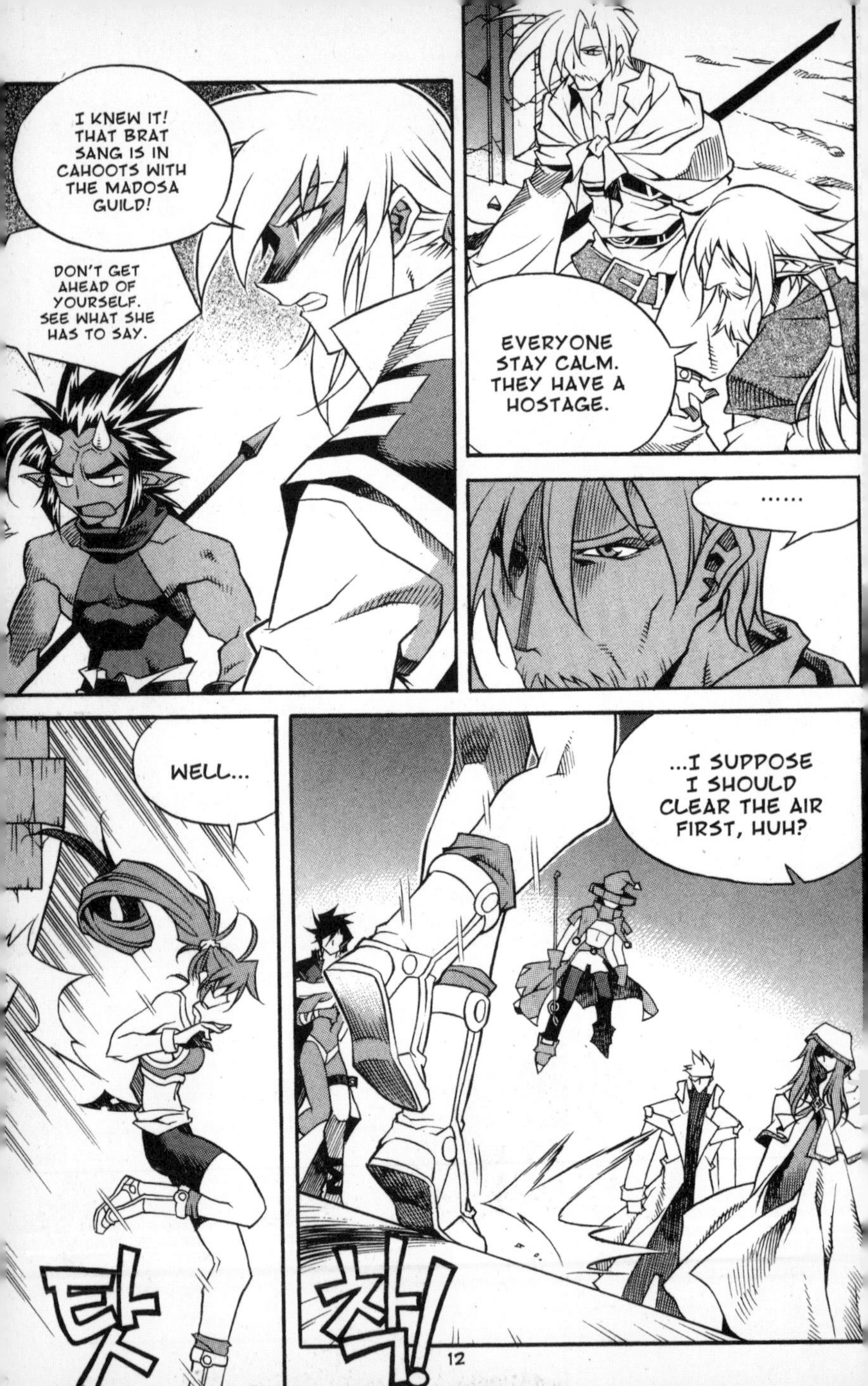
I KNEW IT! THAT BRAT SANG IS IN CAHOOTS WITH THE MADOSA GUILD!
DON'T GET AHEAD OF YOURSELF. SEE WHAT SHE HAS TO SAY.
EVERYONE STAY CALM. THEY HAVE A HOSTAGE.
......
WELL...
...I SUPPOSE I SHOULD CLEAR THE AIR FIRST, HUH?
탓
착!

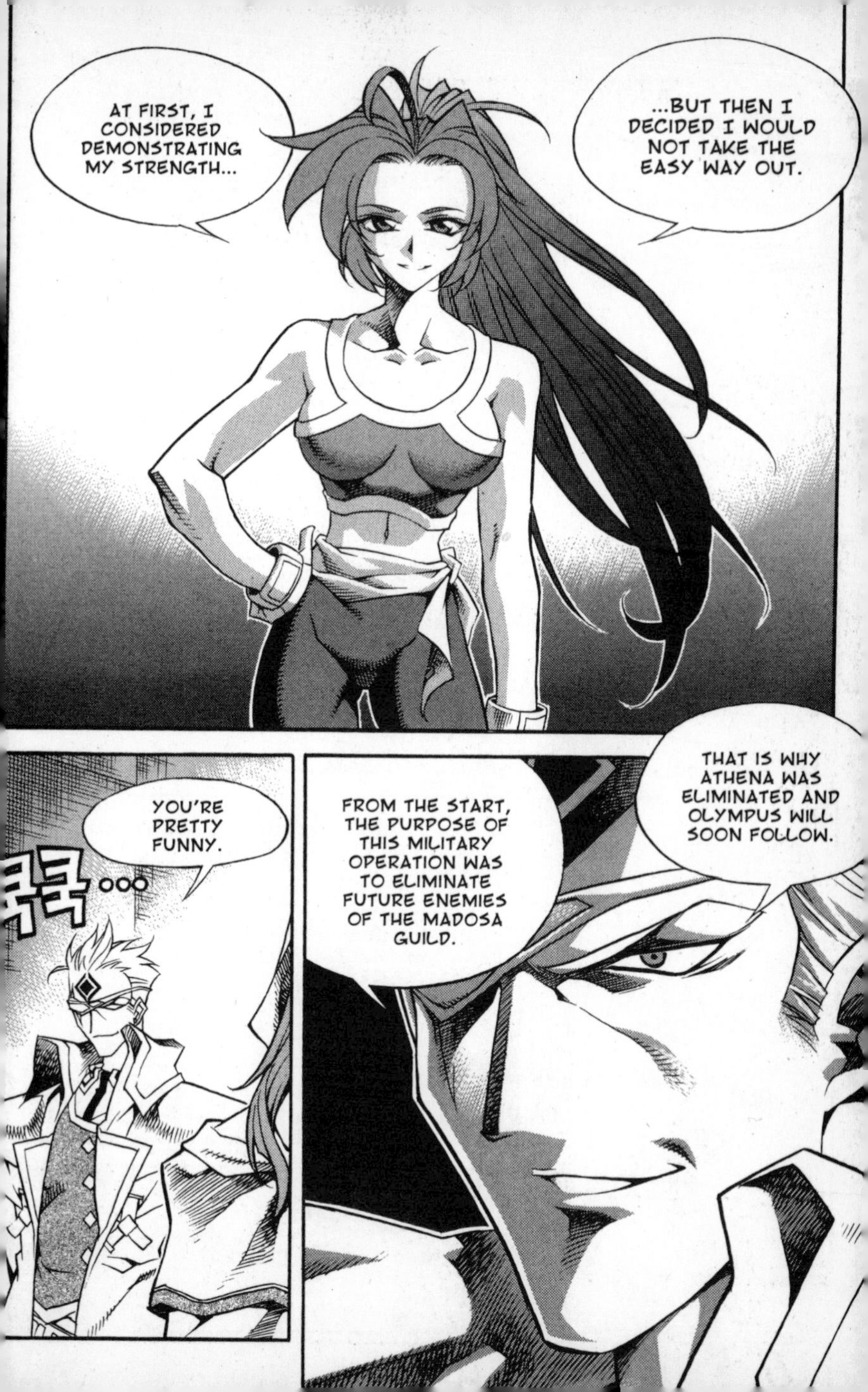
AT FIRST, I CONSIDERED DEMONSTRATING MY STRENGTH...
...BUT THEN I DECIDED I WOULD NOT TAKE THE EASY WAY OUT.
YOU'RE PRETTY FUNNY.
FROM THE START, THE PURPOSE OF THIS MILITARY OPERATION WAS TO ELIMINATE FUTURE ENEMIES OF THE MADOSA GUILD.
THAT IS WHY ATHENA WAS ELIMINATED AND OLYMPUS WILL SOON FOLLOW.

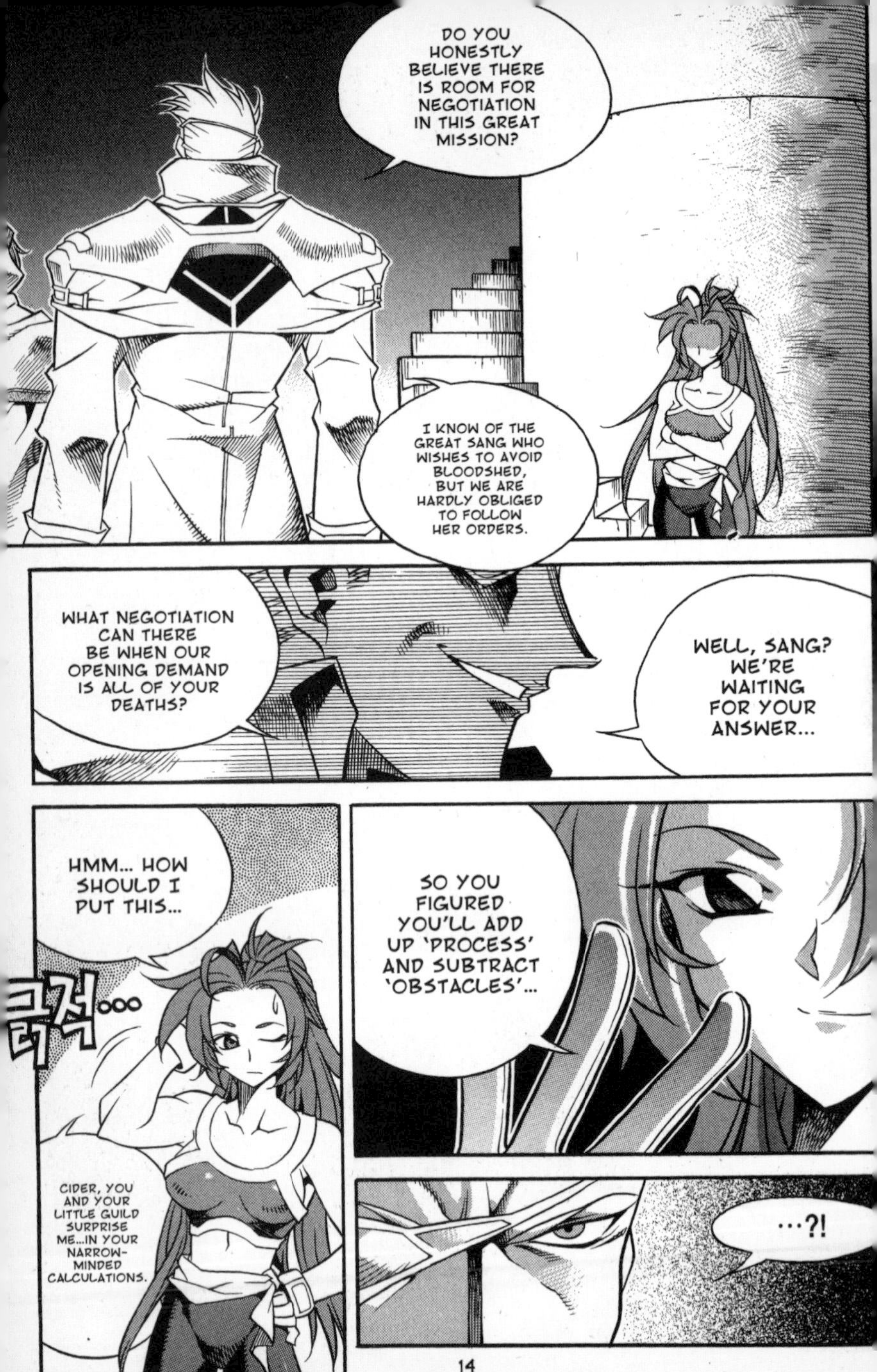
DO YOU HONESTLY BELIEVE THERE IS ROOM FOR NEGOTIATION IN THIS GREAT MISSION?
I KNOW OF THE GREAT SANG WHO WISHES TO AVOID BLOODSHED, BUT WE ARE HARDLY OBLIGED TO FOLLOW HER ORDERS.
WHAT NEGOTIATION CAN THERE BE WHEN OUR OPENING DEMAND IS ALL OF YOUR DEATHS?
WELL, SANG? WE'RE WAITING FOR YOUR ANSWER...
HMM... HOW SHOULD I PUT THIS...
극적...
CIDER, YOU AND YOUR LITTLE GUILD SURPRISE ME...IN YOUR NARROW-MINDED CALCULATIONS.
SO YOU FIGURED YOU'LL ADD UP 'PROCESS' AND SUBTRACT 'OBSTACLES'...
...?!

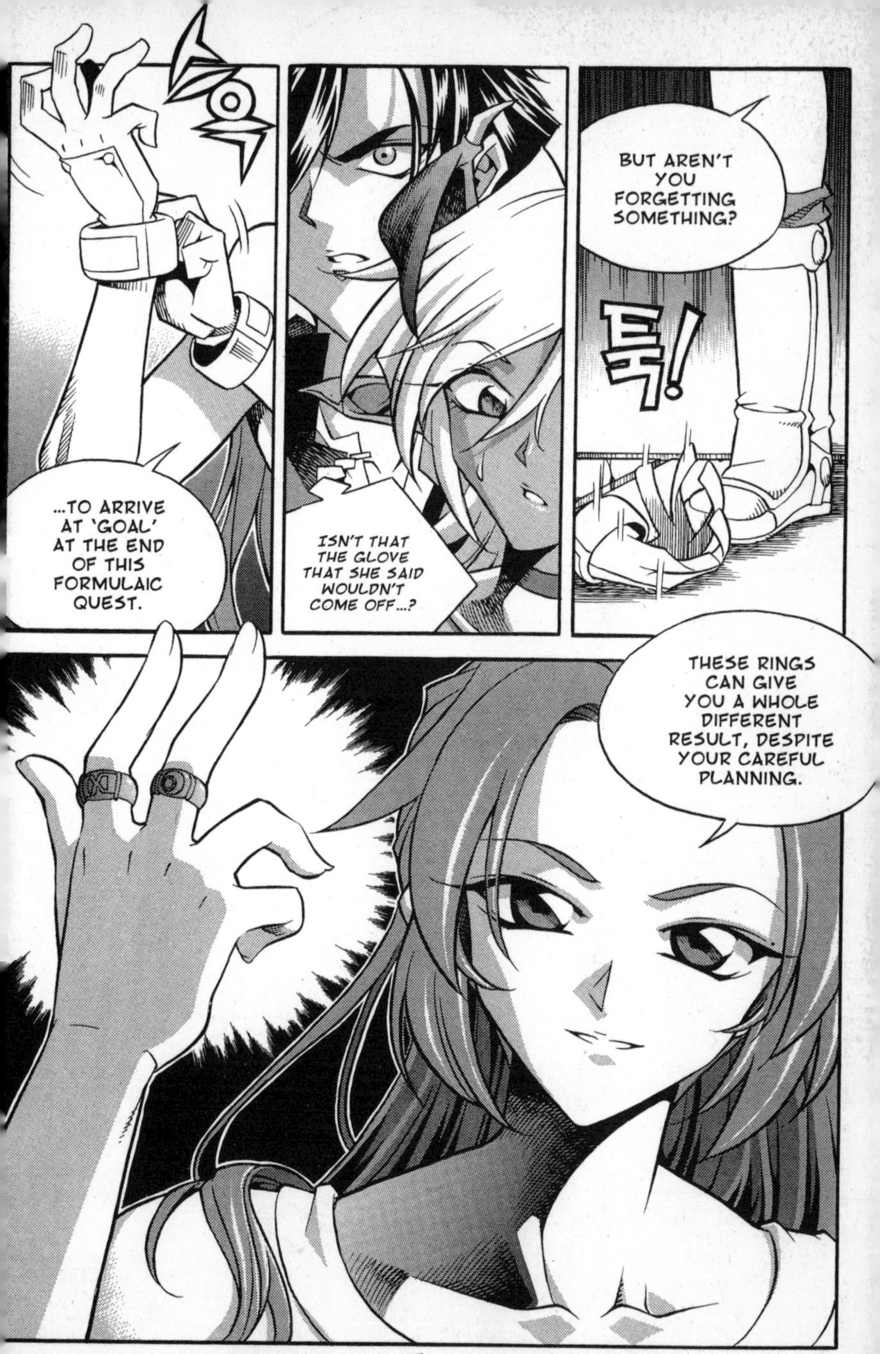
...TO ARRIVE AT 'GOAL' AT THE END OF THIS FORMULAIC QUEST.
ISN'T THAT THE GLOVE THAT SHE SAID WOULDN'T COME OFF...?
BUT AREN'T YOU FORGETTING SOMETHING?
툭!
THESE RINGS CAN GIVE YOU A WHOLE DIFFERENT RESULT, DESPITE YOUR CAREFUL PLANNING.

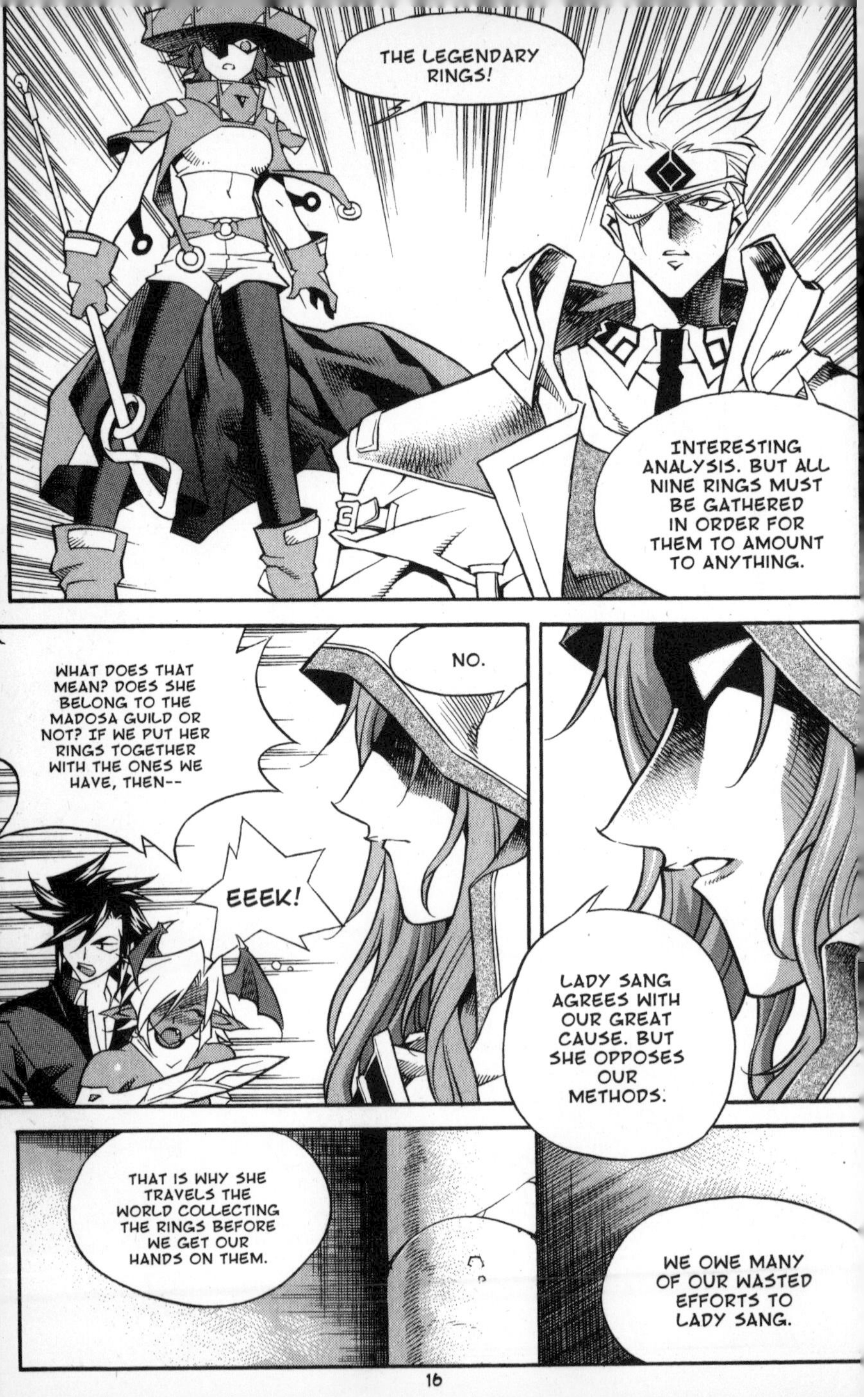
THE LEGENDARY RINGS!
INTERESTING ANALYSIS. BUT ALL NINE RINGS MUST BE GATHERED IN ORDER FOR THEM TO AMOUNT TO ANYTHING.
WHAT DOES THAT MEAN? DOES SHE BELONG TO THE MADOSA GUILD OR NOT? IF WE PUT HER RINGS TOGETHER WITH THE ONES WE HAVE, THEN--
NO.
EEEK!
LADY SANG AGREES WITH OUR GREAT CAUSE. BUT SHE OPPOSES OUR METHODS.
THAT IS WHY SHE TRAVELS THE WORLD COLLECTING THE RINGS BEFORE WE GET OUR HANDS ON THEM.
WE OWE MANY OF OUR WASTED EFFORTS TO LADY SANG.

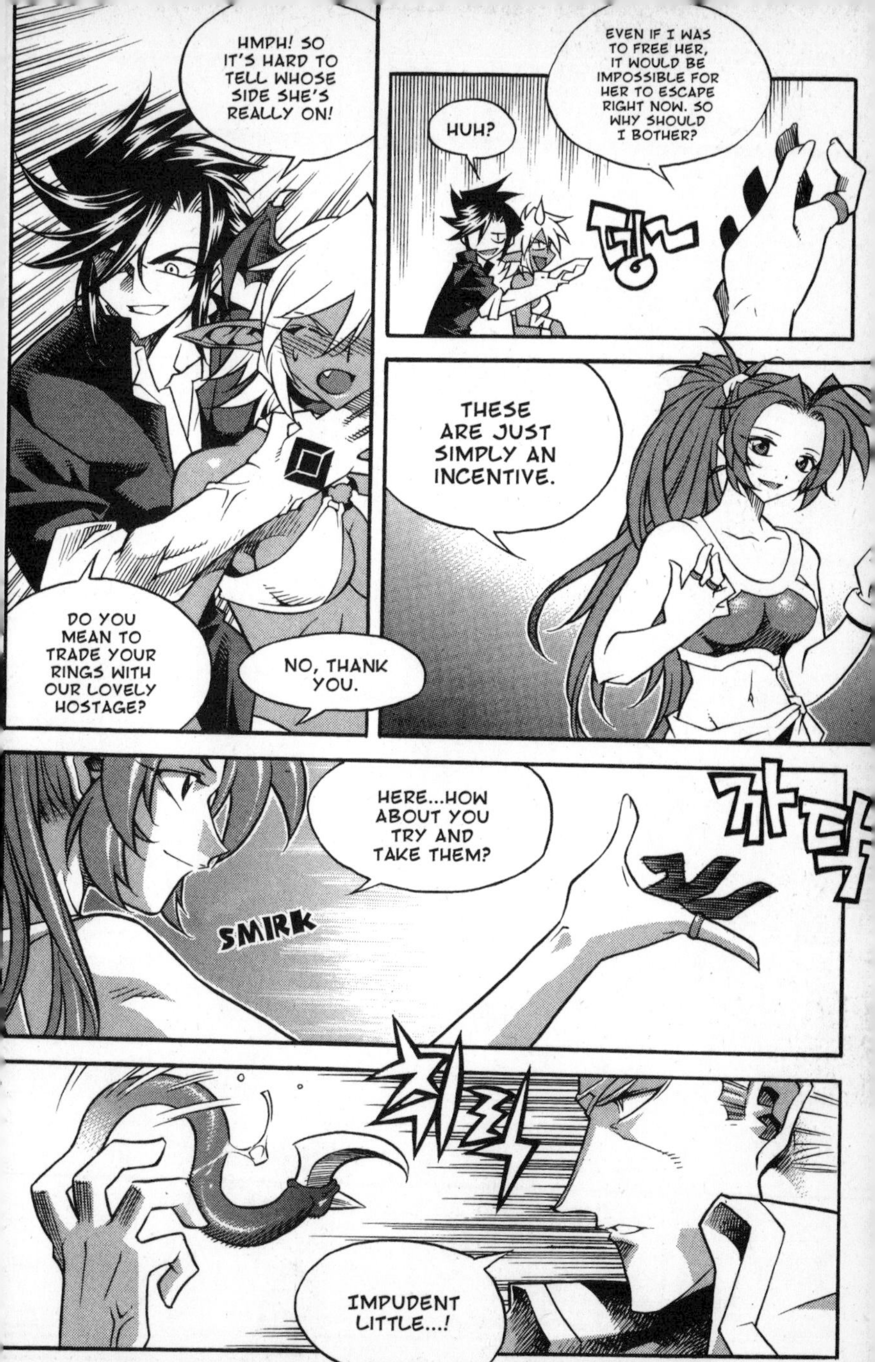
HMPH! SO IT'S HARD TO TELL WHOSE SIDE SHE'S REALLY ON!
DO YOU MEAN TO TRADE YOUR RINGS WITH OUR LOVELY HOSTAGE?
NO, THANK YOU.
EVEN IF I WAS TO FREE HER, IT WOULD BE IMPOSSIBLE FOR HER TO ESCAPE RIGHT NOW. SO WHY SHOULD I BOTHER?
HUH?
THESE ARE JUST SIMPLY AN INCENTIVE.
HERE...HOW ABOUT YOU TRY AND TAKE THEM?
SMIRK
IMPUDENT LITTLE...!

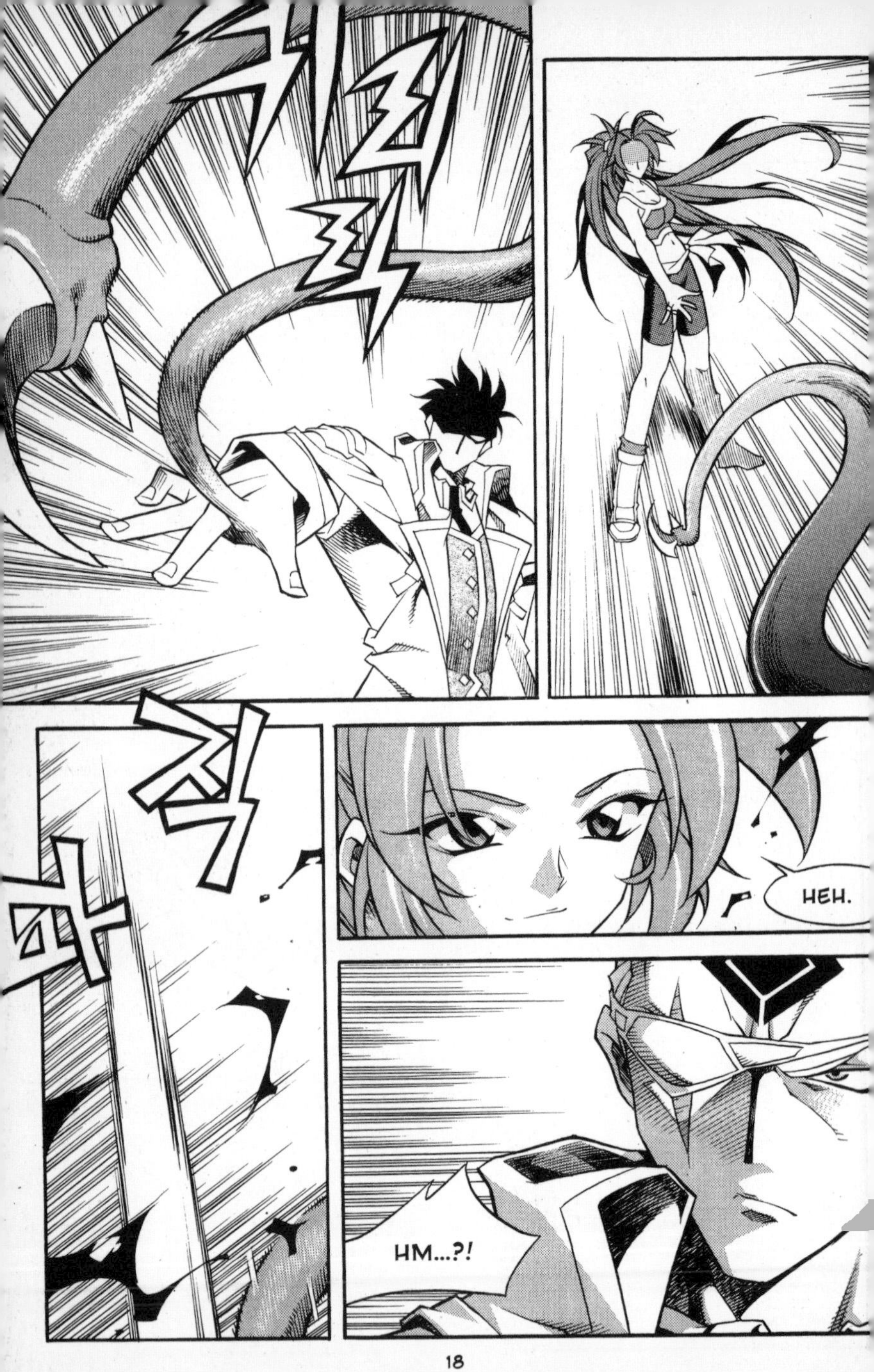
HEH.
HM...?!

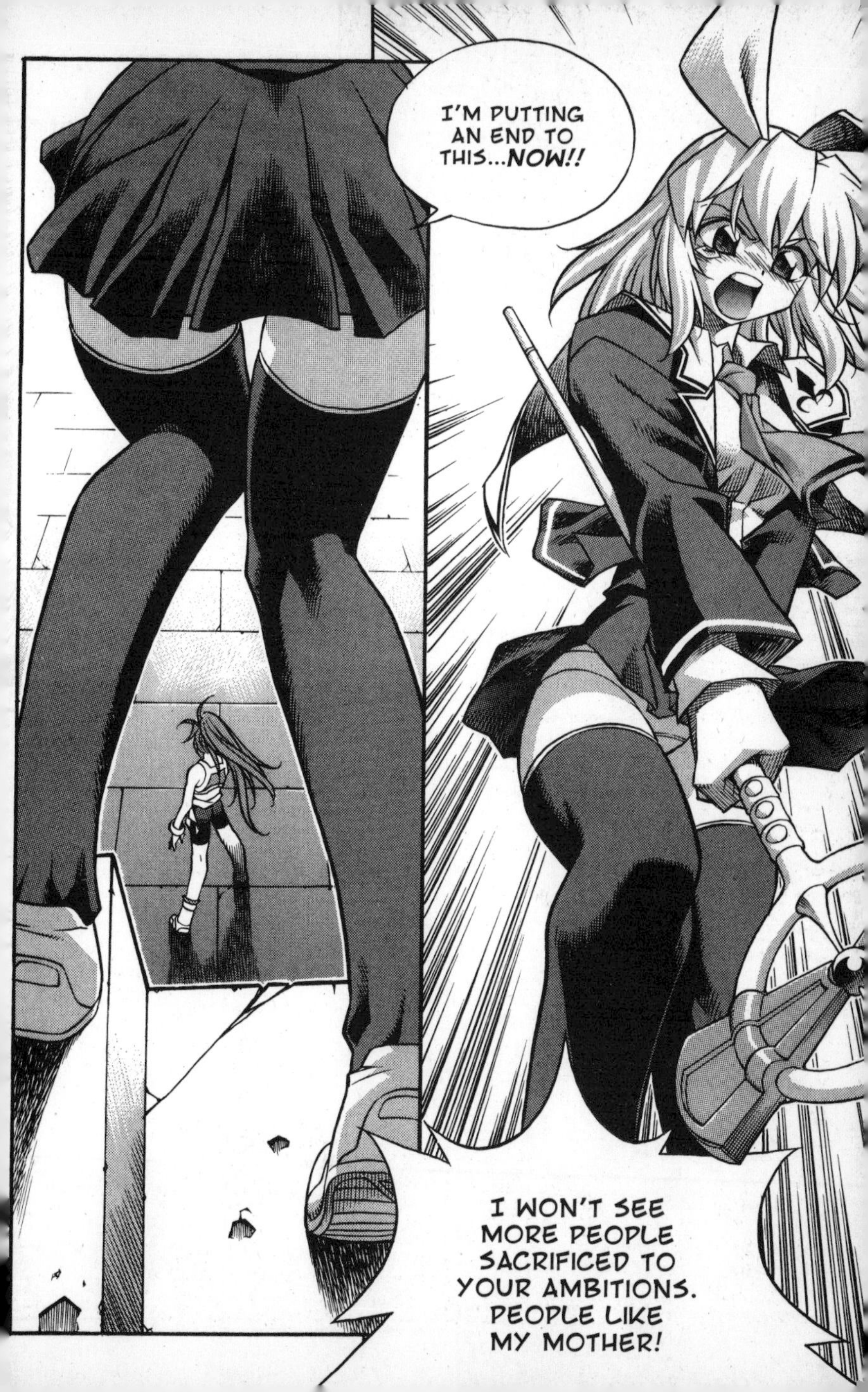
I'M PUTTING AN END TO THIS...NOW!!
I WON'T SEE MORE PEOPLE SACRIFICED TO YOUR AMBITIONS. PEOPLE LIKE MY MOTHER!

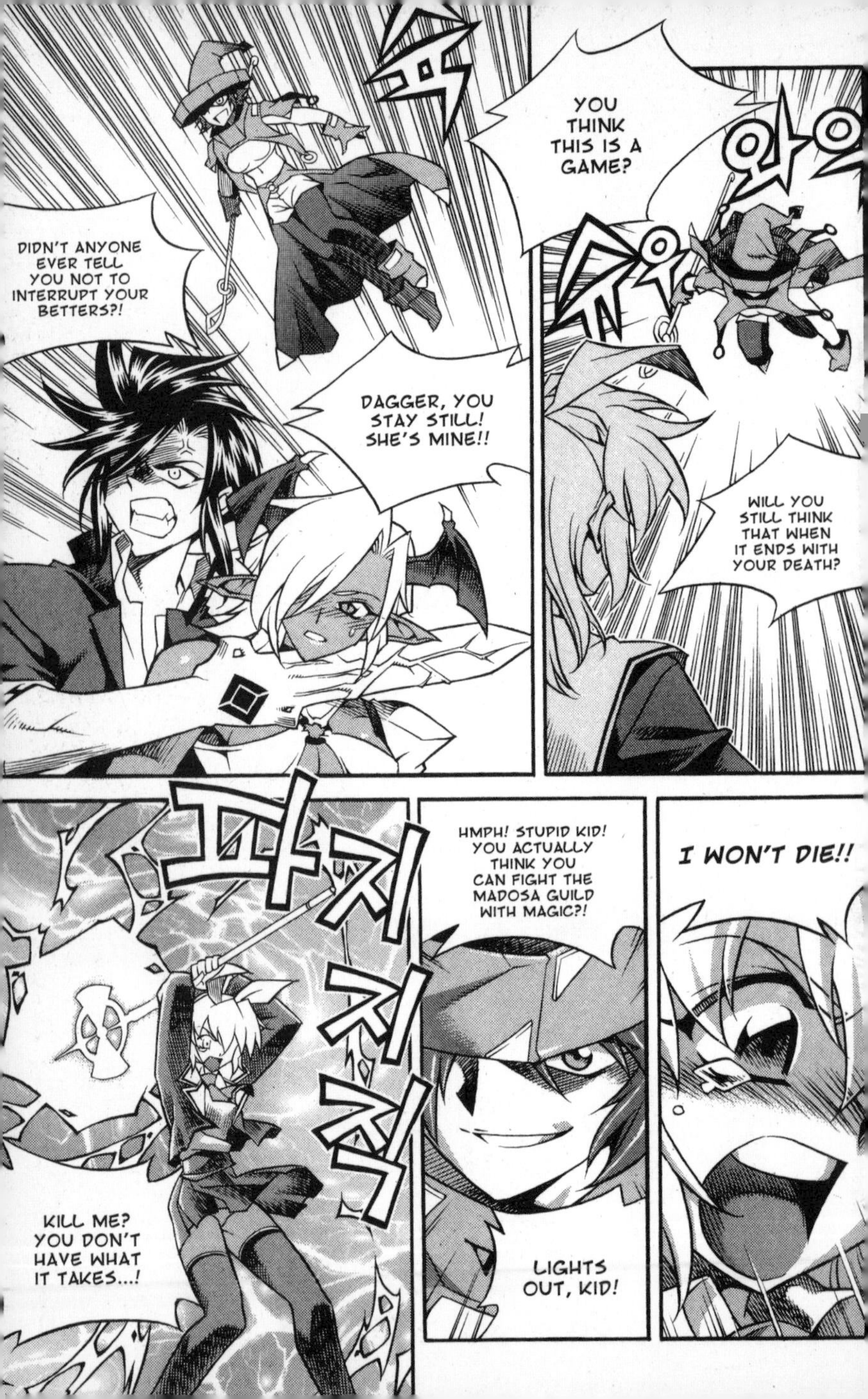
DIDN'T ANYONE EVER TELL YOU NOT TO INTERRUPT YOUR BETTERS?!
DAGGER, YOU STAY STILL! SHE'S MINE!!
YOU THINK THIS IS A GAME?
WILL YOU STILL THINK THAT WHEN IT ENDS WITH YOUR DEATH?
KILL ME? YOU DON'T HAVE WHAT IT TAKES...!
HMPH! STUPID KID! YOU ACTUALLY THINK YOU CAN FIGHT THE MADOSA GUILD WITH MAGIC?!
LIGHTS OUT, KID!
I WON'T DIE!!

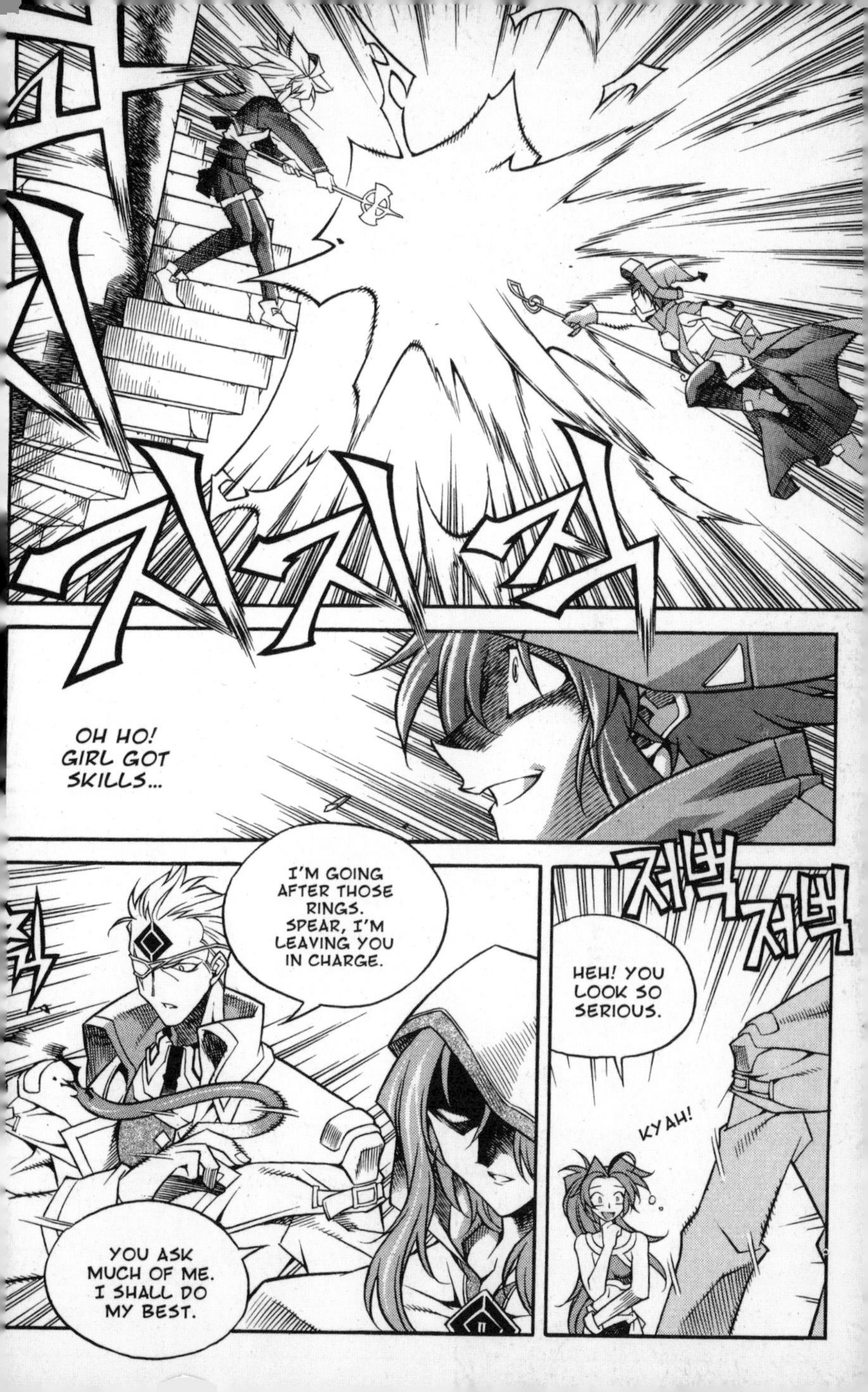

OH HO! GIRL GOT SKILLS...
I'M GOING AFTER THOSE RINGS. SPEAR, I'M LEAVING YOU IN CHARGE.
YOU ASK MUCH OF ME. I SHALL DO MY BEST.
HEH! YOU LOOK SO SERIOUS.
KYAH!

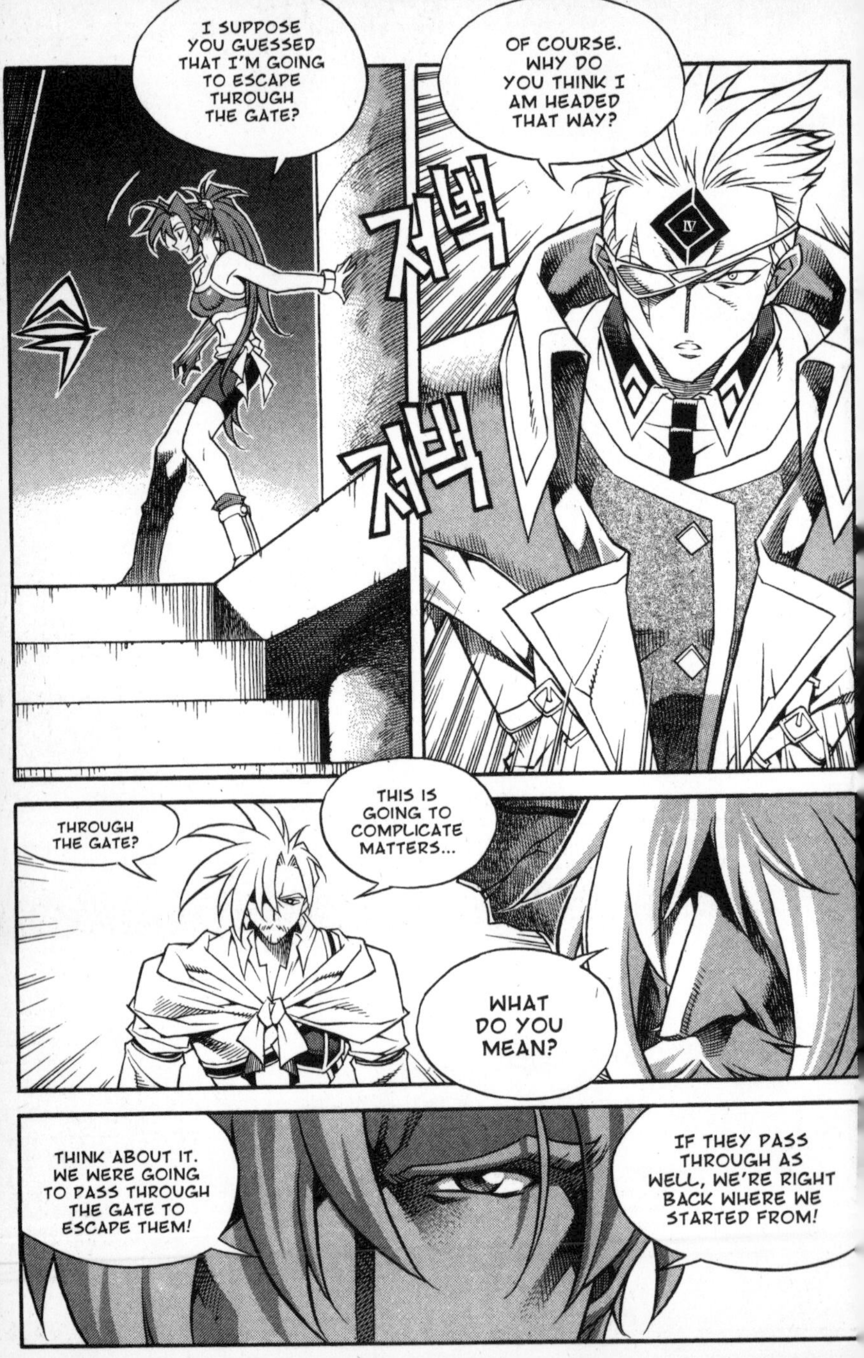
I SUPPOSE YOU GUESSED THAT I'M GOING TO ESCAPE THROUGH THE GATE?
OF COURSE. WHY DO YOU THINK I AM HEADED THAT WAY?
저벅
저벅
THROUGH THE GATE?
THIS IS GOING TO COMPLICATE MATTERS...
WHAT DO YOU MEAN?
THINK ABOUT IT. WE WERE GOING TO PASS THROUGH THE GATE TO ESCAPE THEM!
IF THEY PASS THROUGH AS WELL, WE'RE RIGHT BACK WHERE WE STARTED FROM!

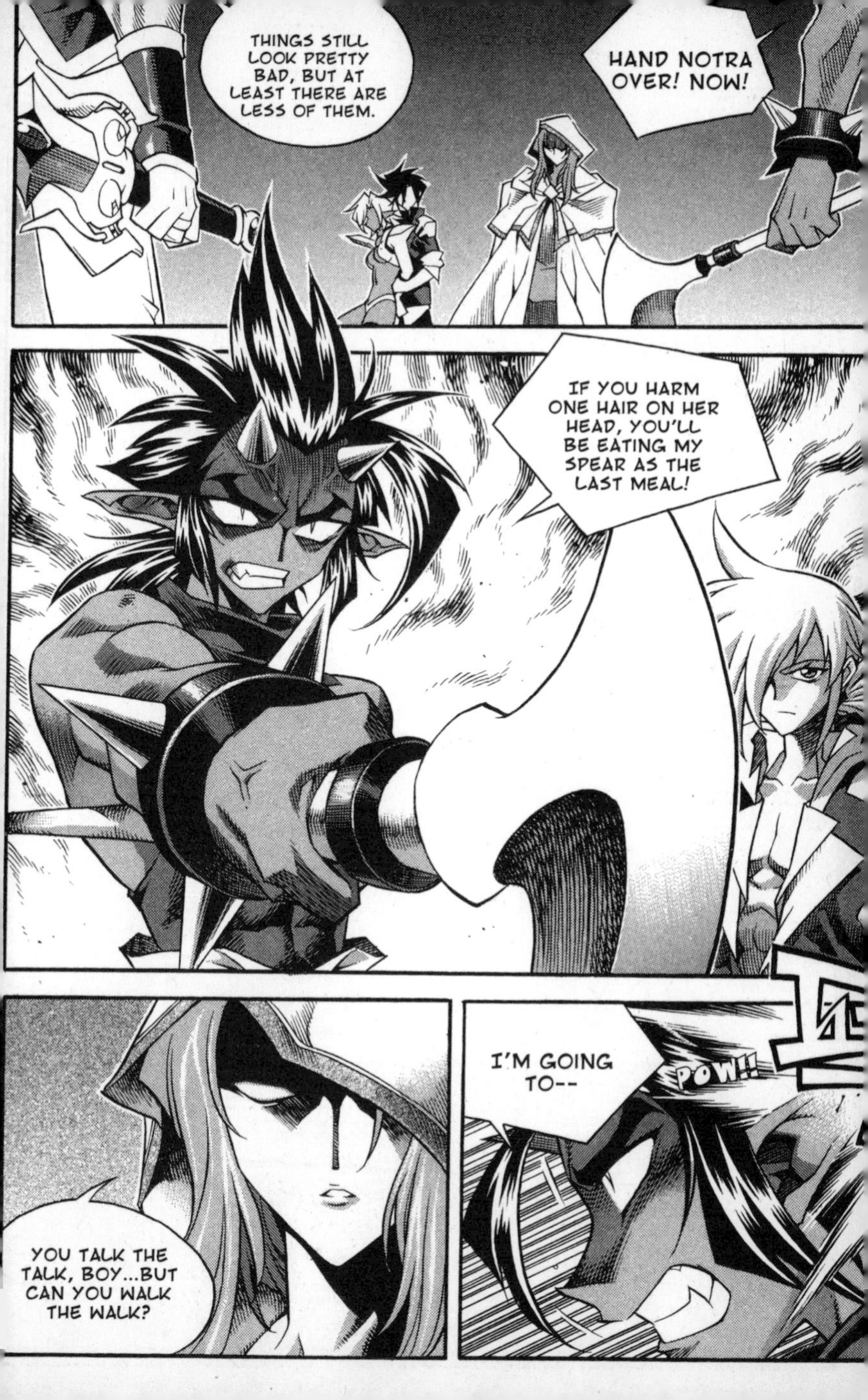
THINGS STILL LOOK PRETTY BAD, BUT AT LEAST THERE ARE LESS OF THEM.
HAND NOTRA OVER! NOW!
IF YOU HARM ONE HAIR ON HER HEAD, YOU'LL BE EATING MY SPEAR AS THE LAST MEAL!
I'M GOING TO--
POW!!
YOU TALK THE TALK, BOY...BUT CAN YOU WALK THE WALK?

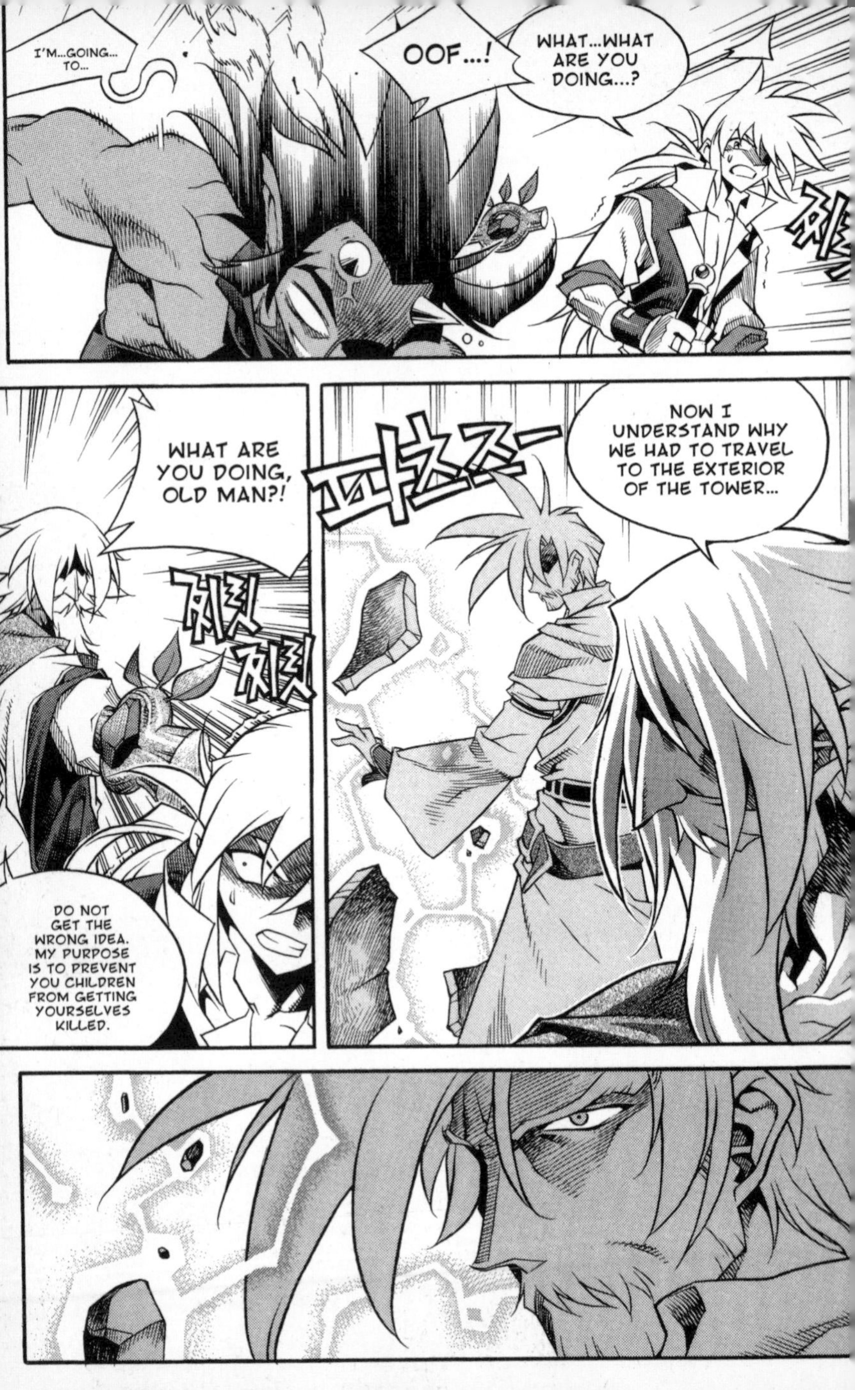
I'M...GOING... TO...
OOF...!
WHAT...WHAT ARE YOU DOING...?
WHAT ARE YOU DOING, OLD MAN?!
DO NOT GET THE WRONG IDEA. MY PURPOSE IS TO PREVENT YOU CHILDREN FROM GETTING YOURSELVES KILLED.
NOW I UNDERSTAND WHY WE HAD TO TRAVEL TO THE EXTERIOR OF THE TOWER...

Quest 89

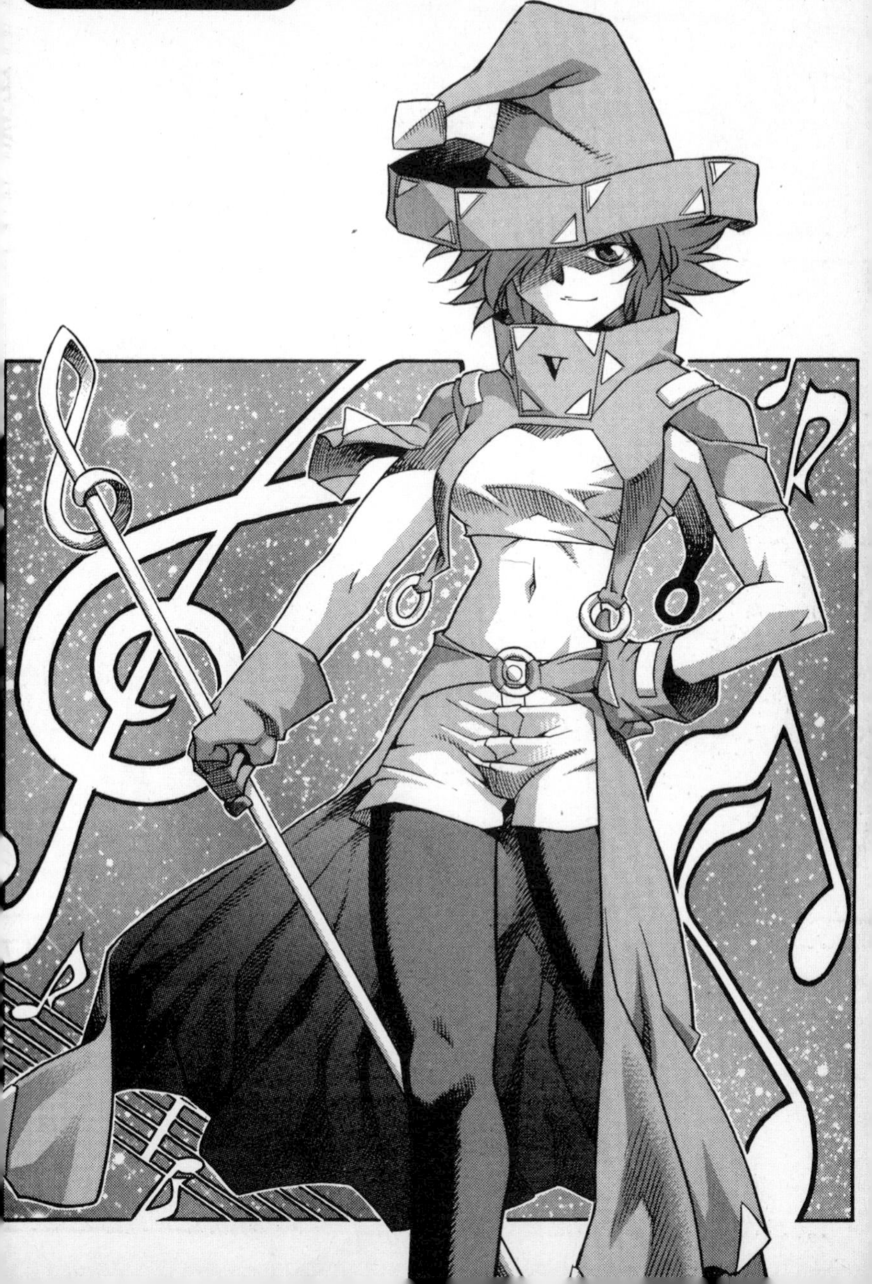

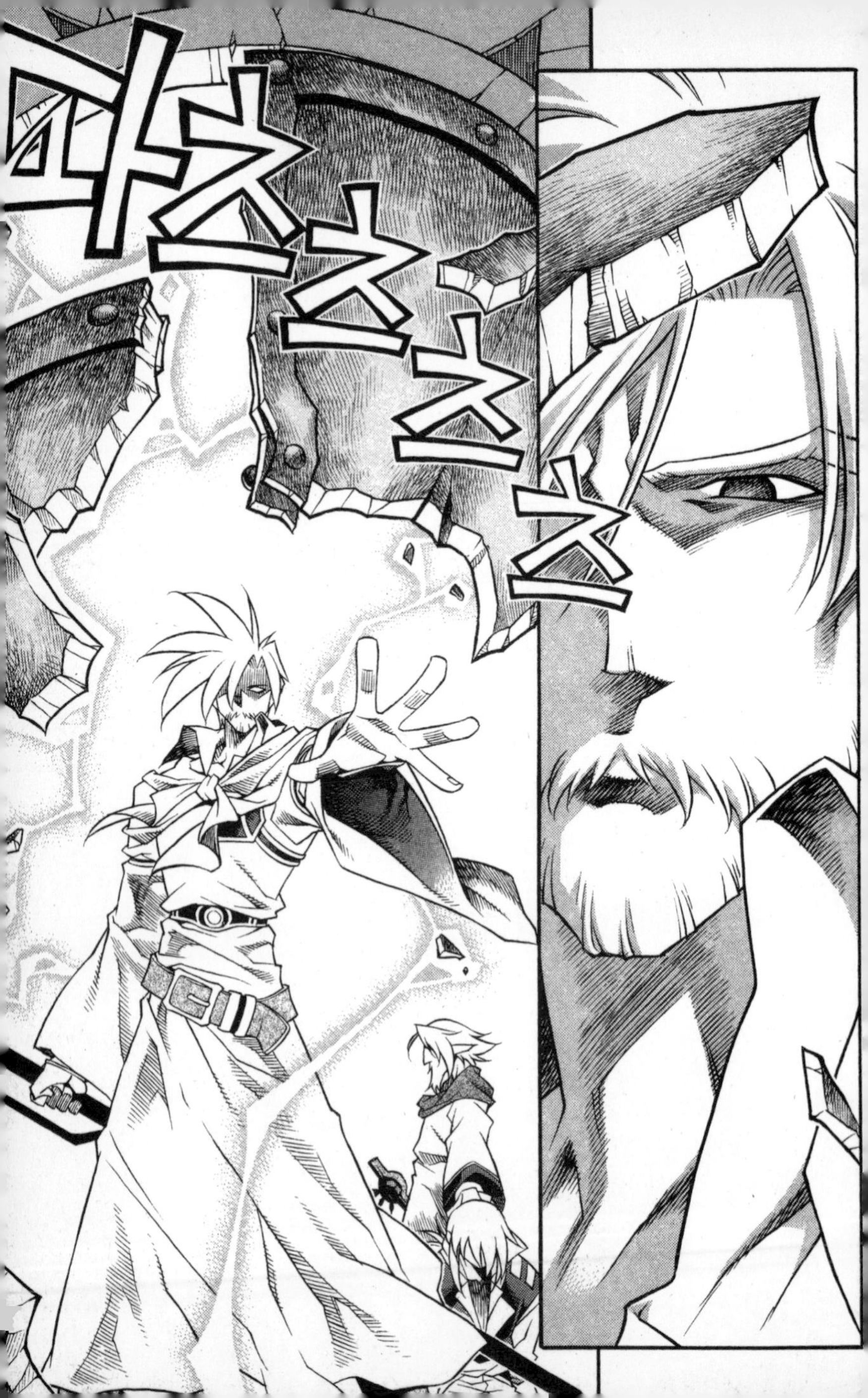

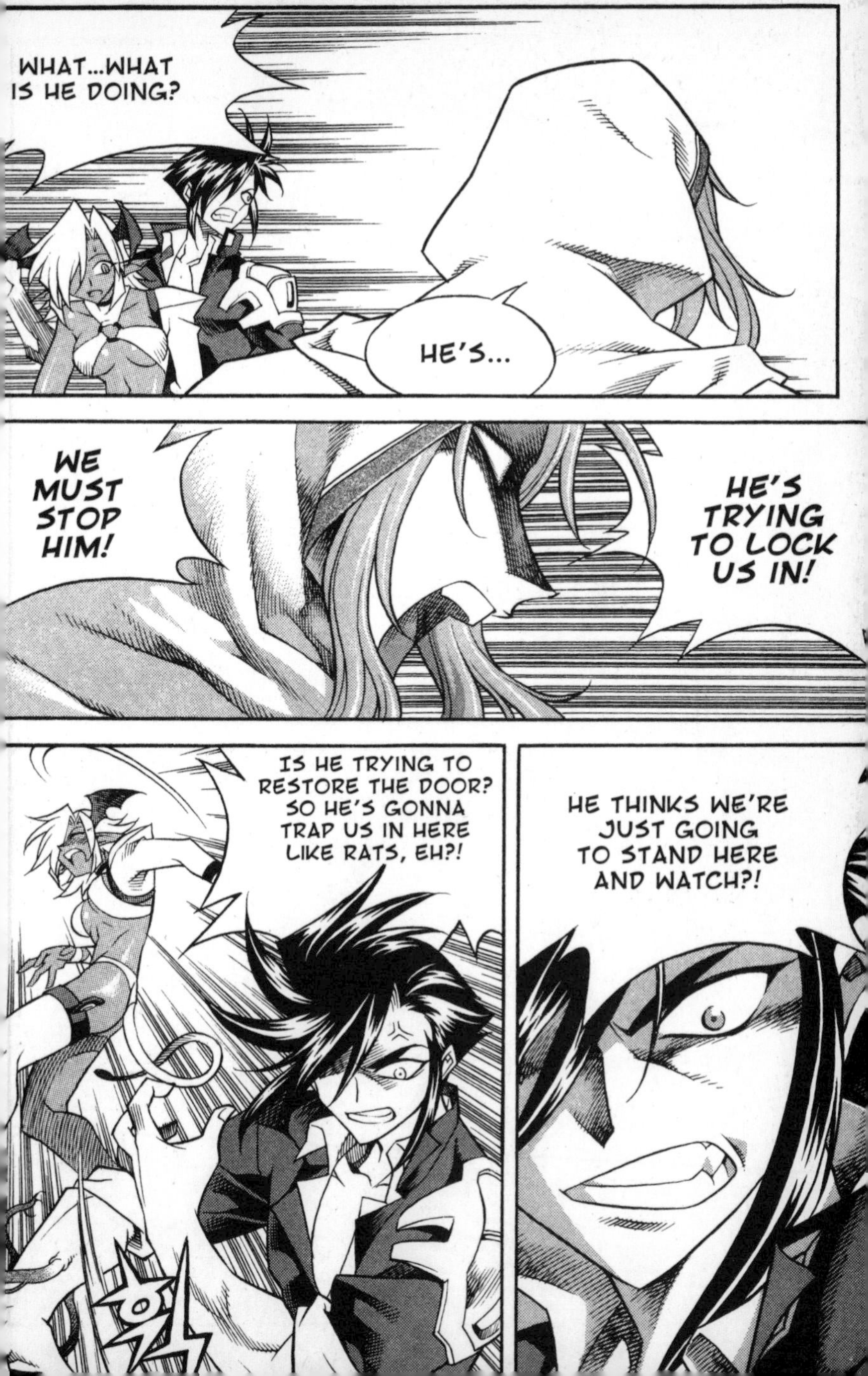
WHAT...WHAT IS HE DOING?
HE'S...
HE'S TRYING TO LOCK US IN!
WE MUST STOP HIM!
IS HE TRYING TO RESTORE THE DOOR? SO HE'S GONNA TRAP US IN HERE LIKE RATS, EH?!
HE THINKS WE'RE JUST GOING TO STAND HERE AND WATCH?!

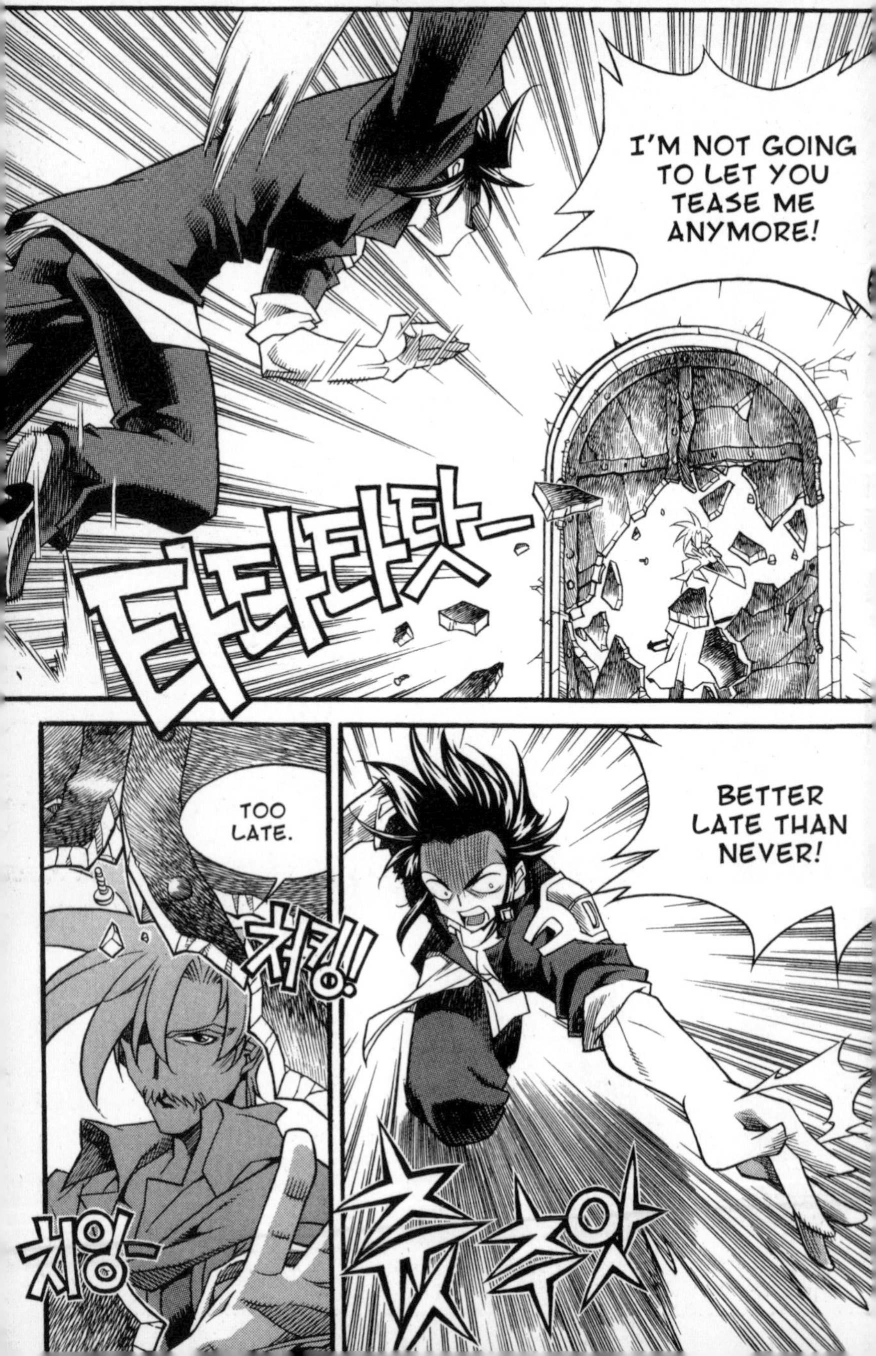

I'M NOT GOING TO LET YOU TEASE ME ANYMORE!
TOO LATE.
BETTER LATE THAN NEVER!

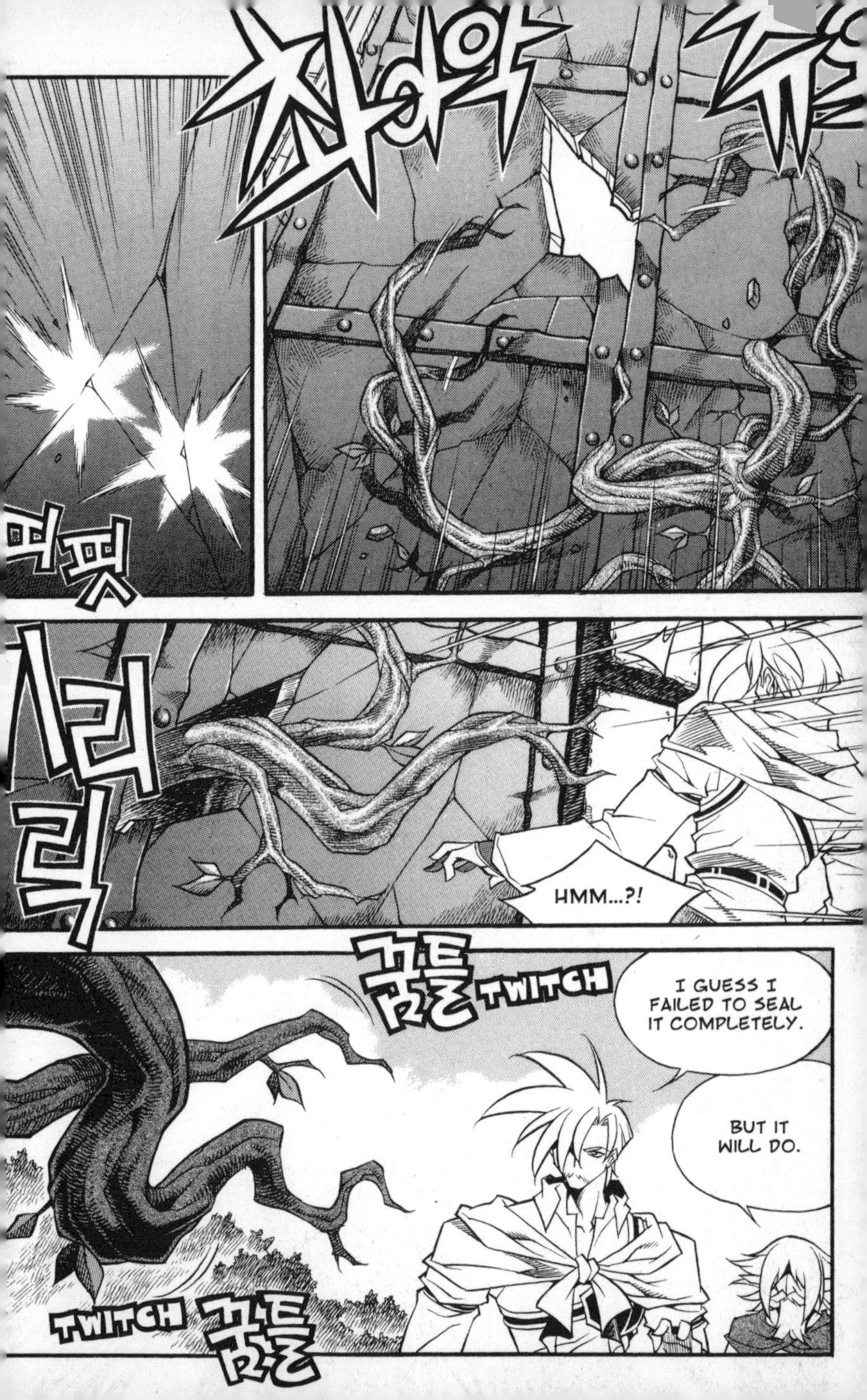
HMM...?!
꿈틀 TWITCH
I GUESS I FAILED TO SEAL IT COMPLETELY.
BUT IT WILL DO.
TWITCH 꿈틀

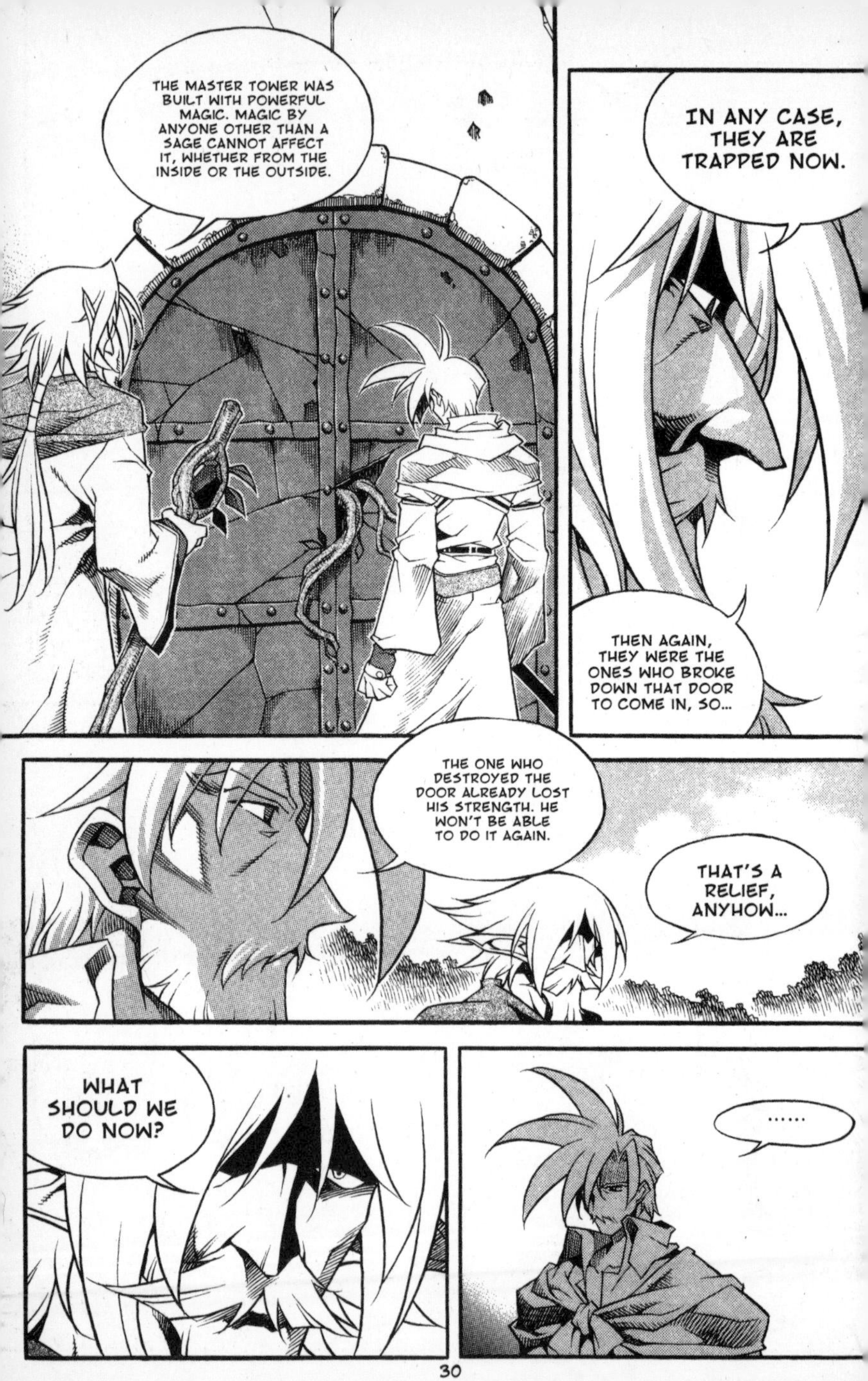
THE MASTER TOWER WAS BUILT WITH POWERFUL MAGIC. MAGIC BY ANYONE OTHER THAN A SAGE CANNOT AFFECT IT, WHETHER FROM THE INSIDE OR THE OUTSIDE.
IN ANY CASE, THEY ARE TRAPPED NOW.
THEN AGAIN, THEY WERE THE ONES WHO BROKE DOWN THAT DOOR TO COME IN, SO...
THE ONE WHO DESTROYED THE DOOR ALREADY LOST HIS STRENGTH. HE WON'T BE ABLE TO DO IT AGAIN.
THAT'S A RELIEF, ANYHOW...
WHAT SHOULD WE DO NOW?
......

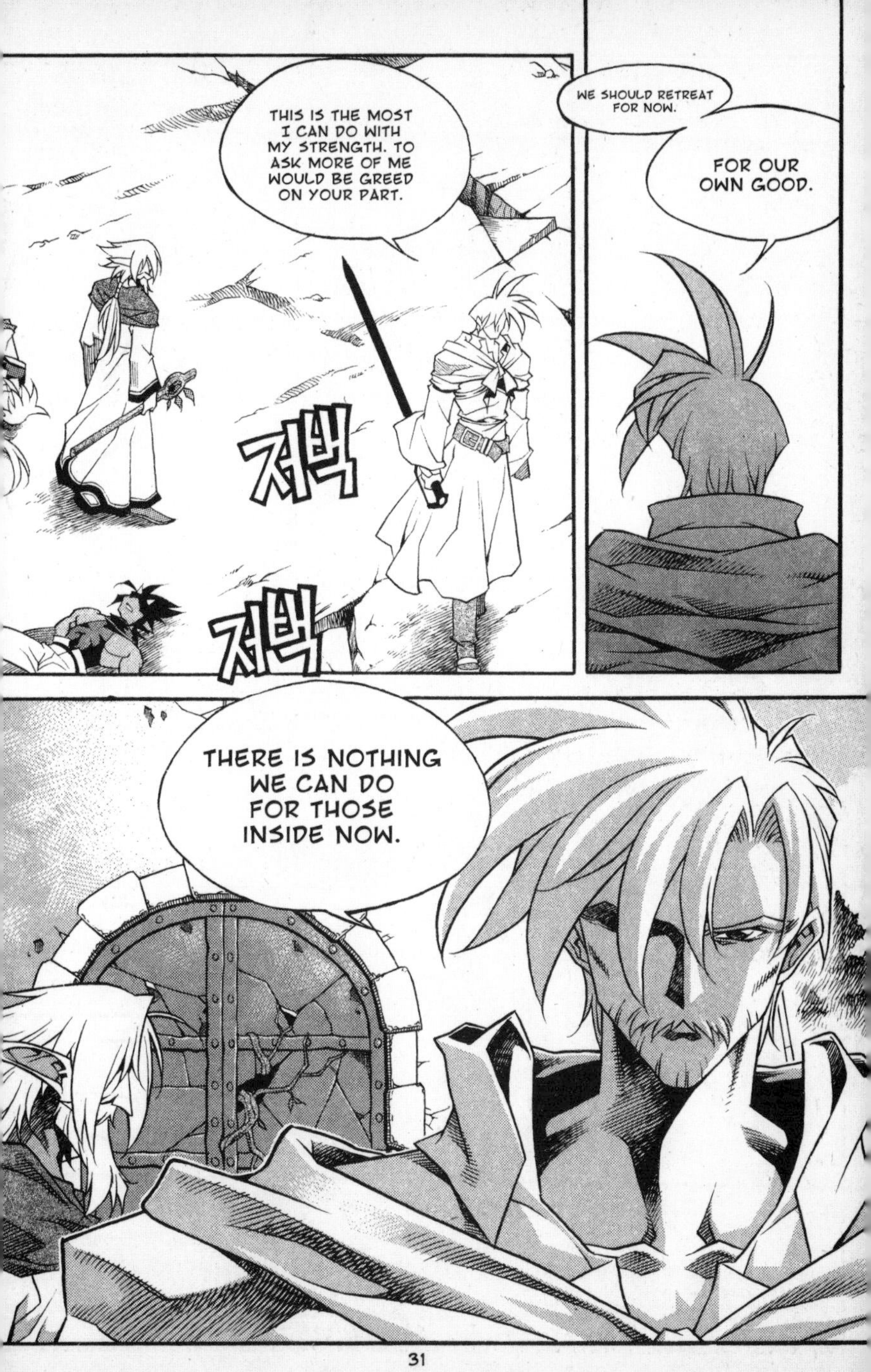
THIS IS THE MOST I CAN DO WITH MY STRENGTH. TO ASK MORE OF ME WOULD BE GREED ON YOUR PART.
저벅
저벅
WE SHOULD RETREAT FOR NOW.
FOR OUR OWN GOOD.
THERE IS NOTHING WE CAN DO FOR THOSE INSIDE NOW.

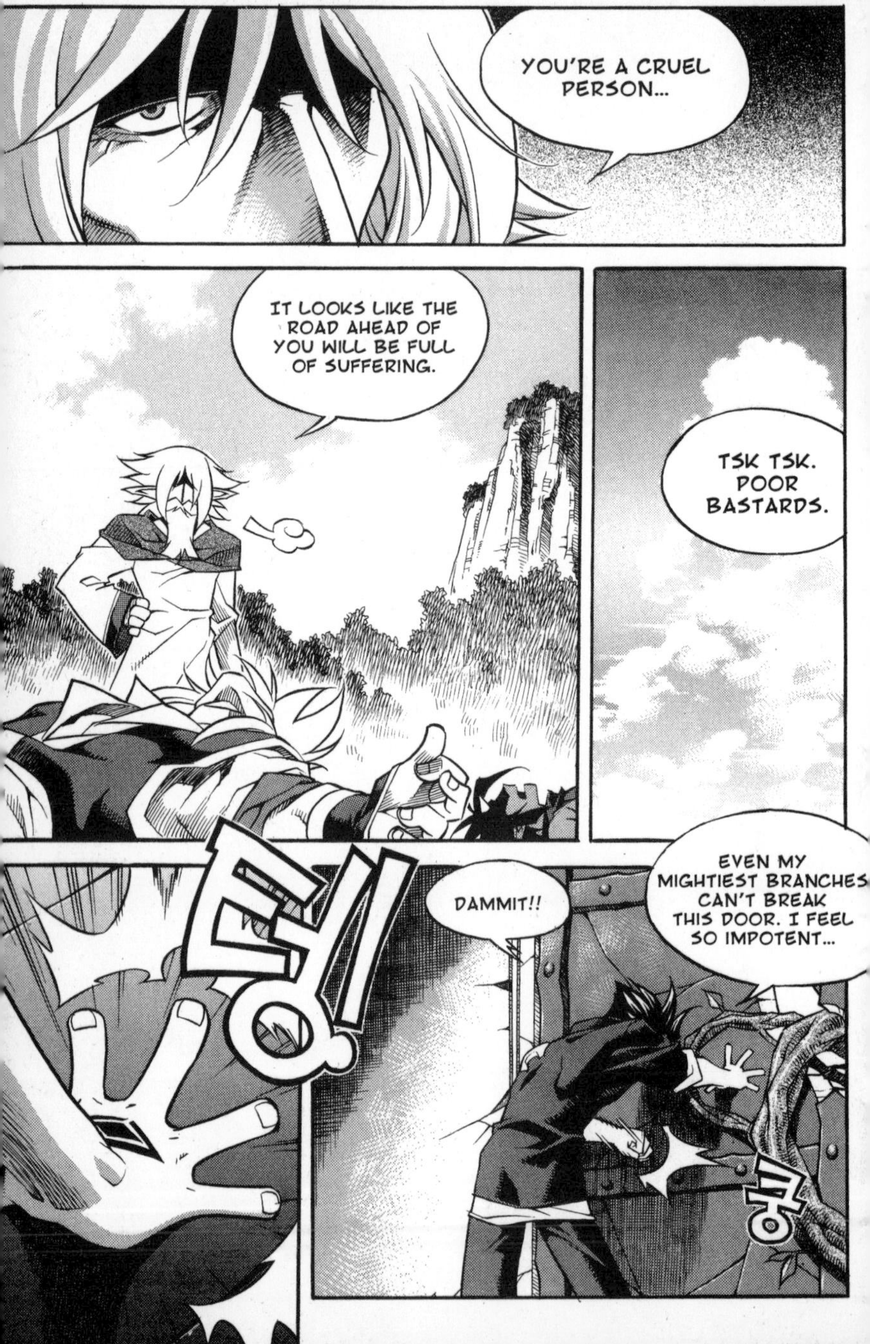
YOU'RE A CRUEL PERSON...
IT LOOKS LIKE THE ROAD AHEAD OF YOU WILL BE FULL OF SUFFERING.
TSK TSK. POOR BASTARDS.
DAMMIT!!
EVEN MY MIGHTIEST BRANCHES CAN'T BREAK THIS DOOR. I FEEL SO IMPOTENT...

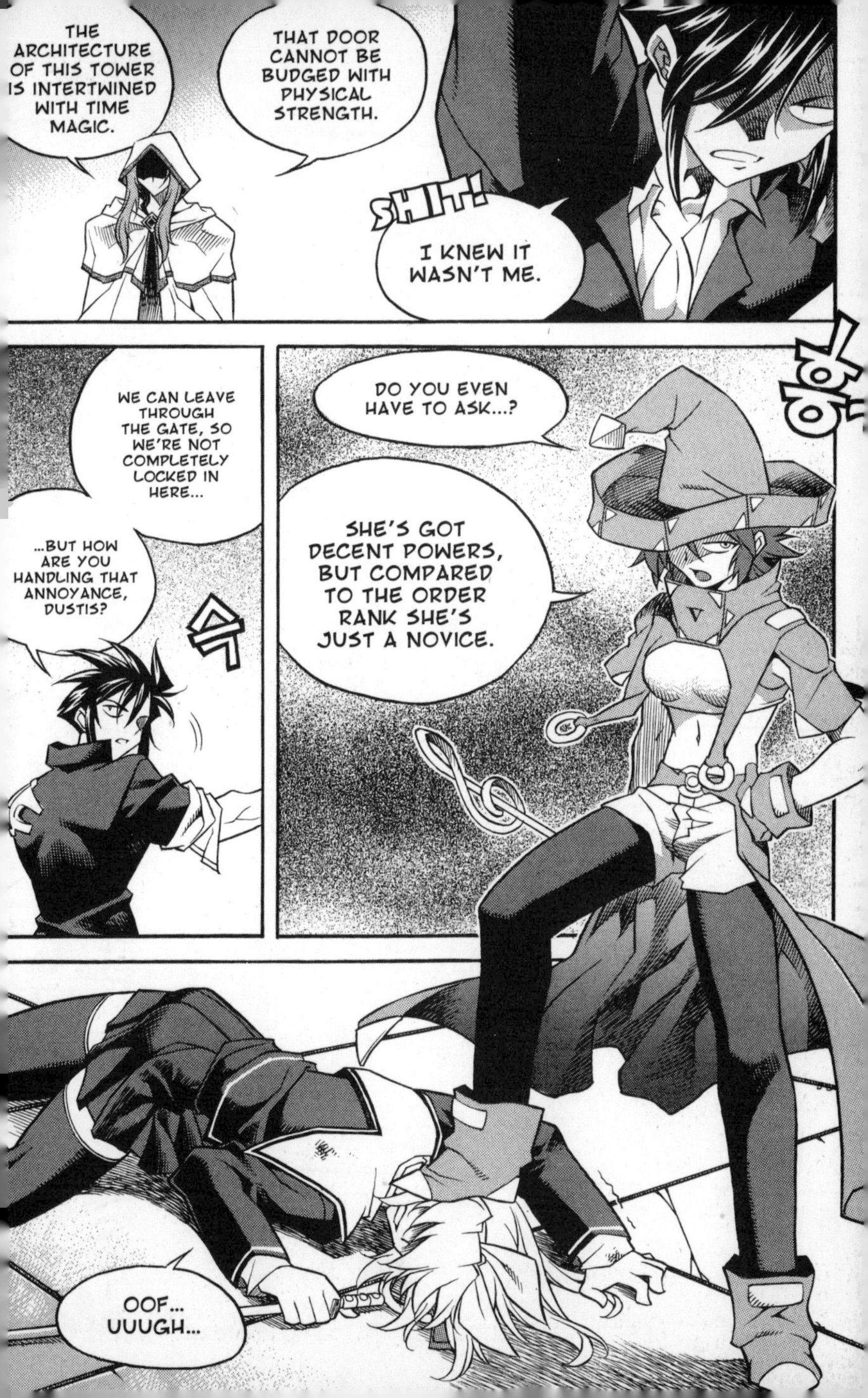
THAT DOOR CANNOT BE BUDGED WITH PHYSICAL STRENGTH.
THE ARCHITECTURE OF THIS TOWER IS INTERTWINED WITH TIME MAGIC.
SHIT!
I KNEW IT WASN'T ME.
DO YOU EVEN HAVE TO ASK...?
SHE'S GOT DECENT POWERS, BUT COMPARED TO THE ORDER RANK SHE'S JUST A NOVICE.
WE CAN LEAVE THROUGH THE GATE, SO WE'RE NOT COMPLETELY LOCKED IN HERE...
...BUT HOW ARE YOU HANDLING THAT ANNOYANCE, DUSTIS?
OOF... UUUGH...

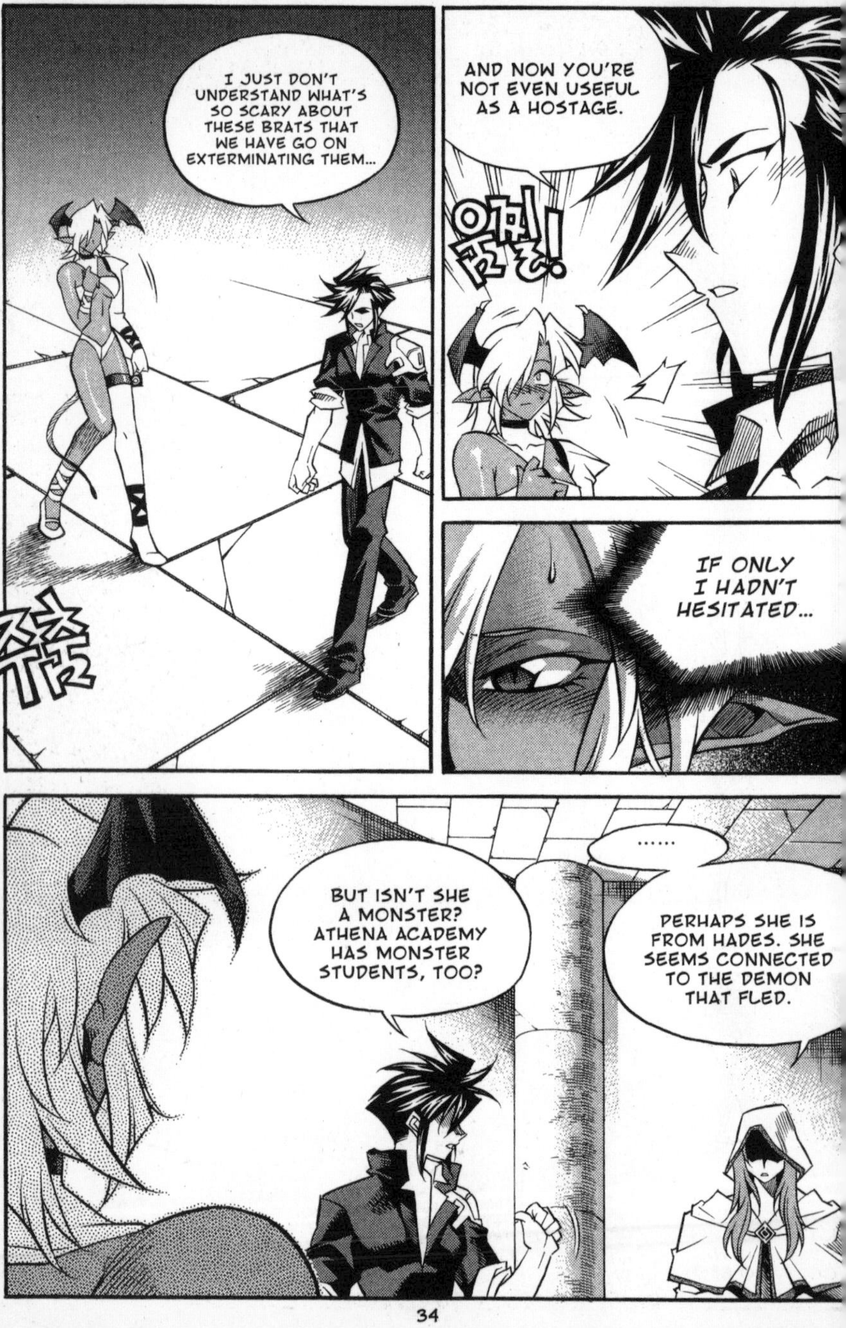

I JUST DON'T UNDERSTAND WHAT'S SO SCARY ABOUT THESE BRATS THAT WE HAVE GO ON EXTERMINATING THEM...
AND NOW YOU'RE NOT EVEN USEFUL AS A HOSTAGE.
IF ONLY I HADN'T HESITATED...
BUT ISN'T SHE A MONSTER? ATHENA ACADEMY HAS MONSTER STUDENTS, TOO?
......
PERHAPS SHE IS FROM HADES. SHE SEEMS CONNECTED TO THE DEMON THAT FLED.

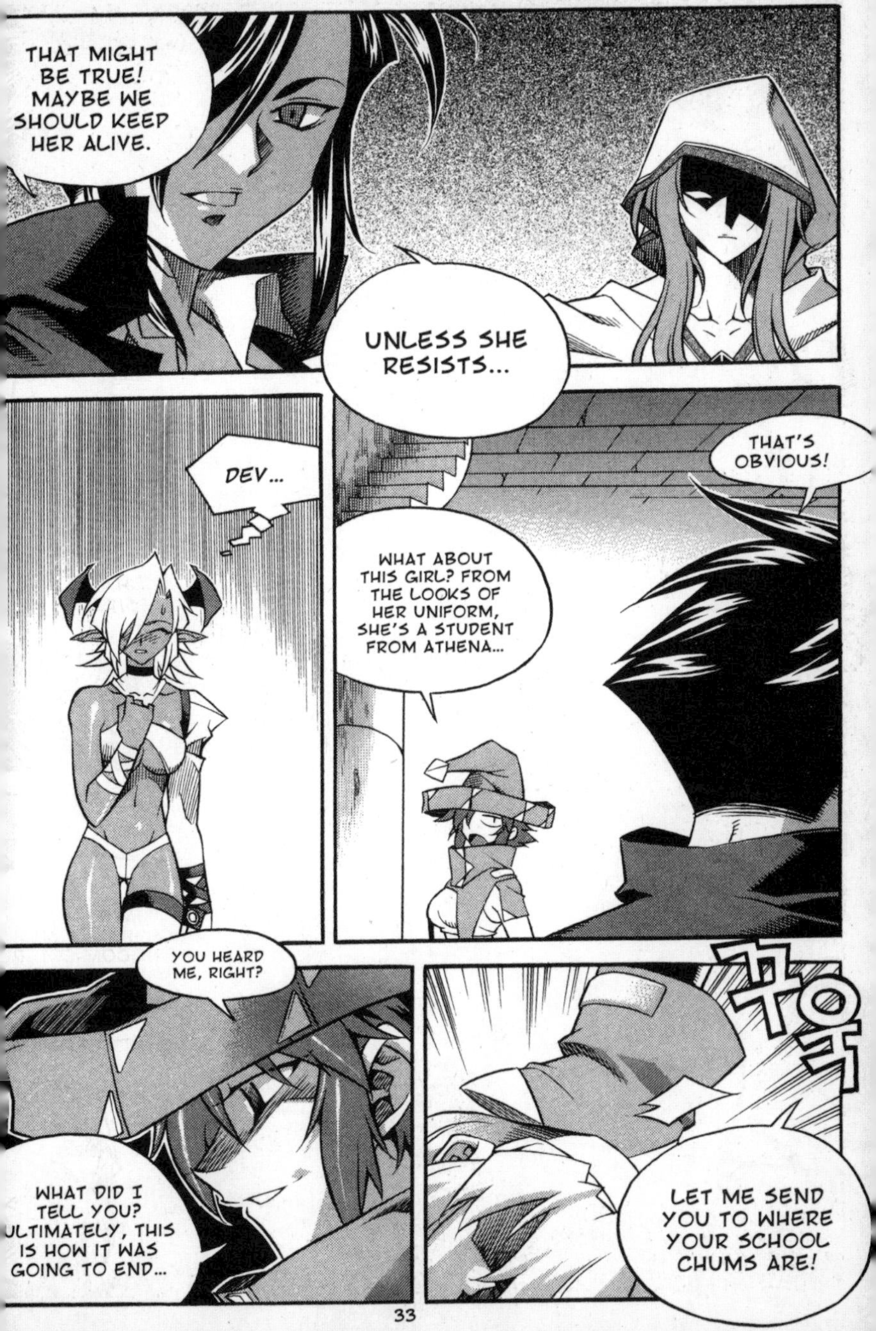
THAT MIGHT BE TRUE! MAYBE WE SHOULD KEEP HER ALIVE.
UNLESS SHE RESISTS...
DEV...
THAT'S OBVIOUS!
WHAT ABOUT THIS GIRL? FROM THE LOOKS OF HER UNIFORM, SHE'S A STUDENT FROM ATHENA...
YOU HEARD ME, RIGHT?
WHAT DID I TELL YOU? ULTIMATELY, THIS IS HOW IT WAS GOING TO END...
LET ME SEND YOU TO WHERE YOUR SCHOOL CHUMS ARE!

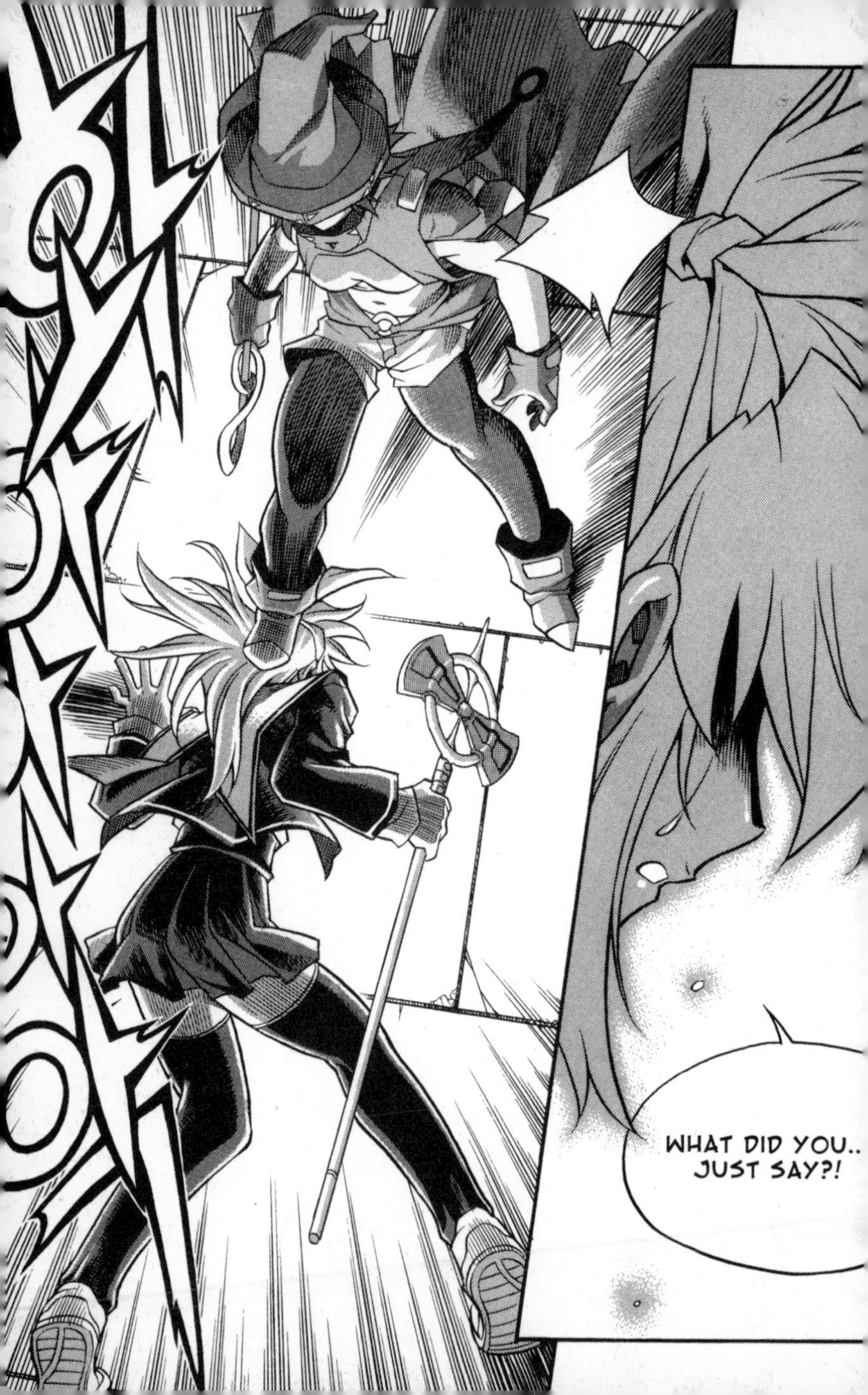
WHAT DID YOU.. JUST SAY?!

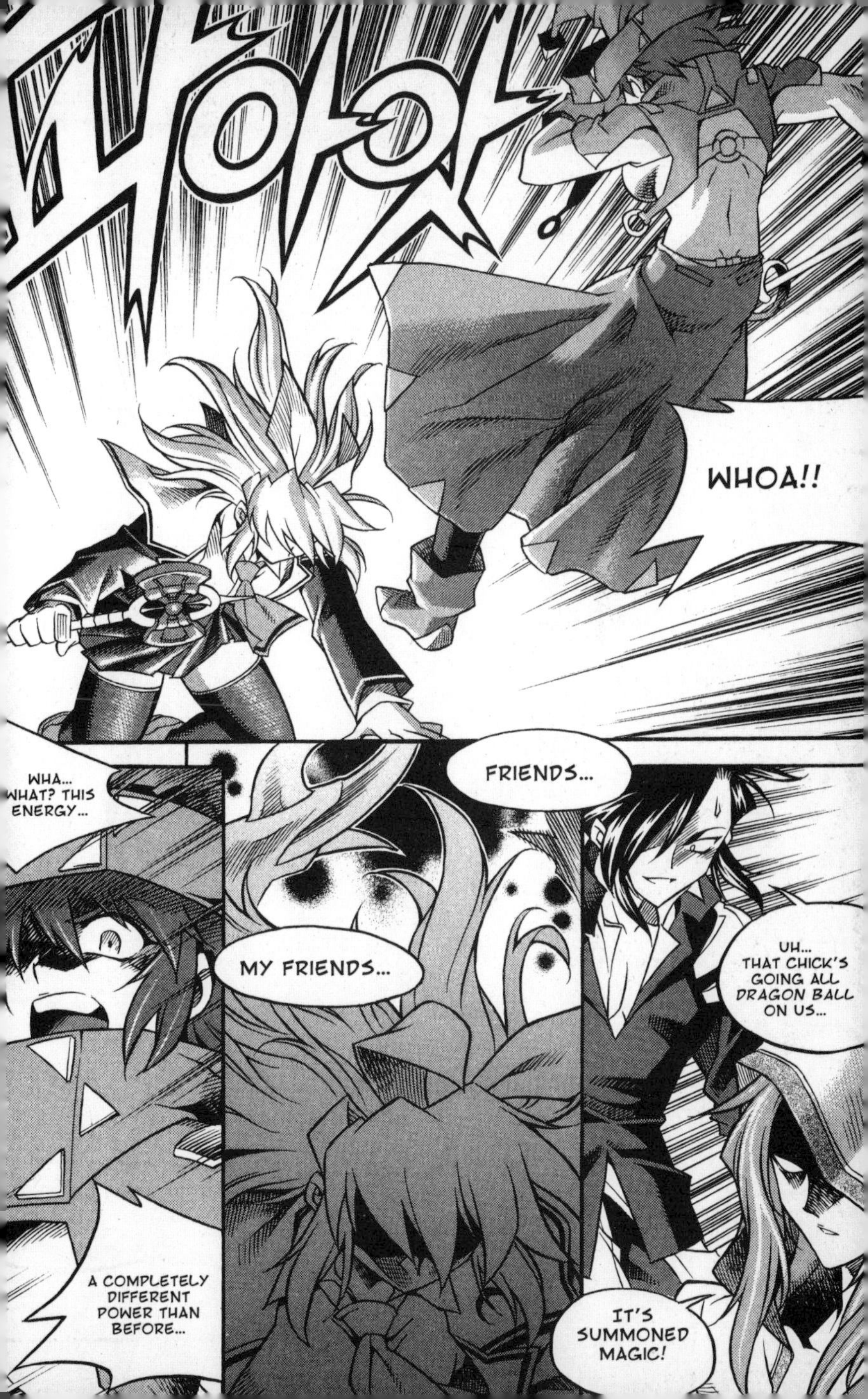
WHOA!!
FRIENDS...
MY FRIENDS...
UH... THAT CHICK'S GOING ALL DRAGON BALL ON US...
IT'S SUMMONED MAGIC!
WHA... WHAT? THIS ENERGY...
A COMPLETELY DIFFERENT POWER THAN BEFORE...

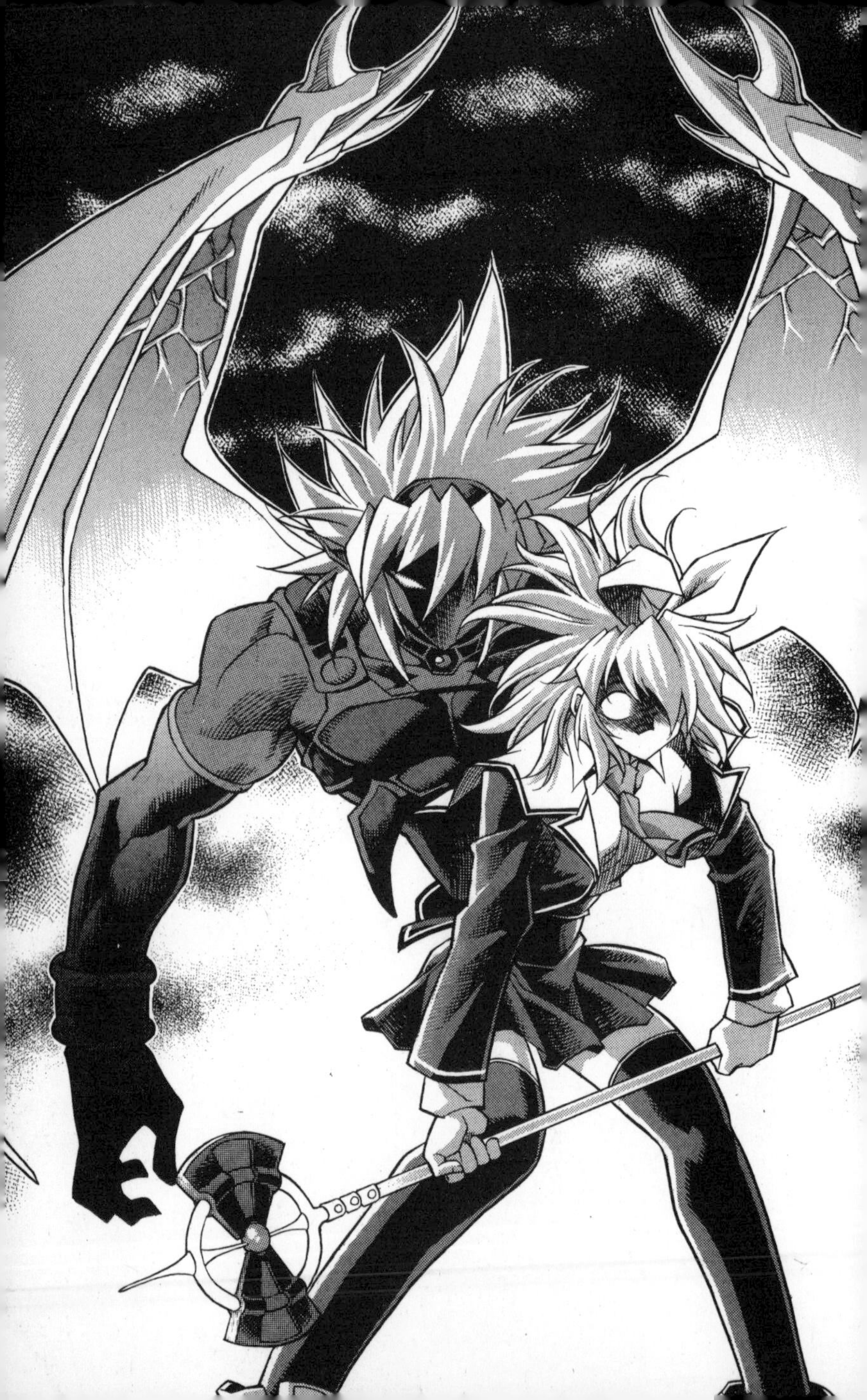

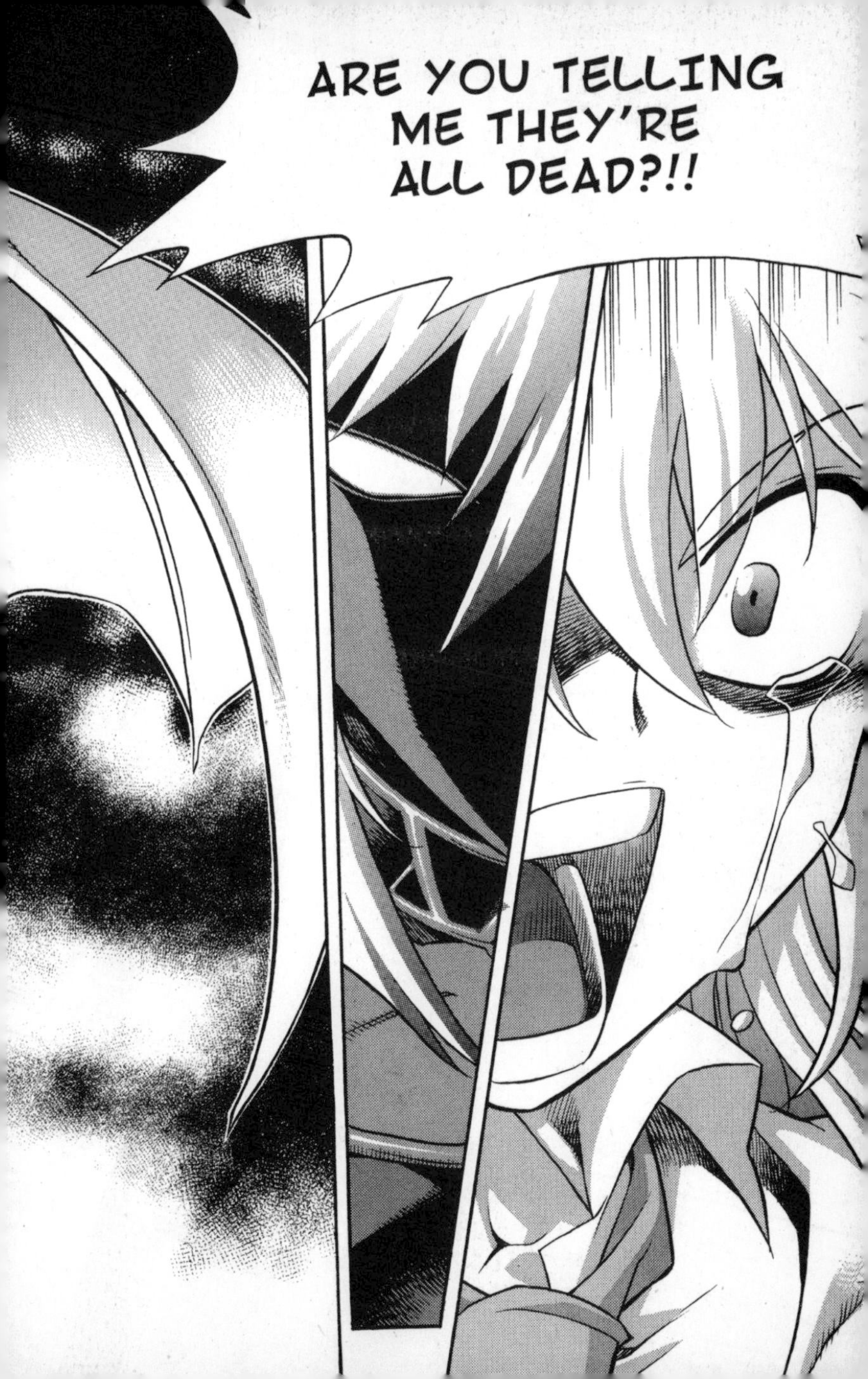
ARE YOU TELLING
ME THEY'RE
ALL DEAD?!!

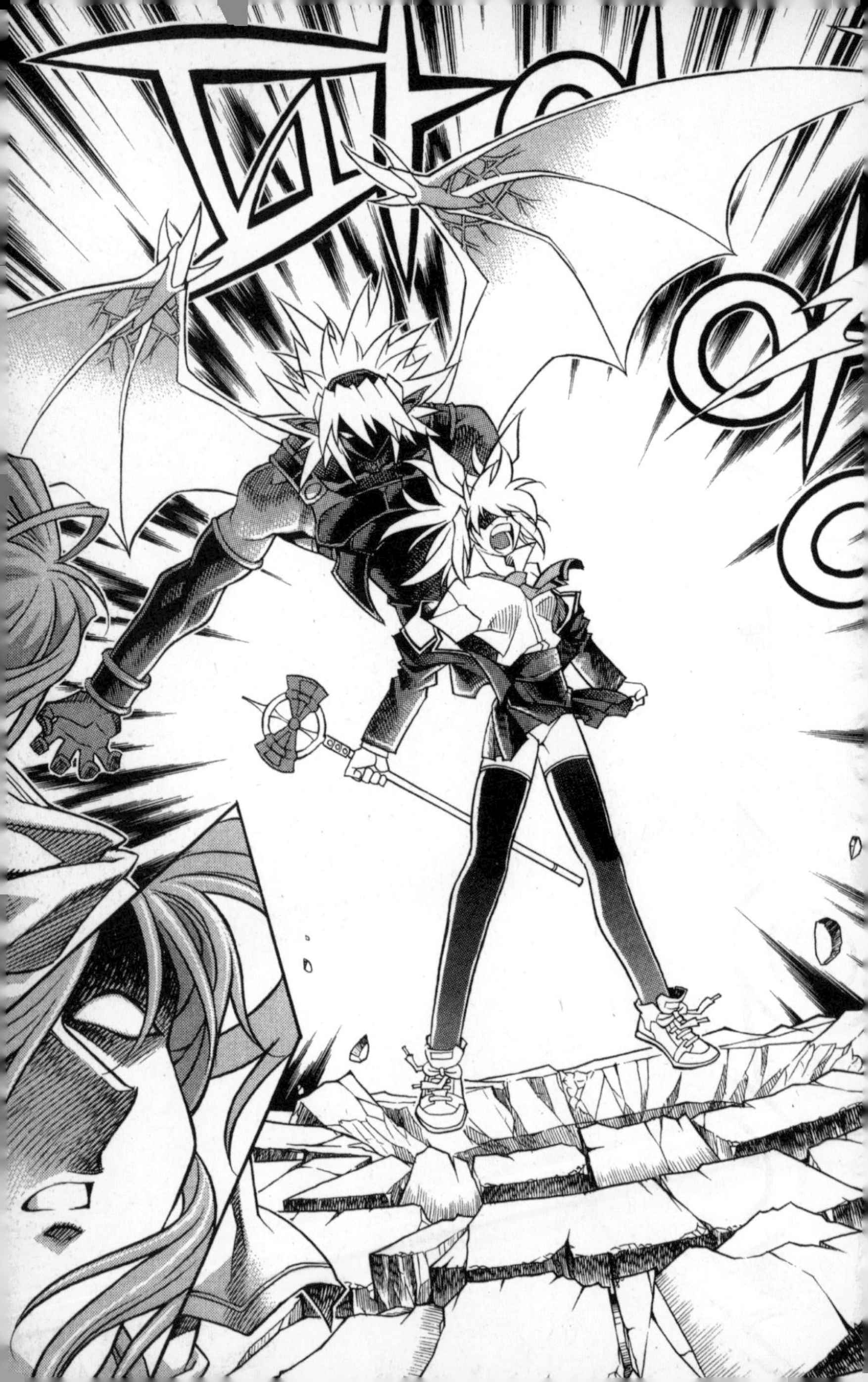

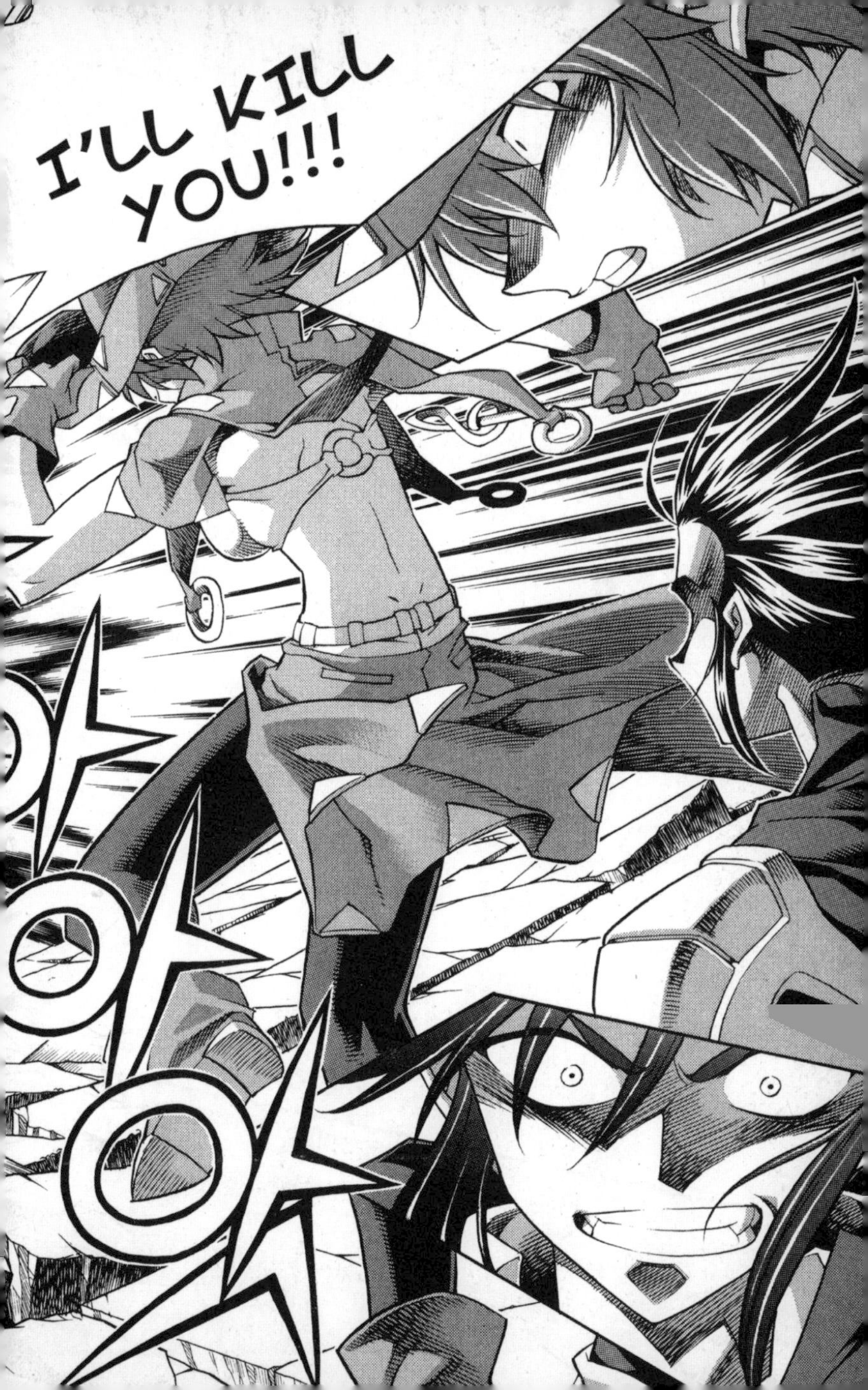
I'LL KILL YOU!!!

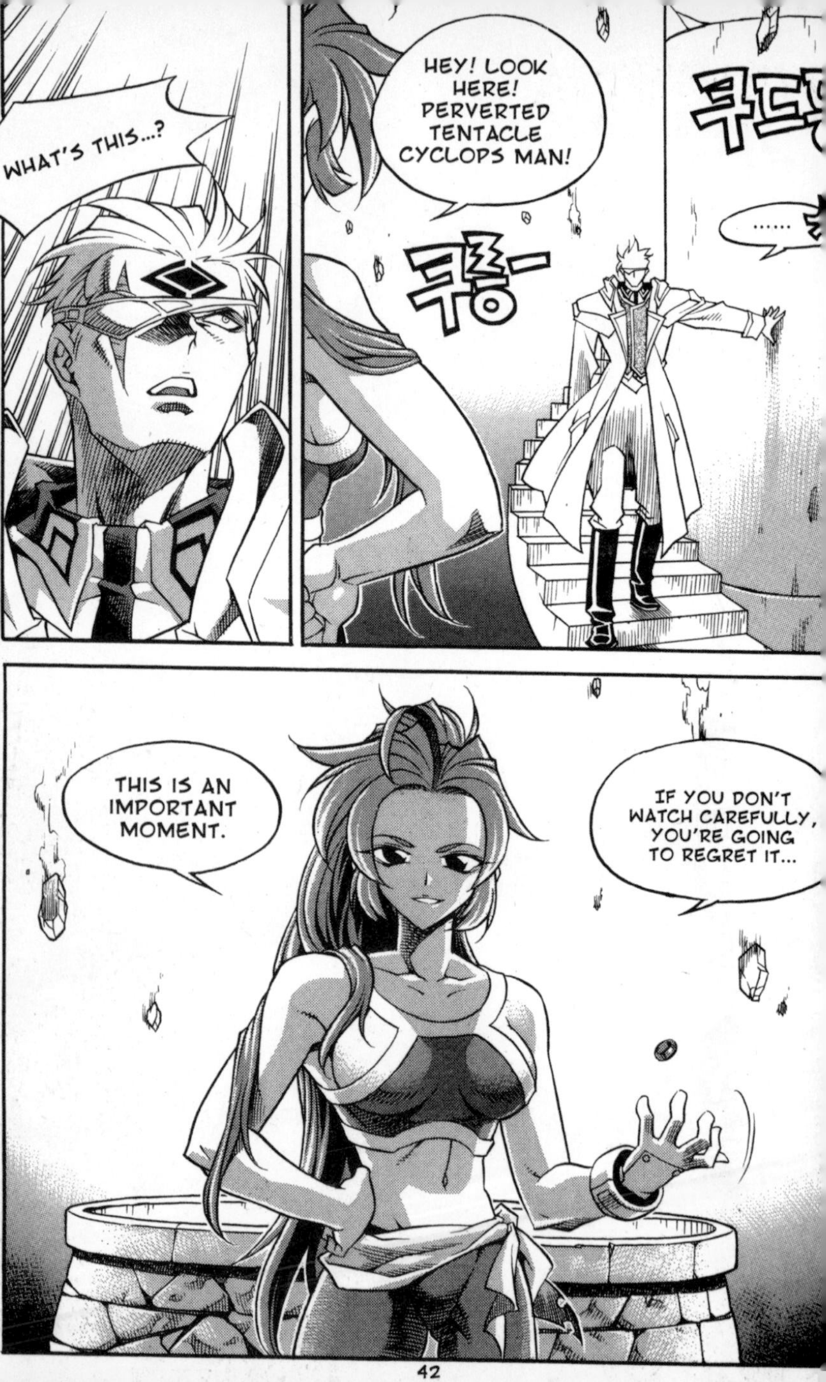
WHAT'S THIS...?
HEY! LOOK HERE! PERVERTED TENTACLE CYCLOPS MAN!
......
THIS IS AN IMPORTANT MOMENT.
IF YOU DON'T WATCH CAREFULLY, YOU'RE GOING TO REGRET IT...

Quest 90

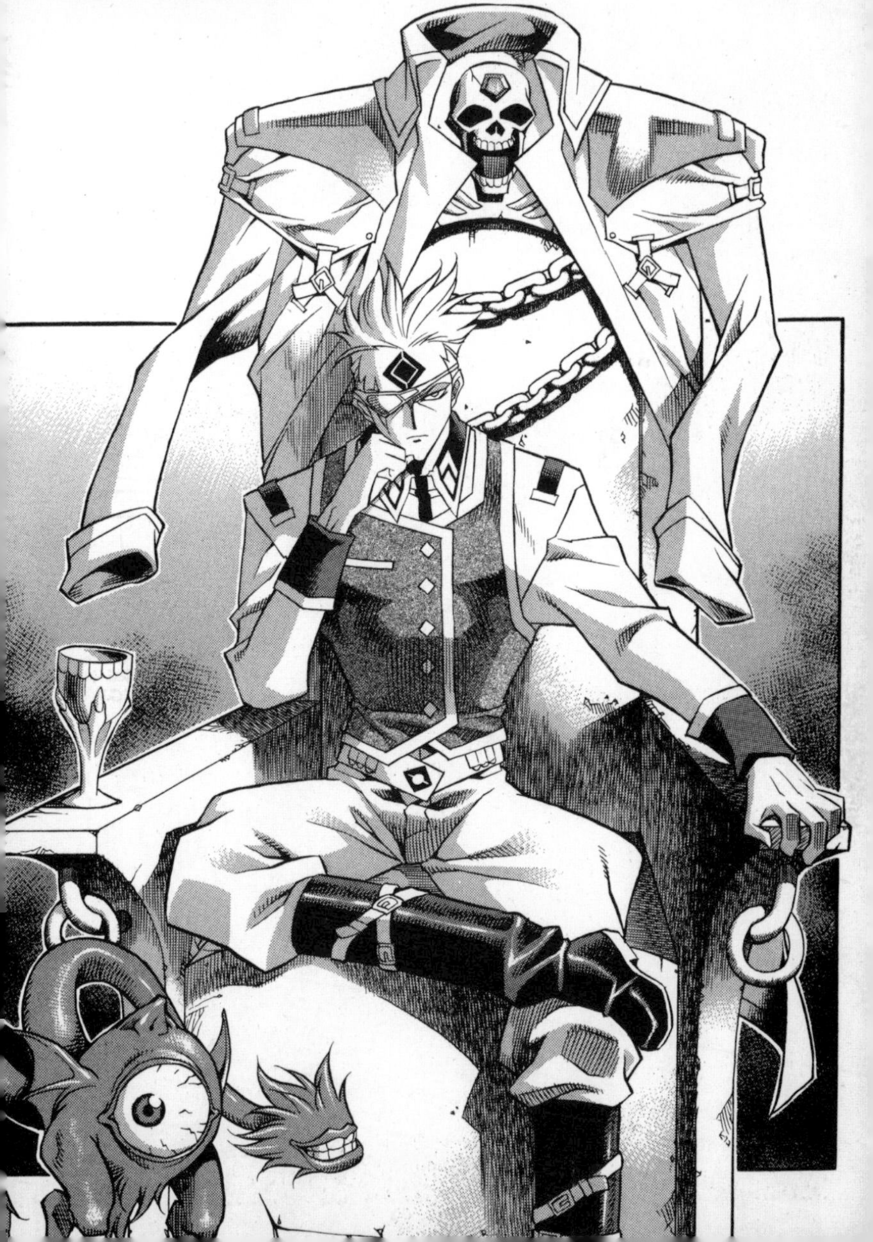

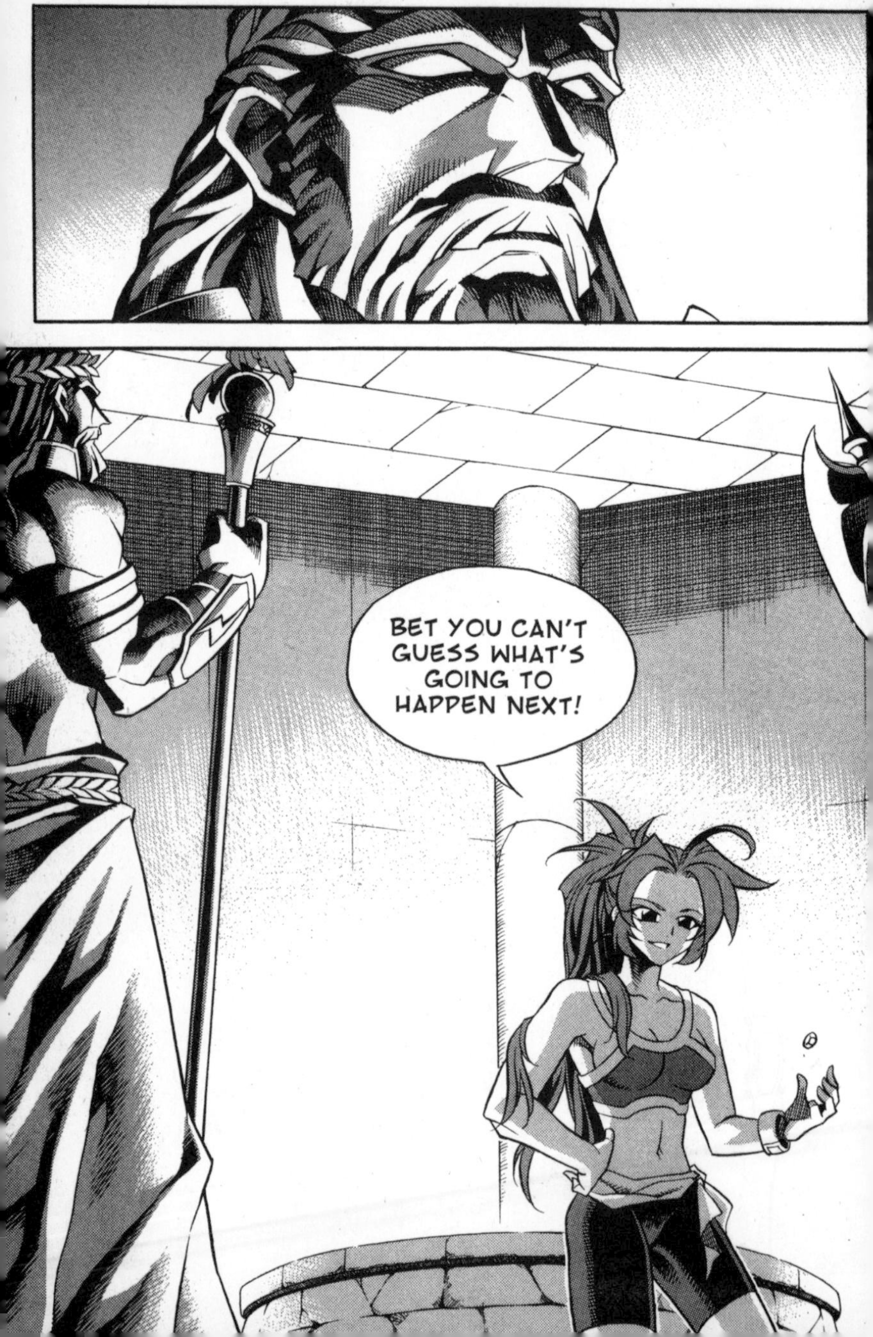
BET YOU CAN'T GUESS WHAT'S GOING TO HAPPEN NEXT!

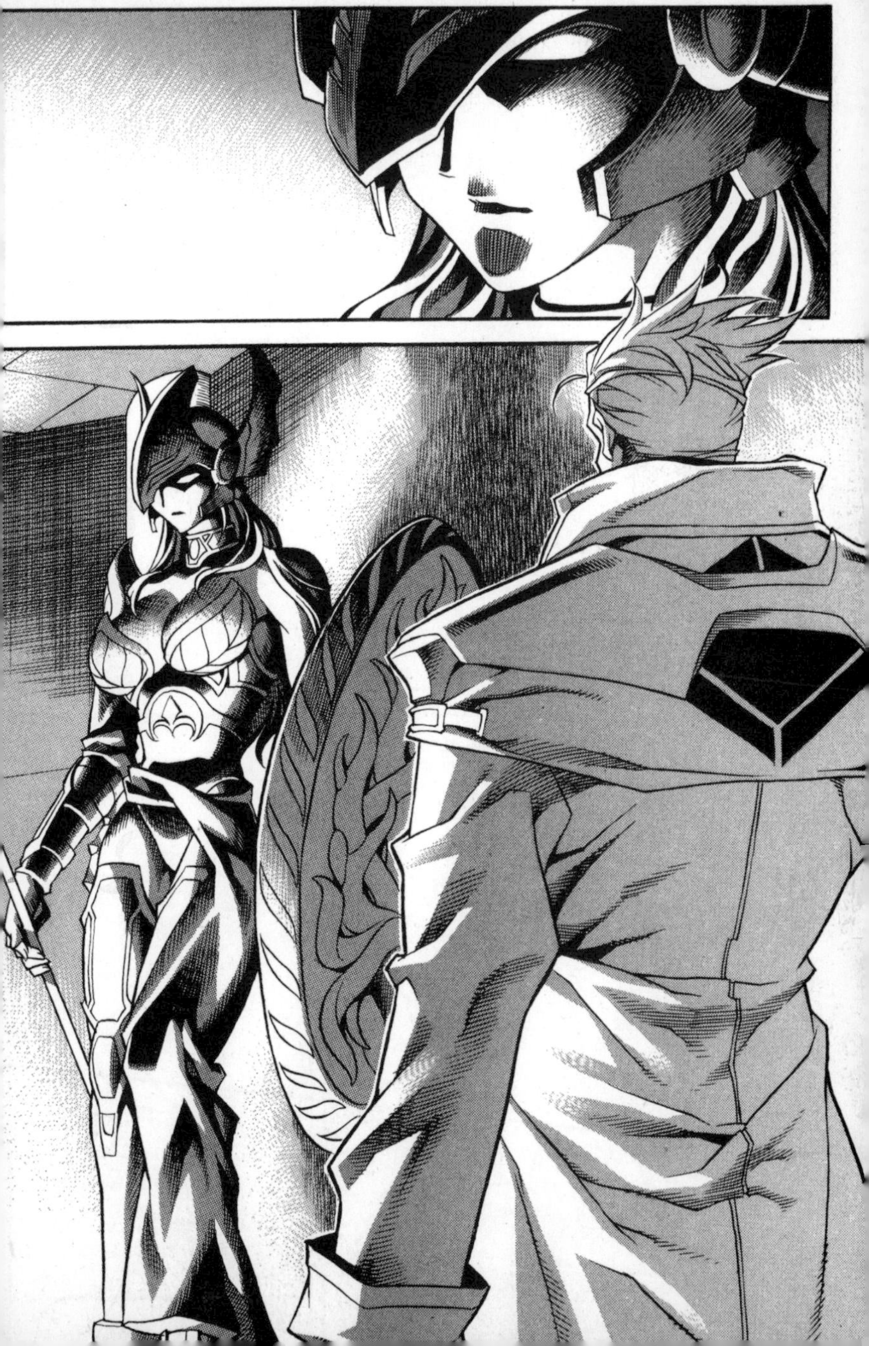

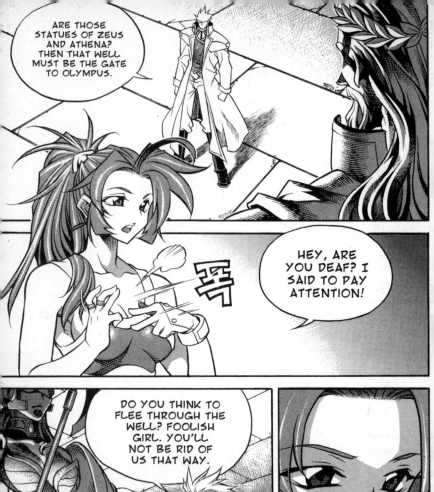

ARE THOSE STATUES OF ZEUS AND ATHENA? THEN THAT WELL MUST BE THE GATE TO OLYMPUS.

HEY, ARE YOU DEAF? I SAID TO PAY ATTENTION!

DO YOU THINK TO FLEE THROUGH THE WELL? FOOLISH GIRL. YOU'LL NOT BE RID OF US THAT WAY.

THE WELL? WHY, WHATEVER DO YOU MEAN?

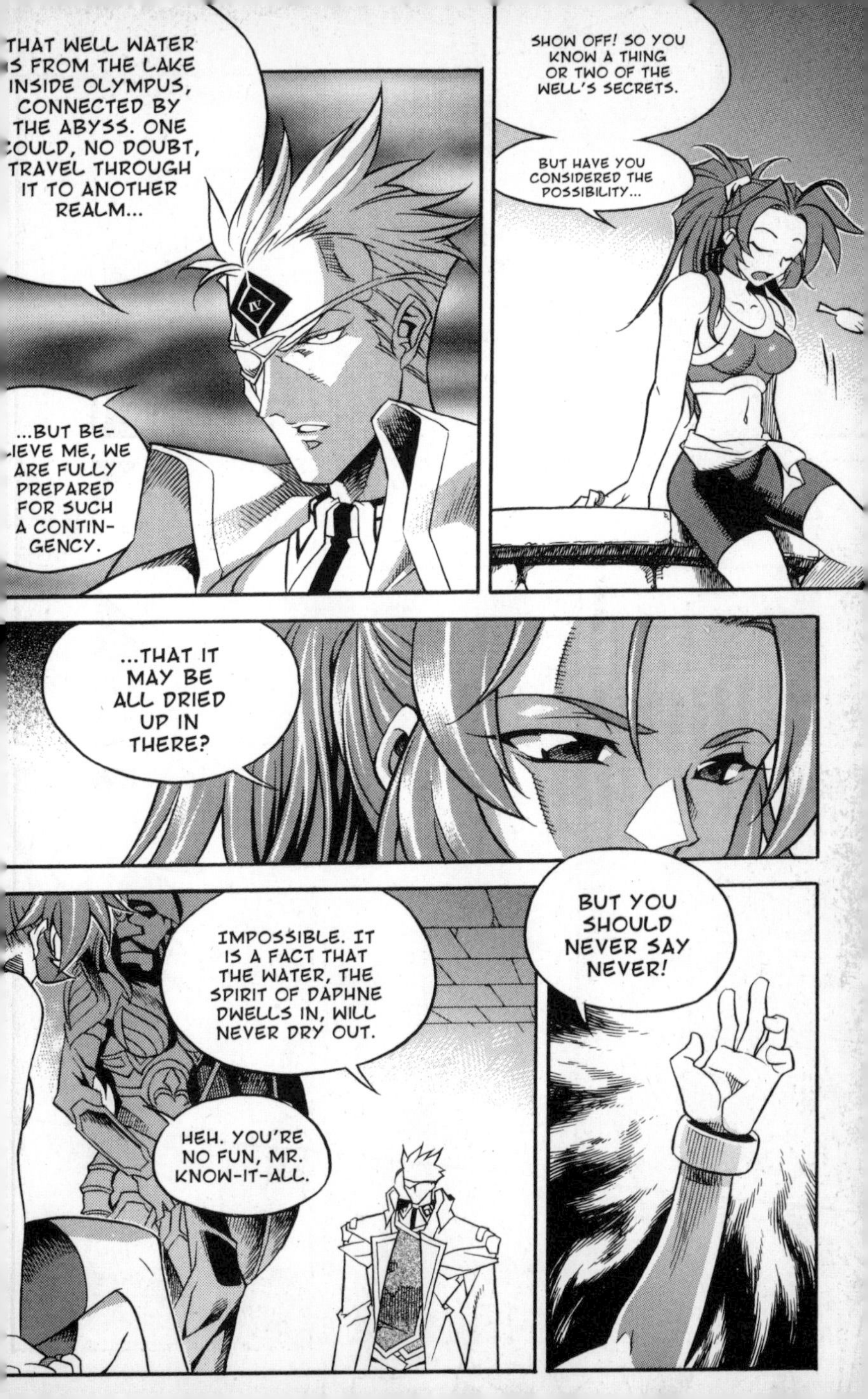
THAT WELL WATER IS FROM THE LAKE INSIDE OLYMPUS, CONNECTED BY THE ABYSS. ONE COULD, NO DOUBT, TRAVEL THROUGH IT TO ANOTHER REALM...
...BUT BE-LIEVE ME, WE ARE FULLY PREPARED FOR SUCH A CONTIN-GENCY.
SHOW OFF! SO YOU KNOW A THING OR TWO OF THE WELL'S SECRETS.
BUT HAVE YOU CONSIDERED THE POSSIBILITY...
...THAT IT MAY BE ALL DRIED UP IN THERE?
BUT YOU SHOULD NEVER SAY NEVER!
IMPOSSIBLE. IT IS A FACT THAT THE WATER, THE SPIRIT OF DAPHNE DWELLS IN, WILL NEVER DRY OUT.
HEH. YOU'RE NO FUN, MR. KNOW-IT-ALL.

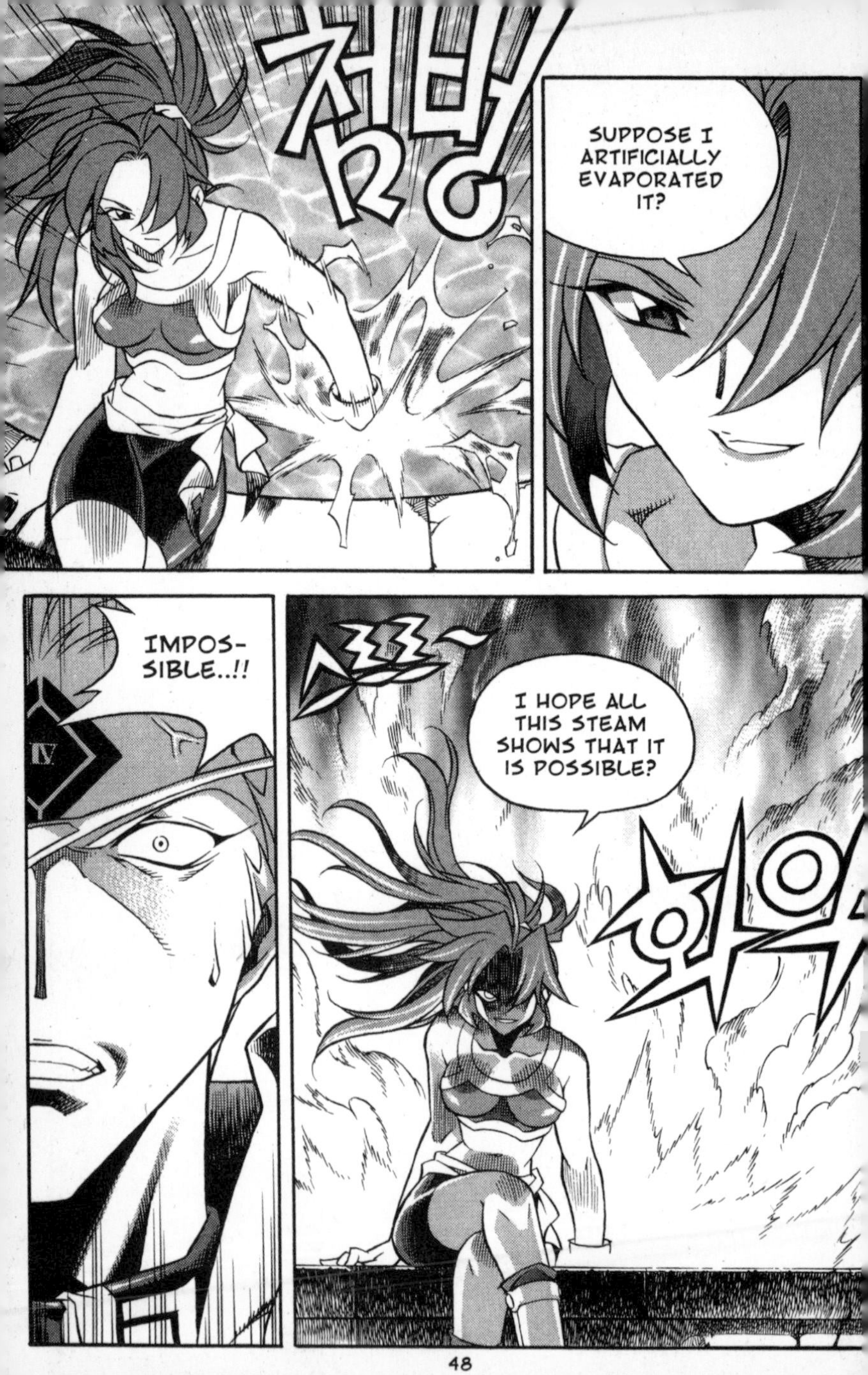
SUPPOSE I ARTIFICIALLY EVAPORATED IT?
IMPOS-SIBLE..!!
I HOPE ALL THIS STEAM SHOWS THAT IT IS POSSIBLE?

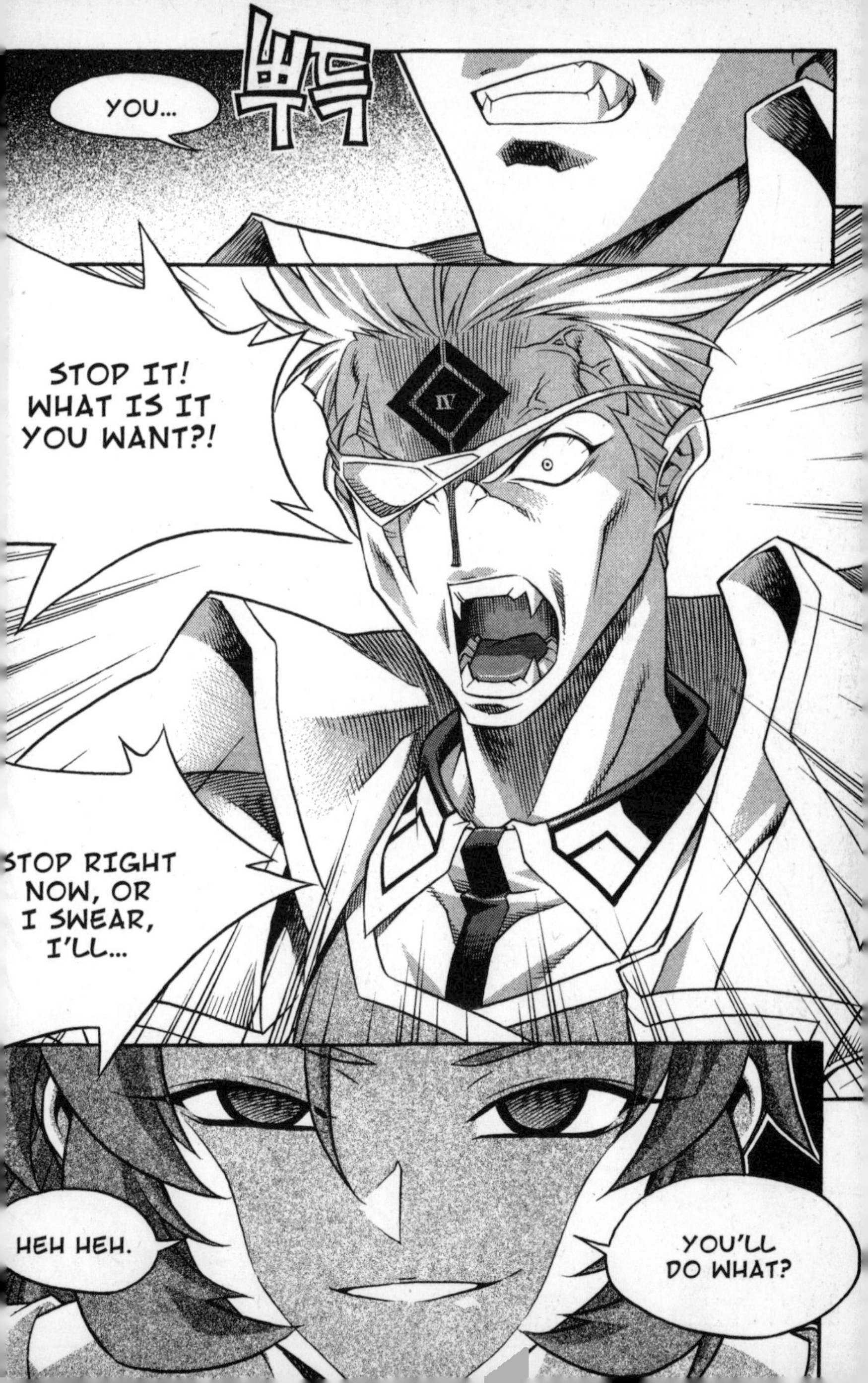
YOU...
STOP IT! WHAT IS IT YOU WANT?!
STOP RIGHT NOW, OR I SWEAR, I'LL...
HEH HEH.
YOU'LL DO WHAT?

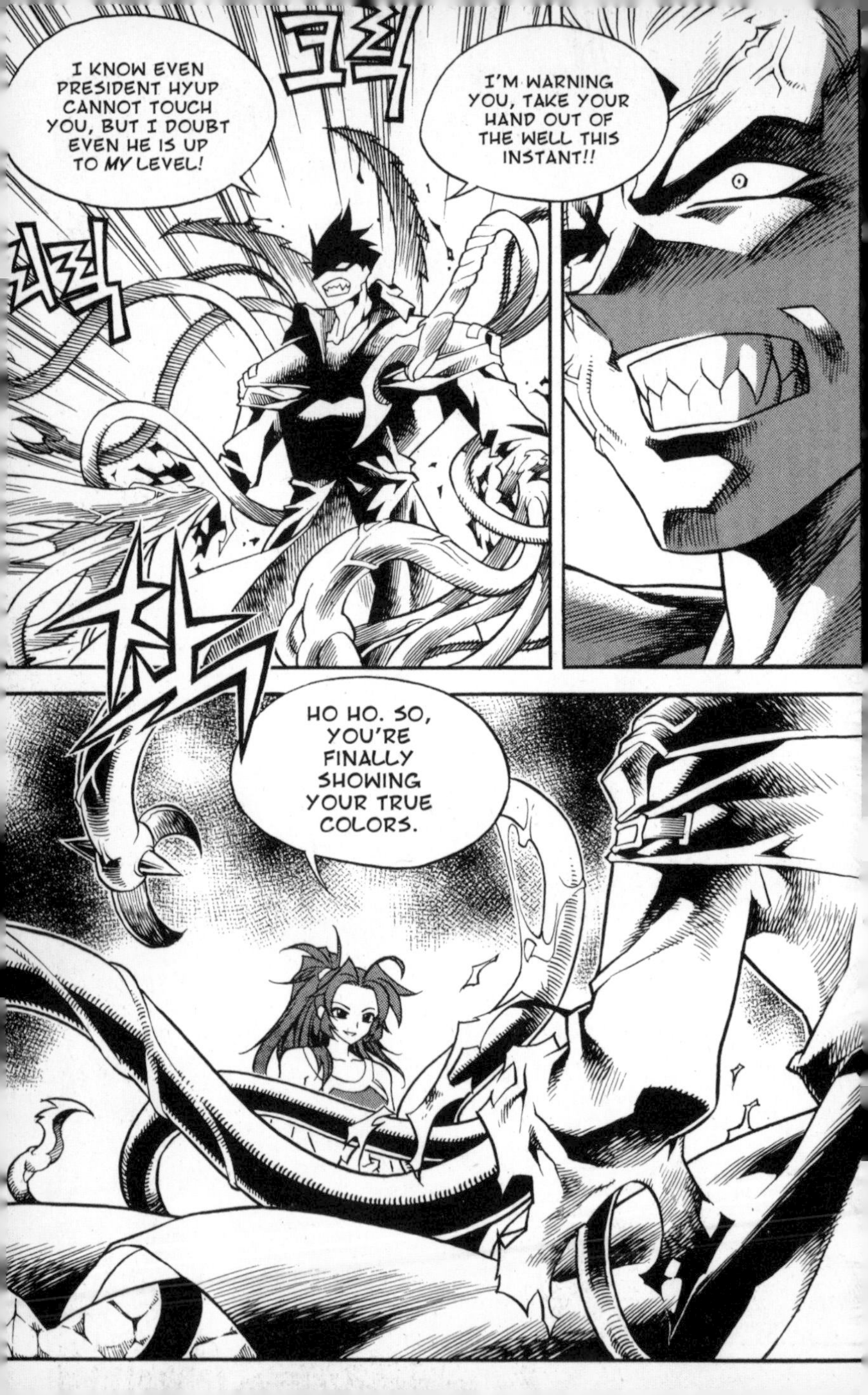
I KNOW EVEN PRESIDENT HYUP CANNOT TOUCH YOU, BUT I DOUBT EVEN HE IS UP TO *MY* LEVEL!
I'M WARNING YOU, TAKE YOUR HAND OUT OF THE WELL THIS INSTANT!!
HO HO. SO, YOU'RE FINALLY SHOWING YOUR TRUE COLORS.

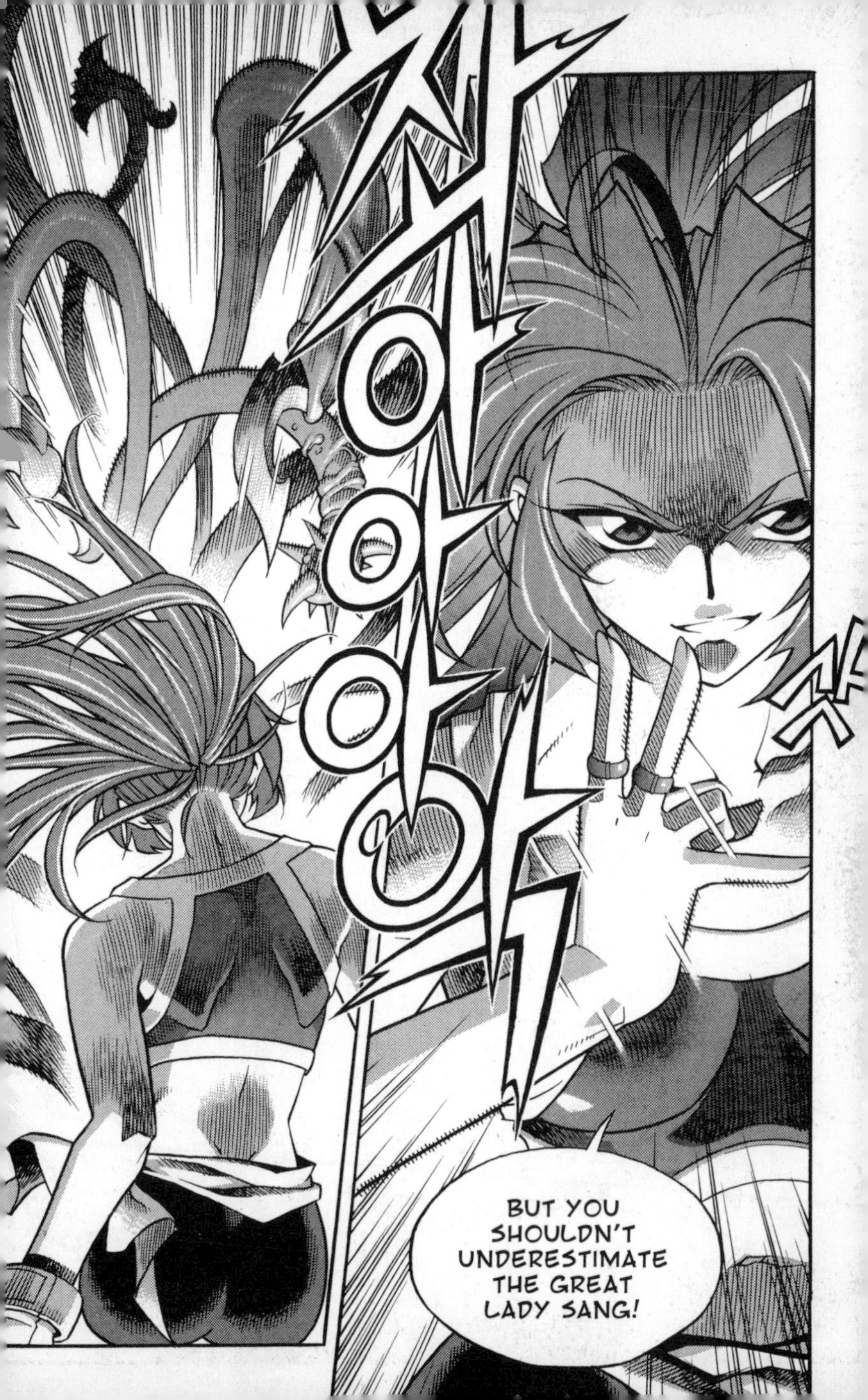
BUT YOU SHOULDN'T UNDERESTIMATE THE GREAT LADY SANG!

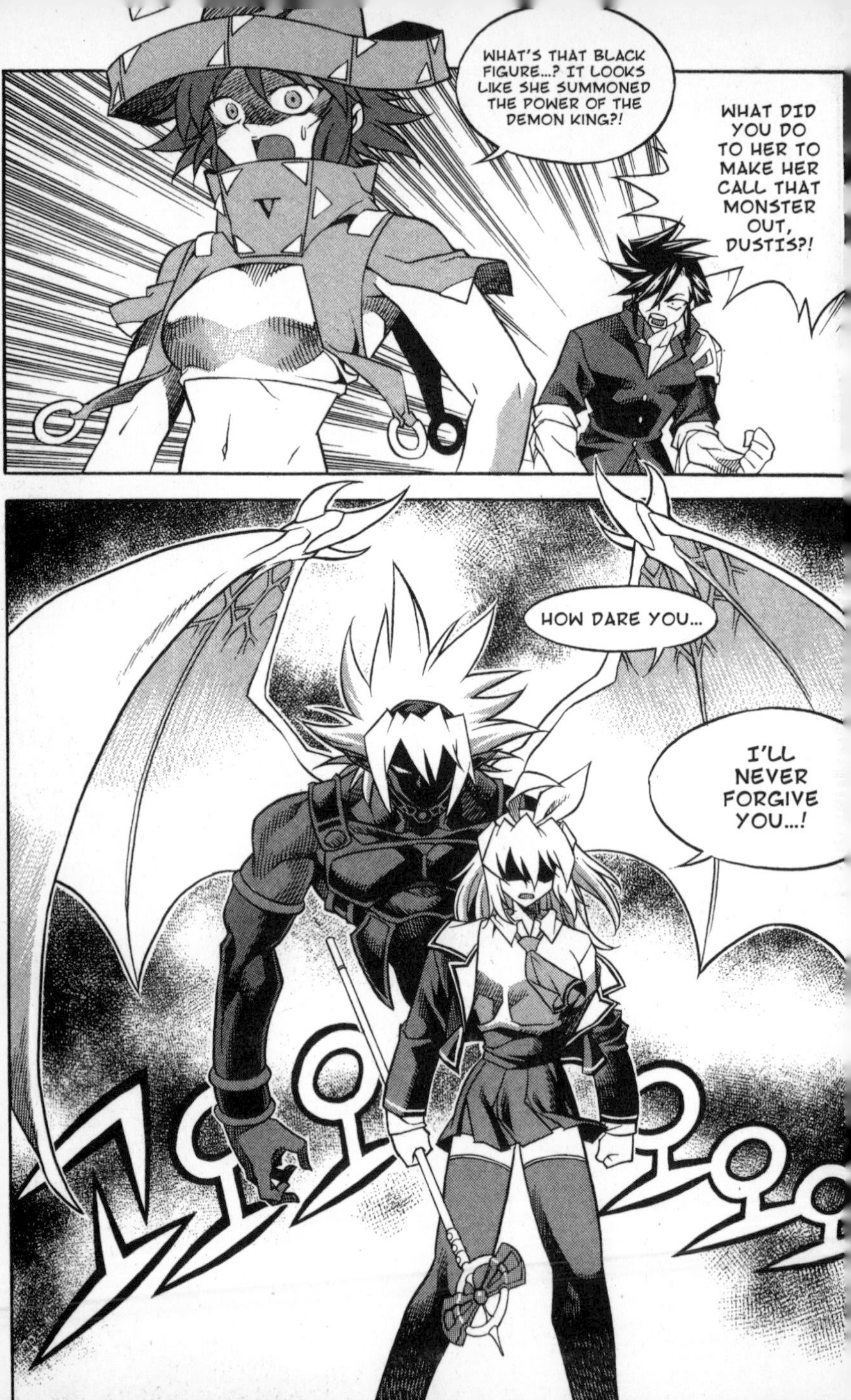
WHAT DID YOU DO TO HER TO MAKE HER CALL THAT MONSTER OUT, DUSTIS?!
WHAT'S THAT BLACK FIGURE...? IT LOOKS LIKE SHE SUMMONED THE POWER OF THE DEMON KING?!
HOW DARE YOU...
I'LL NEVER FORGIVE YOU...!

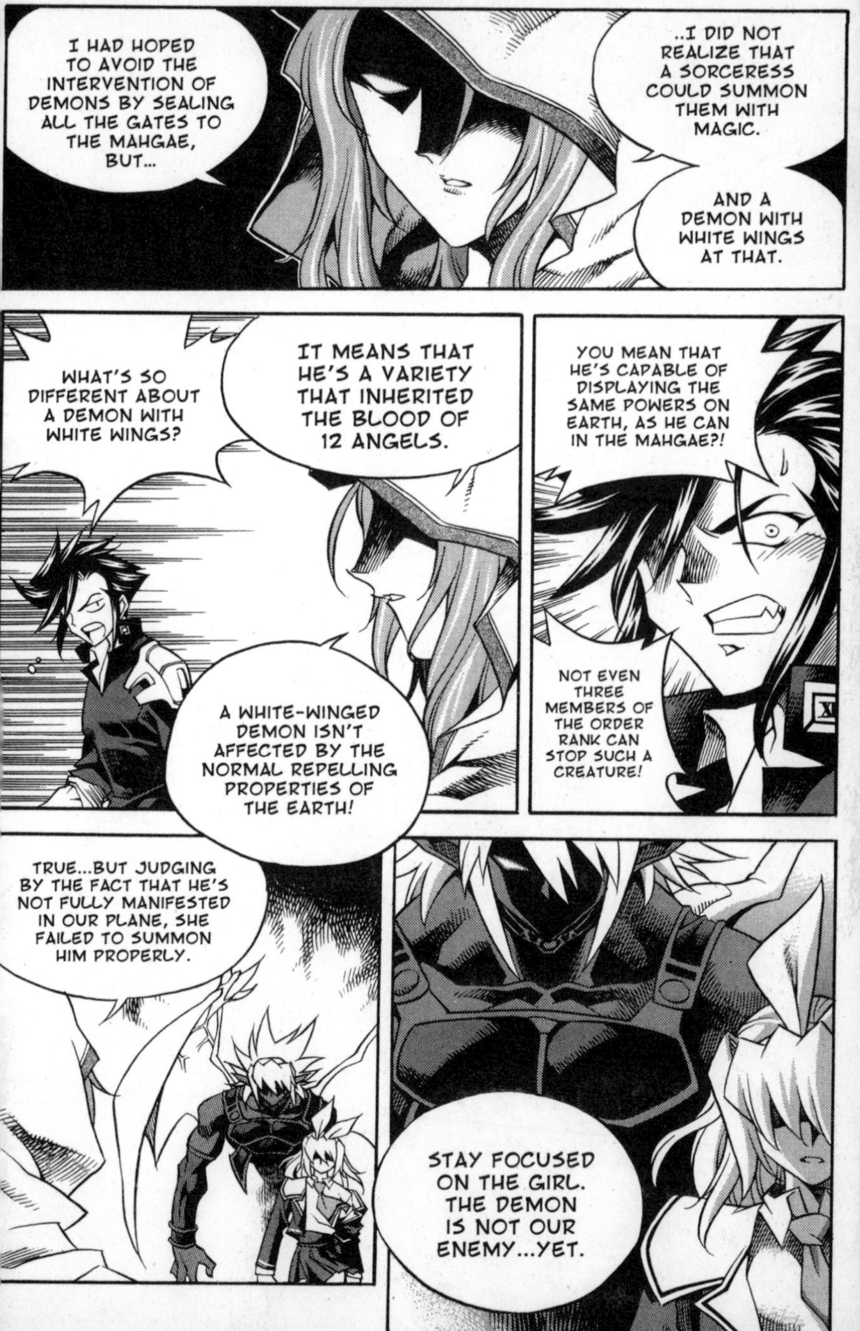
I HAD HOPED TO AVOID THE INTERVENTION OF DEMONS BY SEALING ALL THE GATES TO THE MAHGAE, BUT...
..I DID NOT REALIZE THAT A SORCERESS COULD SUMMON THEM WITH MAGIC.
AND A DEMON WITH WHITE WINGS AT THAT.
WHAT'S SO DIFFERENT ABOUT A DEMON WITH WHITE WINGS?
IT MEANS THAT HE'S A VARIETY THAT INHERITED THE BLOOD OF 12 ANGELS.
A WHITE-WINGED DEMON ISN'T AFFECTED BY THE NORMAL REPELLING PROPERTIES OF THE EARTH!
YOU MEAN THAT HE'S CAPABLE OF DISPLAYING THE SAME POWERS ON EARTH, AS HE CAN IN THE MAHGAE?!
NOT EVEN THREE MEMBERS OF THE ORDER RANK CAN STOP SUCH A CREATURE!
TRUE...BUT JUDGING BY THE FACT THAT HE'S NOT FULLY MANIFESTED IN OUR PLANE, SHE FAILED TO SUMMON HIM PROPERLY.
STAY FOCUSED ON THE GIRL. THE DEMON IS NOT OUR ENEMY...YET.

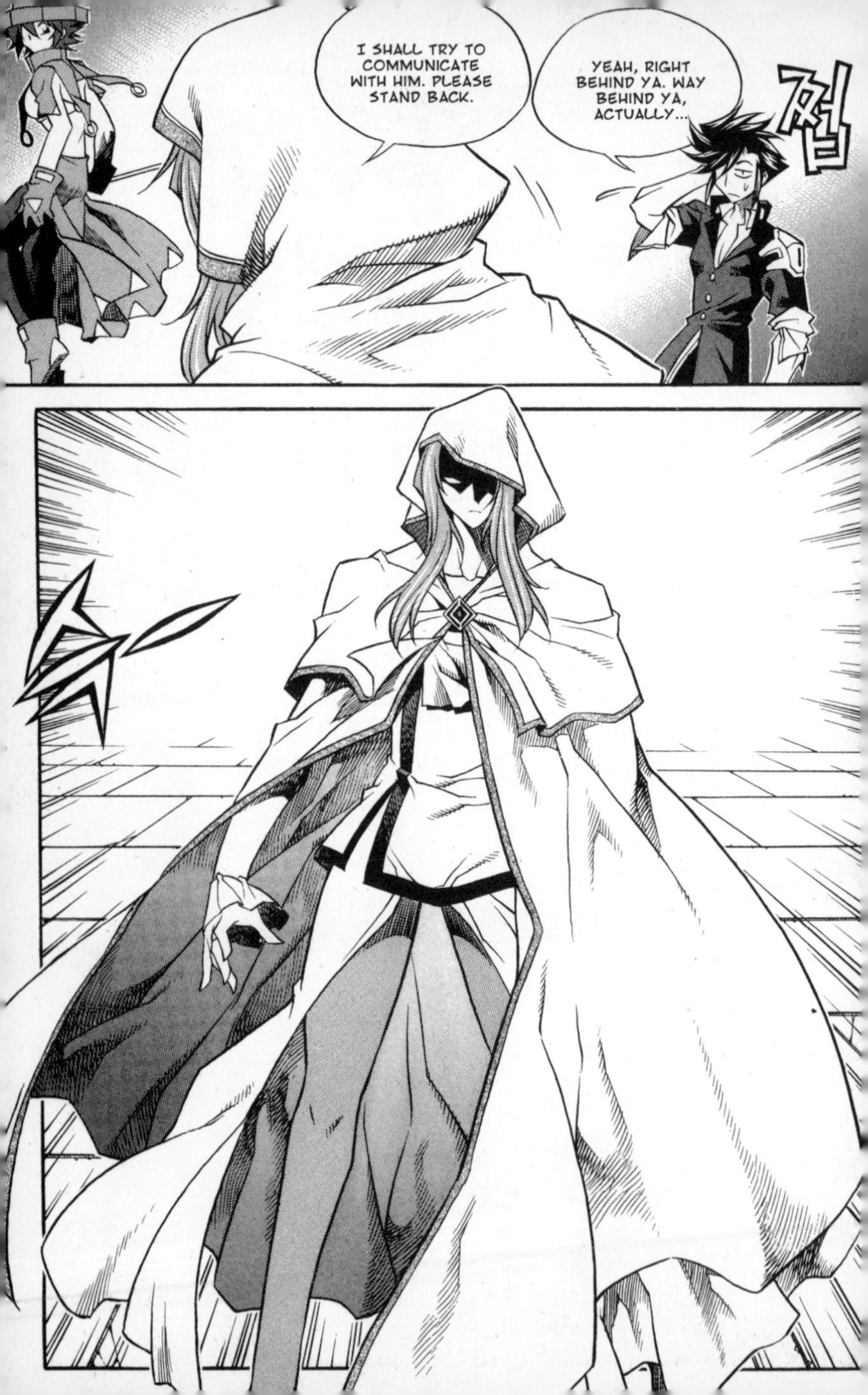
YEAH, RIGHT BEHIND YA. WAY BEHIND YA, ACTUALLY...
I SHALL TRY TO COMMUNICATE WITH HIM. PLEASE STAND BACK.

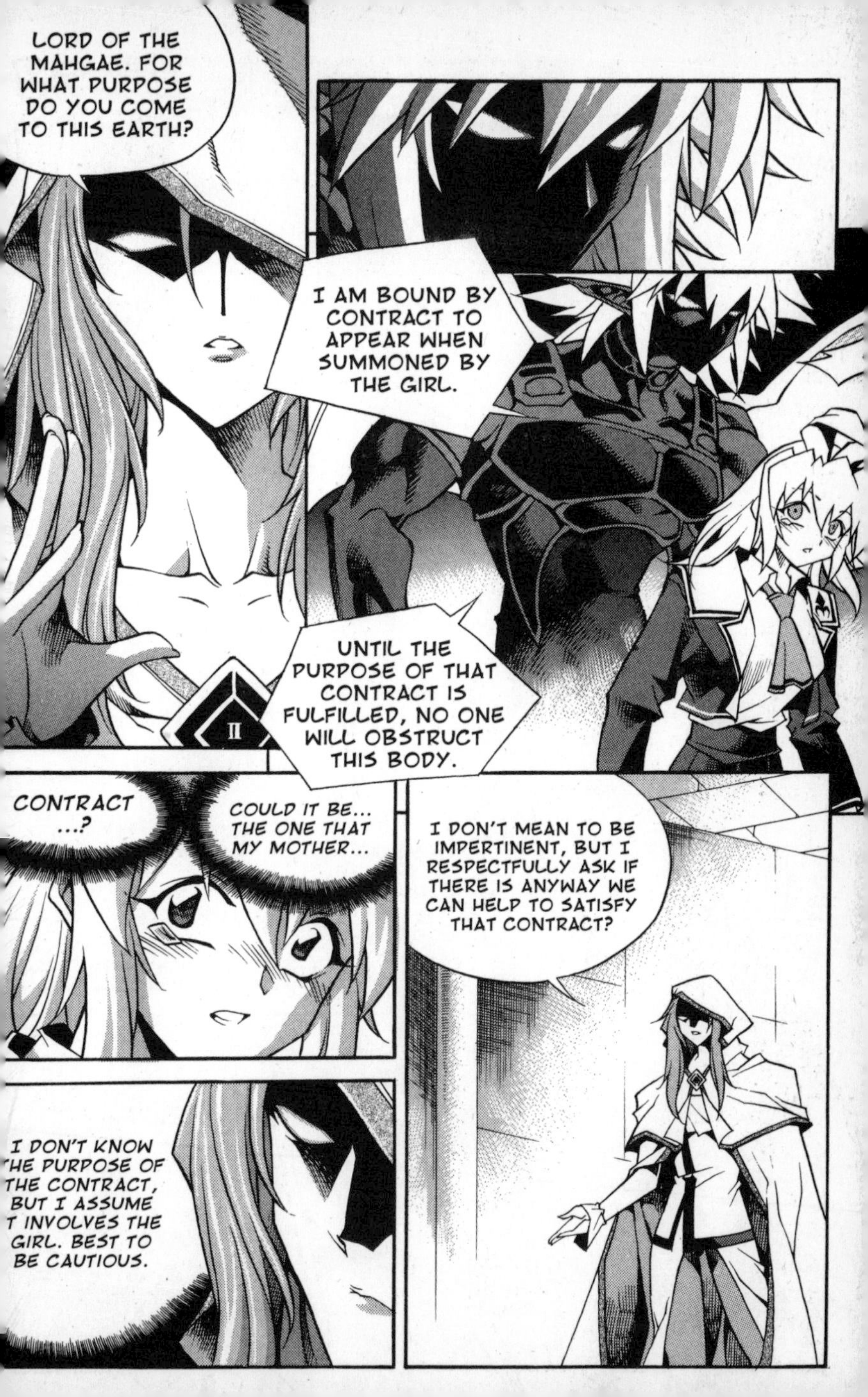
LORD OF THE MAHGAE. FOR WHAT PURPOSE DO YOU COME TO THIS EARTH?
I AM BOUND BY CONTRACT TO APPEAR WHEN SUMMONED BY THE GIRL.
UNTIL THE PURPOSE OF THAT CONTRACT IS FULFILLED, NO ONE WILL OBSTRUCT THIS BODY.
CONTRACT ...?
COULD IT BE... THE ONE THAT MY MOTHER...
I DON'T MEAN TO BE IMPERTINENT, BUT I RESPECTFULLY ASK IF THERE IS ANYWAY WE CAN HELP TO SATISFY THAT CONTRACT?
I DON'T KNOW THE PURPOSE OF THE CONTRACT, BUT I ASSUME IT INVOLVES THE GIRL. BEST TO BE CAUTIOUS.

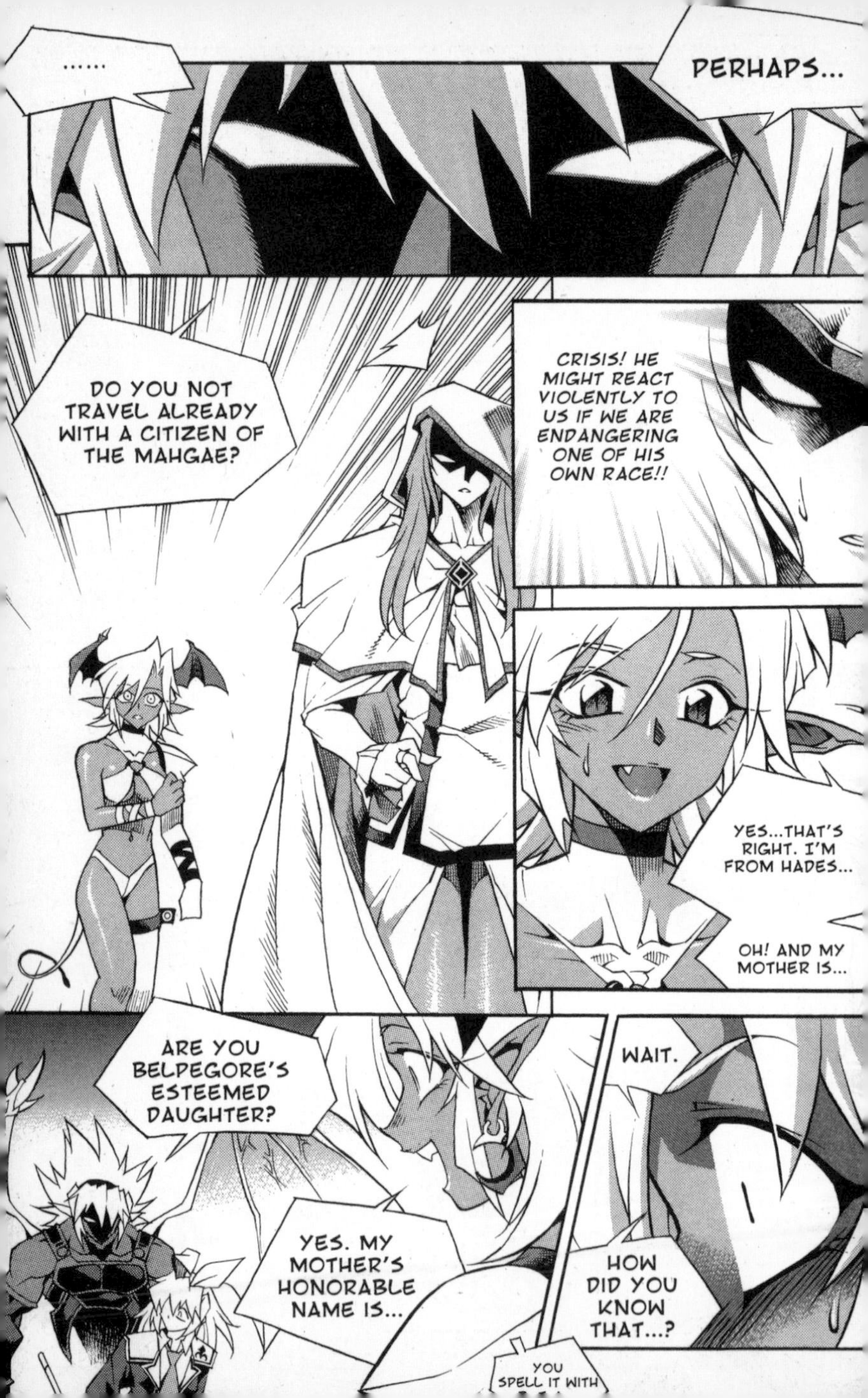

PERHAPS...
......
DO YOU NOT TRAVEL ALREADY WITH A CITIZEN OF THE MAHGAE?
CRISIS! HE MIGHT REACT VIOLENTLY TO US IF WE ARE ENDANGERING ONE OF HIS OWN RACE!!
YES...THAT'S RIGHT. I'M FROM HADES...
OH! AND MY MOTHER IS...
ARE YOU BELPEGORE'S ESTEEMED DAUGHTER?
YES. MY MOTHER'S HONORABLE NAME IS...
WAIT.
HOW DID YOU KNOW THAT...?
YOU SPELL IT WITH

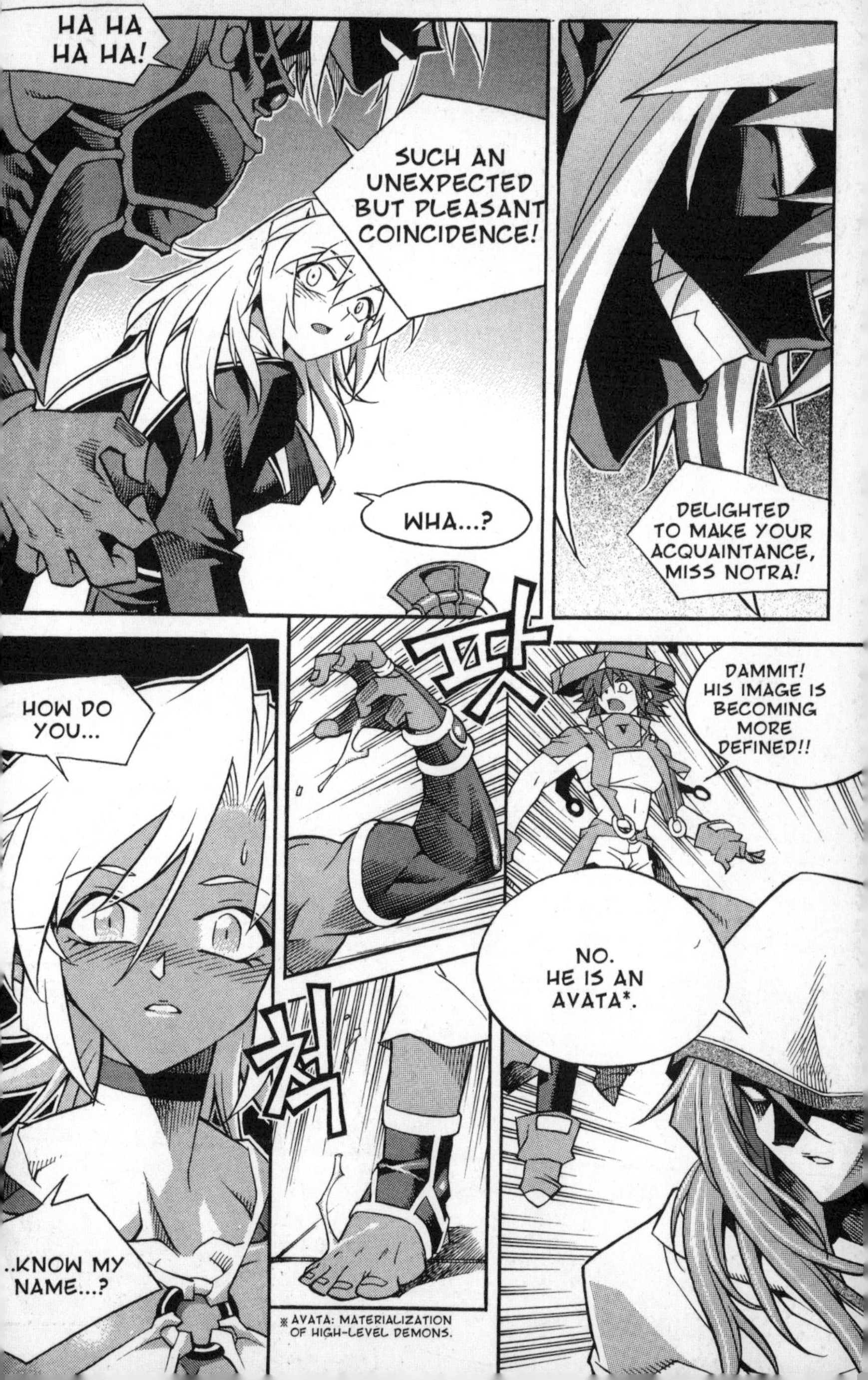
HA HA HA HA!
SUCH AN UNEXPECTED BUT PLEASANT COINCIDENCE!
WHA...?
DELIGHTED TO MAKE YOUR ACQUAINTANCE, MISS NOTRA!
HOW DO YOU...
..KNOW MY NAME...?
DAMMIT! HIS IMAGE IS BECOMING MORE DEFINED!!
NO. HE IS AN AVATA*.

※ AVATA: MATERIALIZATION OF HIGH-LEVEL DEMONS.

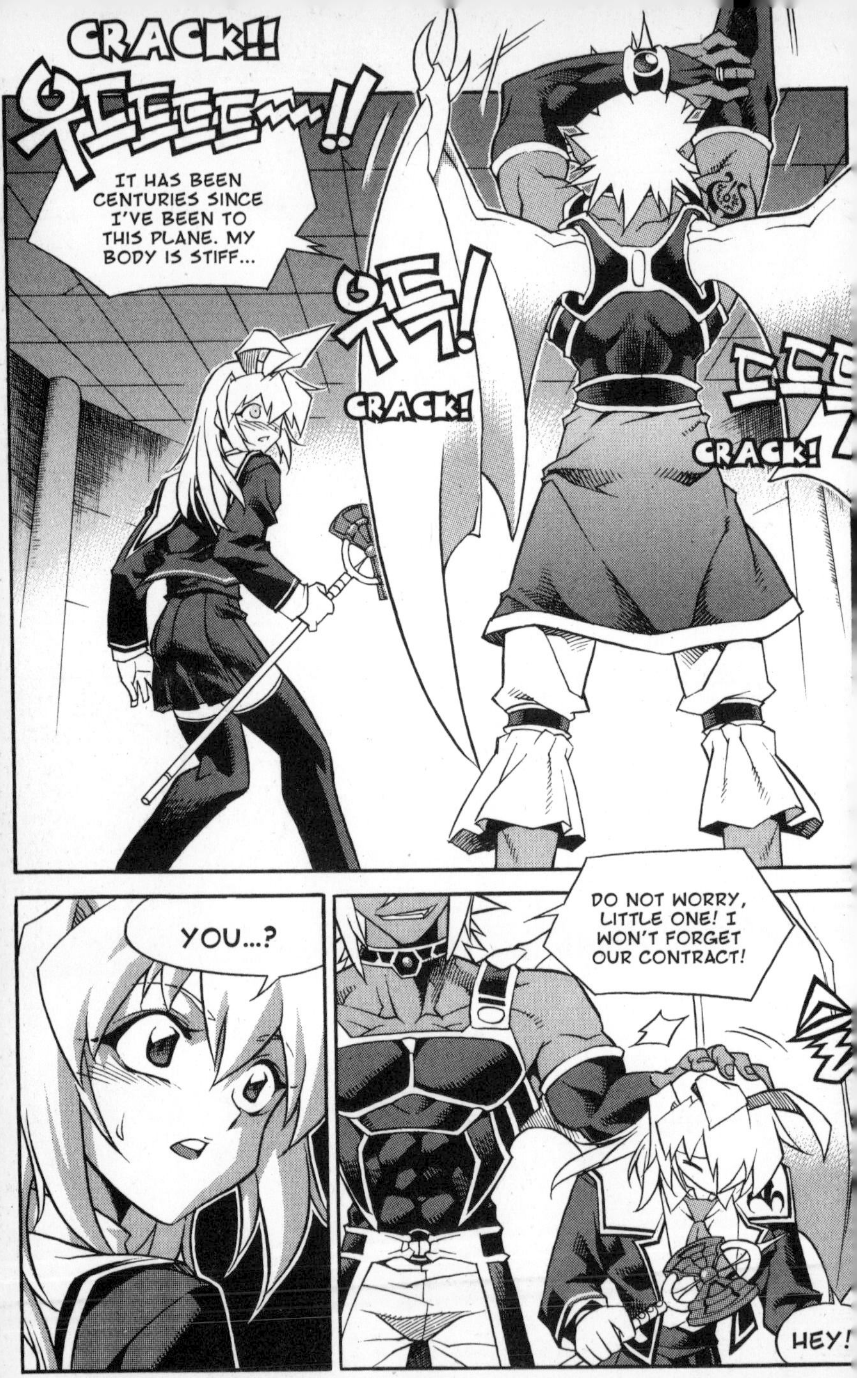
CRACK!!
IT HAS BEEN CENTURIES SINCE I'VE BEEN TO THIS PLANE. MY BODY IS STIFF...
CRACK!
CRACK!
YOU...?
DO NOT WORRY, LITTLE ONE! I WON'T FORGET OUR CONTRACT!
HEY!

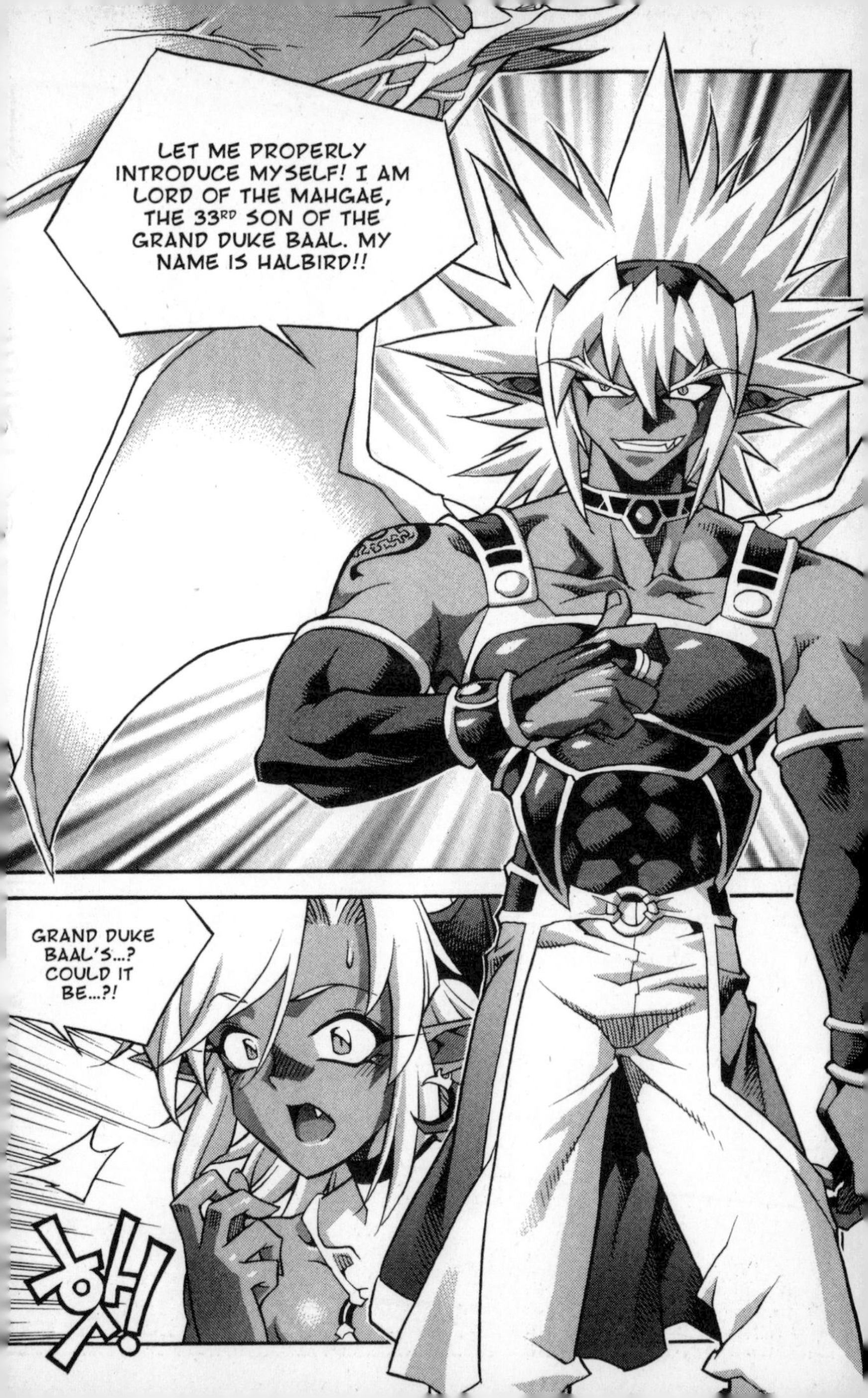
LET ME PROPERLY INTRODUCE MYSELF! I AM LORD OF THE MAHGAE, THE 33RD SON OF THE GRAND DUKE BAAL. MY NAME IS HALBIRD!!
GRAND DUKE BAAL'S...? COULD IT BE...?!

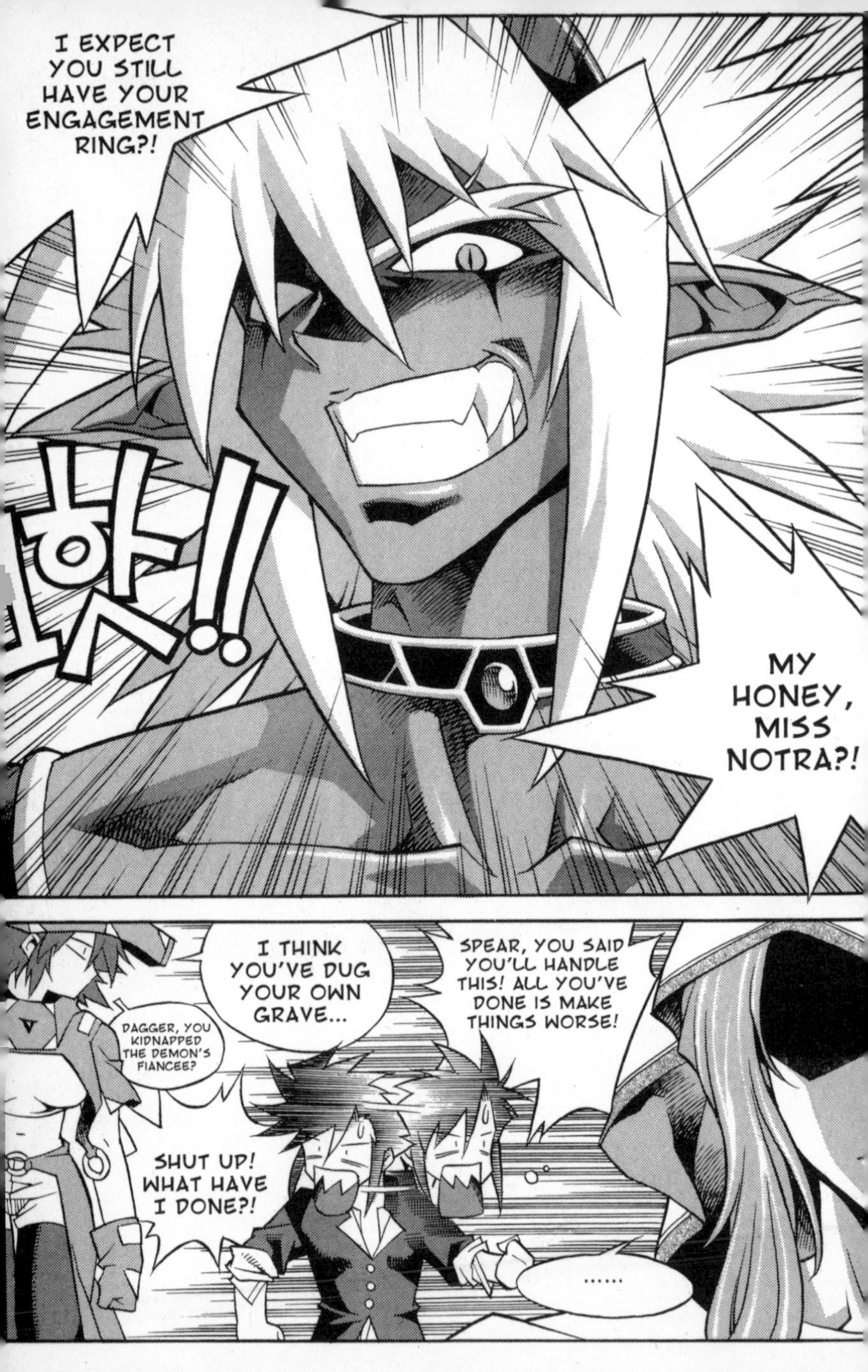
I EXPECT YOU STILL HAVE YOUR ENGAGEMENT RING?!
MY HONEY, MISS NOTRA?!
I THINK YOU'VE DUG YOUR OWN GRAVE...
DAGGER, YOU KIDNAPPED THE DEMON'S FIANCEE?
SPEAR, YOU SAID YOU'LL HANDLE THIS! ALL YOU'VE DONE IS MAKE THINGS WORSE!
SHUT UP! WHAT HAVE I DONE?!
......

Quest 91

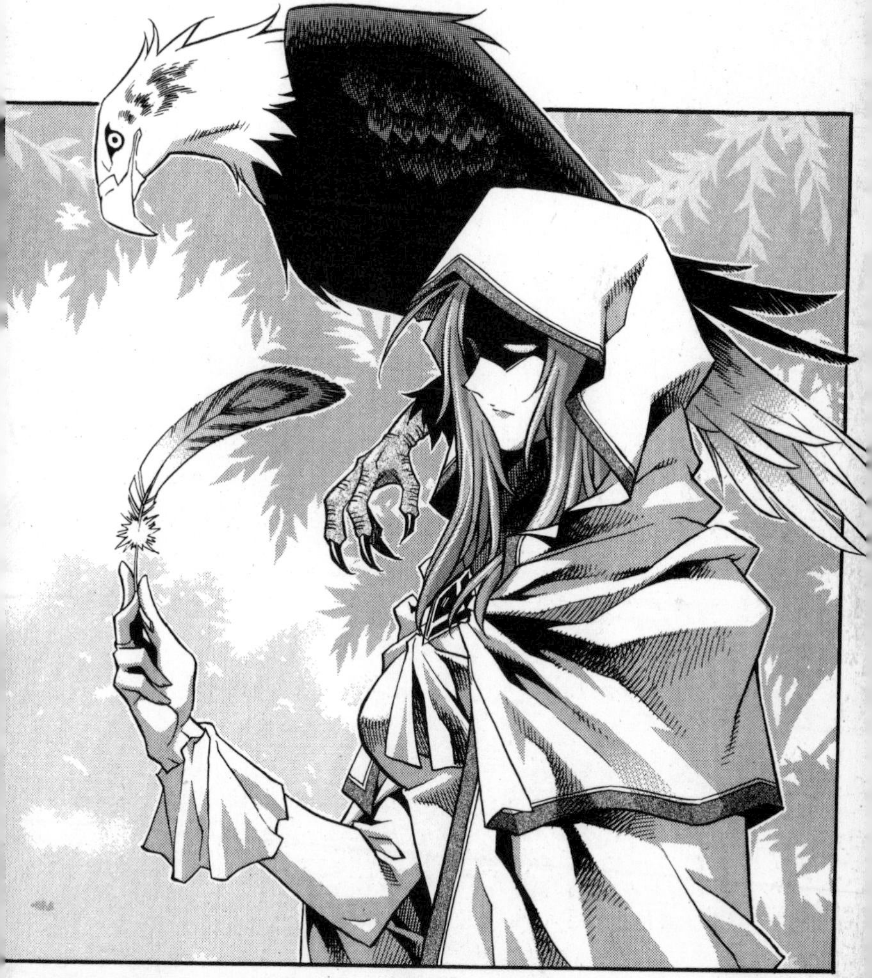

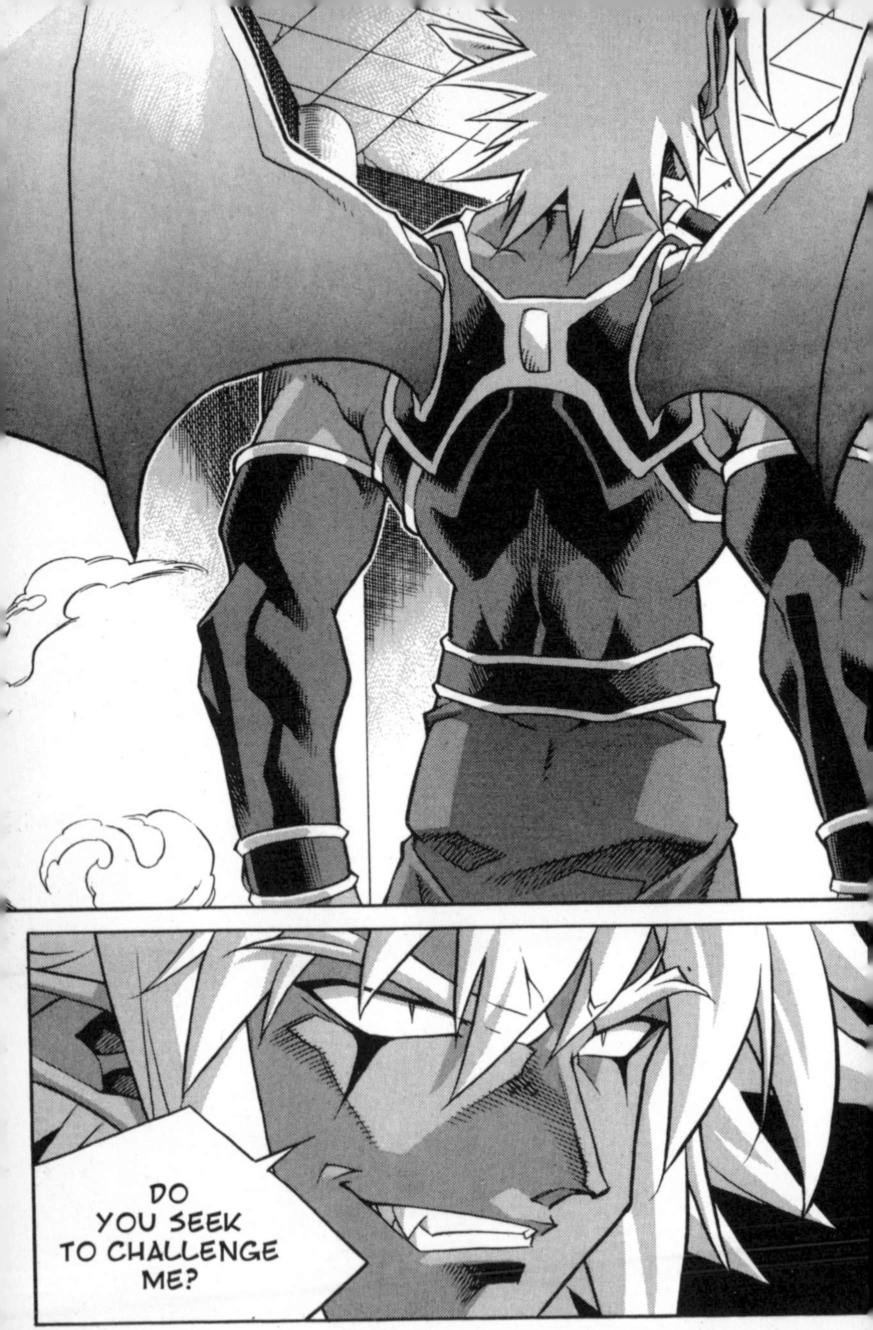
DO YOU SEEK TO CHALLENGE ME?

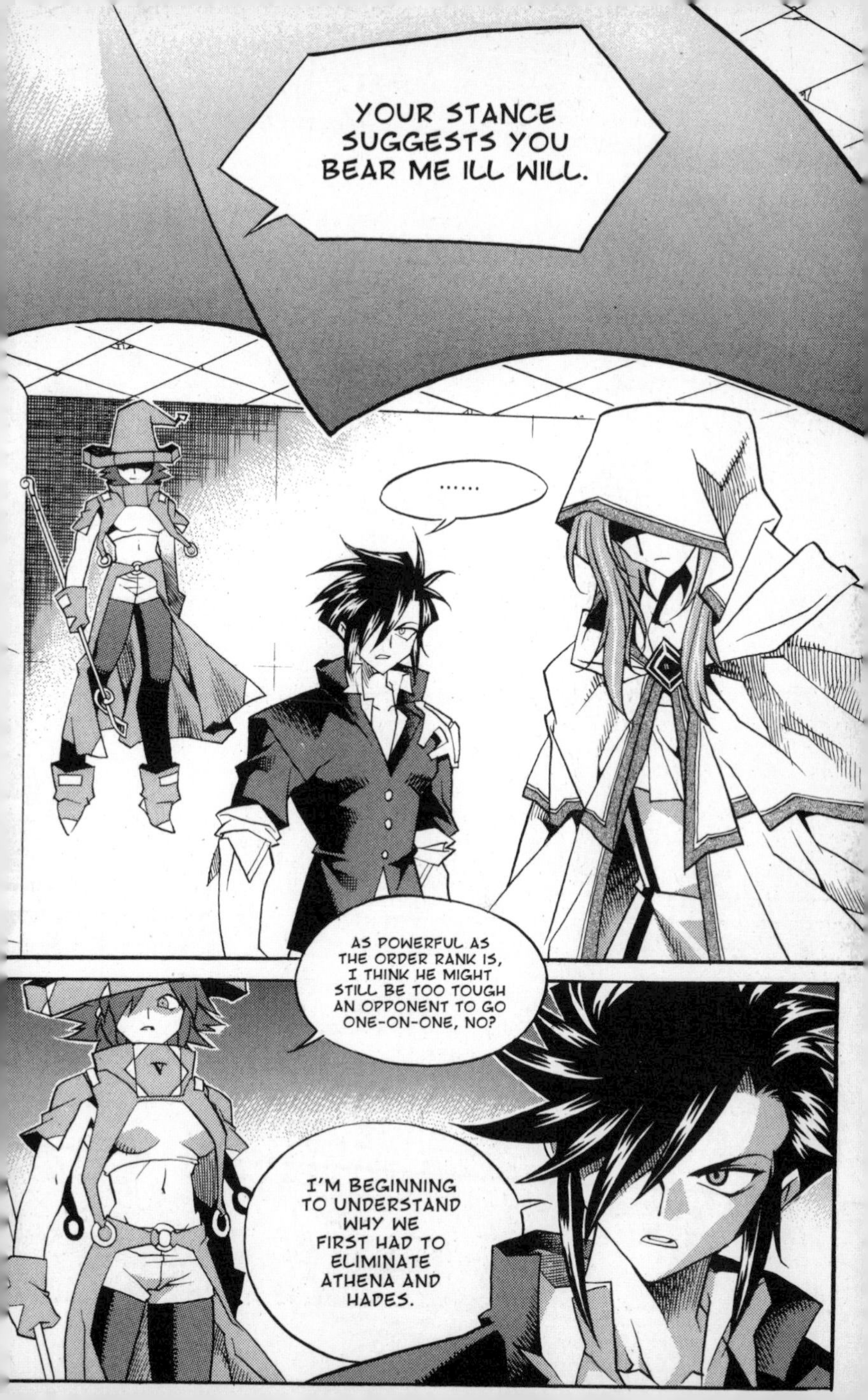
YOUR STANCE SUGGESTS YOU BEAR ME ILL WILL.
......
AS POWERFUL AS THE ORDER RANK IS, I THINK HE MIGHT STILL BE TOO TOUGH AN OPPONENT TO GO ONE-ON-ONE, NO?
I'M BEGINNING TO UNDERSTAND WHY WE FIRST HAD TO ELIMINATE ATHENA AND HADES.

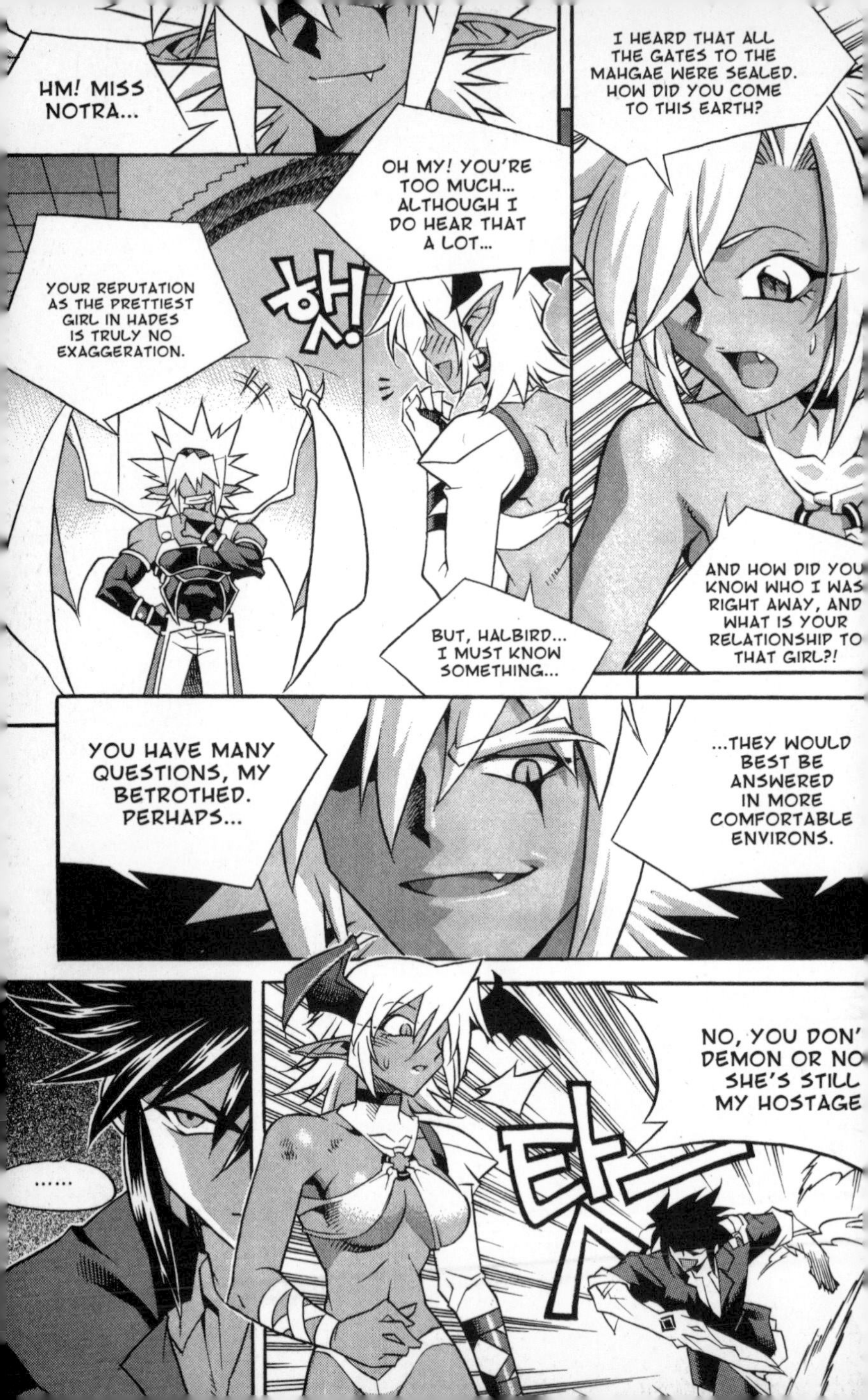
HM! MISS NOTRA...
YOUR REPUTATION AS THE PRETTIEST GIRL IN HADES IS TRULY NO EXAGGERATION.
핫!
OH MY! YOU'RE TOO MUCH... ALTHOUGH I DO HEAR THAT A LOT...
BUT, HALBIRD... I MUST KNOW SOMETHING...
I HEARD THAT ALL THE GATES TO THE MAHGAE WERE SEALED. HOW DID YOU COME TO THIS EARTH?
AND HOW DID YOU KNOW WHO I WAS RIGHT AWAY, AND WHAT IS YOUR RELATIONSHIP TO THAT GIRL?!
YOU HAVE MANY QUESTIONS, MY BETROTHED. PERHAPS...
...THEY WOULD BEST BE ANSWERED IN MORE COMFORTABLE ENVIRONS.
......
탓—
NO, YOU DON'
DEMON OR NO
SHE'S STILL
MY HOSTAGE

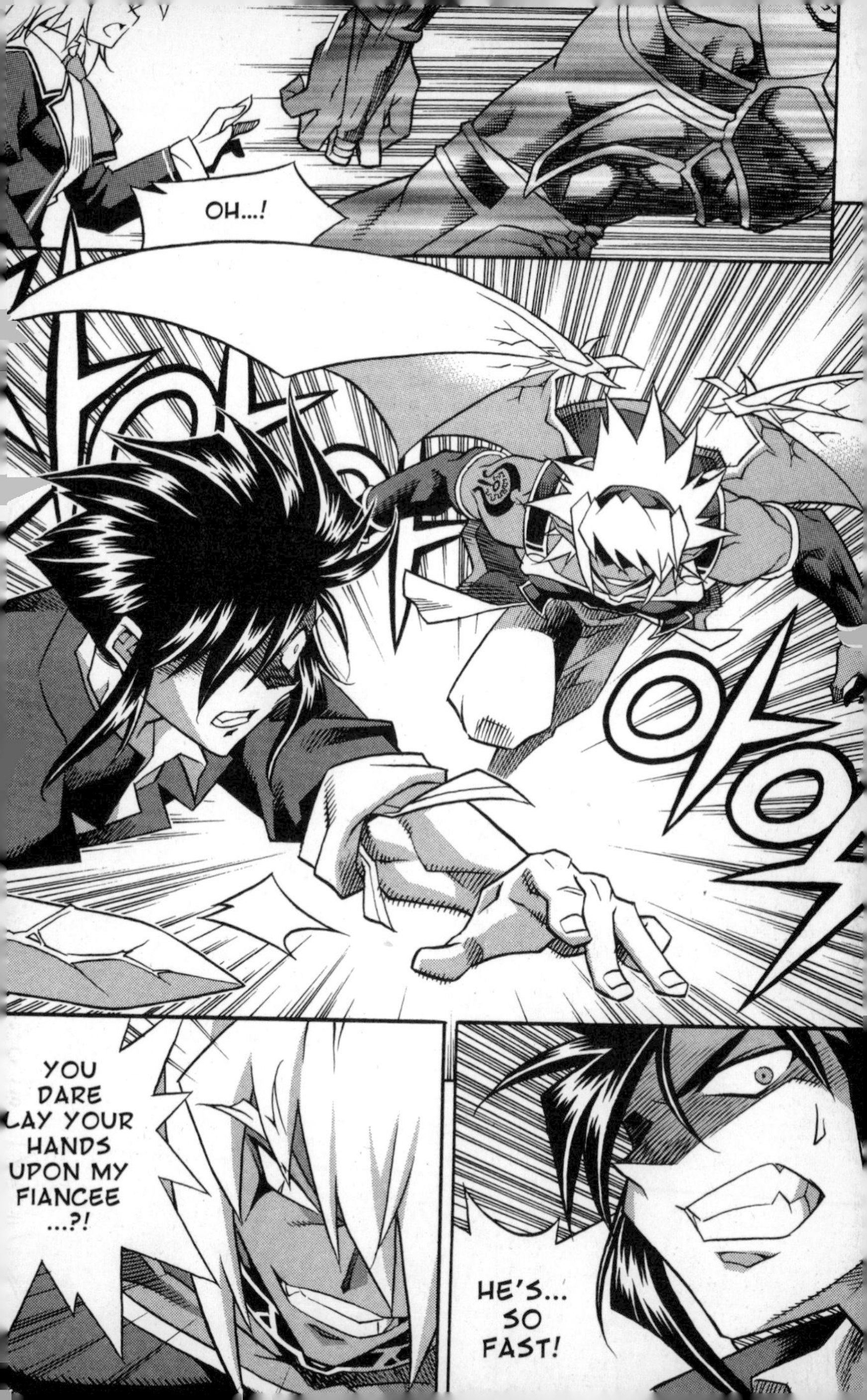
OH...!
HE'S... SO FAST!
YOU DARE LAY YOUR HANDS UPON MY FIANCEE ...?!

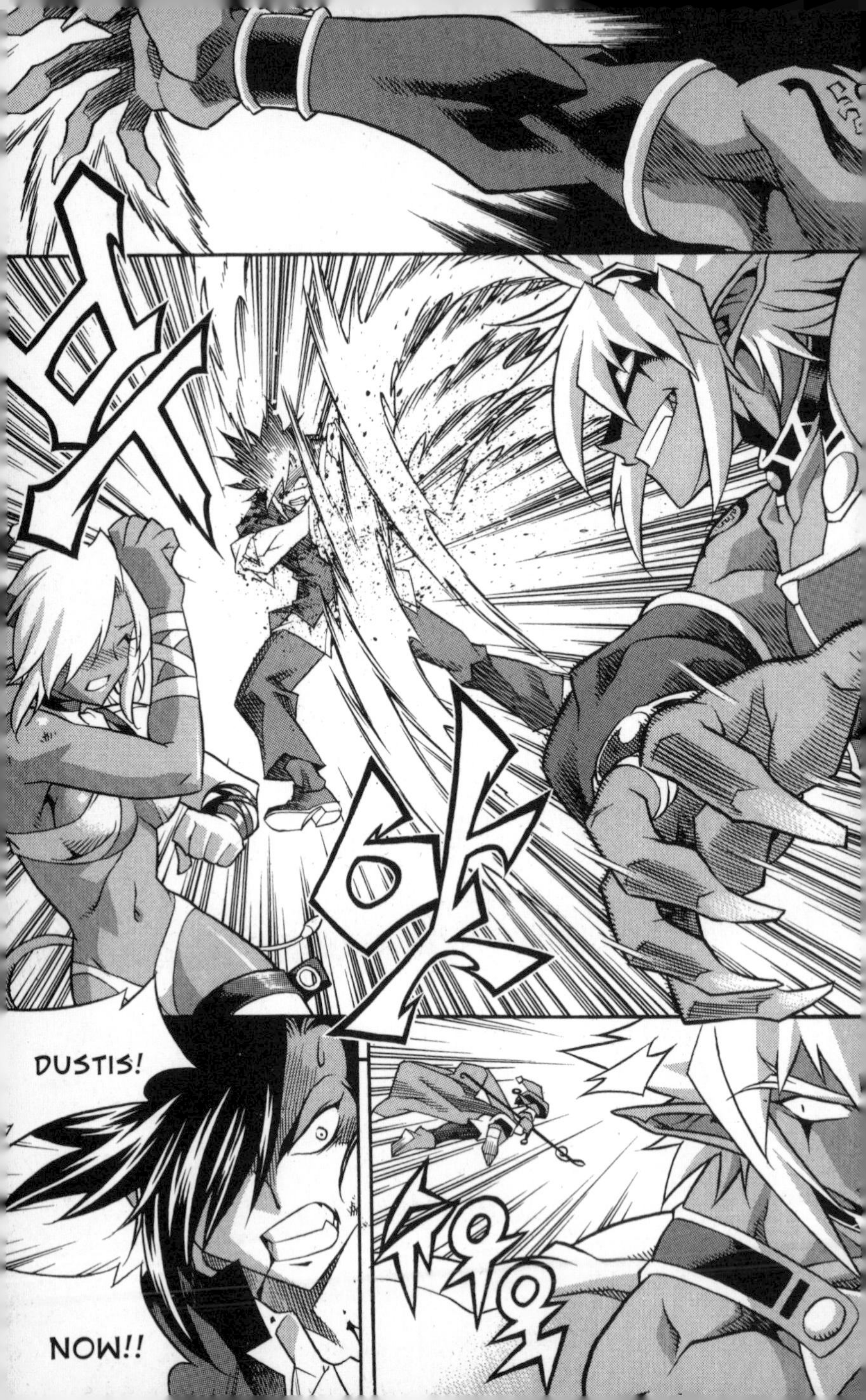
DUSTIS!
NOW!!

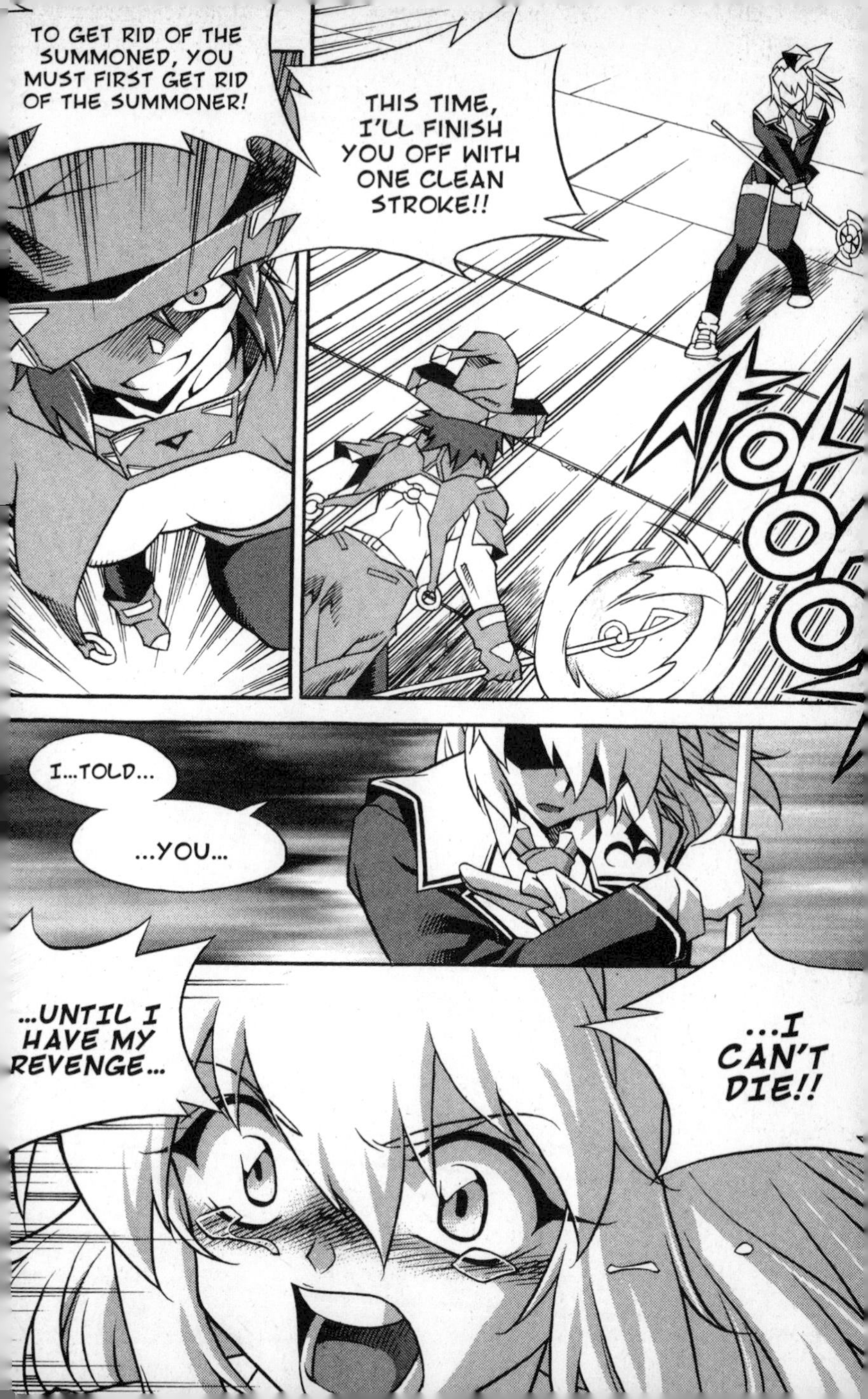
TO GET RID OF THE SUMMONED, YOU MUST FIRST GET RID OF THE SUMMONER!
THIS TIME, I'LL FINISH YOU OFF WITH ONE CLEAN STROKE!!
I...TOLD...
...YOU...
...UNTIL I HAVE MY REVENGE...
...I CAN'T DIE!!

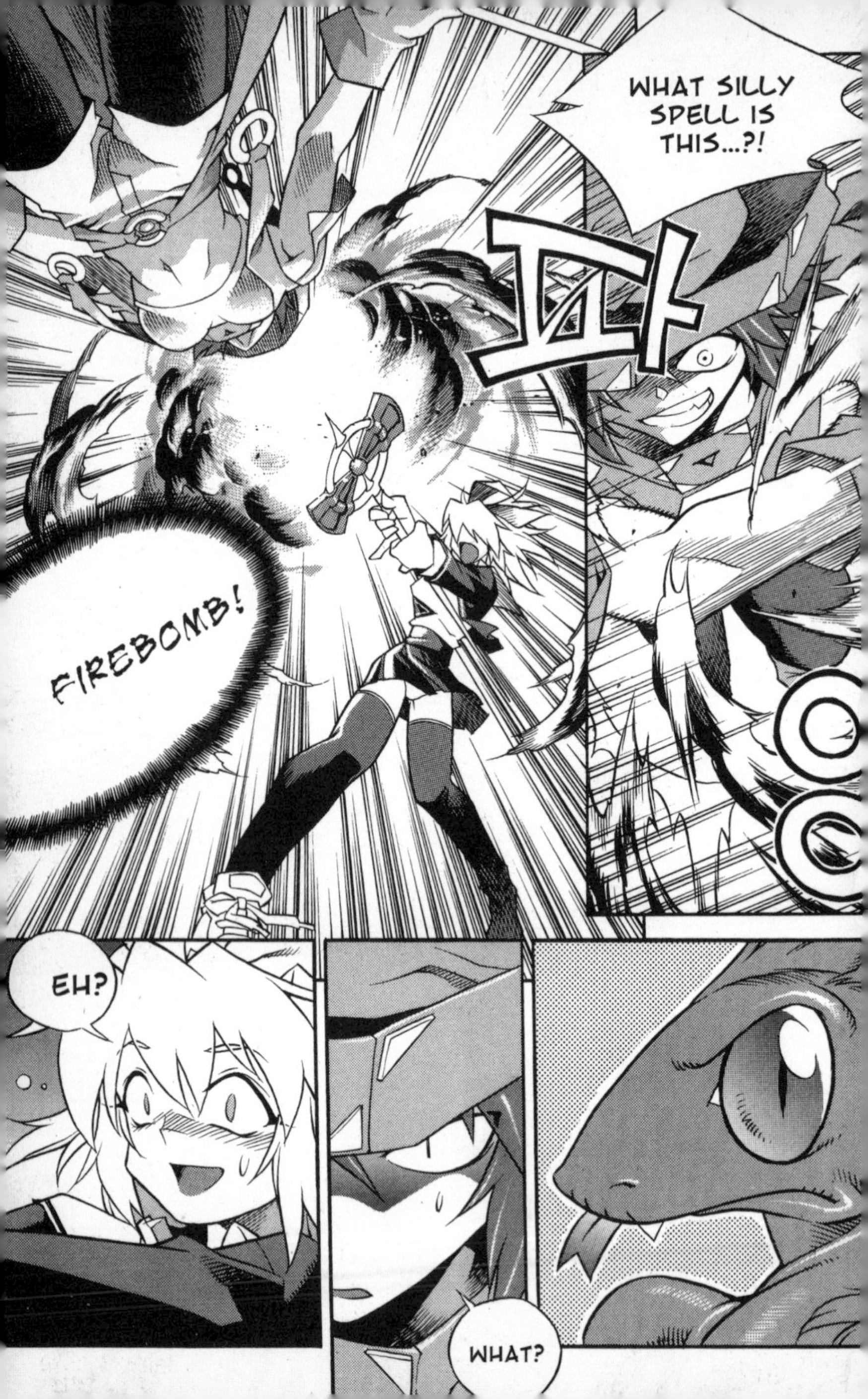
WHAT SILLY SPELL IS THIS...?!
FIREBOMB!
WHAT?
EH?

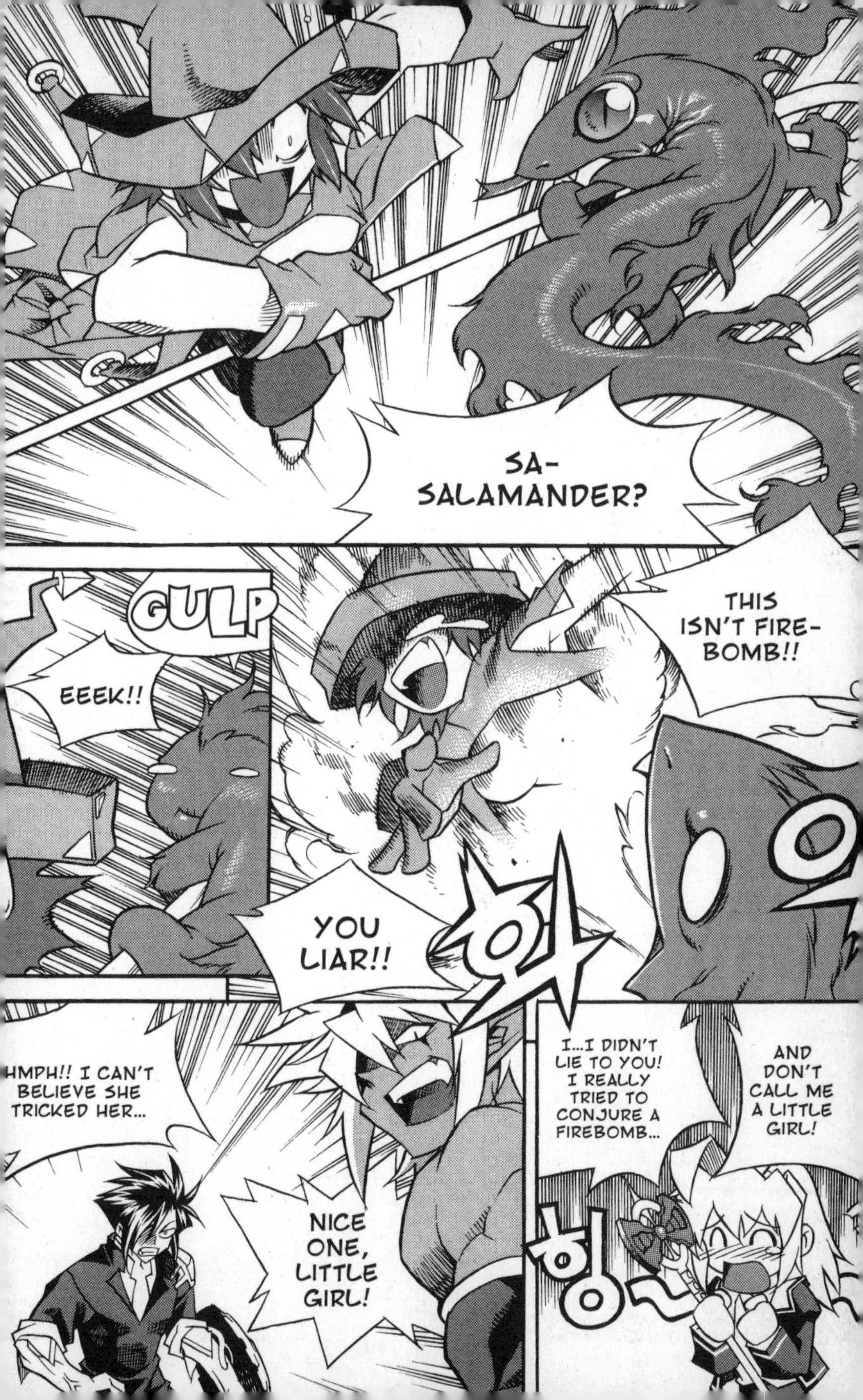
SA-
SALAMANDER?
THIS ISN'T FIRE-BOMB!!
GULP
EEEK!!
YOU LIAR!!
HMPH!! I CAN'T BELIEVE SHE TRICKED HER...
NICE ONE, LITTLE GIRL!
I...I DIDN'T LIE TO YOU! I REALLY TRIED TO CONJURE A FIREBOMB...
AND DON'T CALL ME A LITTLE GIRL!

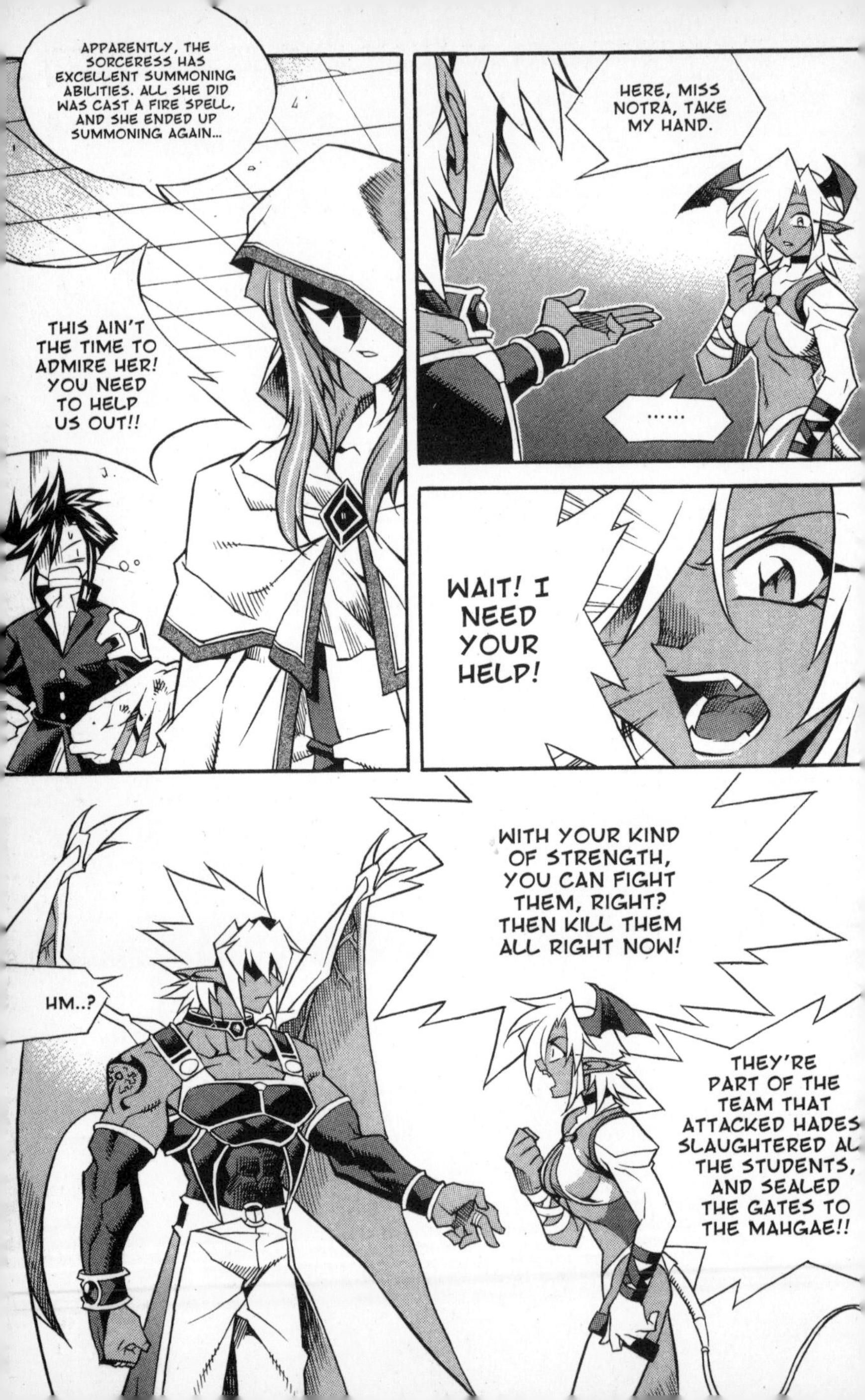
APPARENTLY, THE SORCERESS HAS EXCELLENT SUMMONING ABILITIES. ALL SHE DID WAS CAST A FIRE SPELL, AND SHE ENDED UP SUMMONING AGAIN...
THIS AIN'T THE TIME TO ADMIRE HER! YOU NEED TO HELP US OUT!!
HERE, MISS NOTRA, TAKE MY HAND.
......
WAIT! I NEED YOUR HELP!
WITH YOUR KIND OF STRENGTH, YOU CAN FIGHT THEM, RIGHT? THEN KILL THEM ALL RIGHT NOW!
HM..?
THEY'RE PART OF THE TEAM THAT ATTACKED HADES SLAUGHTERED AL THE STUDENTS, AND SEALED THE GATES TO THE MAHGAE!!

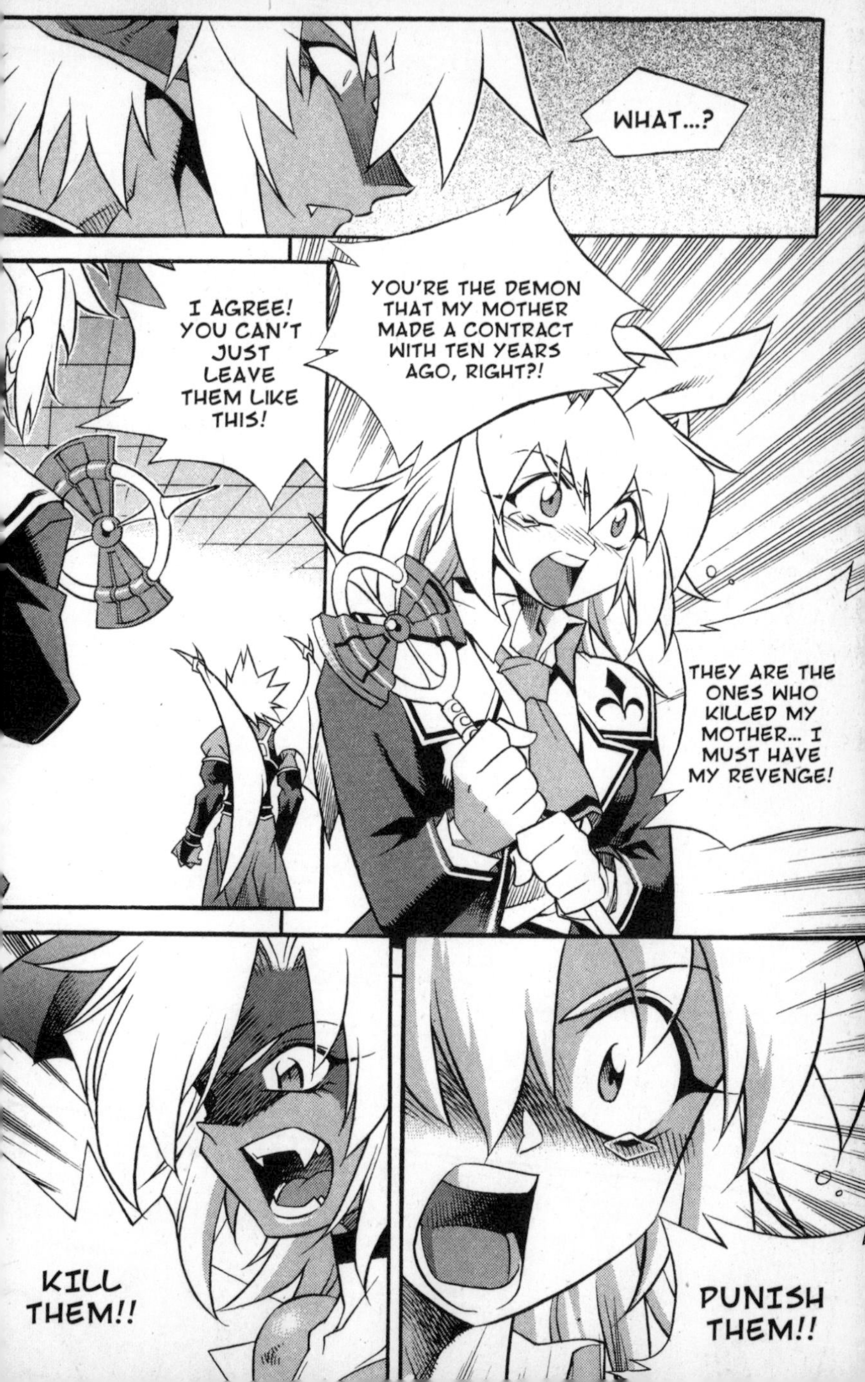
WHAT...?
YOU'RE THE DEMON THAT MY MOTHER MADE A CONTRACT WITH TEN YEARS AGO, RIGHT?!
I AGREE! YOU CAN'T JUST LEAVE THEM LIKE THIS!
THEY ARE THE ONES WHO KILLED MY MOTHER... I MUST HAVE MY REVENGE!
PUNISH THEM!!
KILL THEM!!

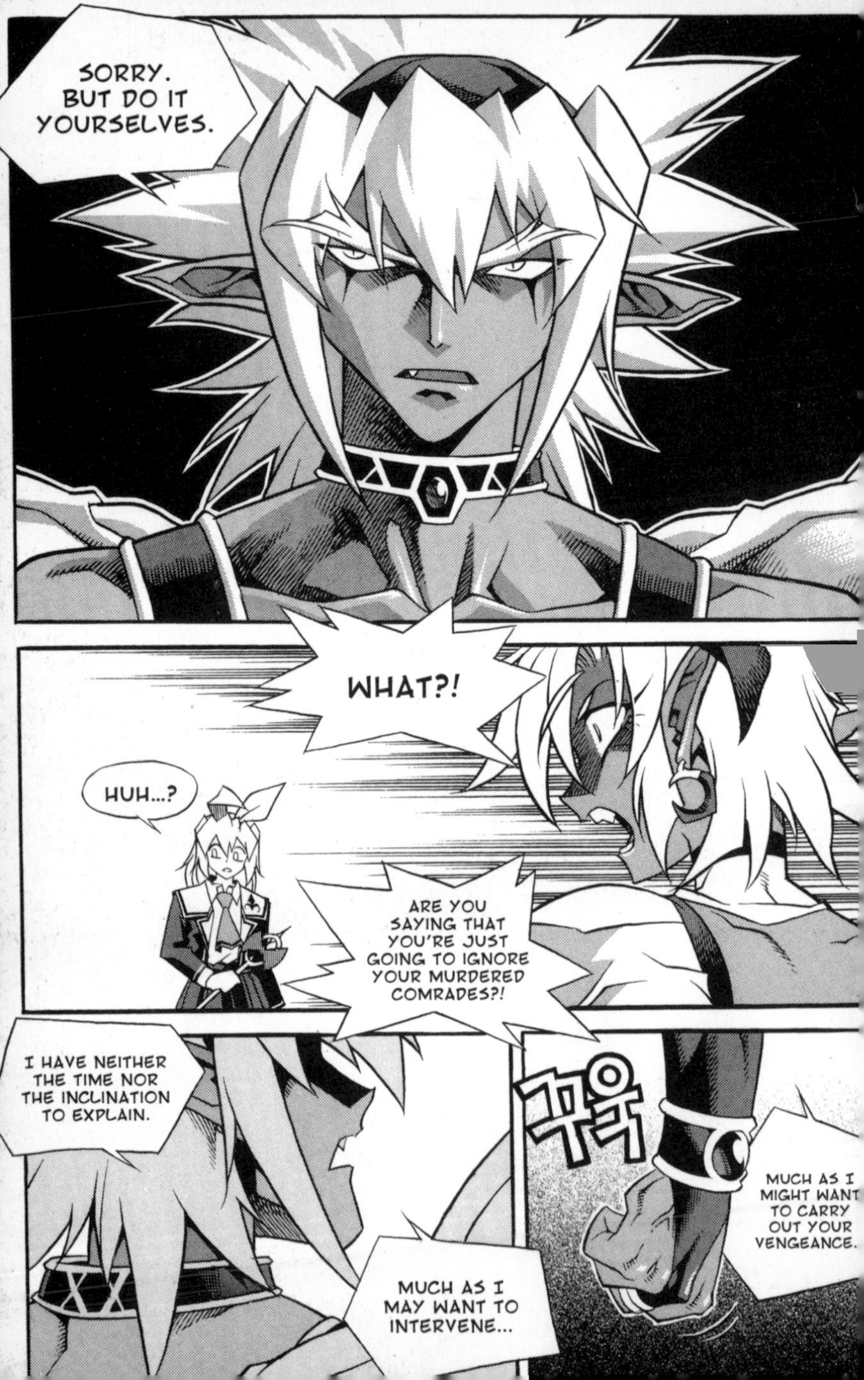
SORRY. BUT DO IT YOURSELVES.
WHAT?!
HUH...?
ARE YOU SAYING THAT YOU'RE JUST GOING TO IGNORE YOUR MURDERED COMRADES?!
I HAVE NEITHER THE TIME NOR THE INCLINATION TO EXPLAIN.
MUCH AS I MAY WANT TO INTERVENE...
MUCH AS I MIGHT WANT TO CARRY OUT YOUR VENGEANCE.

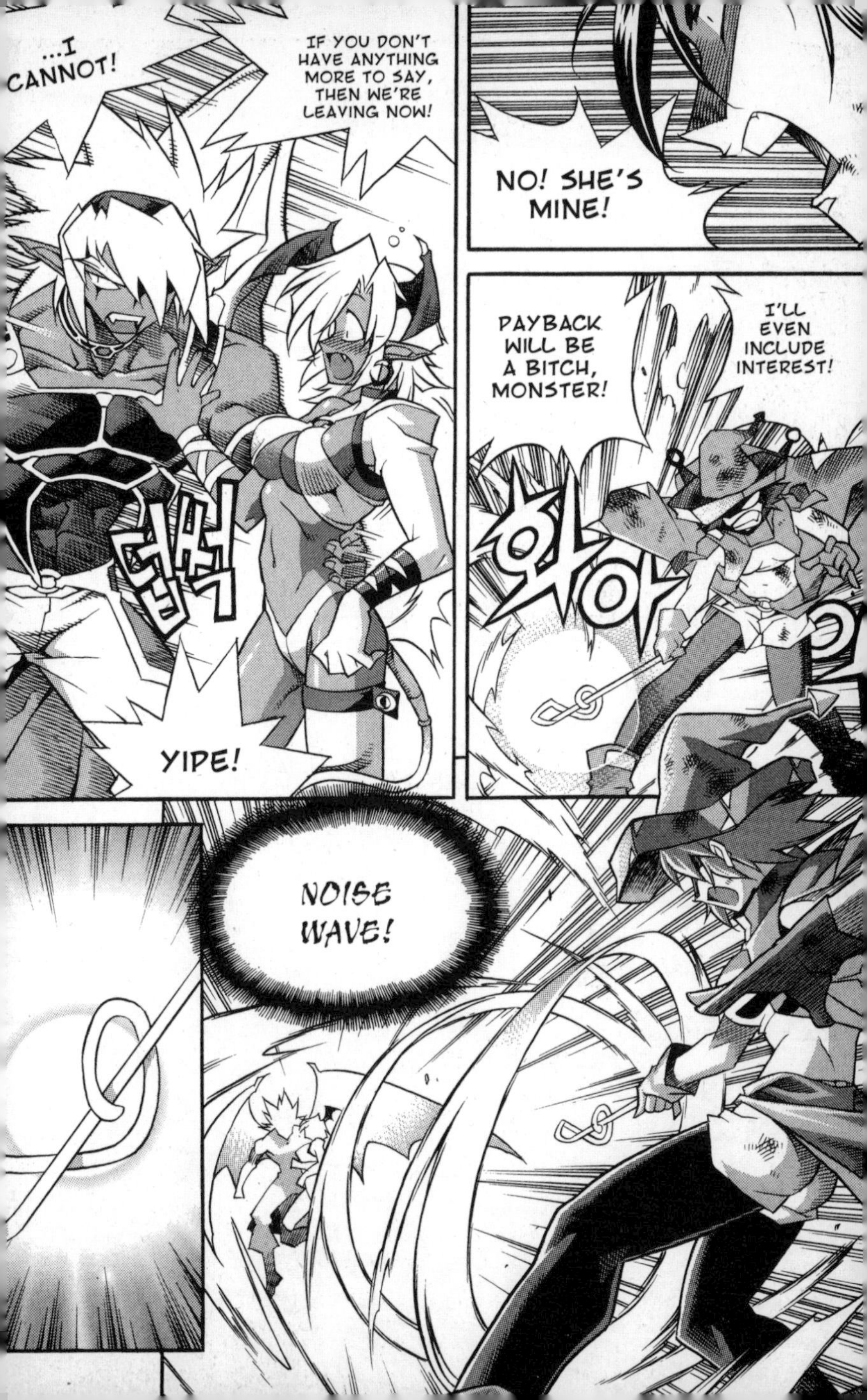
...I CANNOT!
IF YOU DON'T HAVE ANYTHING MORE TO SAY, THEN WE'RE LEAVING NOW!
YIPE!
NO! SHE'S MINE!
PAYBACK WILL BE A BITCH, MONSTER!
I'LL EVEN INCLUDE INTEREST!
NOISE WAVE!

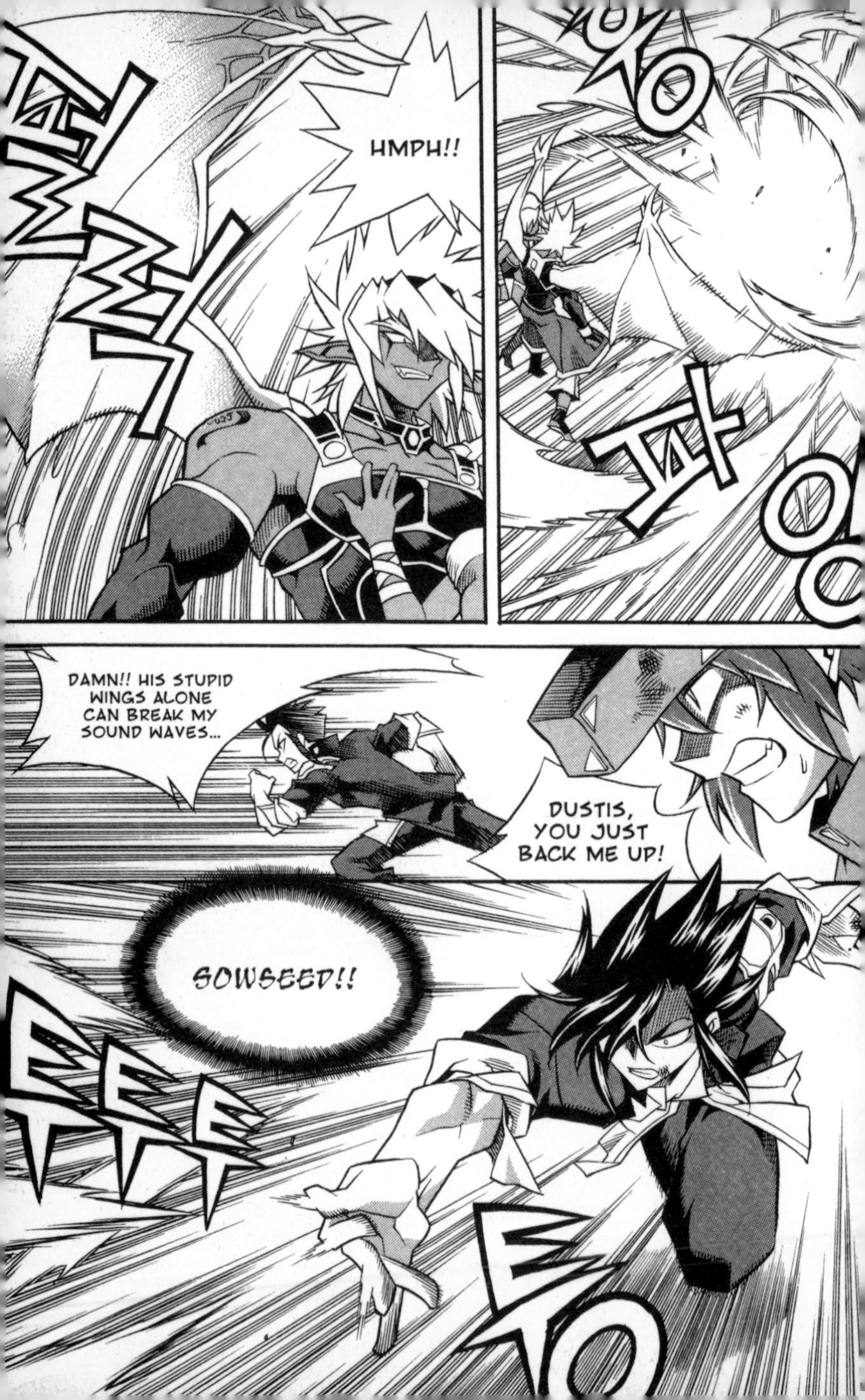
HMPH!!
DAMN!! HIS STUPID WINGS ALONE CAN BREAK MY SOUND WAVES...
DUSTIS, YOU JUST BACK ME UP!
SOWSEED!!

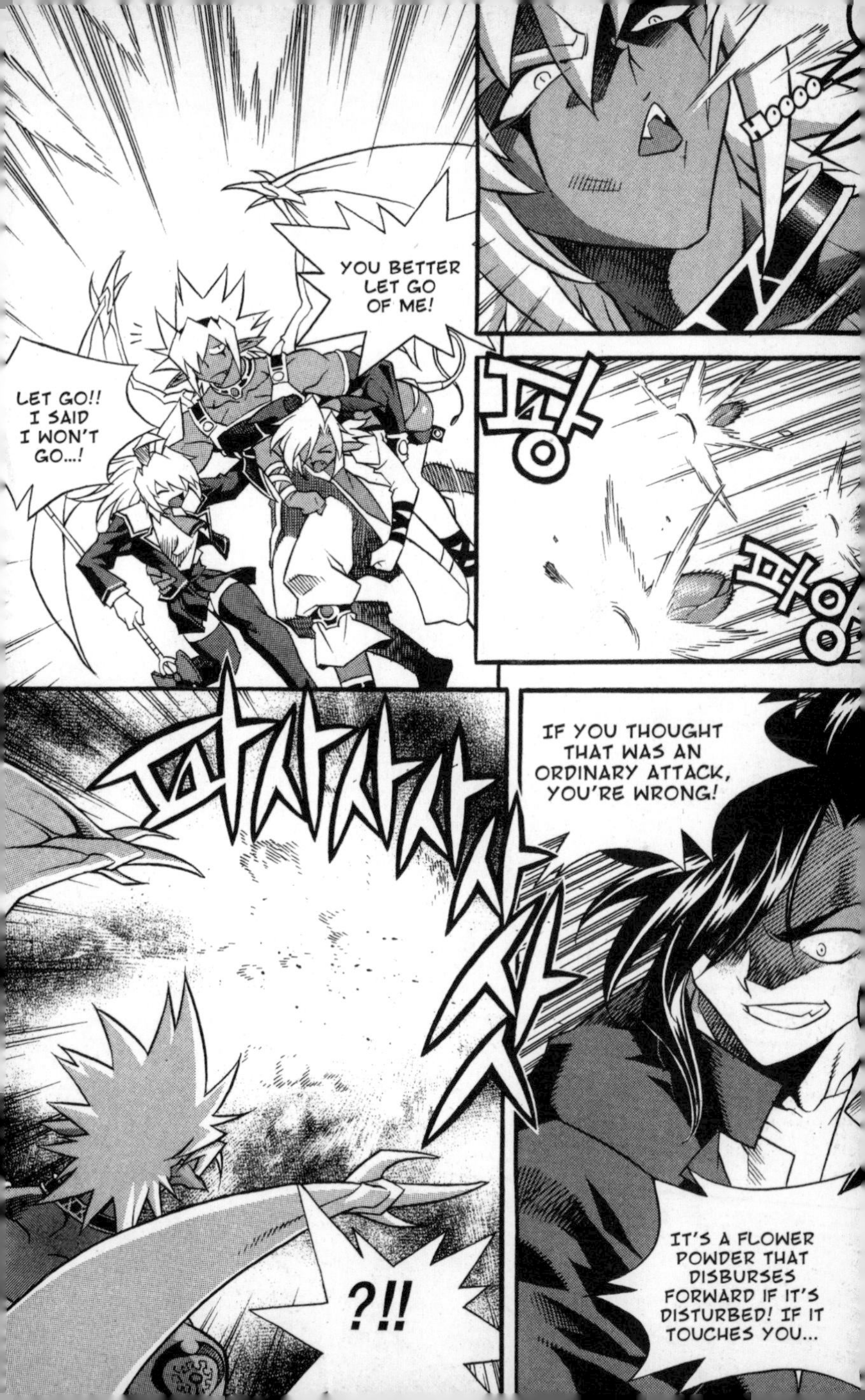
LET GO!! I SAID I WON'T GO...!
YOU BETTER LET GO OF ME!
HOOOO
?!!
IF YOU THOUGHT THAT WAS AN ORDINARY ATTACK, YOU'RE WRONG!
IT'S A FLOWER POWDER THAT DISBURSES FORWARD IF IT'S DISTURBED! IF IT TOUCHES YOU...

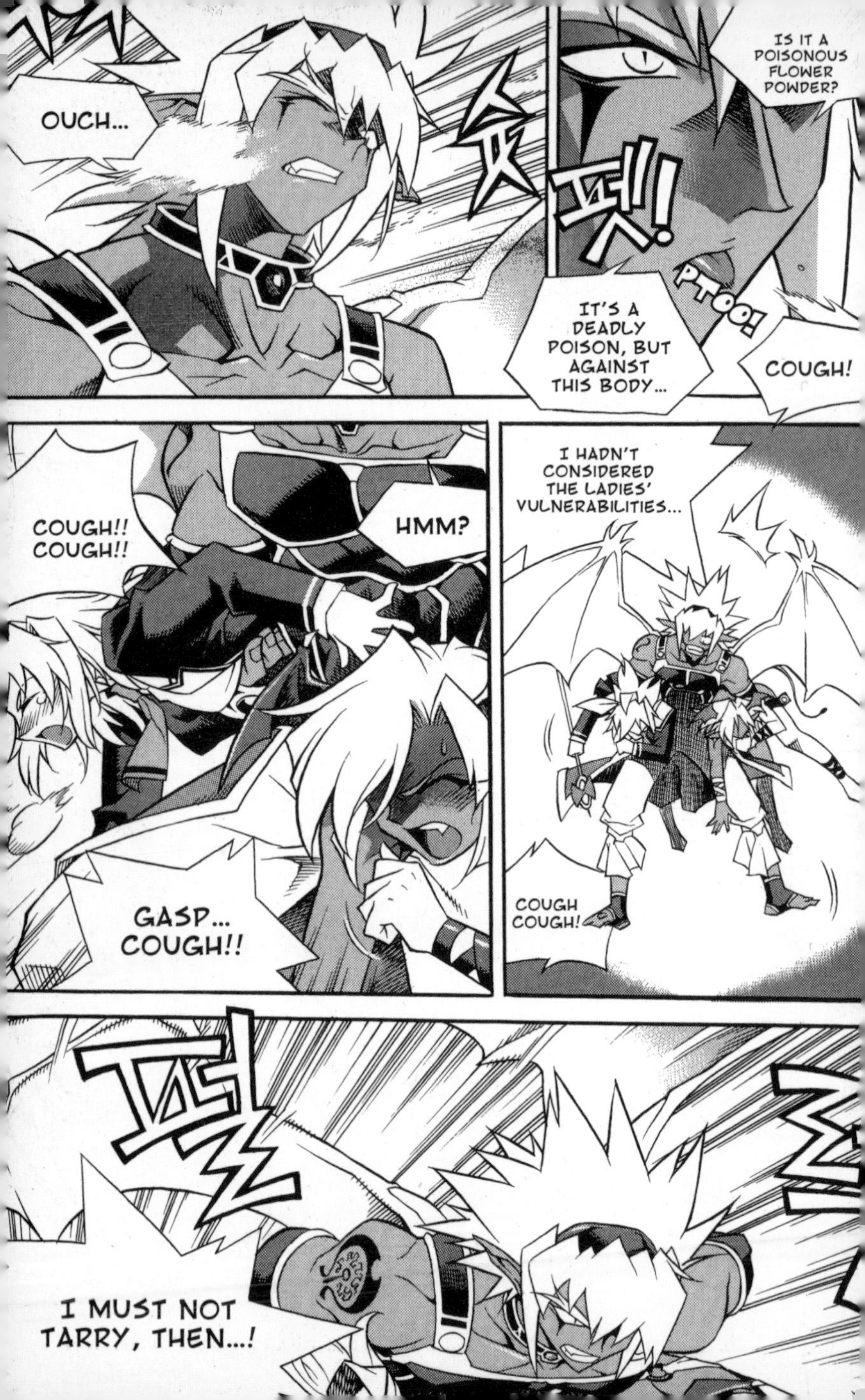

IS IT A POISONOUS FLOWER POWDER?
PTOO!
IT'S A DEADLY POISON, BUT AGAINST THIS BODY...
COUGH!
OUCH...
I HADN'T CONSIDERED THE LADIES' VULNERABILITIES...
COUGH COUGH!
HMM?
COUGH!! COUGH!!
GASP... COUGH!!
I MUST NOT TARRY, THEN...!

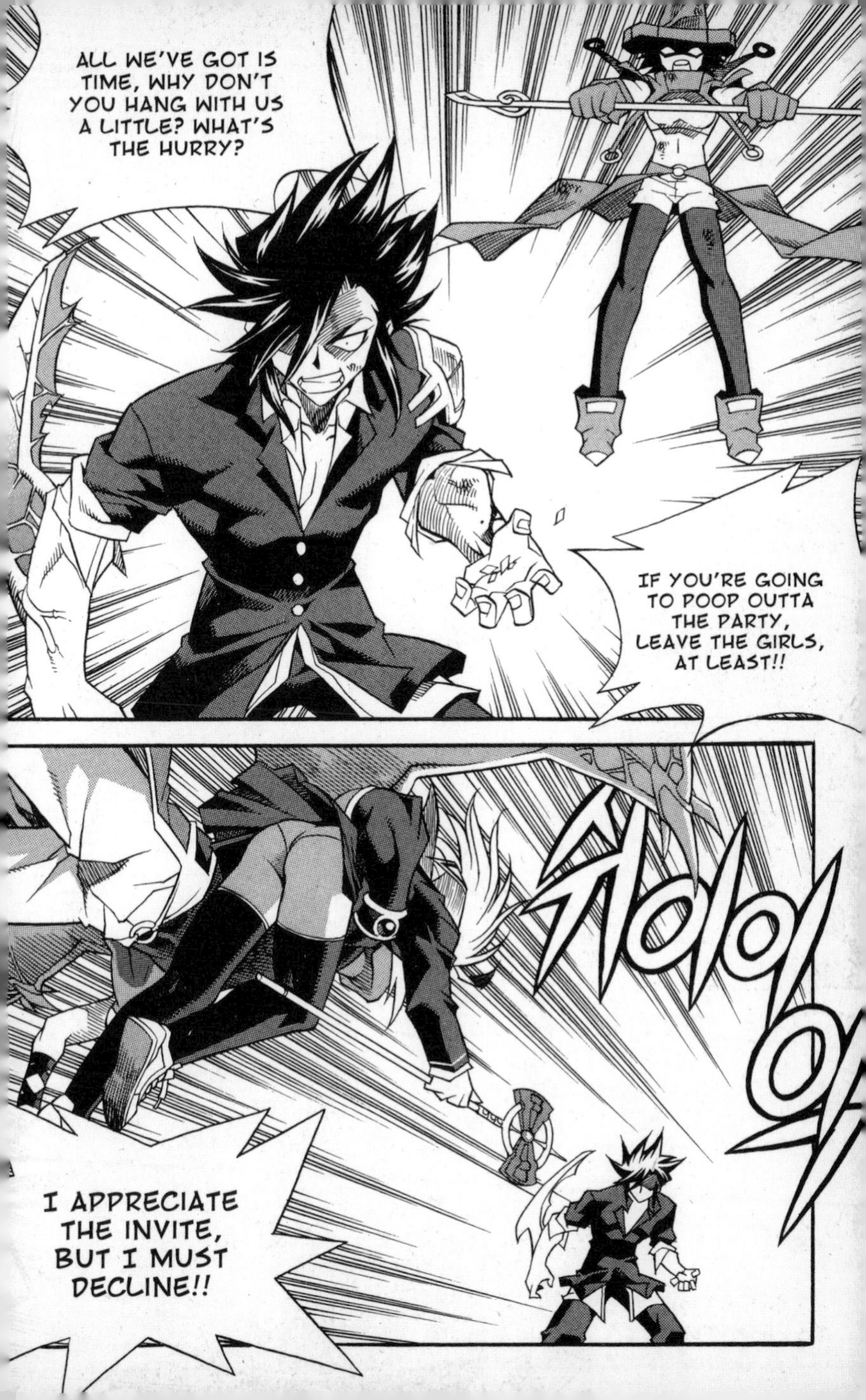
ALL WE'VE GOT IS TIME, WHY DON'T YOU HANG WITH US A LITTLE? WHAT'S THE HURRY?
IF YOU'RE GOING TO POOP OUTTA THE PARTY, LEAVE THE GIRLS, AT LEAST!!
I APPRECIATE THE INVITE, BUT I MUST DECLINE!!

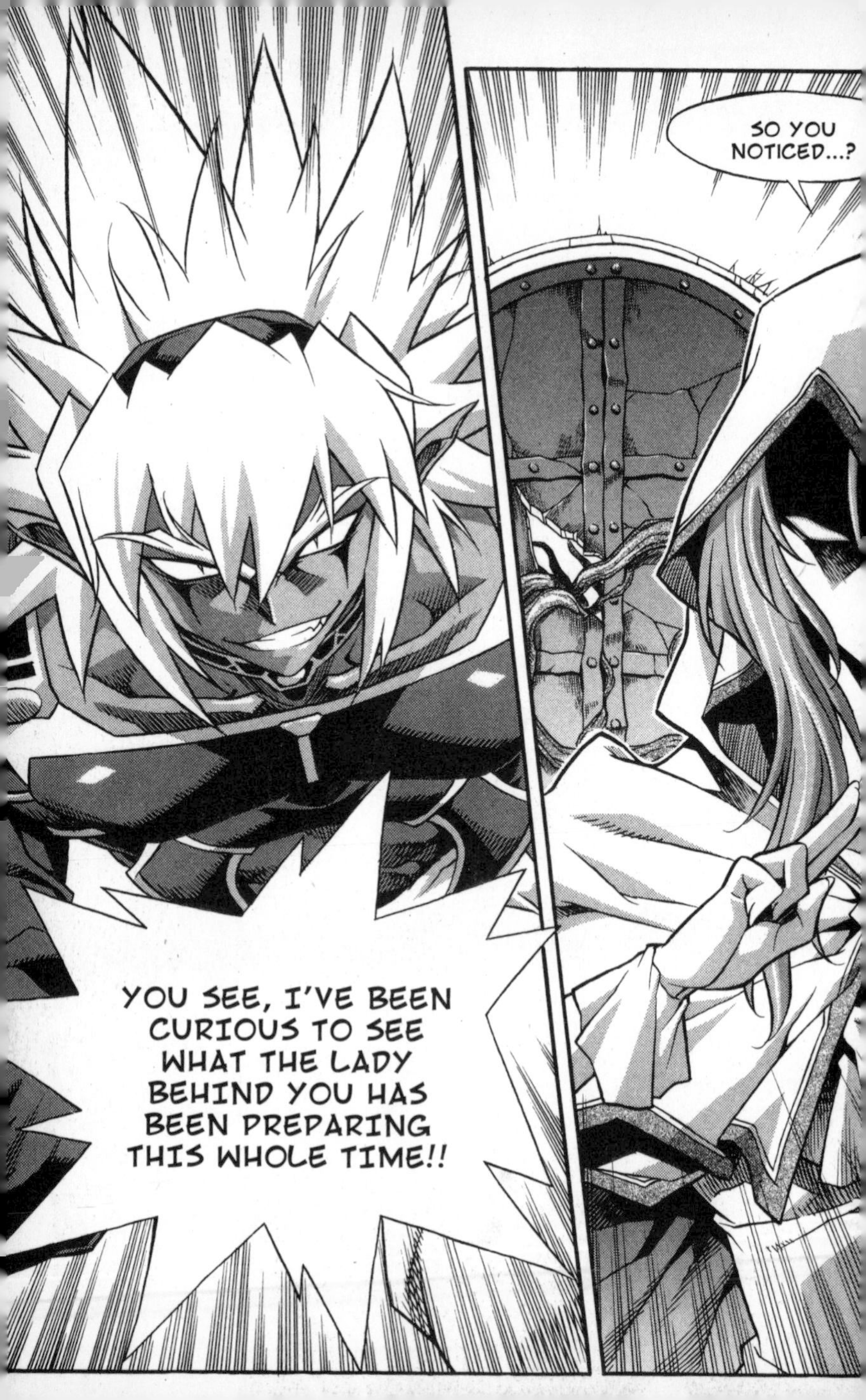
SO YOU NOTICED...?
YOU SEE, I'VE BEEN CURIOUS TO SEE WHAT THE LADY BEHIND YOU HAS BEEN PREPARING THIS WHOLE TIME!!

Quest 92

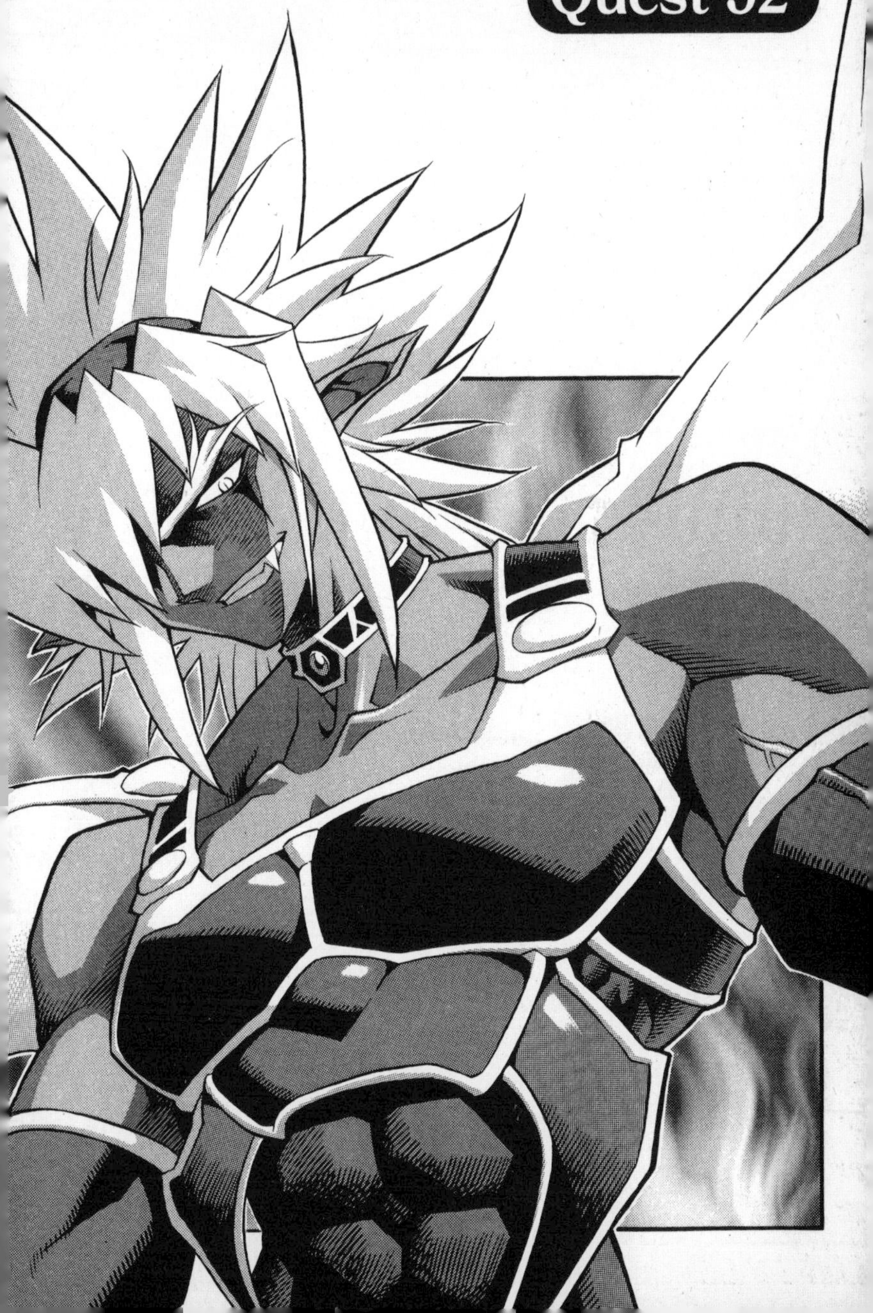

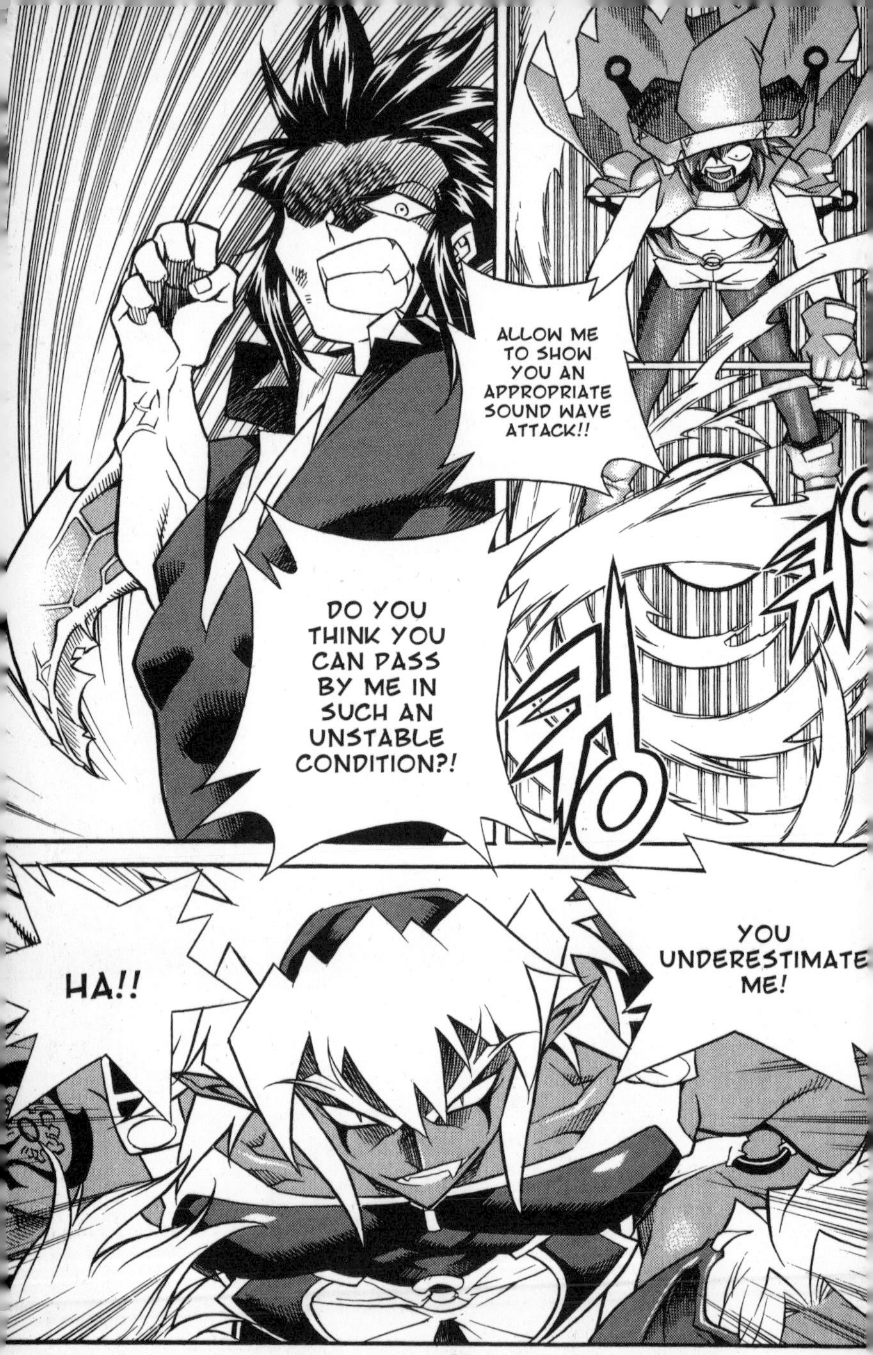
ALLOW ME TO SHOW YOU AN APPROPRIATE SOUND WAVE ATTACK!!
DO YOU THINK YOU CAN PASS BY ME IN SUCH AN UNSTABLE CONDITION?!
YOU UNDERESTIMATE ME!
HA!!

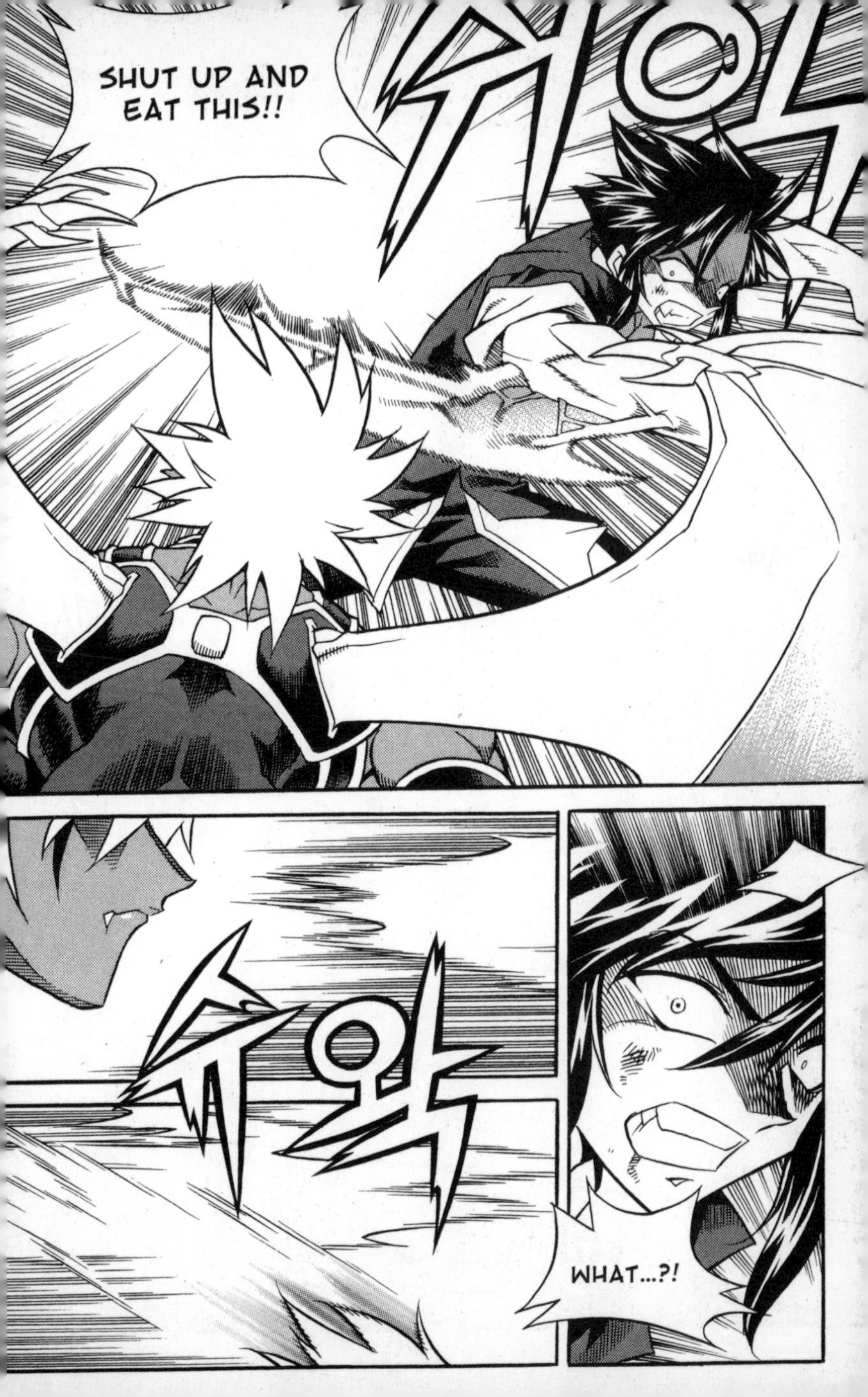
SHUT UP AND EAT THIS!!
WHAT...?!

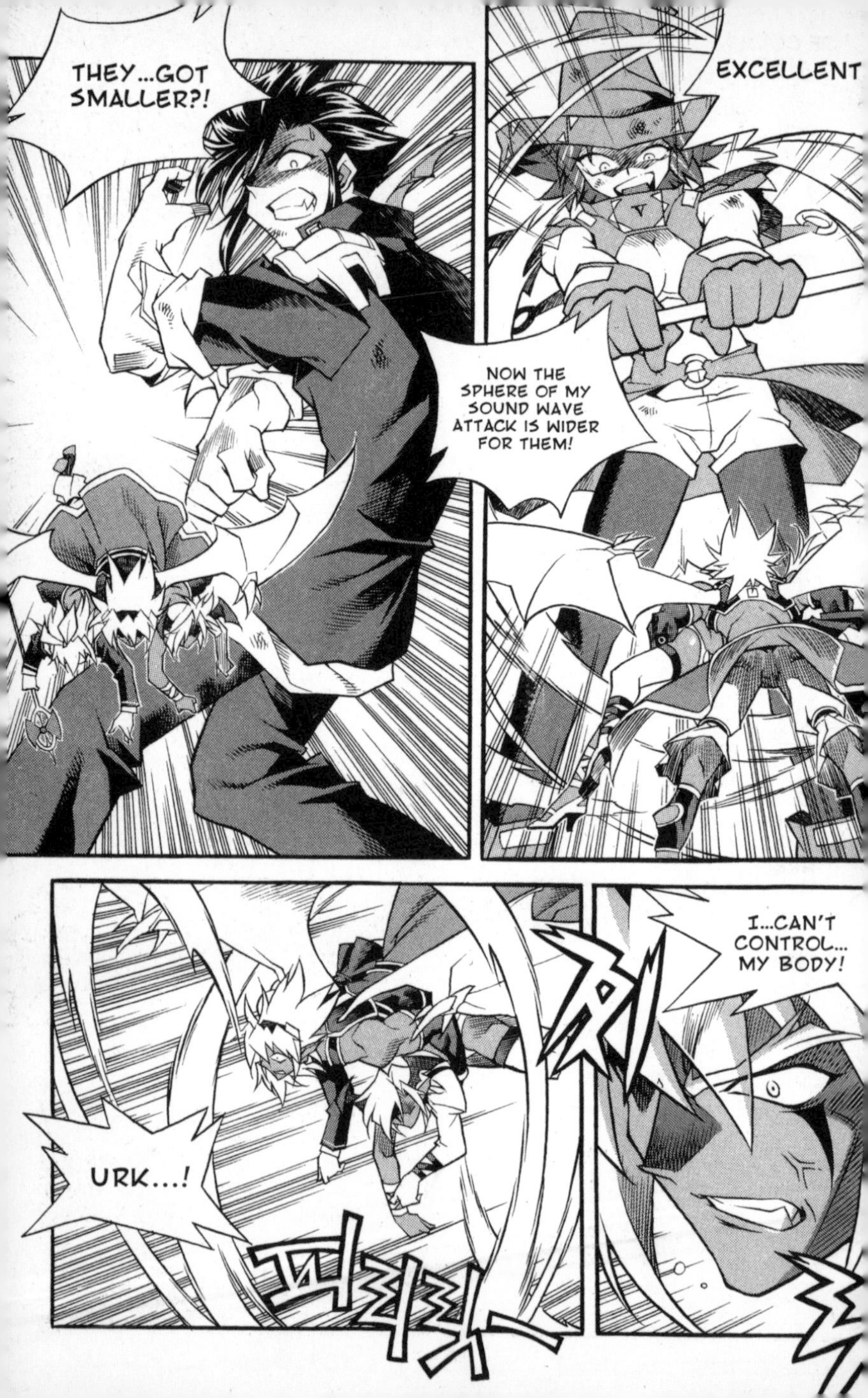
EXCELLENT
THEY...GOT SMALLER?!
NOW THE SPHERE OF MY SOUND WAVE ATTACK IS WIDER FOR THEM!
I...CAN'T CONTROL... MY BODY!
URK...!

OF COURSE NOT!!

BANG!

IF YOU EXPERIENCE EVEN A PART OF MY TREMORS, YOUR WHOLE BODY WILL GO INTO CONVULSIONS! AND AFTER THAT...

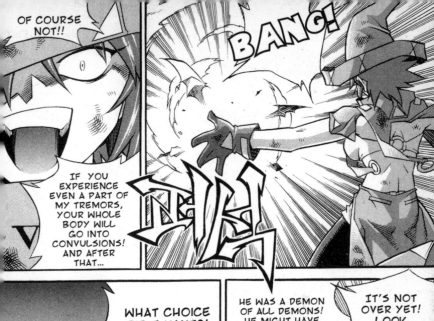

WHAT CHOICE DID I HAVE?! IT WAS EITHER THEM OR US!

DID...DID YOU KILL THEM? ALL THREE?

HE WAS A DEMON OF ALL DEMONS! HE MIGHT HAVE BEEN AN AVATA OR WHATEVER, BUT...

IT'S NOT OVER YET! LOOK BEHIND YOU!

WHAT?

83

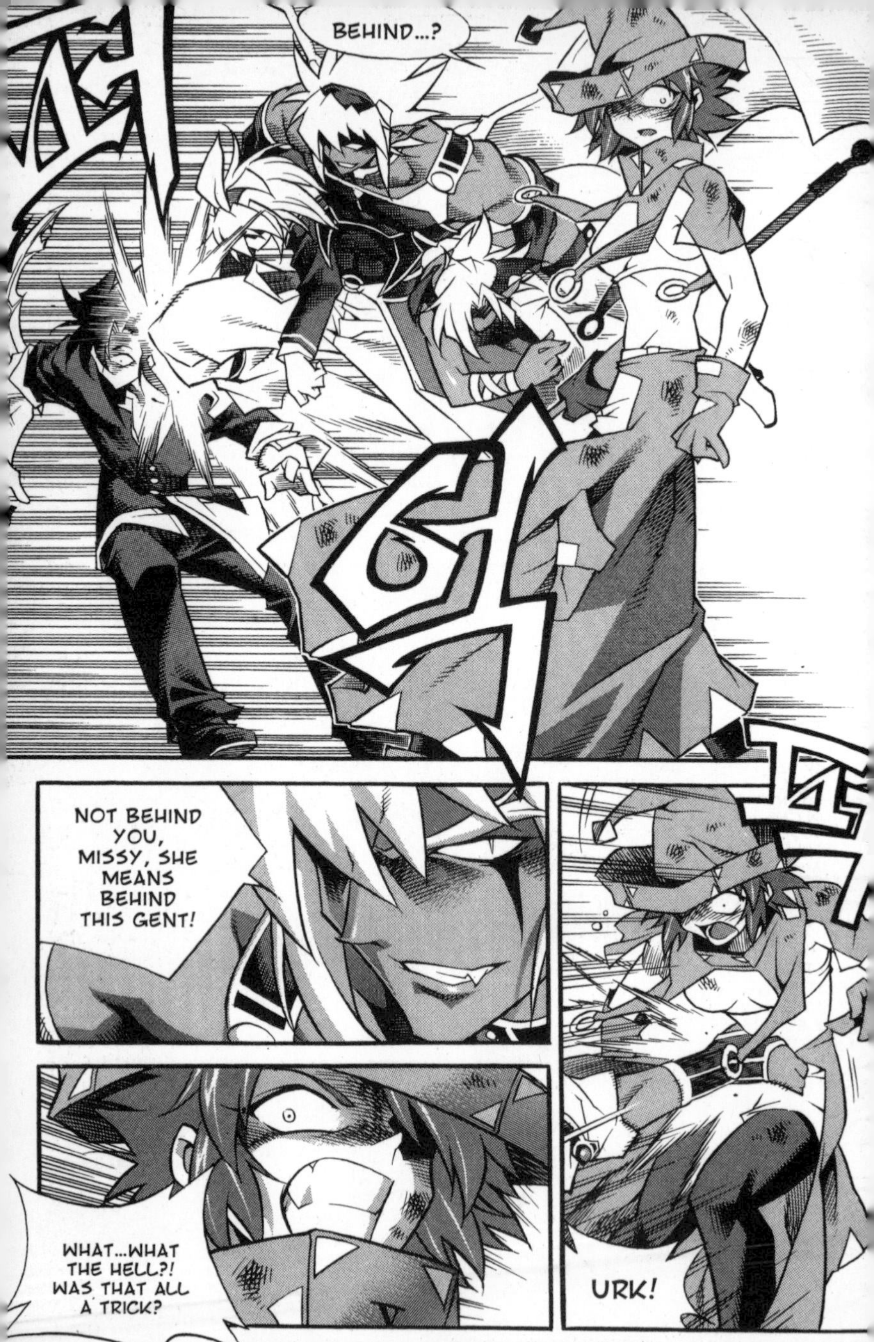

BEHIND...?
NOT BEHIND YOU, MISSY, SHE MEANS BEHIND THIS GENT!
URK!
WHAT...WHAT THE HELL?! WAS THAT ALL A TRICK?

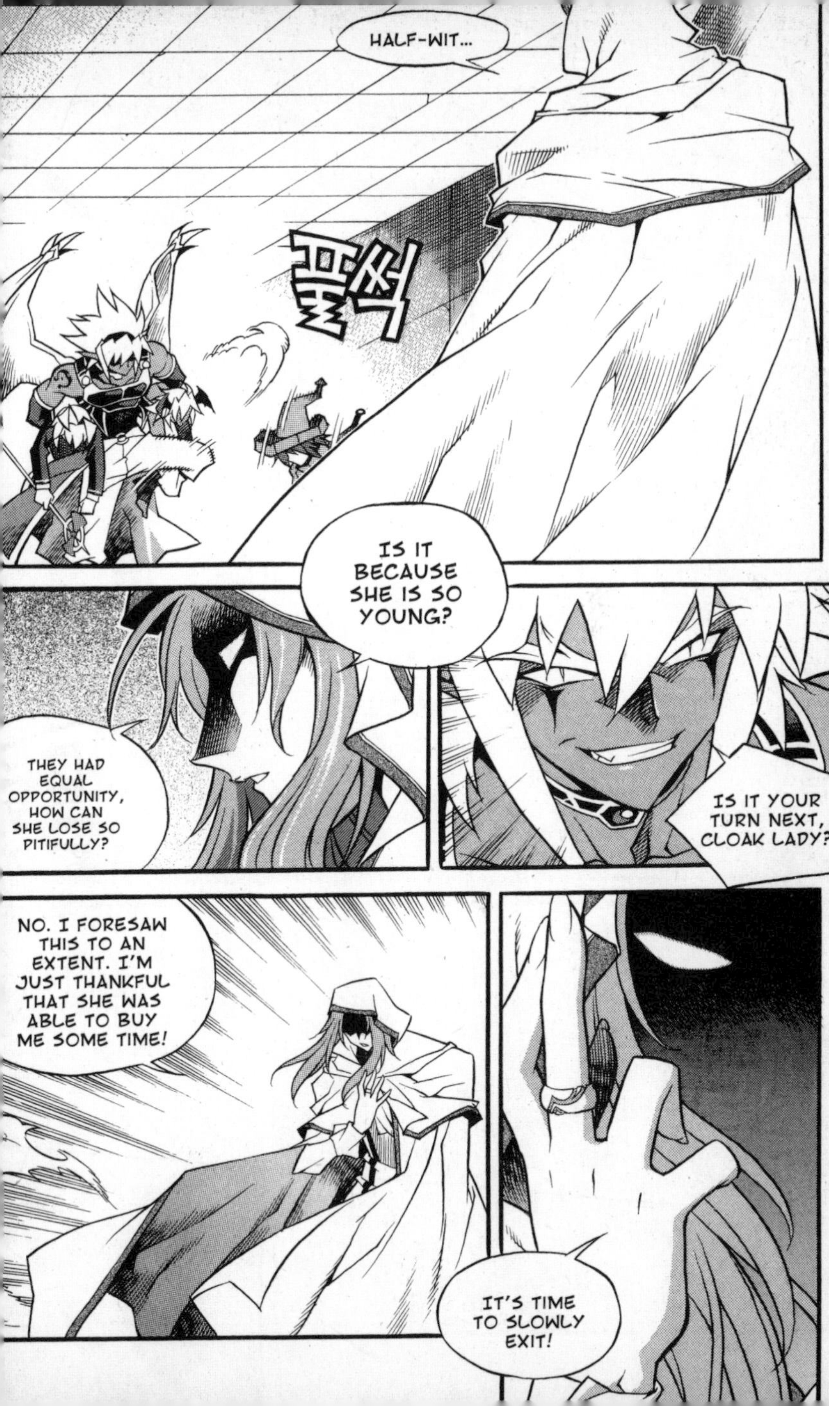
HALF-WIT...
IS IT BECAUSE SHE IS SO YOUNG?
THEY HAD EQUAL OPPORTUNITY, HOW CAN SHE LOSE SO PITIFULLY?
IS IT YOUR TURN NEXT, CLOAK LADY?
NO. I FORESAW THIS TO AN EXTENT. I'M JUST THANKFUL THAT SHE WAS ABLE TO BUY ME SOME TIME!
IT'S TIME TO SLOWLY EXIT!

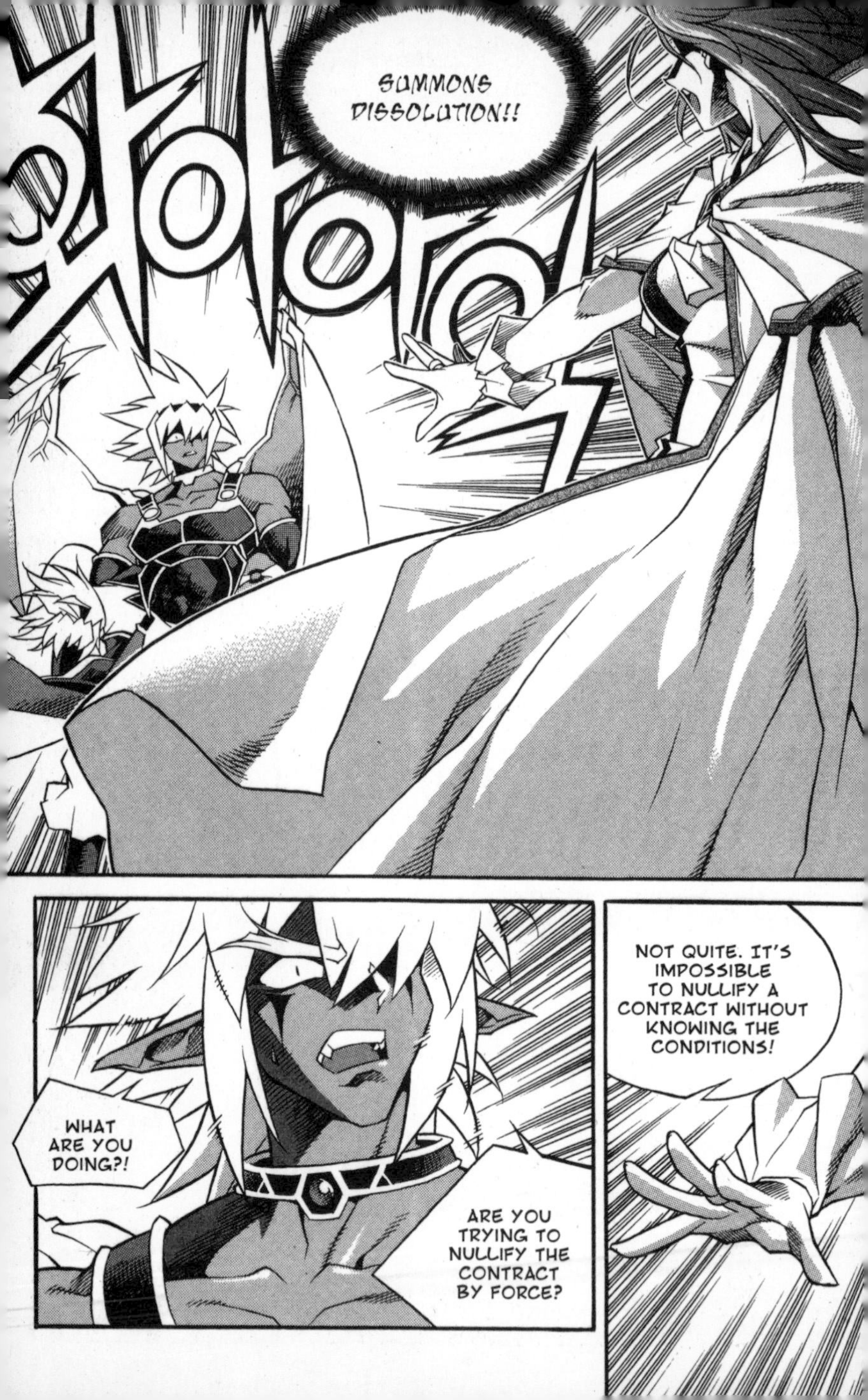
SUMMONS DISSOLUTION!!
WHAT ARE YOU DOING?!
ARE YOU TRYING TO NULLIFY THE CONTRACT BY FORCE?
NOT QUITE. IT'S IMPOSSIBLE TO NULLIFY A CONTRACT WITHOUT KNOWING THE CONDITIONS!

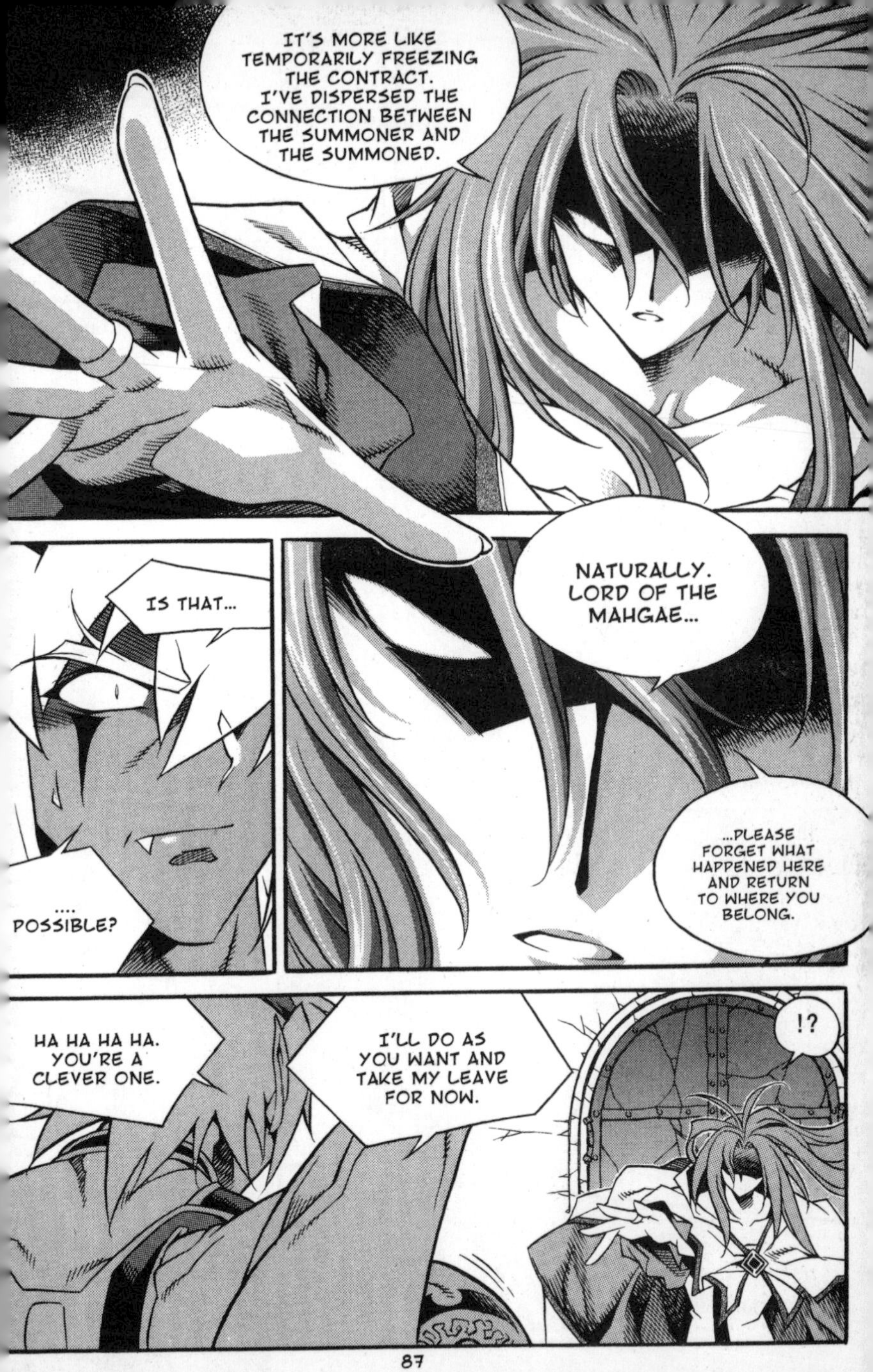
IT'S MORE LIKE TEMPORARILY FREEZING THE CONTRACT. I'VE DISPERSED THE CONNECTION BETWEEN THE SUMMONER AND THE SUMMONED.
IS THAT...
.... POSSIBLE?
NATURALLY. LORD OF THE MAHGAE...
...PLEASE FORGET WHAT HAPPENED HERE AND RETURN TO WHERE YOU BELONG.
HA HA HA HA. YOU'RE A CLEVER ONE.
I'LL DO AS YOU WANT AND TAKE MY LEAVE FOR NOW.
!?

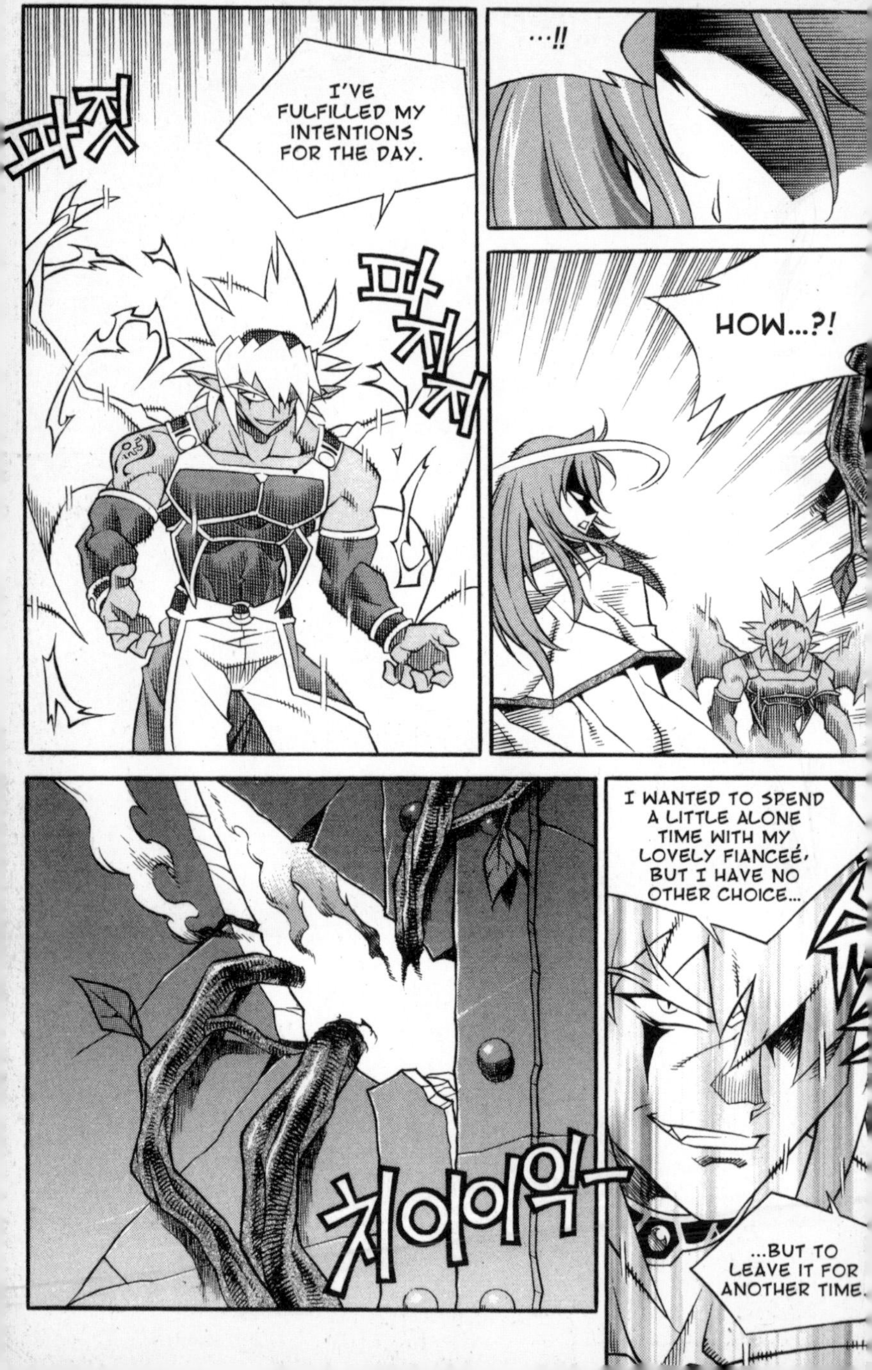
I'VE FULFILLED MY INTENTIONS FOR THE DAY.
...!!
HOW...?!
치이이익—
I WANTED TO SPEND A LITTLE ALONE TIME WITH MY LOVELY FIANCEÉ, BUT I HAVE NO OTHER CHOICE...
...BUT TO LEAVE IT FOR ANOTHER TIME.

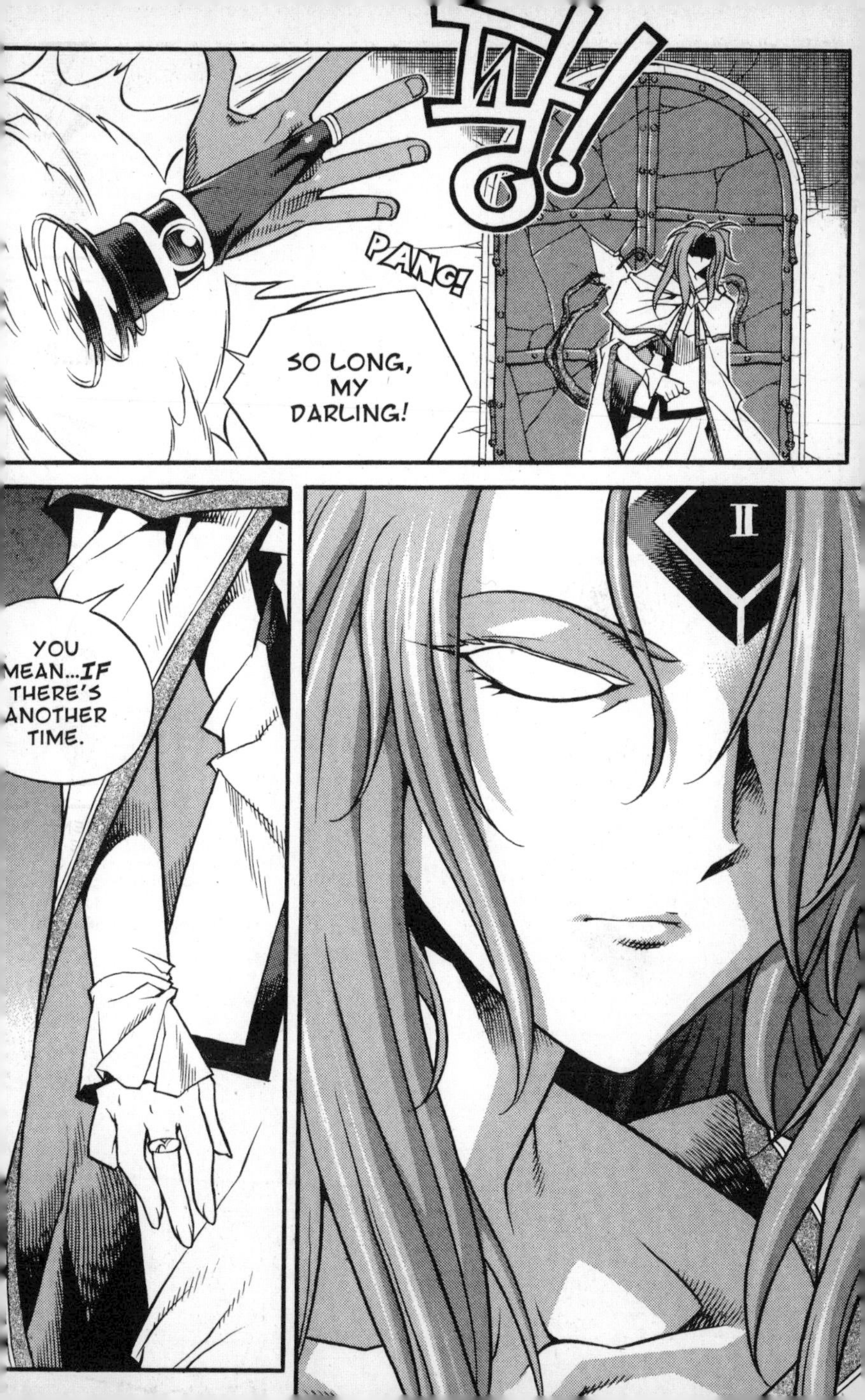
PANG!
SO LONG, MY DARLING!
YOU MEAN...IF THERE'S ANOTHER TIME.

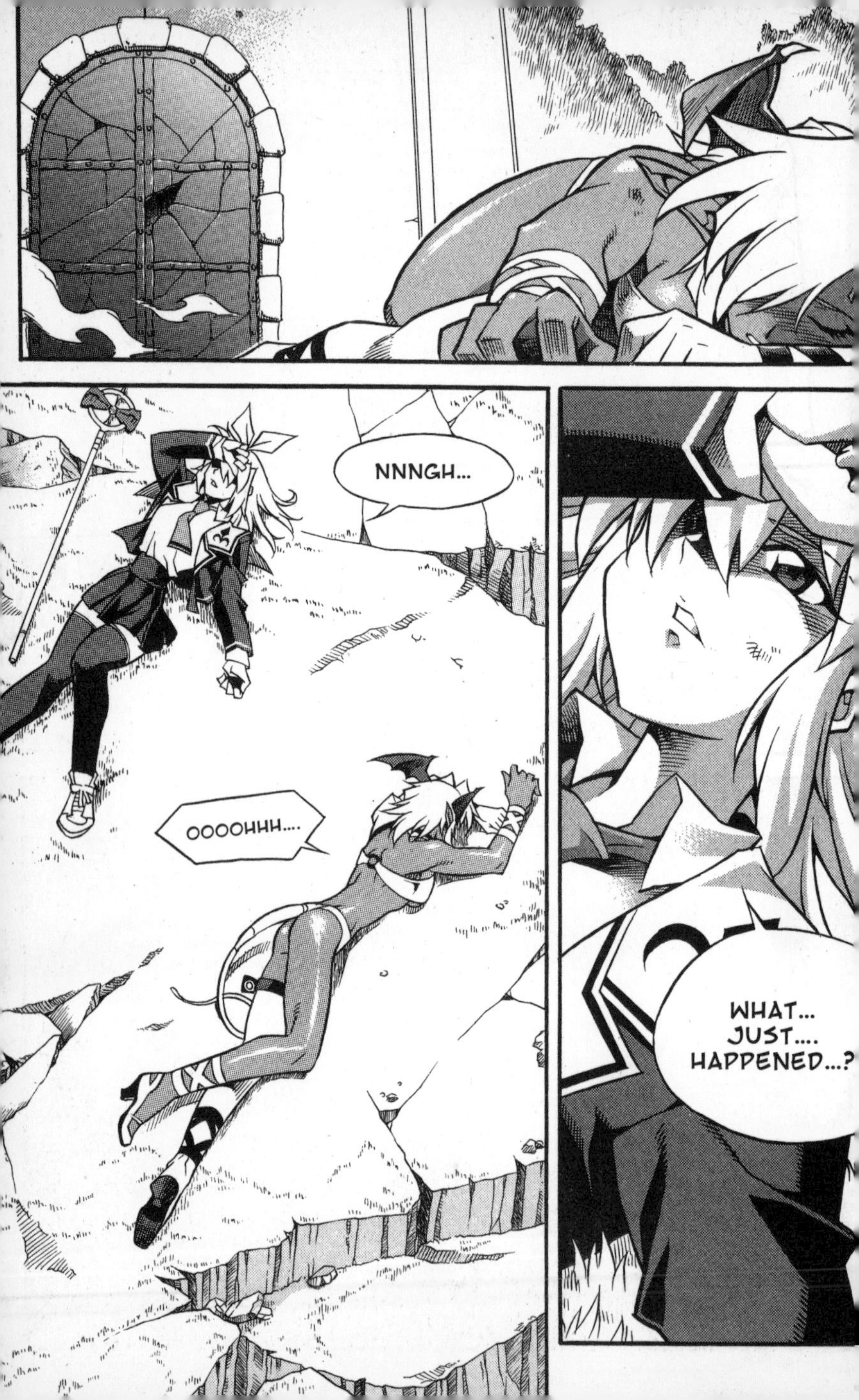
NNNGH...
OOOOHHH....
WHAT... JUST.... HAPPENED...?

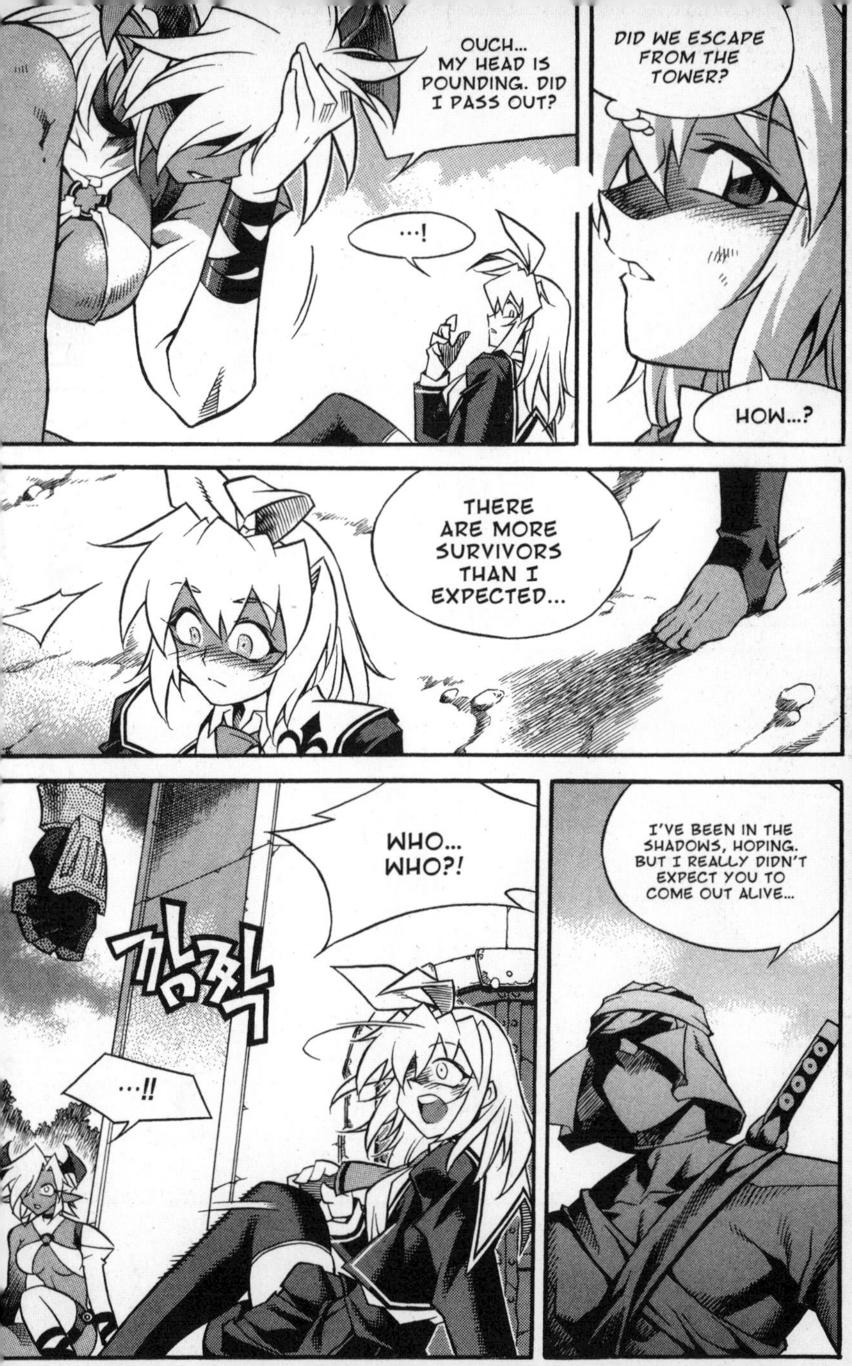
OUCH... MY HEAD IS POUNDING. DID I PASS OUT?
...!
DID WE ESCAPE FROM THE TOWER?
HOW...?
THERE ARE MORE SURVIVORS THAN I EXPECTED...
WHO... WHO?!
깜짝
...!!
I'VE BEEN IN THE SHADOWS, HOPING. BUT I REALLY DIDN'T EXPECT YOU TO COME OUT ALIVE...

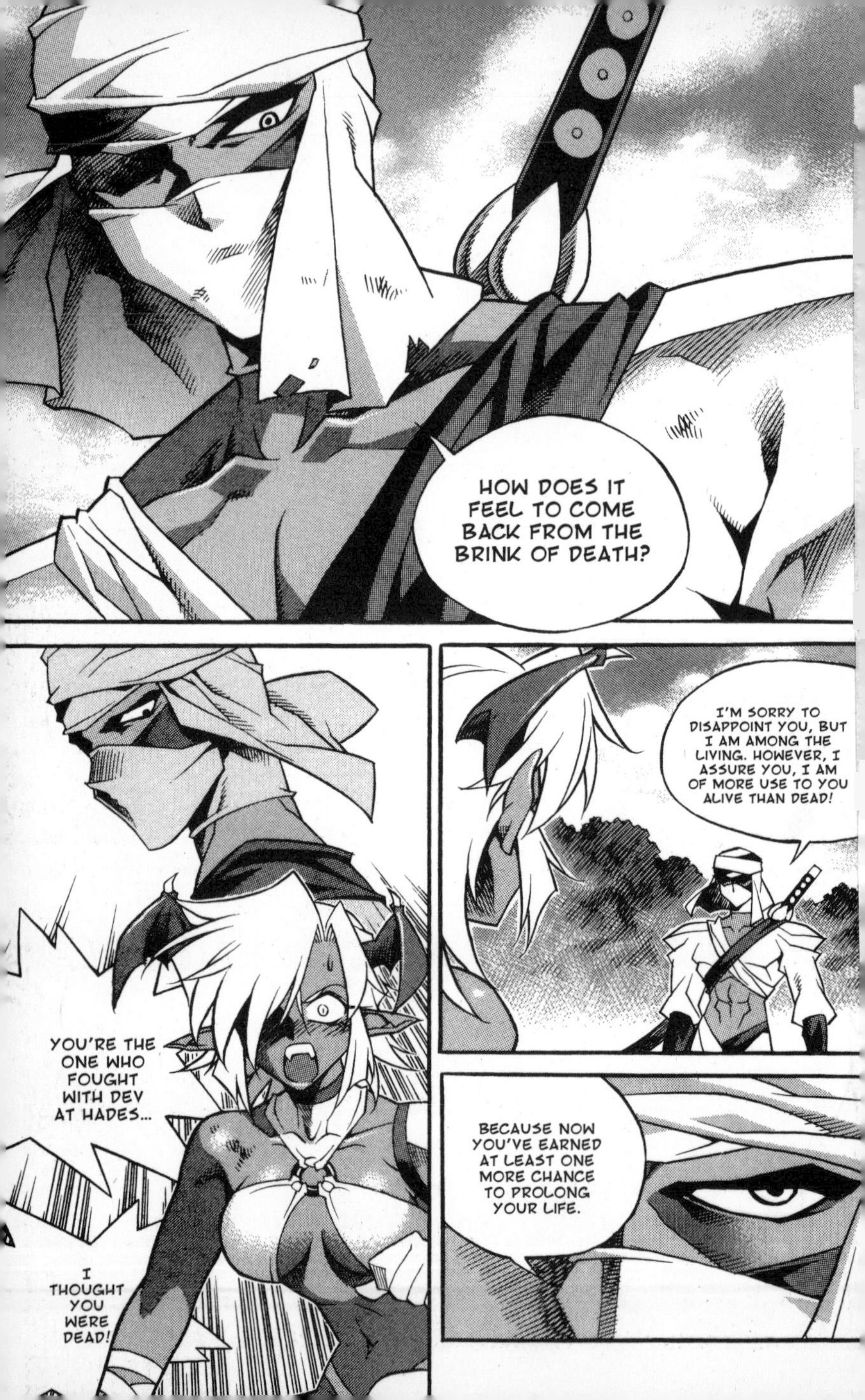
HOW DOES IT FEEL TO COME BACK FROM THE BRINK OF DEATH?
YOU'RE THE ONE WHO FOUGHT WITH DEV AT HADES...
I THOUGHT YOU WERE DEAD!
I'M SORRY TO DISAPPOINT YOU, BUT I AM AMONG THE LIVING. HOWEVER, I ASSURE YOU, I AM OF MORE USE TO YOU ALIVE THAN DEAD!
BECAUSE NOW YOU'VE EARNED AT LEAST ONE MORE CHANCE TO PROLONG YOUR LIFE.

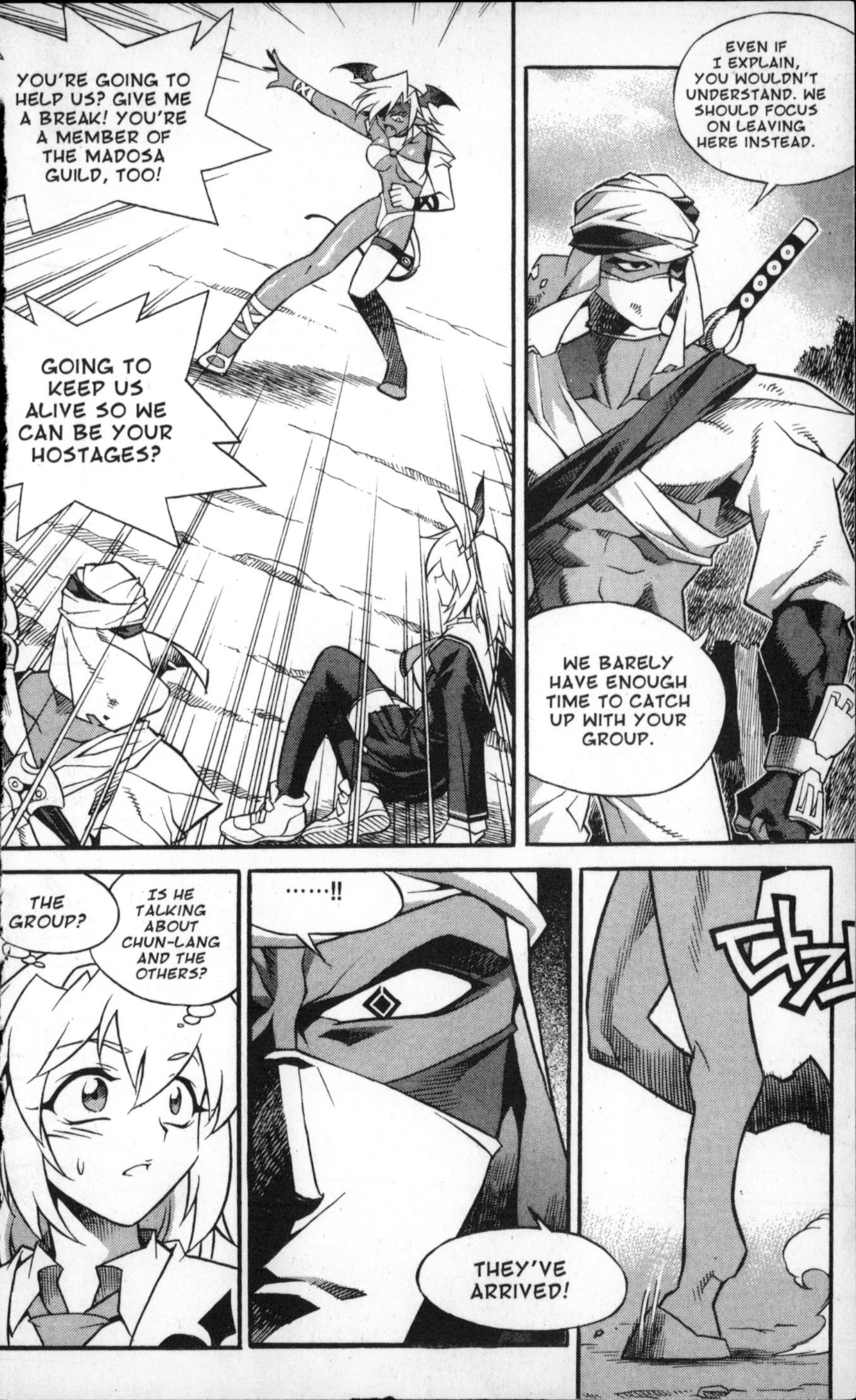
YOU'RE GOING TO HELP US? GIVE ME A BREAK! YOU'RE A MEMBER OF THE MADOSA GUILD, TOO!
GOING TO KEEP US ALIVE SO WE CAN BE YOUR HOSTAGES?
EVEN IF I EXPLAIN, YOU WOULDN'T UNDERSTAND. WE SHOULD FOCUS ON LEAVING HERE INSTEAD.
WE BARELY HAVE ENOUGH TIME TO CATCH UP WITH YOUR GROUP.
THE GROUP?
IS HE TALKING ABOUT CHUN-LANG AND THE OTHERS?
......!!
THEY'VE ARRIVED!

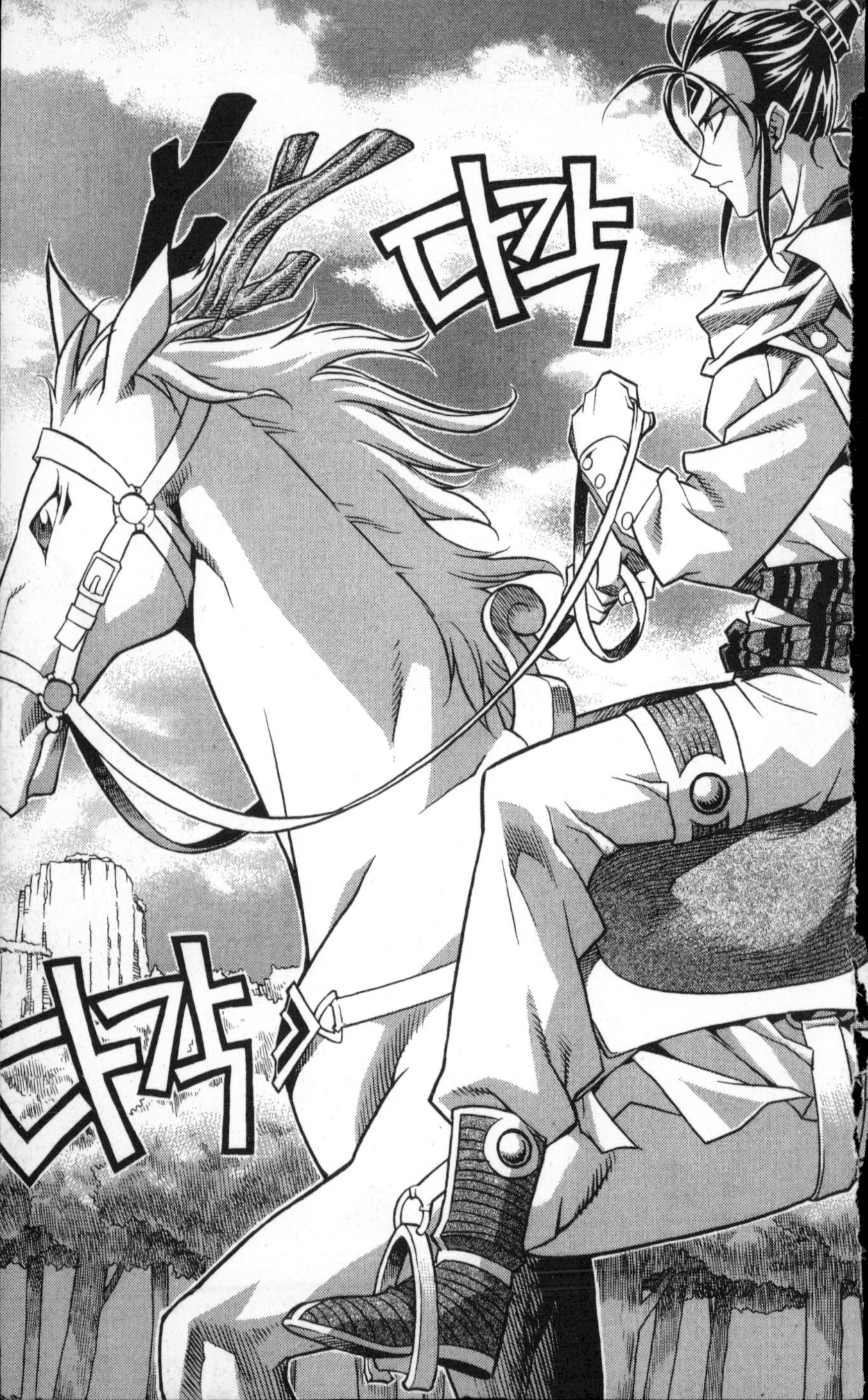
다각
다각

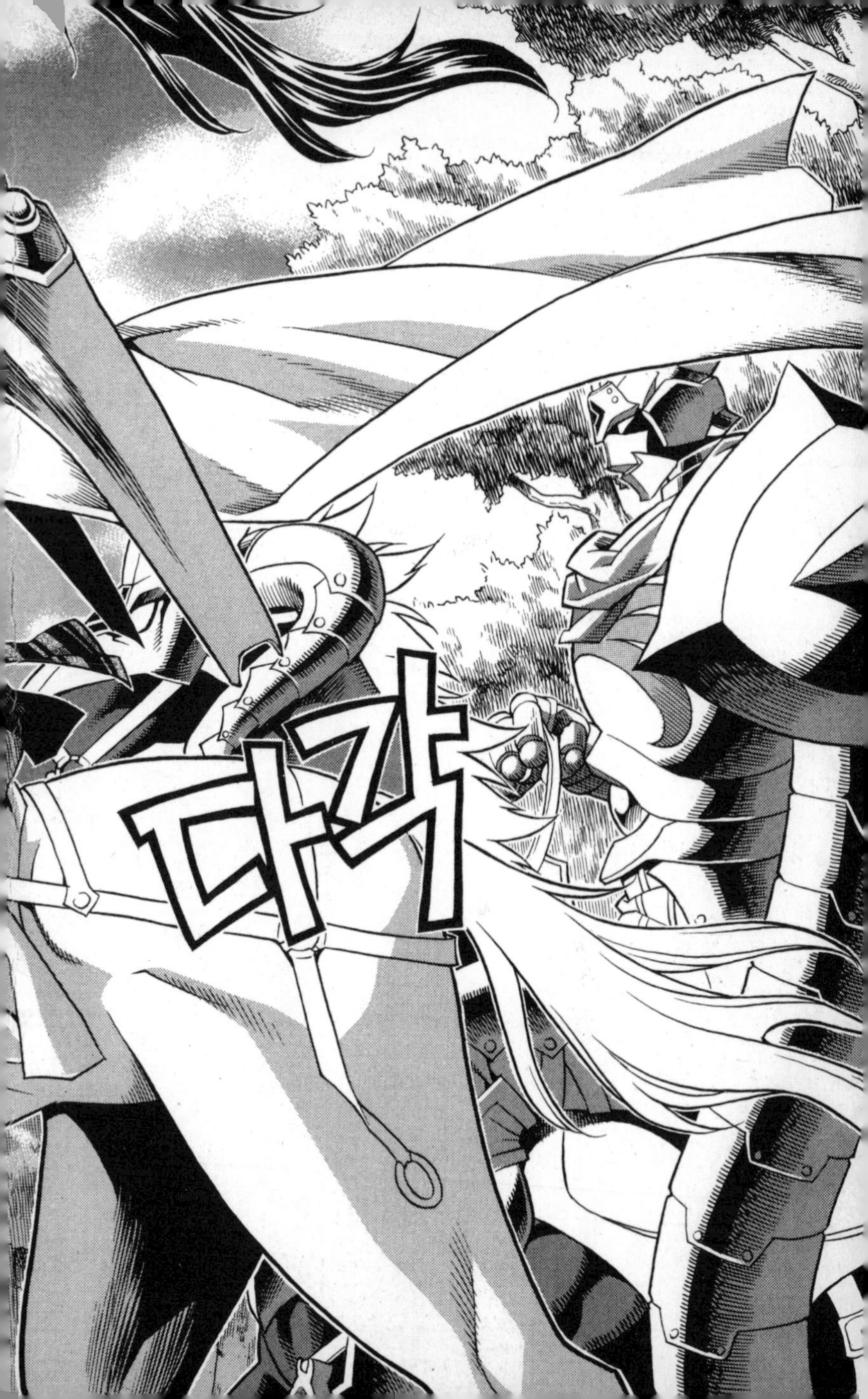
다각

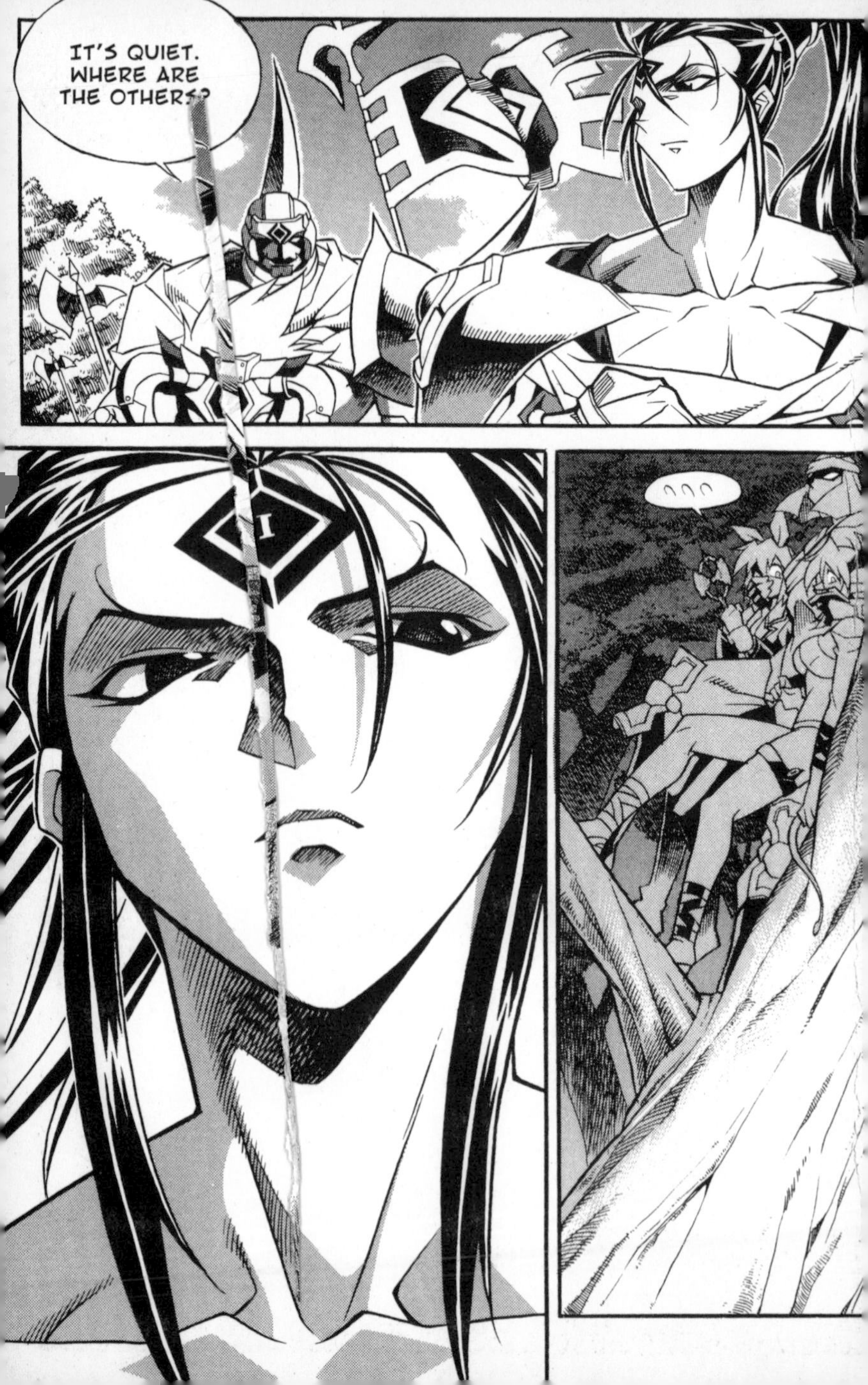
IT'S QUIET. WHERE ARE THE OTHERS?

Quest 93

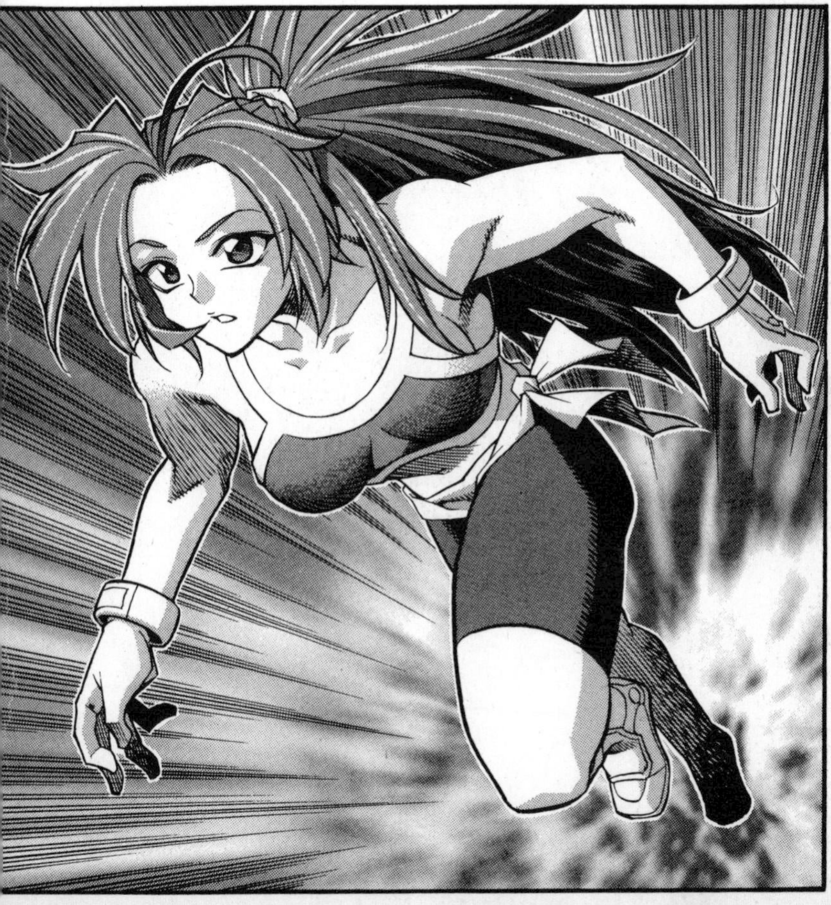

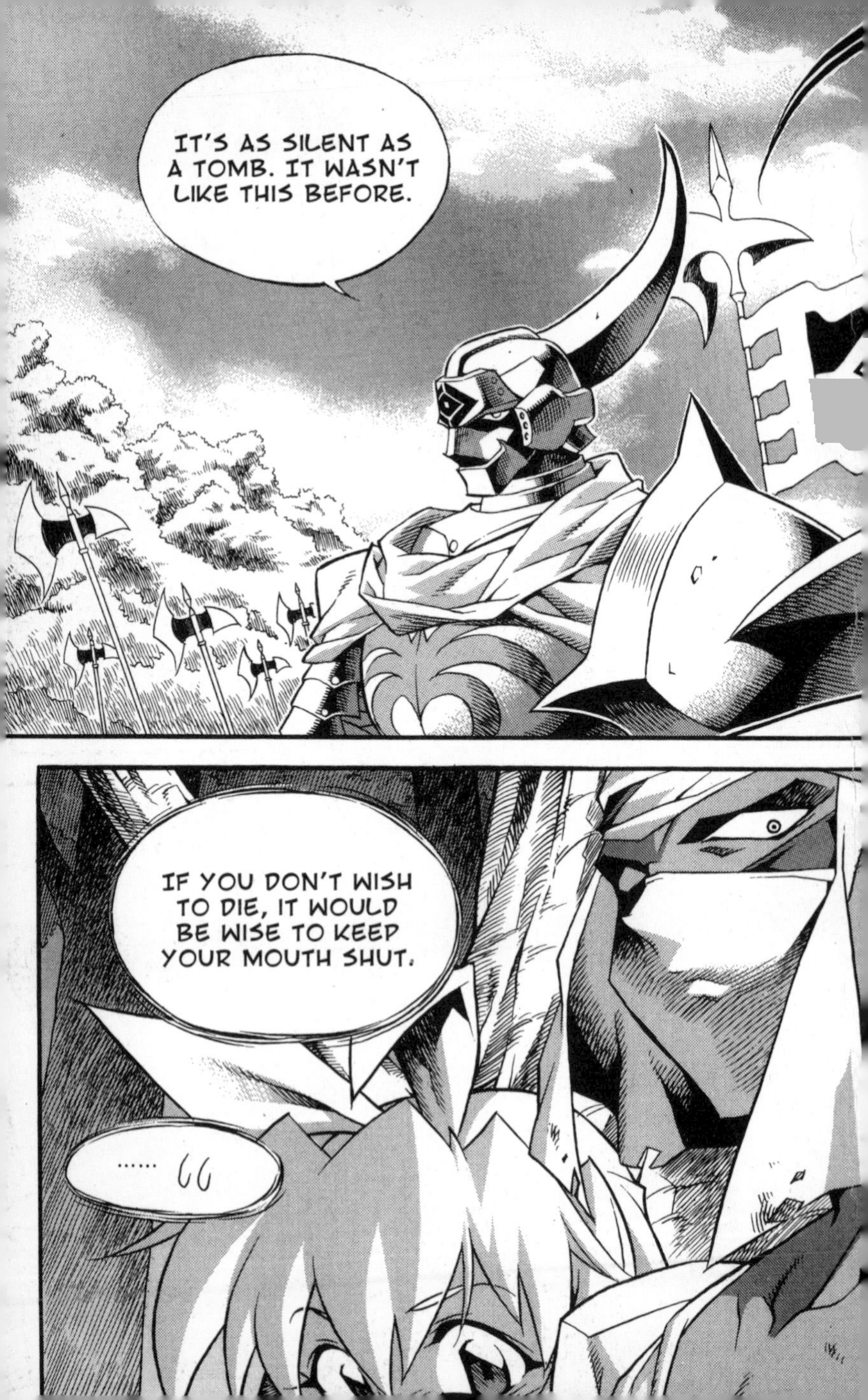
IT'S AS SILENT AS A TOMB. IT WASN'T LIKE THIS BEFORE.
IF YOU DON'T WISH TO DIE, IT WOULD BE WISE TO KEEP YOUR MOUTH SHUT.
......

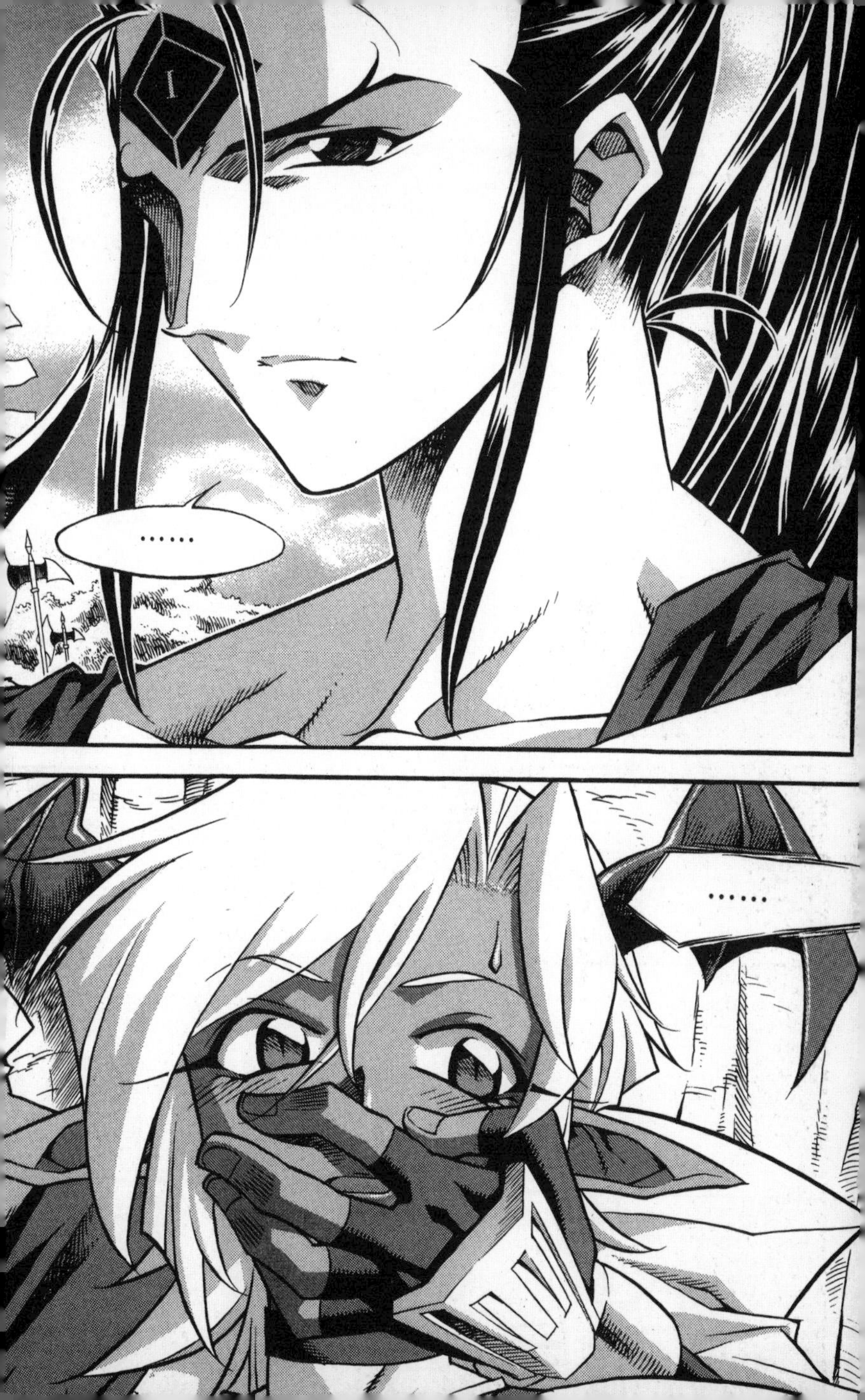

......
......

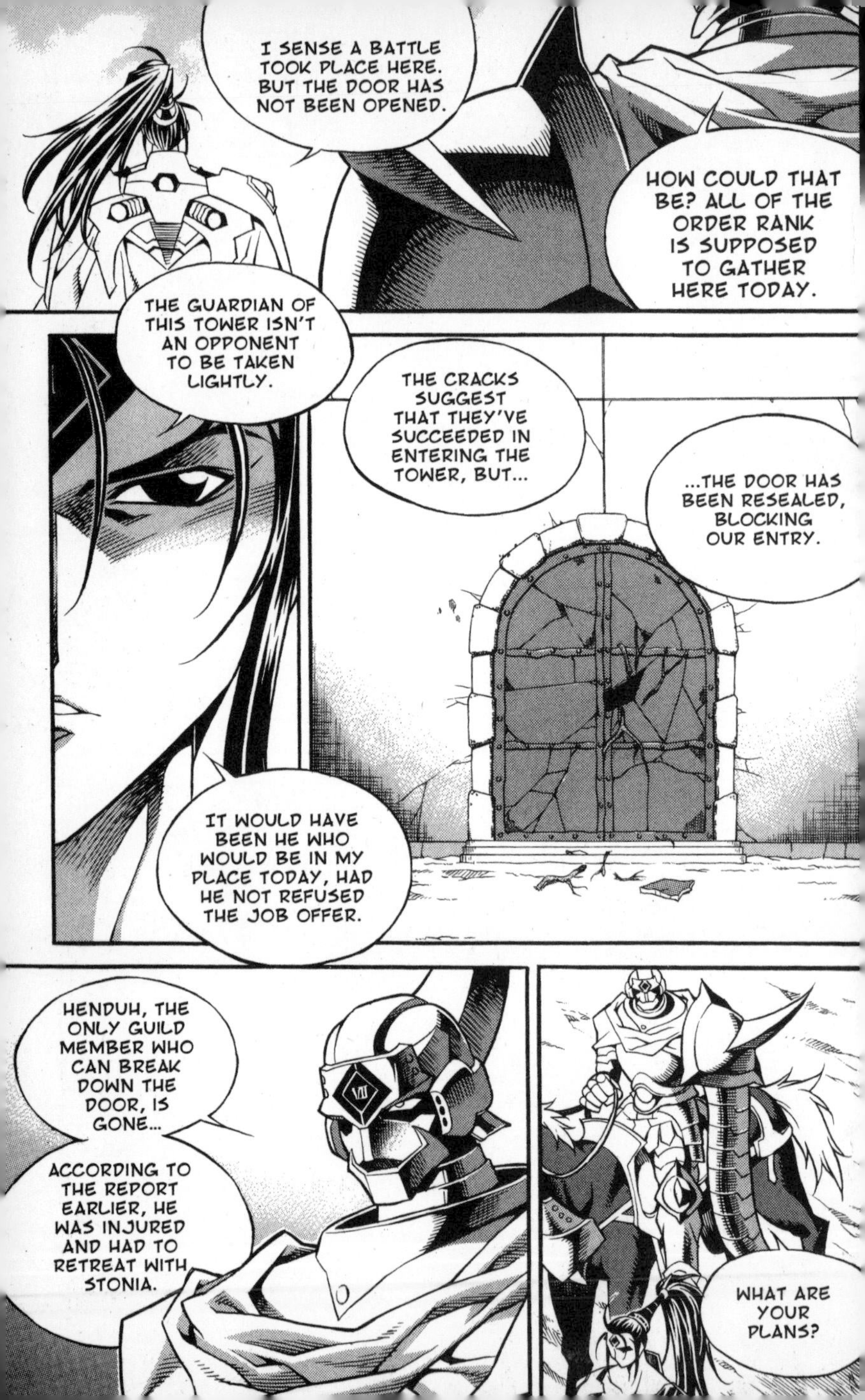
I SENSE A BATTLE TOOK PLACE HERE. BUT THE DOOR HAS NOT BEEN OPENED.
HOW COULD THAT BE? ALL OF THE ORDER RANK IS SUPPOSED TO GATHER HERE TODAY.
THE GUARDIAN OF THIS TOWER ISN'T AN OPPONENT TO BE TAKEN LIGHTLY.
THE CRACKS SUGGEST THAT THEY'VE SUCCEEDED IN ENTERING THE TOWER, BUT...
...THE DOOR HAS BEEN RESEALED, BLOCKING OUR ENTRY.
IT WOULD HAVE BEEN HE WHO WOULD BE IN MY PLACE TODAY, HAD HE NOT REFUSED THE JOB OFFER.
HENDUH, THE ONLY GUILD MEMBER WHO CAN BREAK DOWN THE DOOR, IS GONE...
ACCORDING TO THE REPORT EARLIER, HE WAS INJURED AND HAD TO RETREAT WITH STONIA.
WHAT ARE YOUR PLANS?

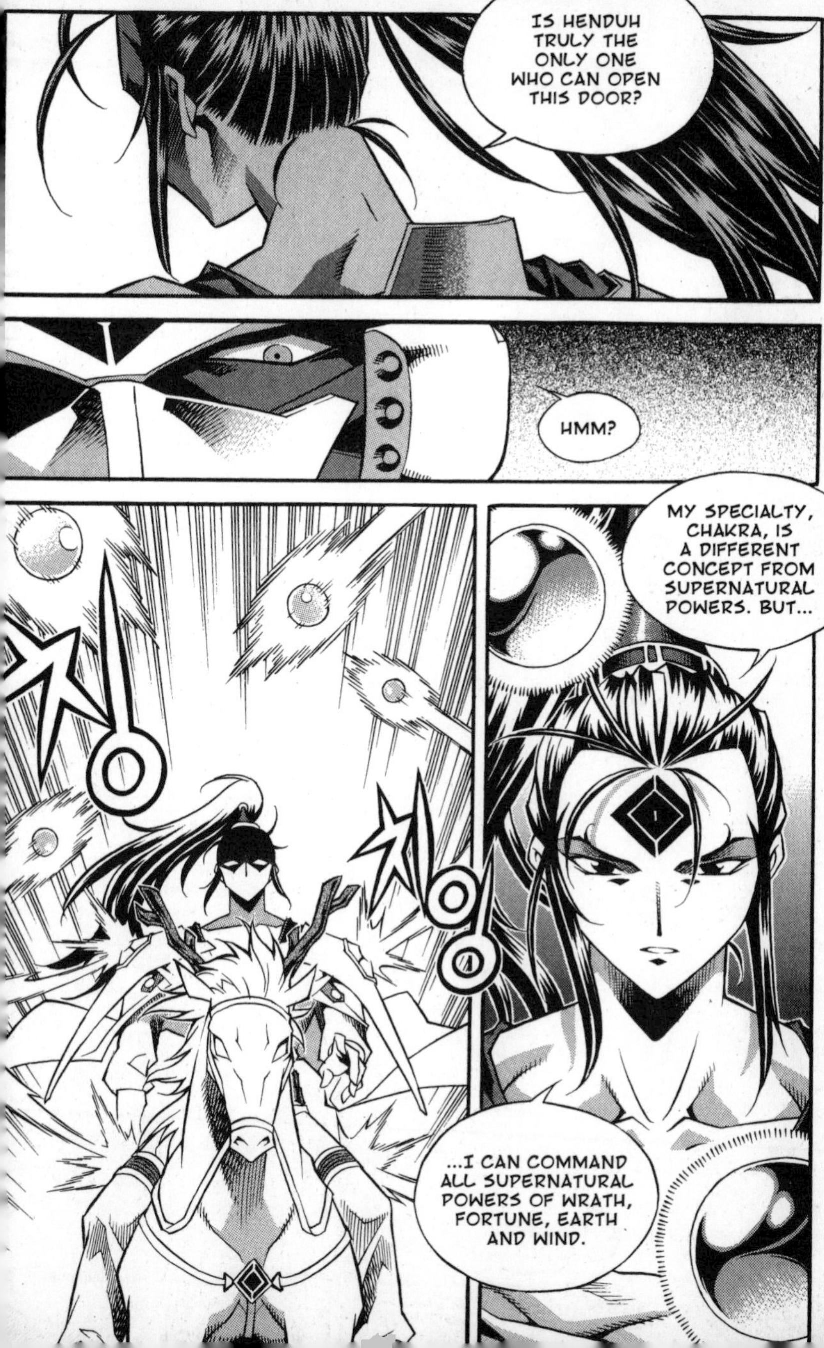
IS HENDUH TRULY THE ONLY ONE WHO CAN OPEN THIS DOOR?
HMM?
MY SPECIALTY, CHAKRA, IS A DIFFERENT CONCEPT FROM SUPERNATURAL POWERS. BUT...
...I CAN COMMAND ALL SUPERNATURAL POWERS OF WRATH, FORTUNE, EARTH AND WIND.

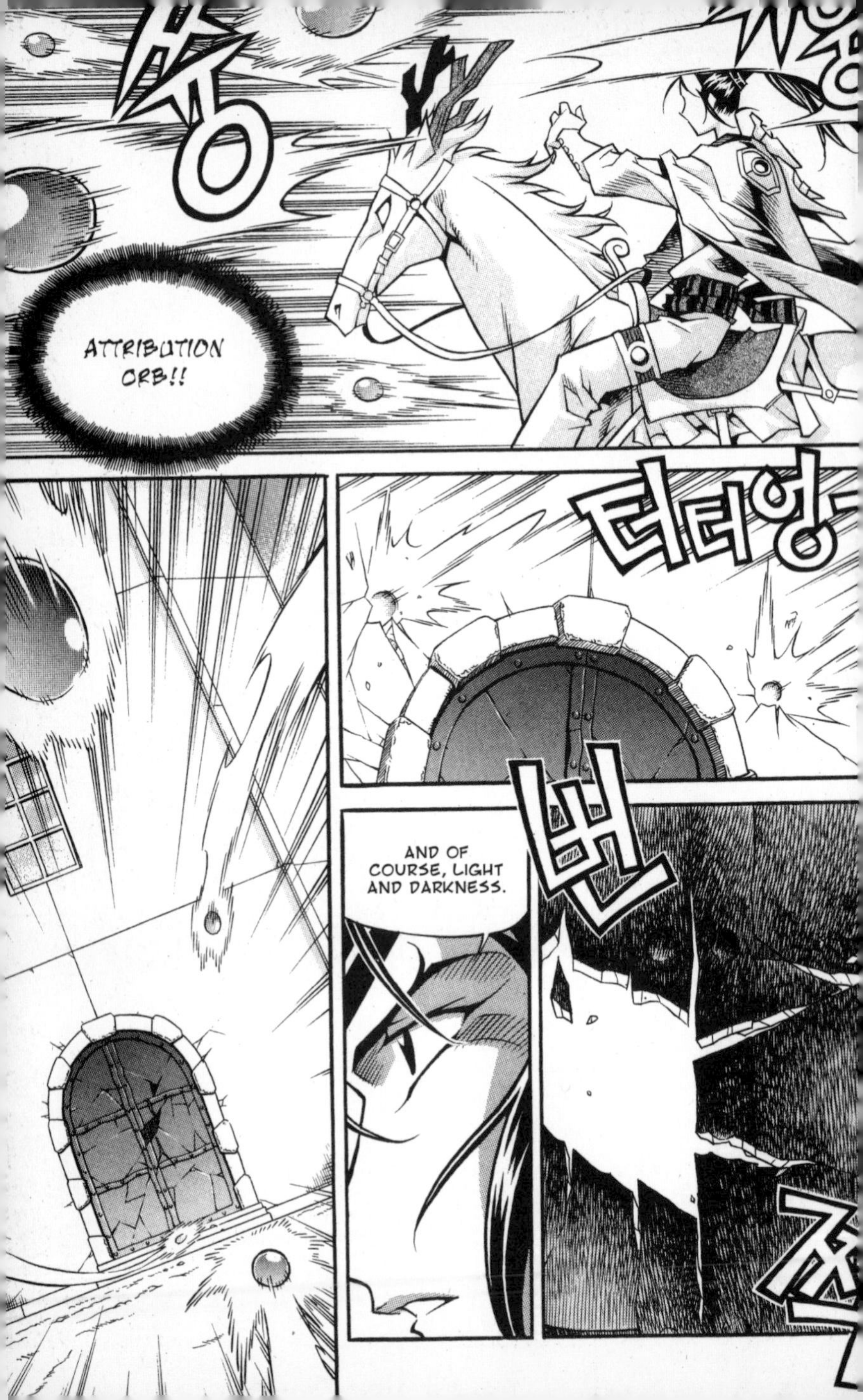
ATTRIBUTION ORB!!
AND OF COURSE, LIGHT AND DARKNESS.

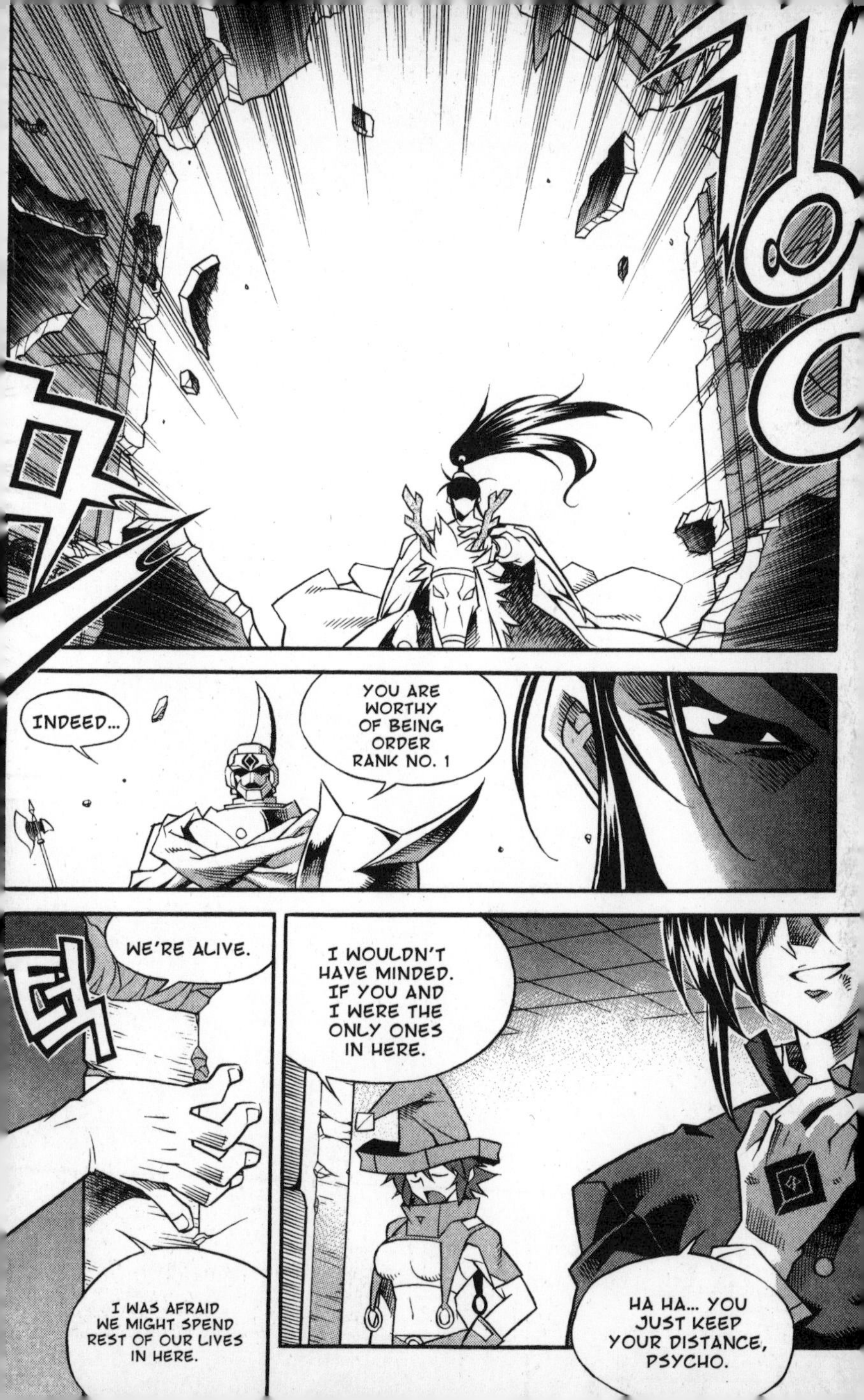
YOU ARE WORTHY OF BEING ORDER RANK NO. 1
INDEED...
WE'RE ALIVE.
I WAS AFRAID WE MIGHT SPEND REST OF OUR LIVES IN HERE.
I WOULDN'T HAVE MINDED. IF YOU AND I WERE THE ONLY ONES IN HERE.
HA HA... YOU JUST KEEP YOUR DISTANCE, PSYCHO.

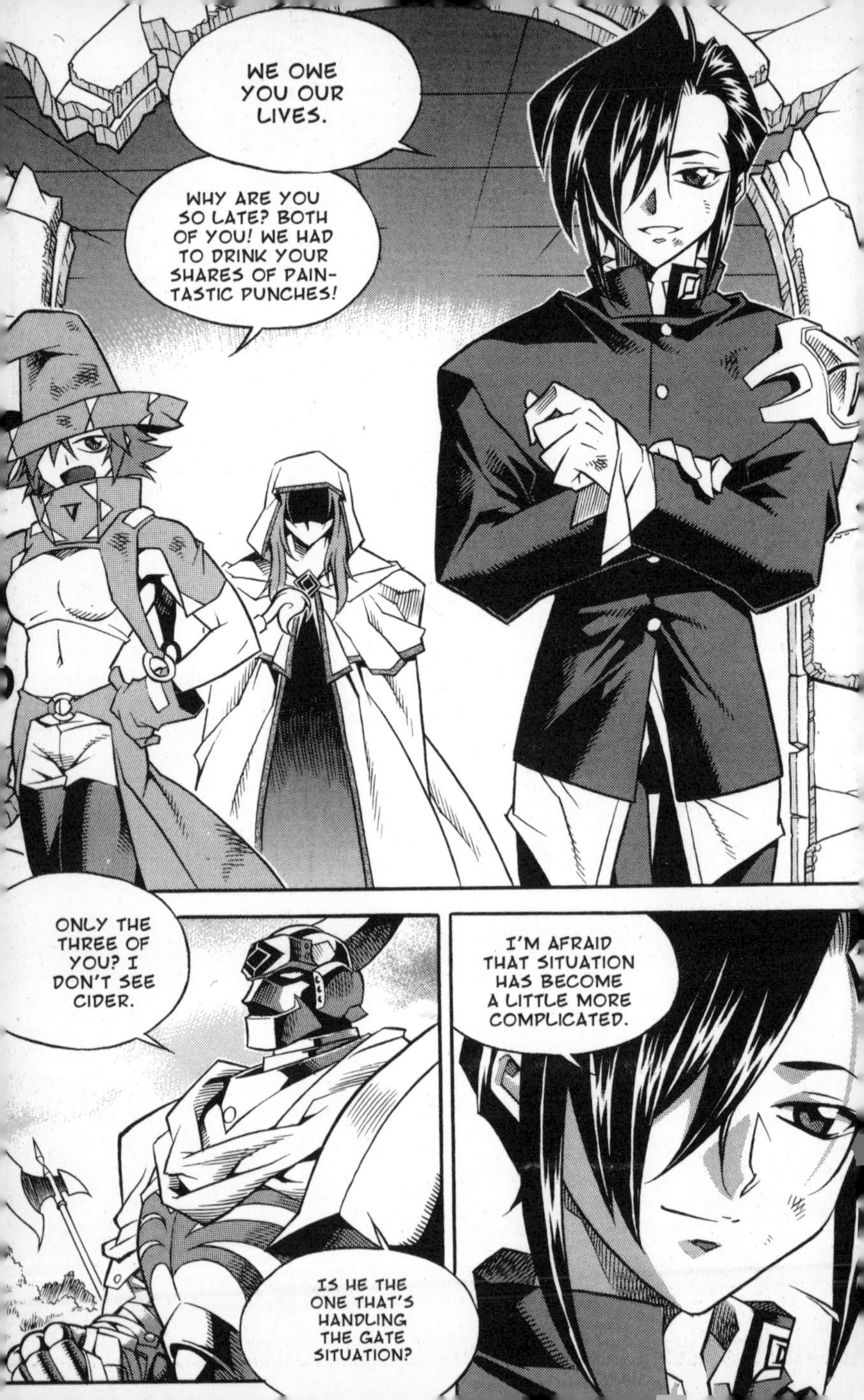
WE OWE YOU OUR LIVES.
WHY ARE YOU SO LATE? BOTH OF YOU! WE HAD TO DRINK YOUR SHARES OF PAIN-TASTIC PUNCHES!
ONLY THE THREE OF YOU? I DON'T SEE CIDER.
IS HE THE ONE THAT'S HANDLING THE GATE SITUATION?
I'M AFRAID THAT SITUATION HAS BECOME A LITTLE MORE COMPLICATED.

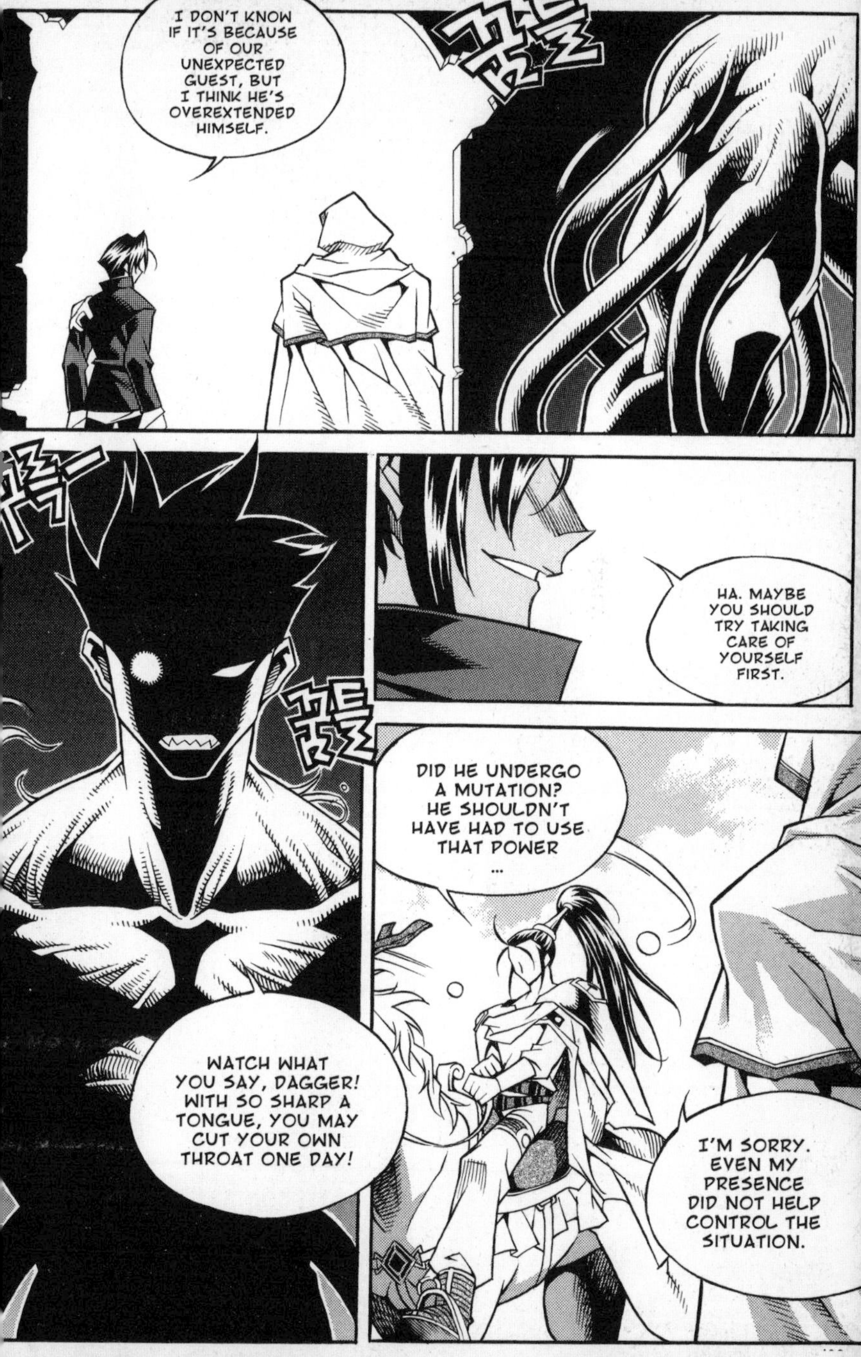
I DON'T KNOW IF IT'S BECAUSE OF OUR UNEXPECTED GUEST, BUT I THINK HE'S OVEREXTENDED HIMSELF.
HA. MAYBE YOU SHOULD TRY TAKING CARE OF YOURSELF FIRST.
WATCH WHAT YOU SAY, DAGGER! WITH SO SHARP A TONGUE, YOU MAY CUT YOUR OWN THROAT ONE DAY!
DID HE UNDERGO A MUTATION? HE SHOULDN'T HAVE HAD TO USE THAT POWER ...
I'M SORRY. EVEN MY PRESENCE DID NOT HELP CONTROL THE SITUATION.

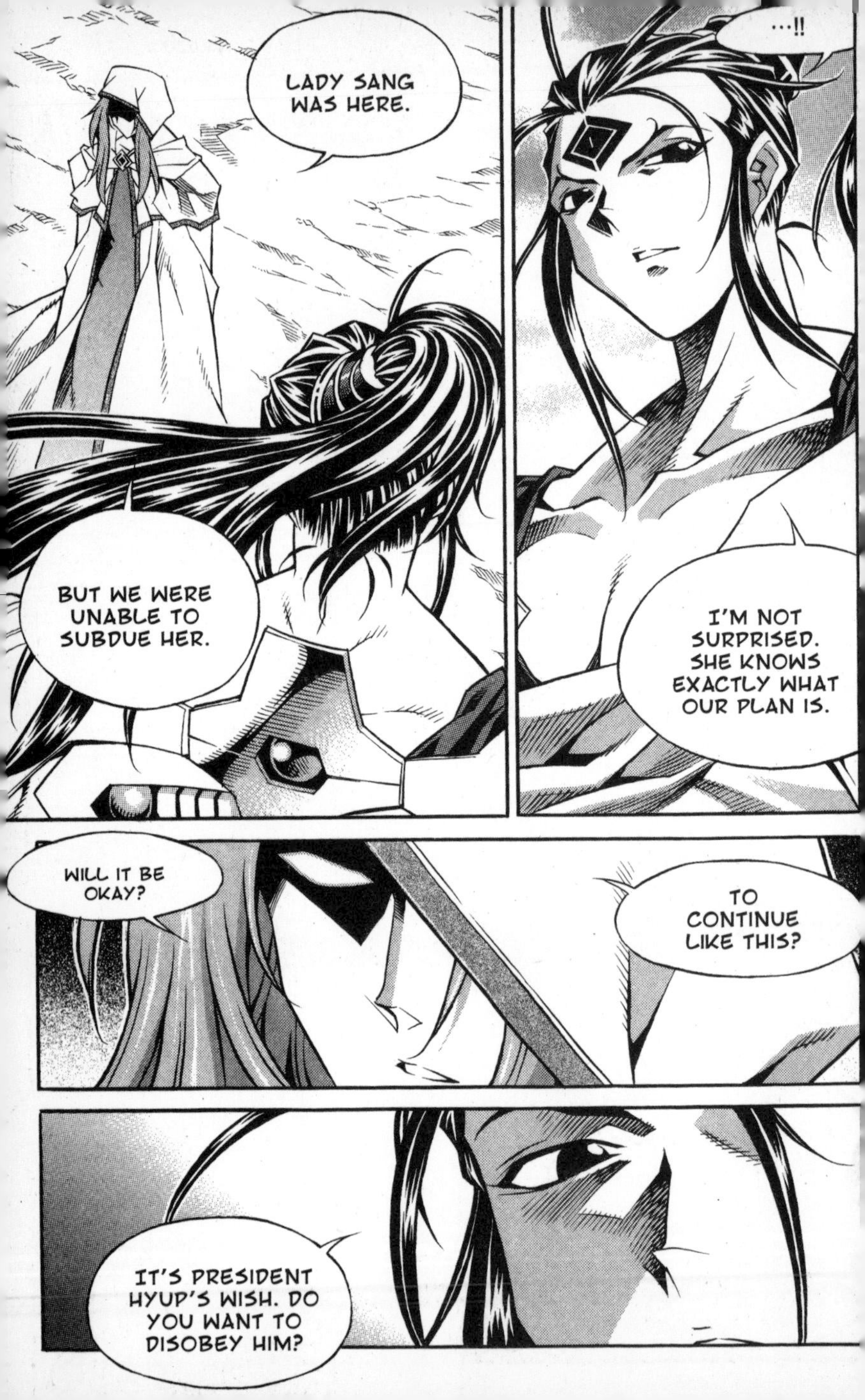
LADY SANG WAS HERE.
...!!
BUT WE WERE UNABLE TO SUBDUE HER.
I'M NOT SURPRISED. SHE KNOWS EXACTLY WHAT OUR PLAN IS.
WILL IT BE OKAY?
TO CONTINUE LIKE THIS?
IT'S PRESIDENT HYUP'S WISH. DO YOU WANT TO DISOBEY HIM?

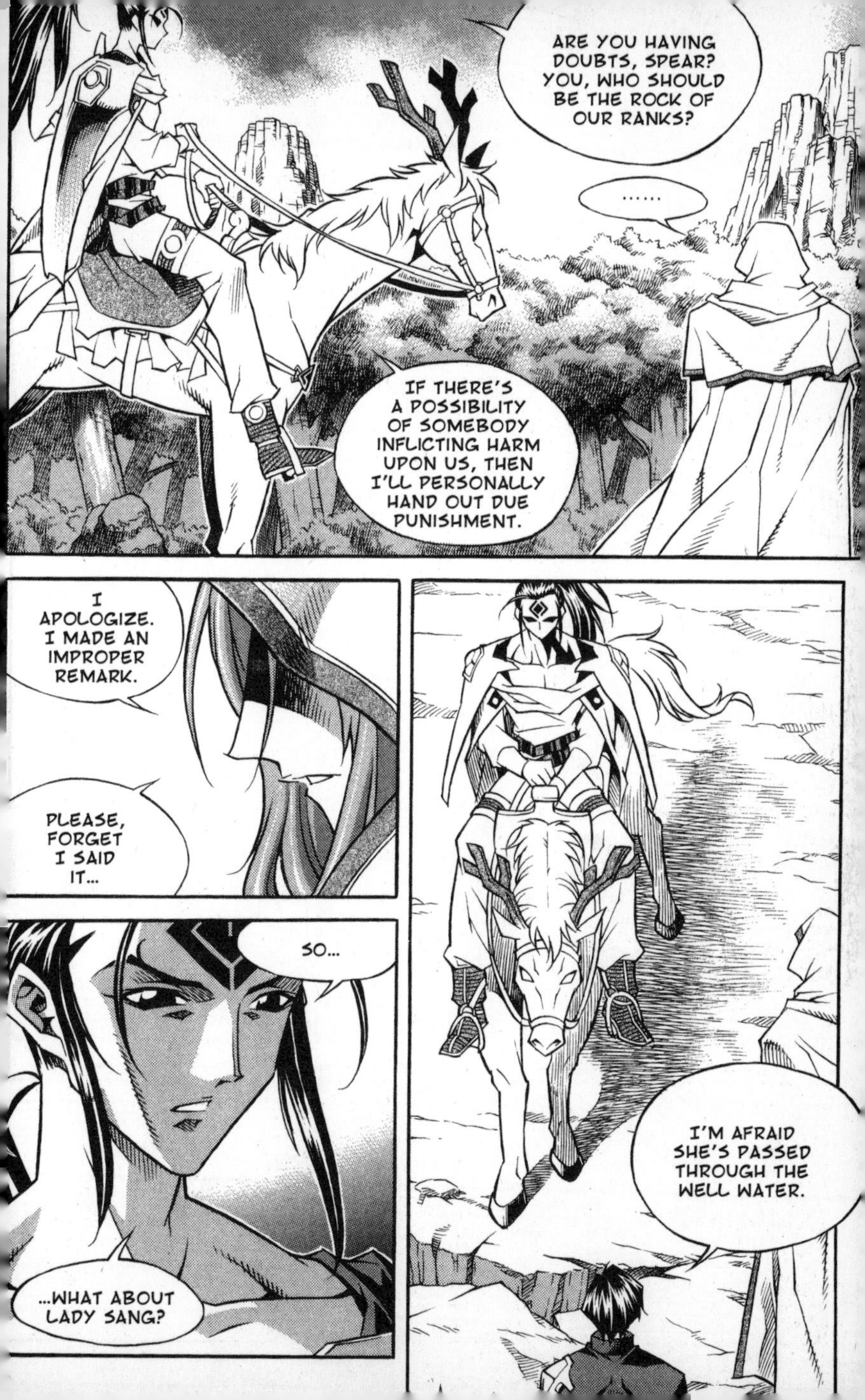
ARE YOU HAVING DOUBTS, SPEAR? YOU, WHO SHOULD BE THE ROCK OF OUR RANKS?
......
IF THERE'S A POSSIBILITY OF SOMEBODY INFLICTING HARM UPON US, THEN I'LL PERSONALLY HAND OUT DUE PUNISHMENT.
I APOLOGIZE. I MADE AN IMPROPER REMARK.
PLEASE, FORGET I SAID IT...
SO...
...WHAT ABOUT LADY SANG?
I'M AFRAID SHE'S PASSED THROUGH THE WELL WATER.

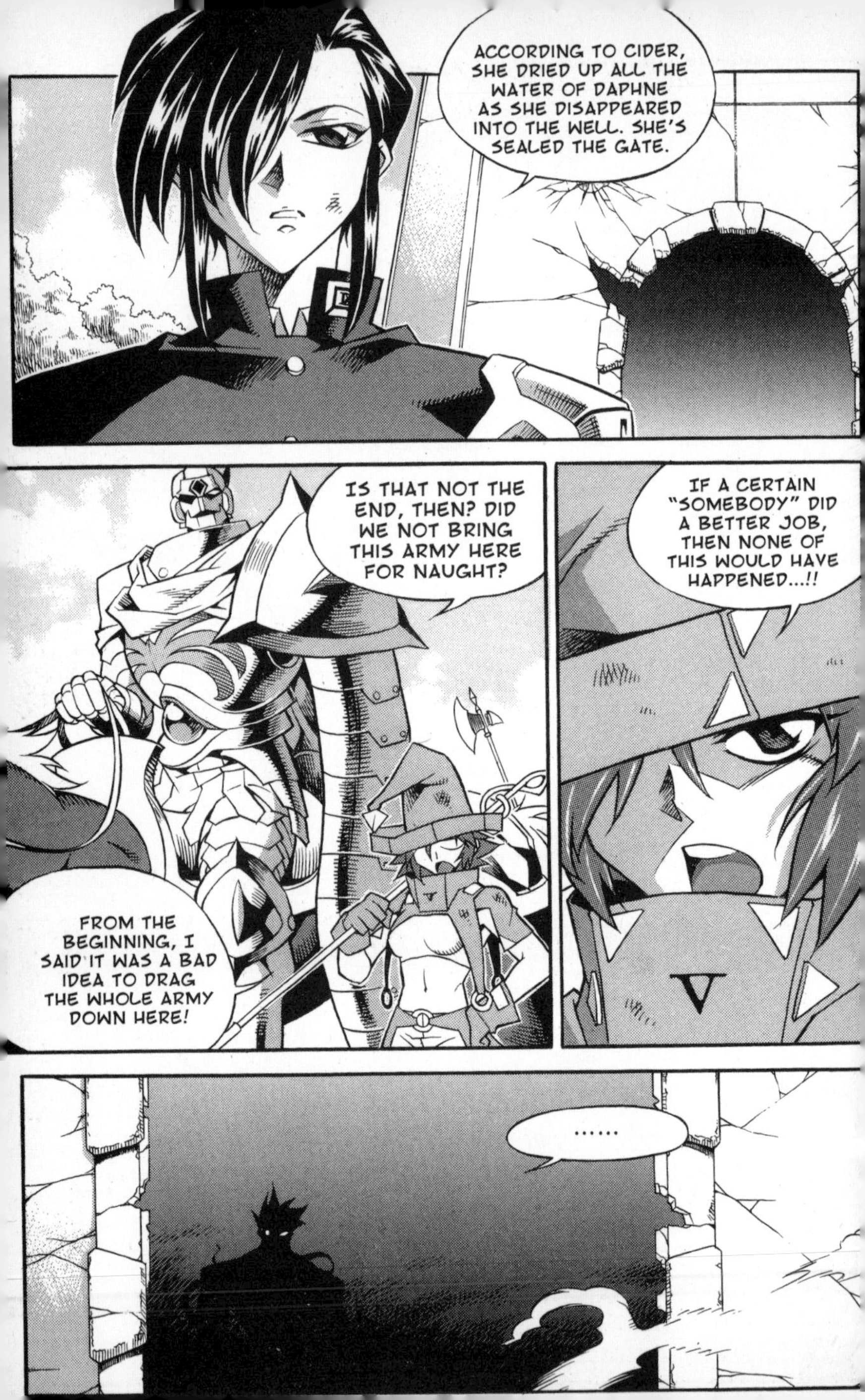
ACCORDING TO CIDER, SHE DRIED UP ALL THE WATER OF DAPHNE AS SHE DISAPPEARED INTO THE WELL. SHE'S SEALED THE GATE.
IS THAT NOT THE END, THEN? DID WE NOT BRING THIS ARMY HERE FOR NAUGHT?
FROM THE BEGINNING, I SAID IT WAS A BAD IDEA TO DRAG THE WHOLE ARMY DOWN HERE!
IF A CERTAIN "SOMEBODY" DID A BETTER JOB, THEN NONE OF THIS WOULD HAVE HAPPENED...!!
......

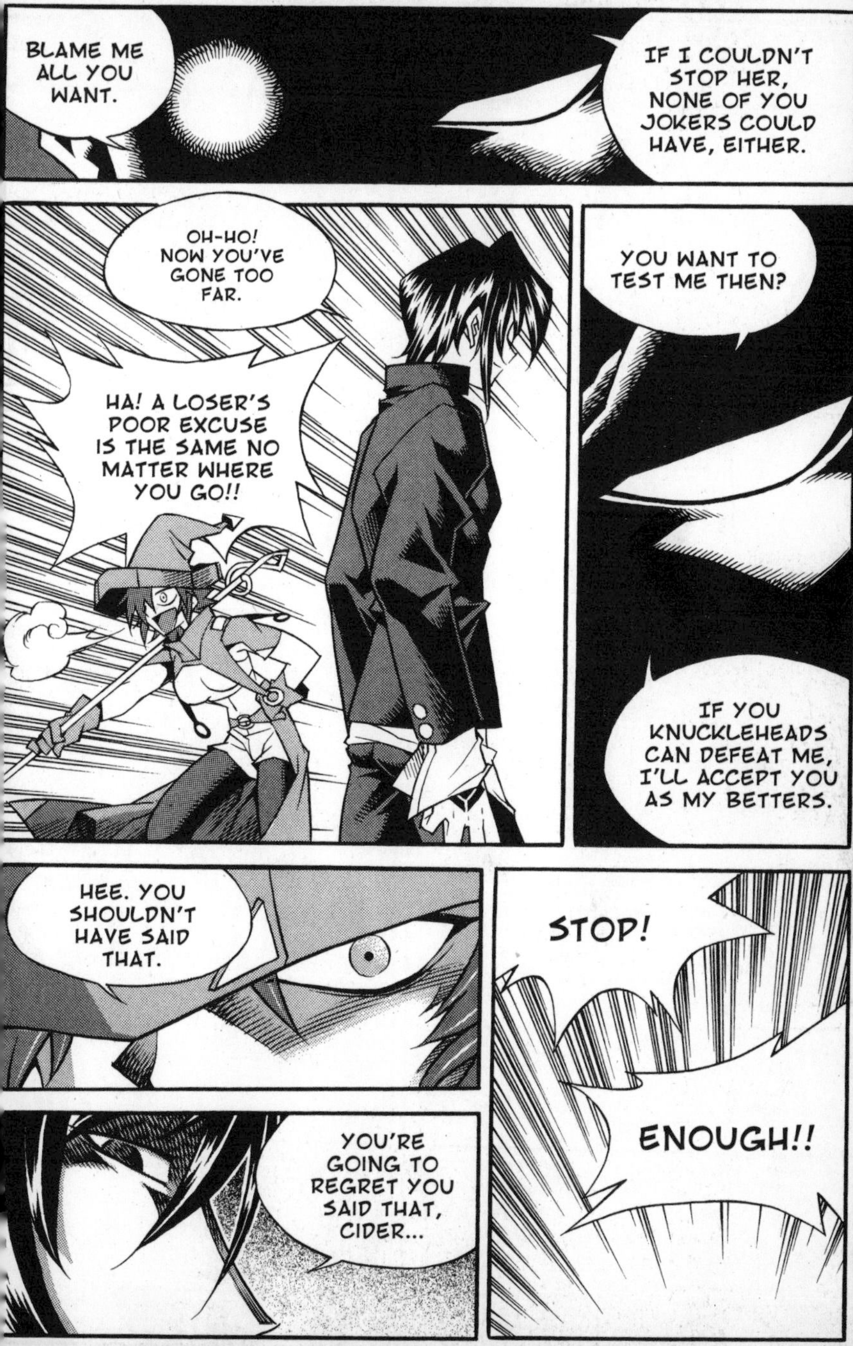
BLAME ME ALL YOU WANT.
IF I COULDN'T STOP HER, NONE OF YOU JOKERS COULD HAVE, EITHER.
OH-HO! NOW YOU'VE GONE TOO FAR.
HA! A LOSER'S POOR EXCUSE IS THE SAME NO MATTER WHERE YOU GO!!
YOU WANT TO TEST ME THEN?
IF YOU KNUCKLEHEADS CAN DEFEAT ME, I'LL ACCEPT YOU AS MY BETTERS.
HEE. YOU SHOULDN'T HAVE SAID THAT.
YOU'RE GOING TO REGRET YOU SAID THAT, CIDER...
STOP!
ENOUGH!!

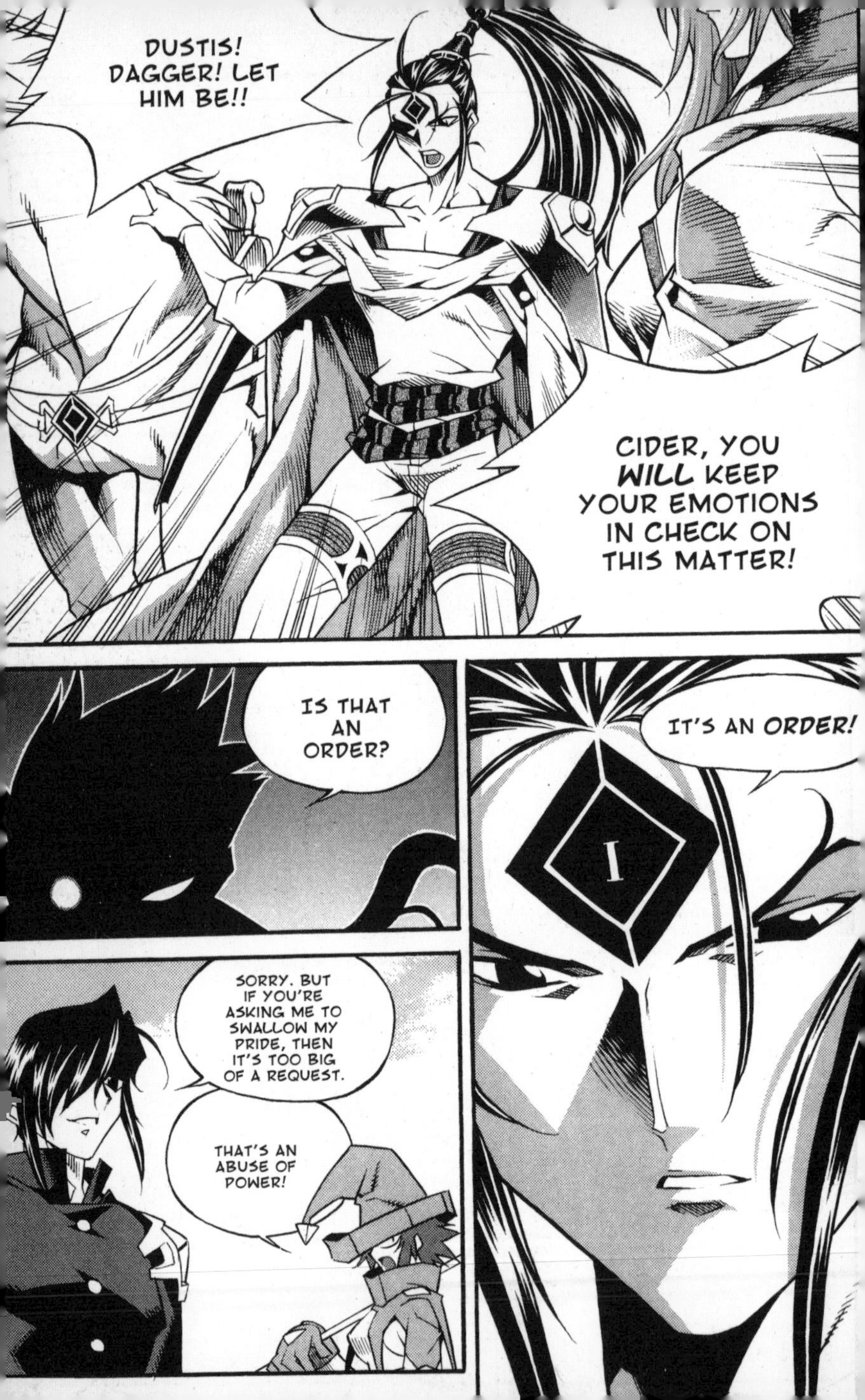
DUSTIS! DAGGER! LET HIM BE!!
CIDER, YOU WILL KEEP YOUR EMOTIONS IN CHECK ON THIS MATTER!
IS THAT AN ORDER?
IT'S AN ORDER!
SORRY. BUT IF YOU'RE ASKING ME TO SWALLOW MY PRIDE, THEN IT'S TOO BIG OF A REQUEST.
THAT'S AN ABUSE OF POWER!

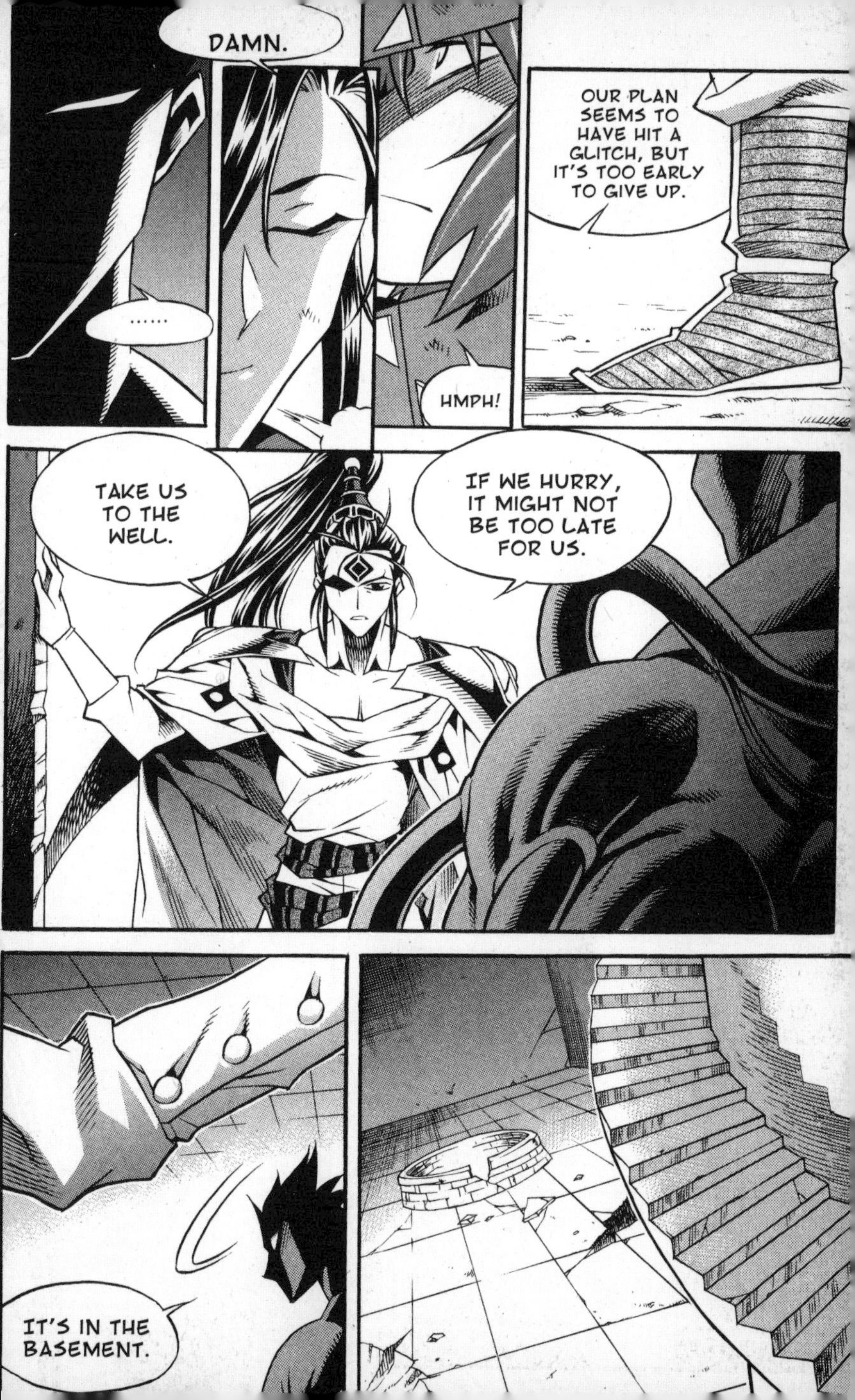
DAMN.
......
HMPH!
OUR PLAN SEEMS TO HAVE HIT A GLITCH, BUT IT'S TOO EARLY TO GIVE UP.
TAKE US TO THE WELL.
IF WE HURRY, IT MIGHT NOT BE TOO LATE FOR US.
IT'S IN THE BASEMENT.

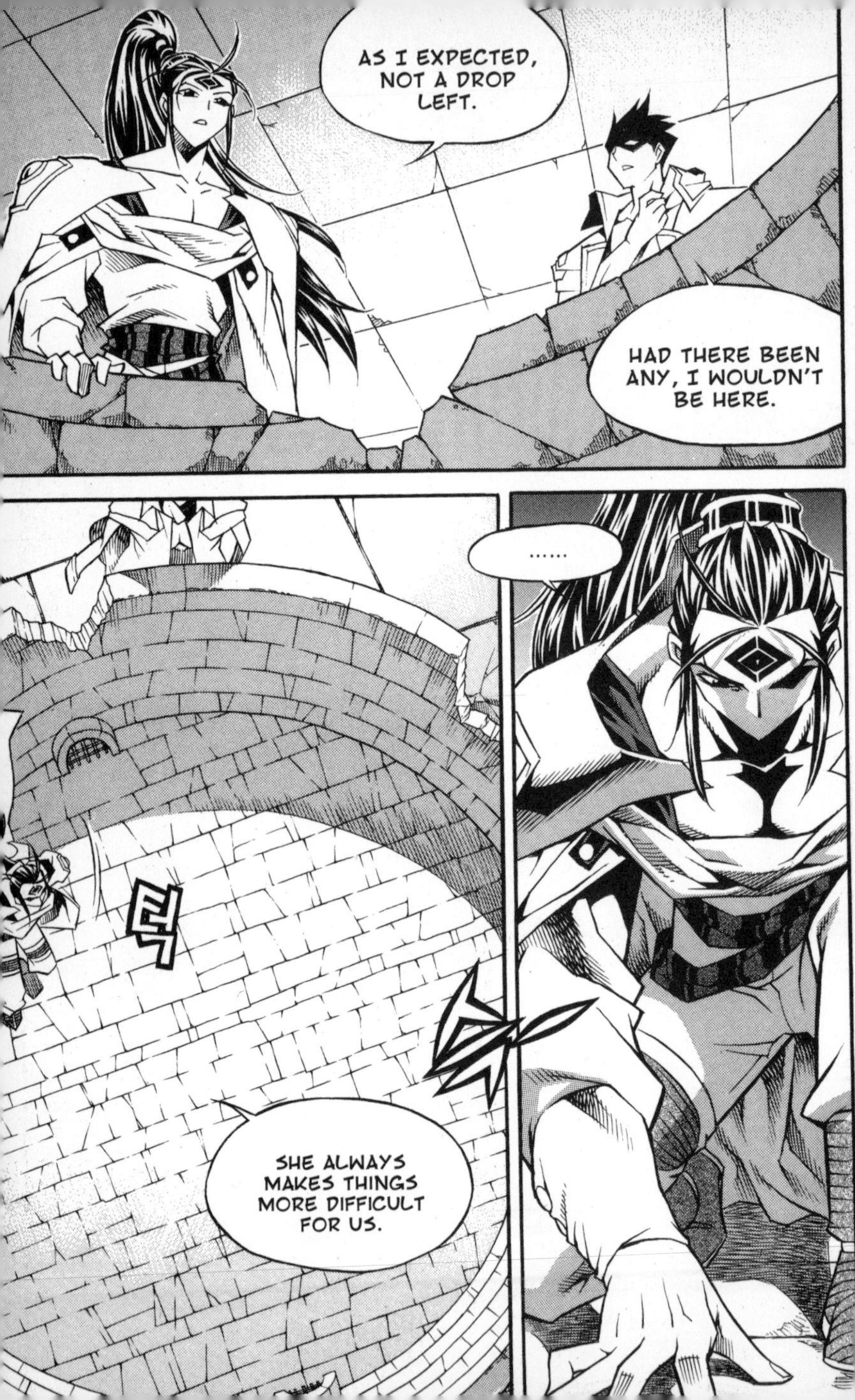
AS I EXPECTED, NOT A DROP LEFT.
HAD THERE BEEN ANY, I WOULDN'T BE HERE.
탁
SHE ALWAYS MAKES THINGS MORE DIFFICULT FOR US.
......

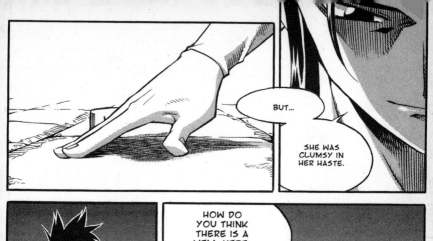

BUT...

SHE WAS CLUMSY IN HER HASTE.

HOW DO YOU THINK THERE IS A WELL HERE, WHERE IT DOESN'T EVEN RAIN?

WHAT...?

WATER VEIN UNDERNEATH. SHE SHOULD HAVE SEALED THAT AS WELL.

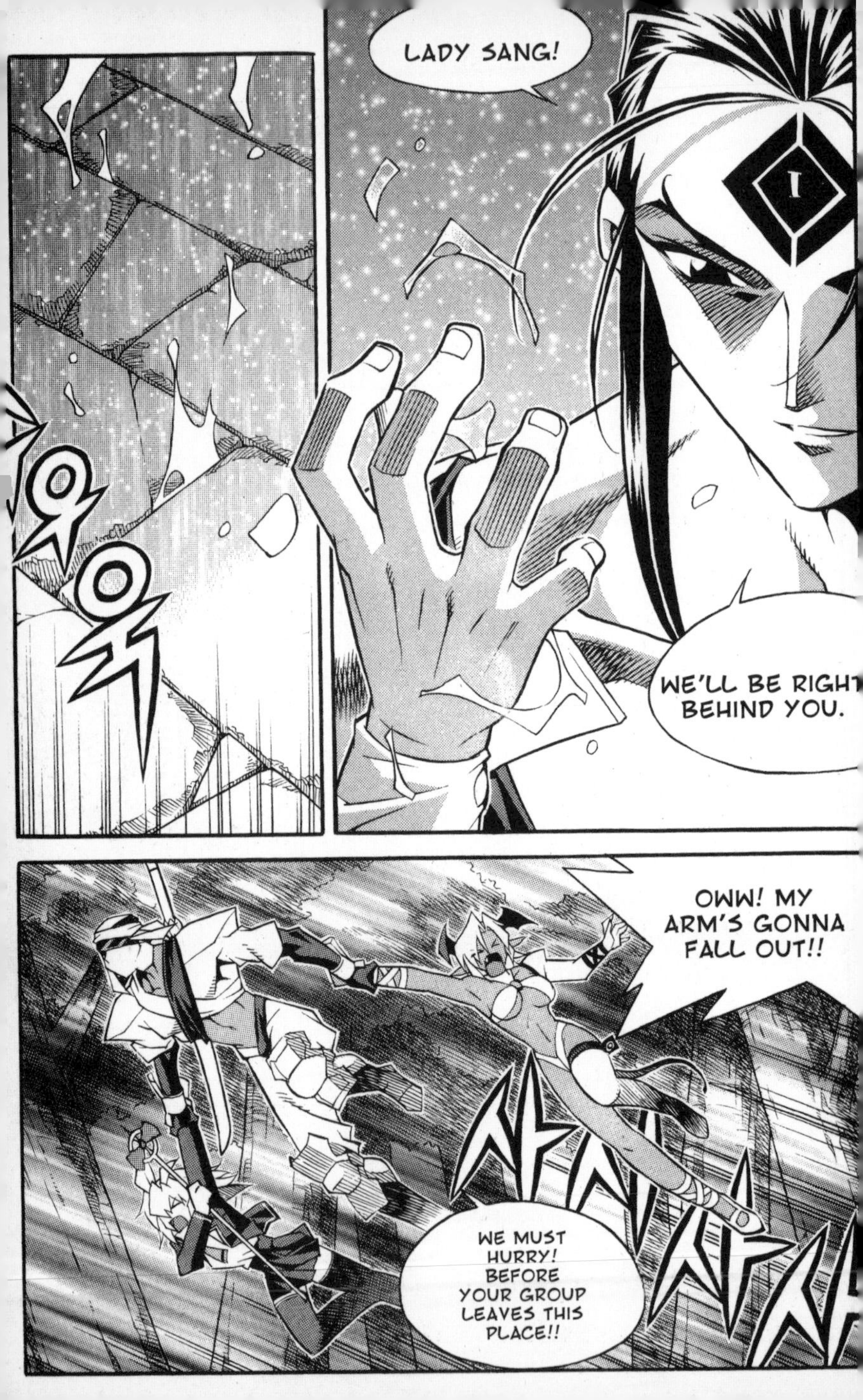
LADY SANG!
WE'LL BE RIGHT BEHIND YOU.
OWW! MY ARM'S GONNA FALL OUT!!
WE MUST HURRY! BEFORE YOUR GROUP LEAVES THIS PLACE!!

Quest 94

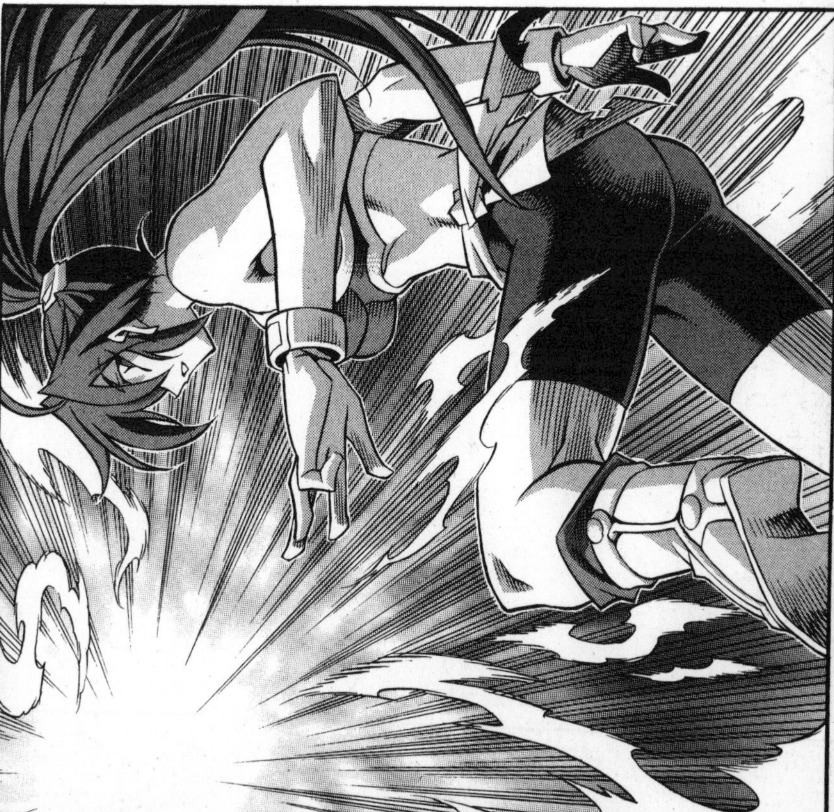

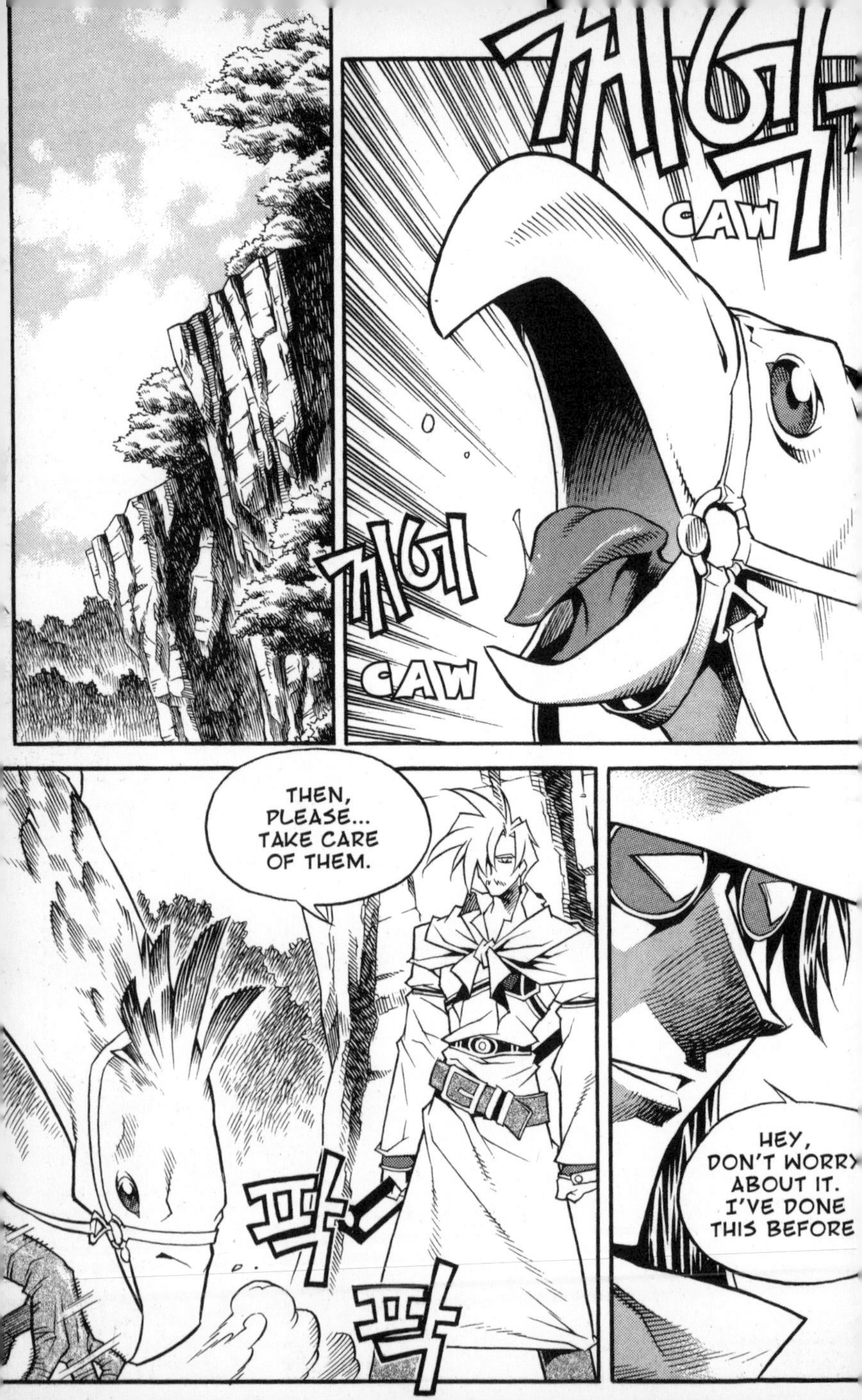
CAW
CAW
THEN, PLEASE... TAKE CARE OF THEM.
HEY, DON'T WORRY ABOUT IT. I'VE DONE THIS BEFORE

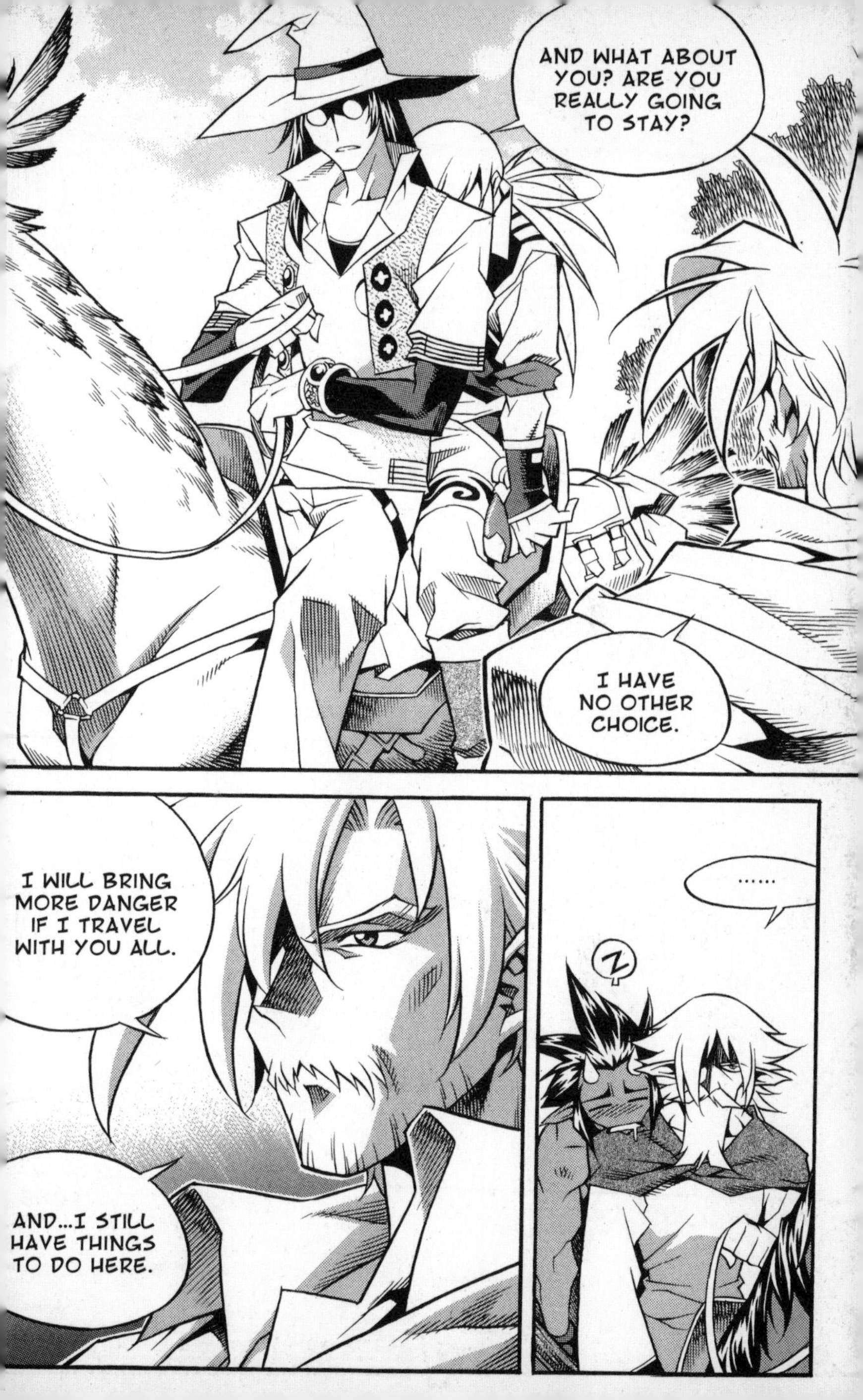
AND WHAT ABOUT YOU? ARE YOU REALLY GOING TO STAY?
I HAVE NO OTHER CHOICE.
I WILL BRING MORE DANGER IF I TRAVEL WITH YOU ALL.
AND...I STILL HAVE THINGS TO DO HERE.
......
Z

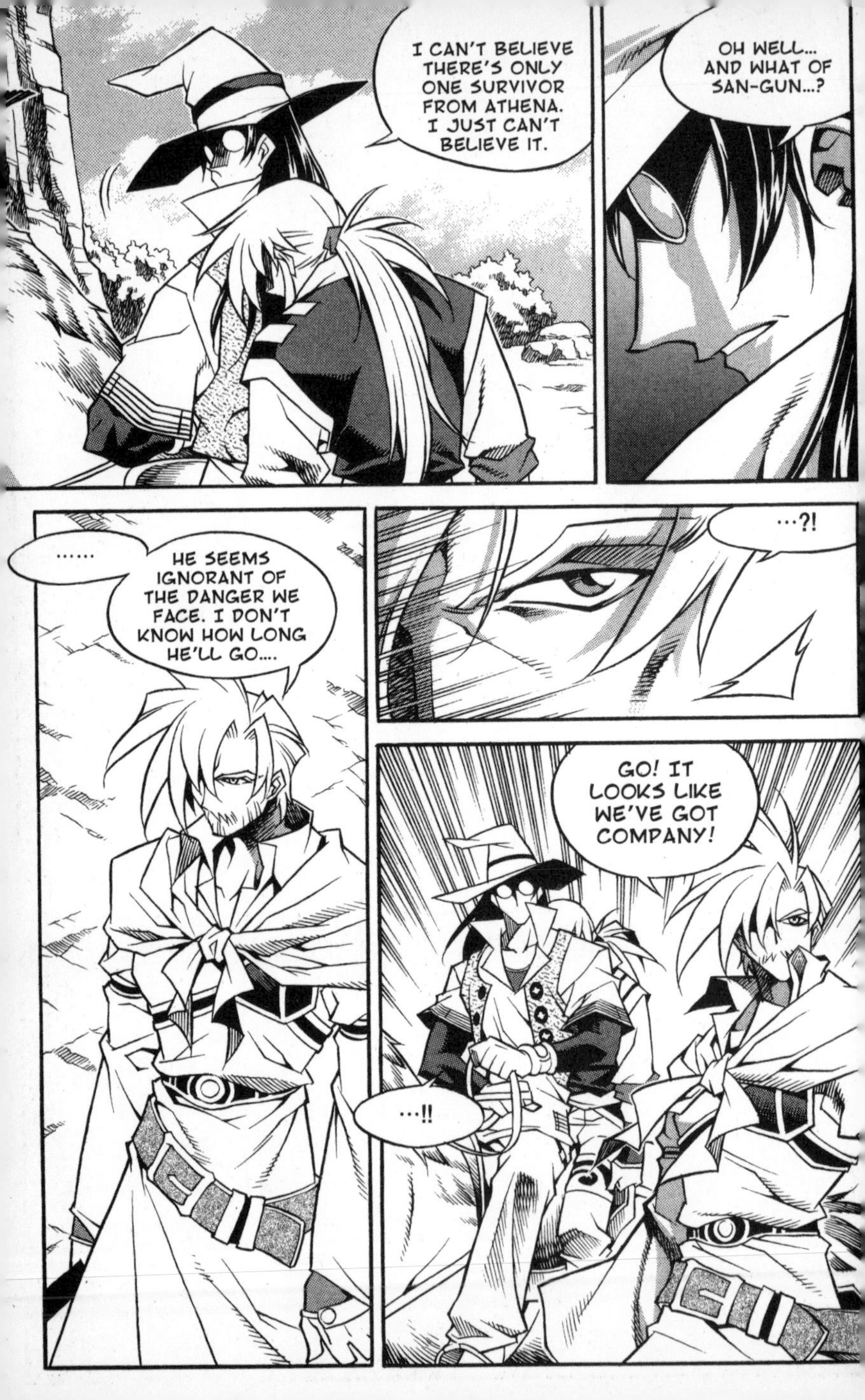

I CAN'T BELIEVE THERE'S ONLY ONE SURVIVOR FROM ATHENA. I JUST CAN'T BELIEVE IT.
OH WELL... AND WHAT OF SAN-GUN...?
......
HE SEEMS IGNORANT OF THE DANGER WE FACE. I DON'T KNOW HOW LONG HE'LL GO....
...?!
GO! IT LOOKS LIKE WE'VE GOT COMPANY!
...!!

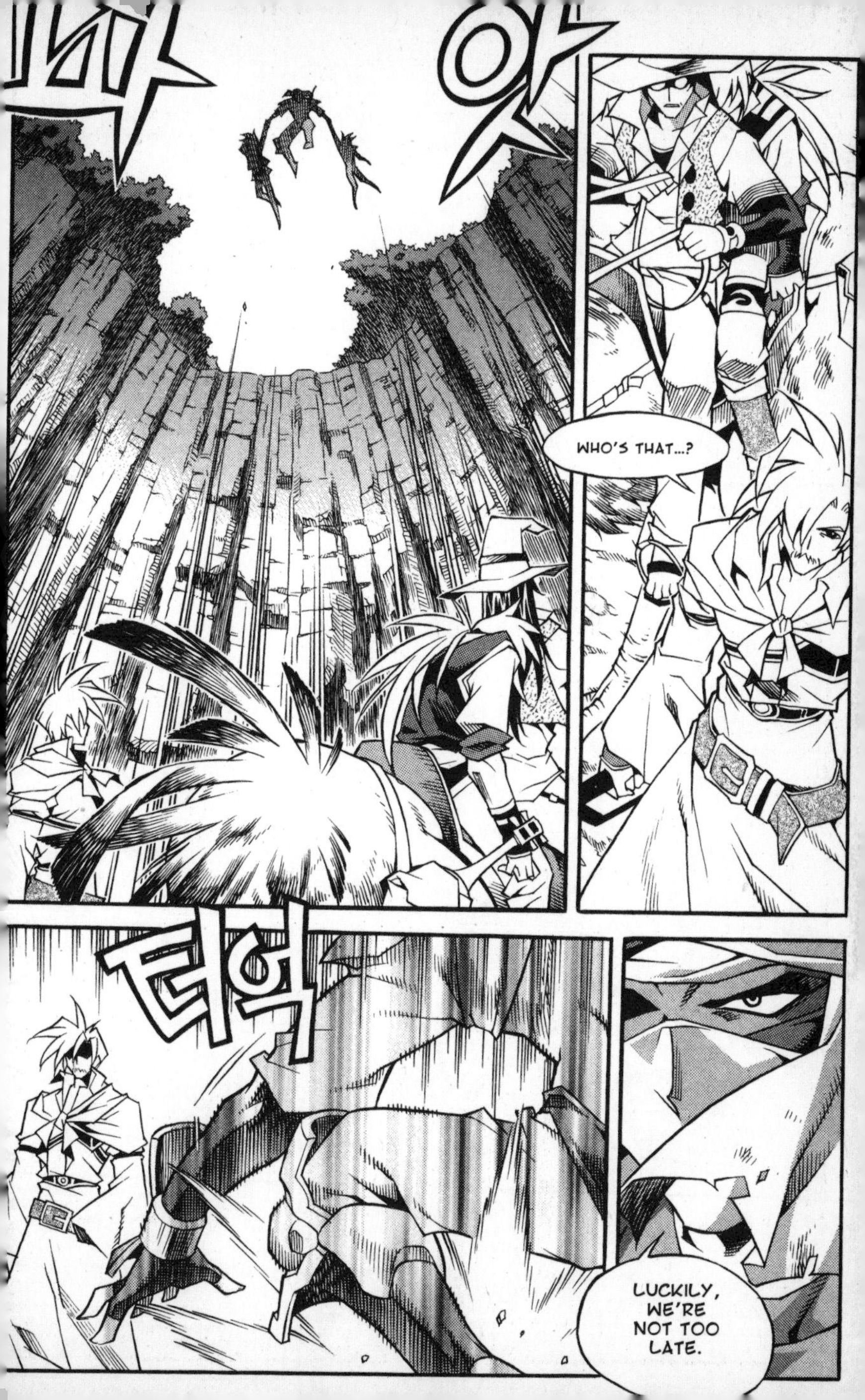

WHO'S THAT...?
LUCKILY, WE'RE NOT TOO LATE.

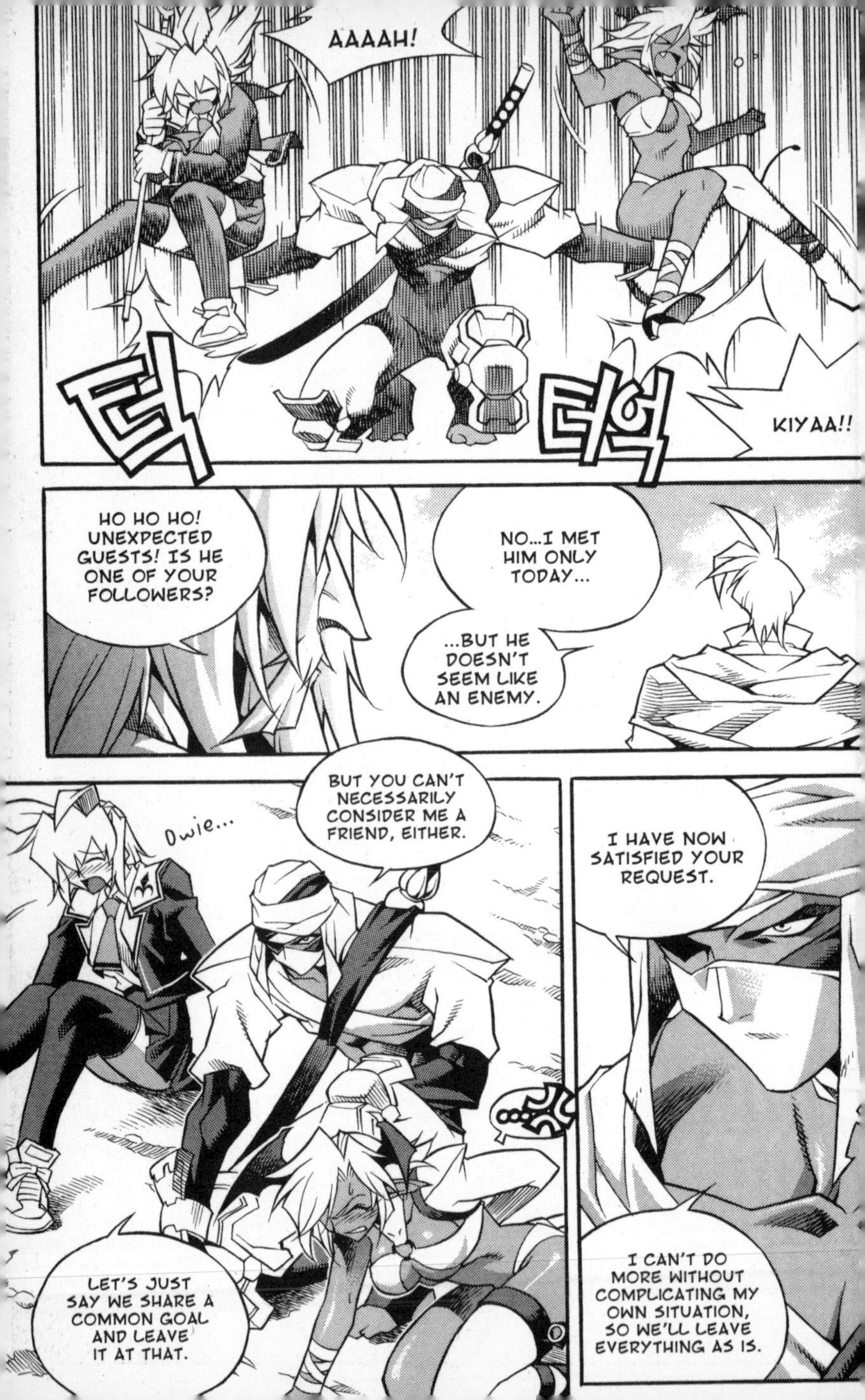

AAAAH!
KIYAA!!
HO HO HO! UNEXPECTED GUESTS! IS HE ONE OF YOUR FOLLOWERS?
NO...I MET HIM ONLY TODAY...
...BUT HE DOESN'T SEEM LIKE AN ENEMY.
Owie...
BUT YOU CAN'T NECESSARILY CONSIDER ME A FRIEND, EITHER.
LET'S JUST SAY WE SHARE A COMMON GOAL AND LEAVE IT AT THAT.
I HAVE NOW SATISFIED YOUR REQUEST.
I CAN'T DO MORE WITHOUT COMPLICATING MY OWN SITUATION, SO WE'LL LEAVE EVERYTHING AS IS.

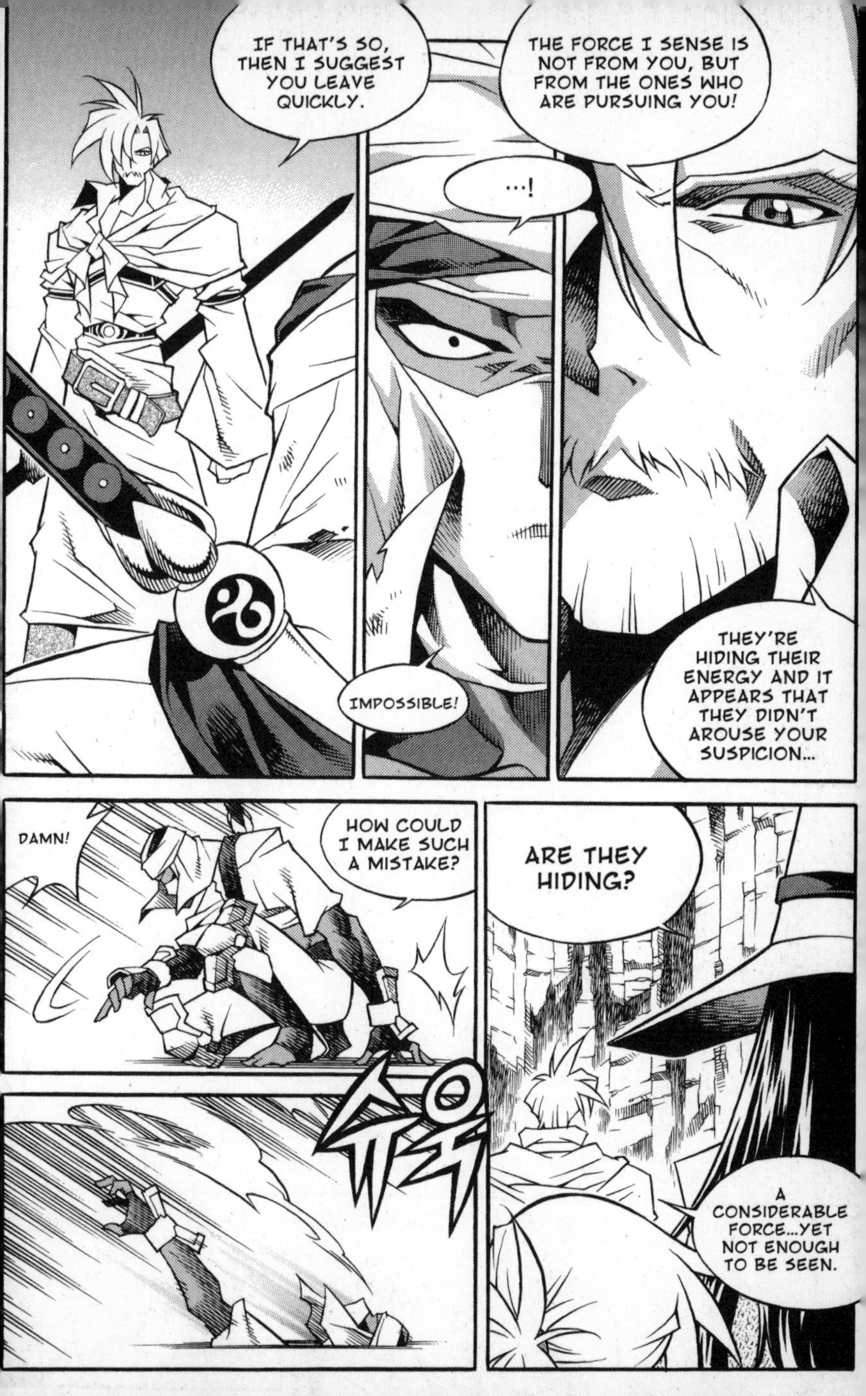
IF THAT'S SO, THEN I SUGGEST YOU LEAVE QUICKLY.
THE FORCE I SENSE IS NOT FROM YOU, BUT FROM THE ONES WHO ARE PURSUING YOU!
...!
IMPOSSIBLE!
THEY'RE HIDING THEIR ENERGY AND IT APPEARS THAT THEY DIDN'T AROUSE YOUR SUSPICION...
DAMN!
HOW COULD I MAKE SUCH A MISTAKE?
ARE THEY HIDING?
A CONSIDERABLE FORCE...YET NOT ENOUGH TO BE SEEN.

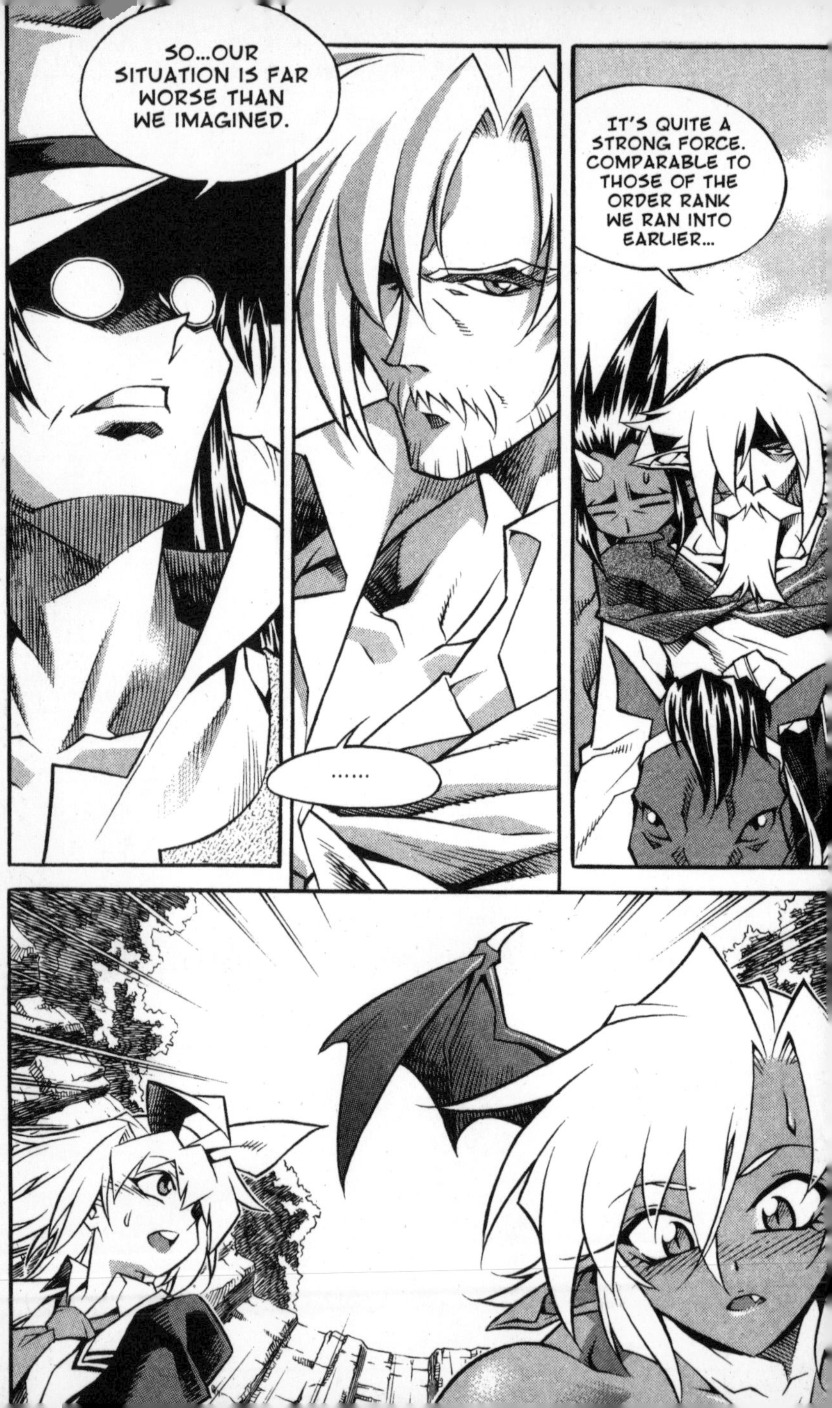

SO...OUR SITUATION IS FAR WORSE THAN WE IMAGINED.
......
IT'S QUITE A STRONG FORCE. COMPARABLE TO THOSE OF THE ORDER RANK WE RAN INTO EARLIER...

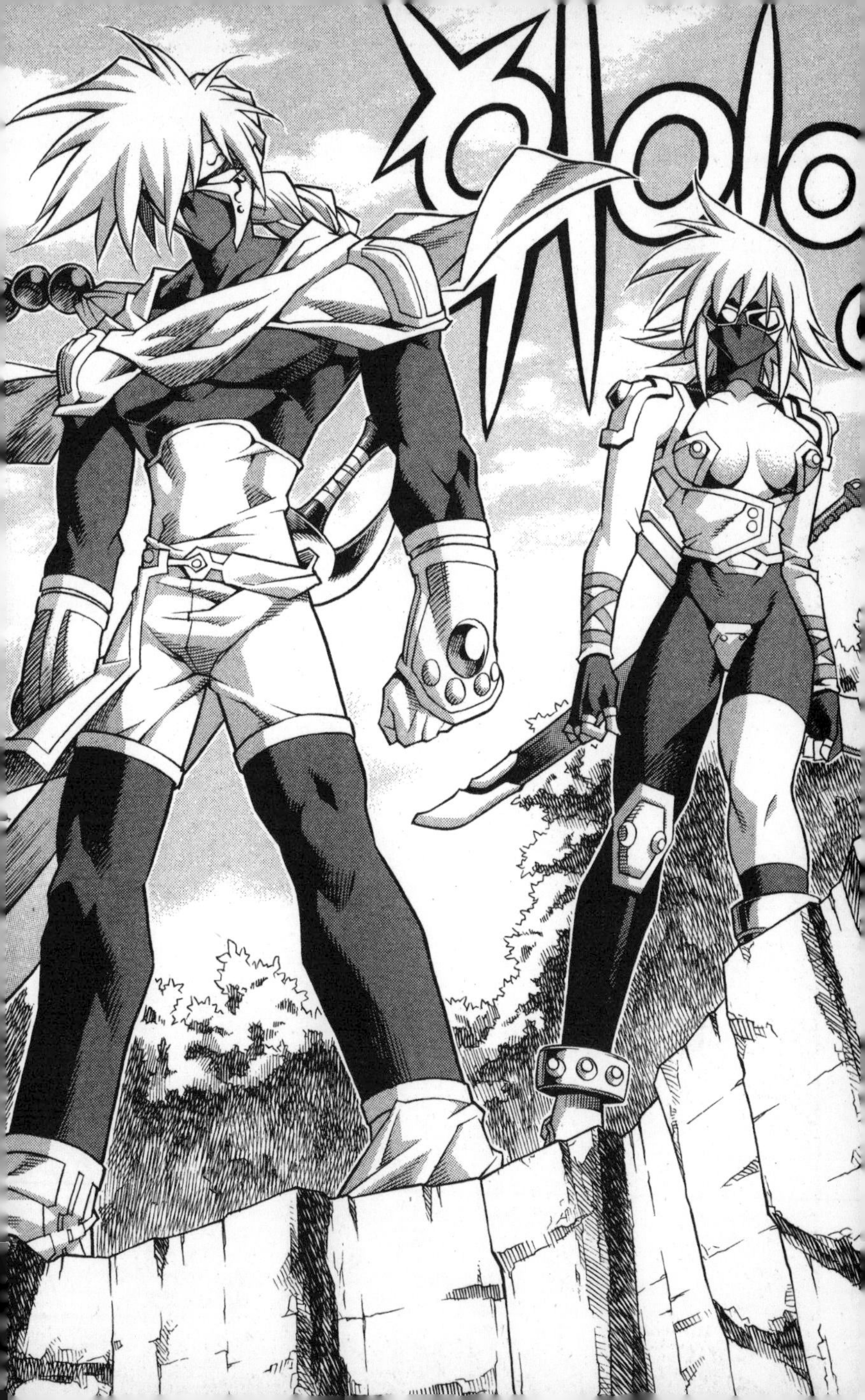

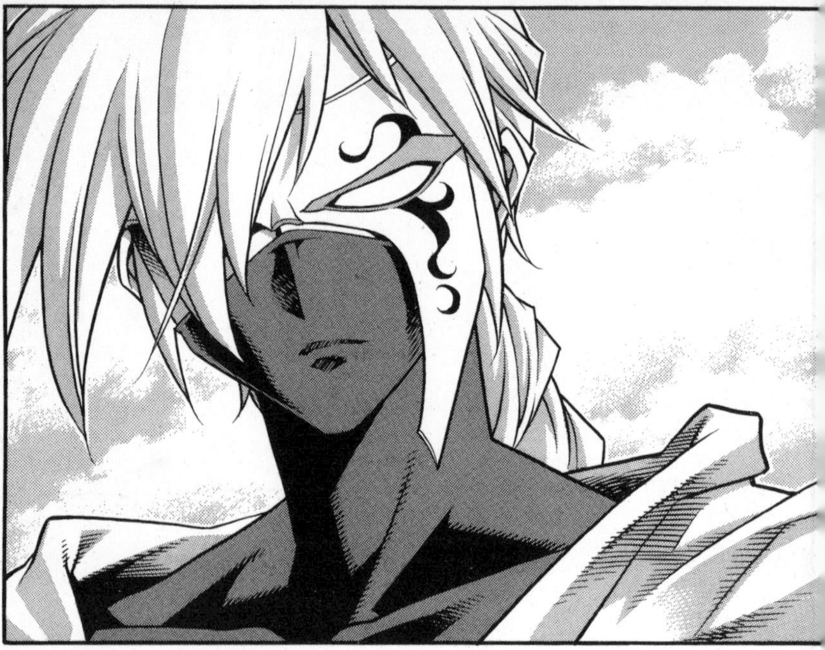

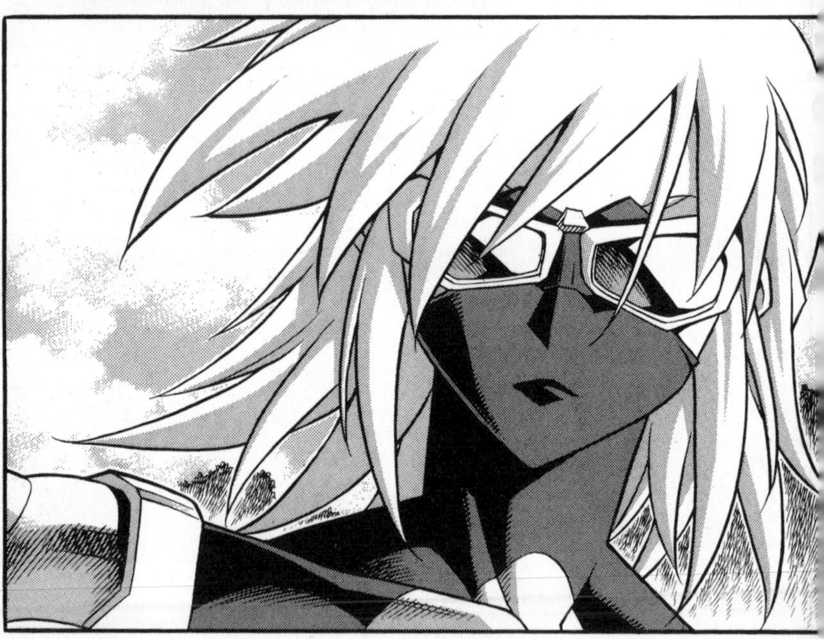

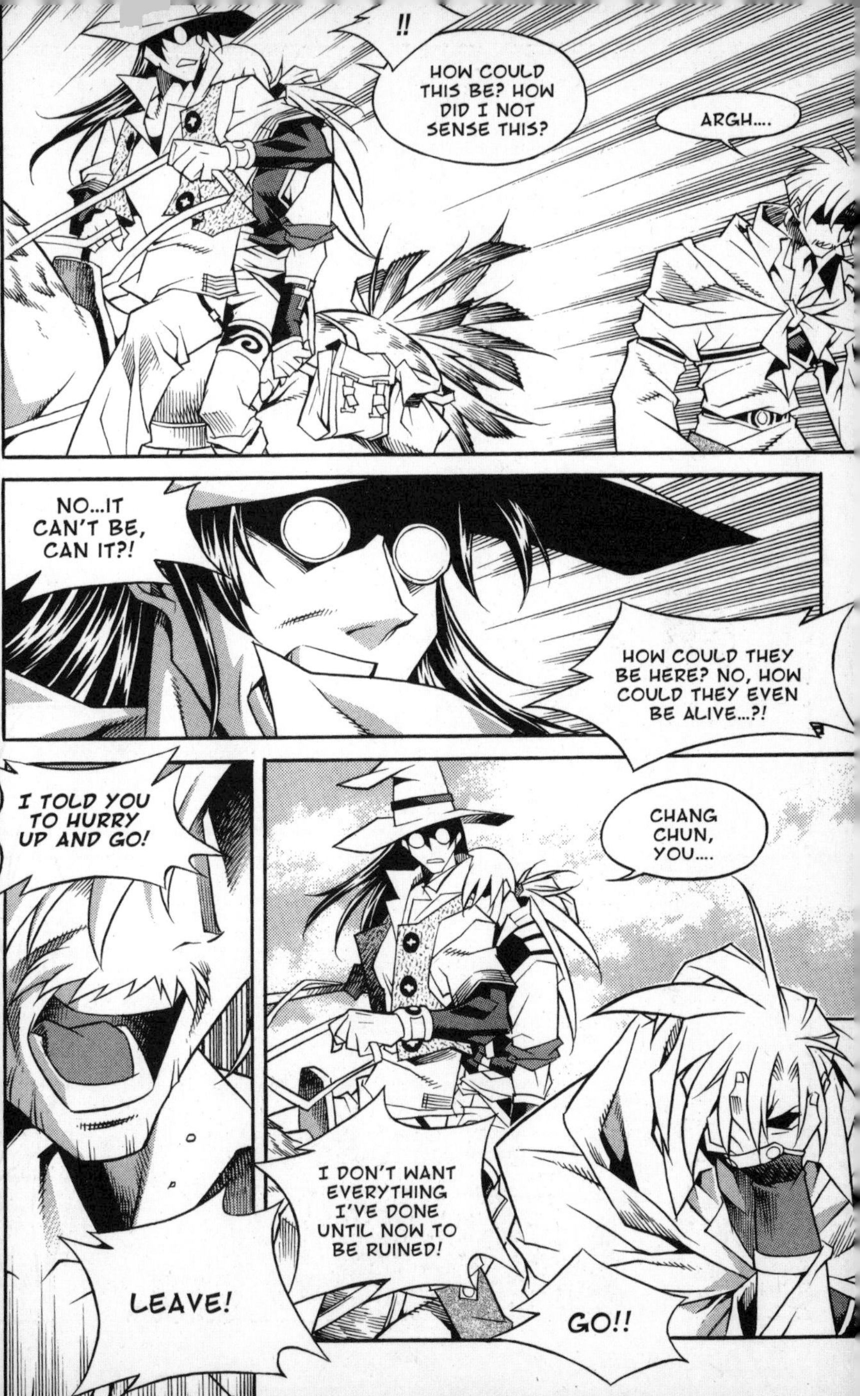
!!
HOW COULD THIS BE? HOW DID I NOT SENSE THIS?
ARGH....
NO...IT CAN'T BE, CAN IT?!
HOW COULD THEY BE HERE? NO, HOW COULD THEY EVEN BE ALIVE...?!
I TOLD YOU TO HURRY UP AND GO!
CHANG CHUN, YOU....
I DON'T WANT EVERYTHING I'VE DONE UNTIL NOW TO BE RUINED!
LEAVE!
GO!!

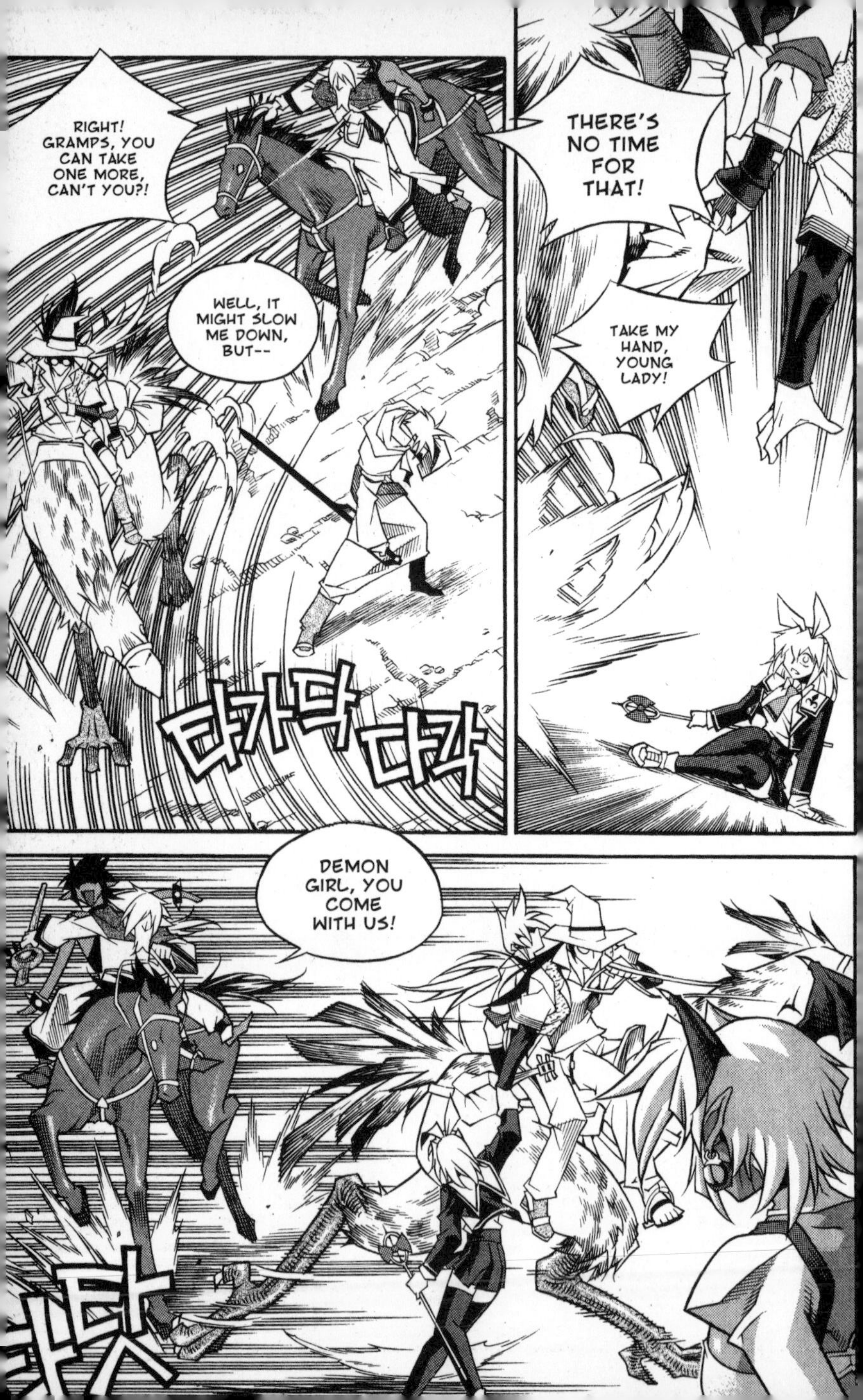
RIGHT! GRAMPS, YOU CAN TAKE ONE MORE, CAN'T YOU?!
WELL, IT MIGHT SLOW ME DOWN, BUT--
THERE'S NO TIME FOR THAT!
TAKE MY HAND, YOUNG LADY!
DEMON GIRL, YOU COME WITH US!

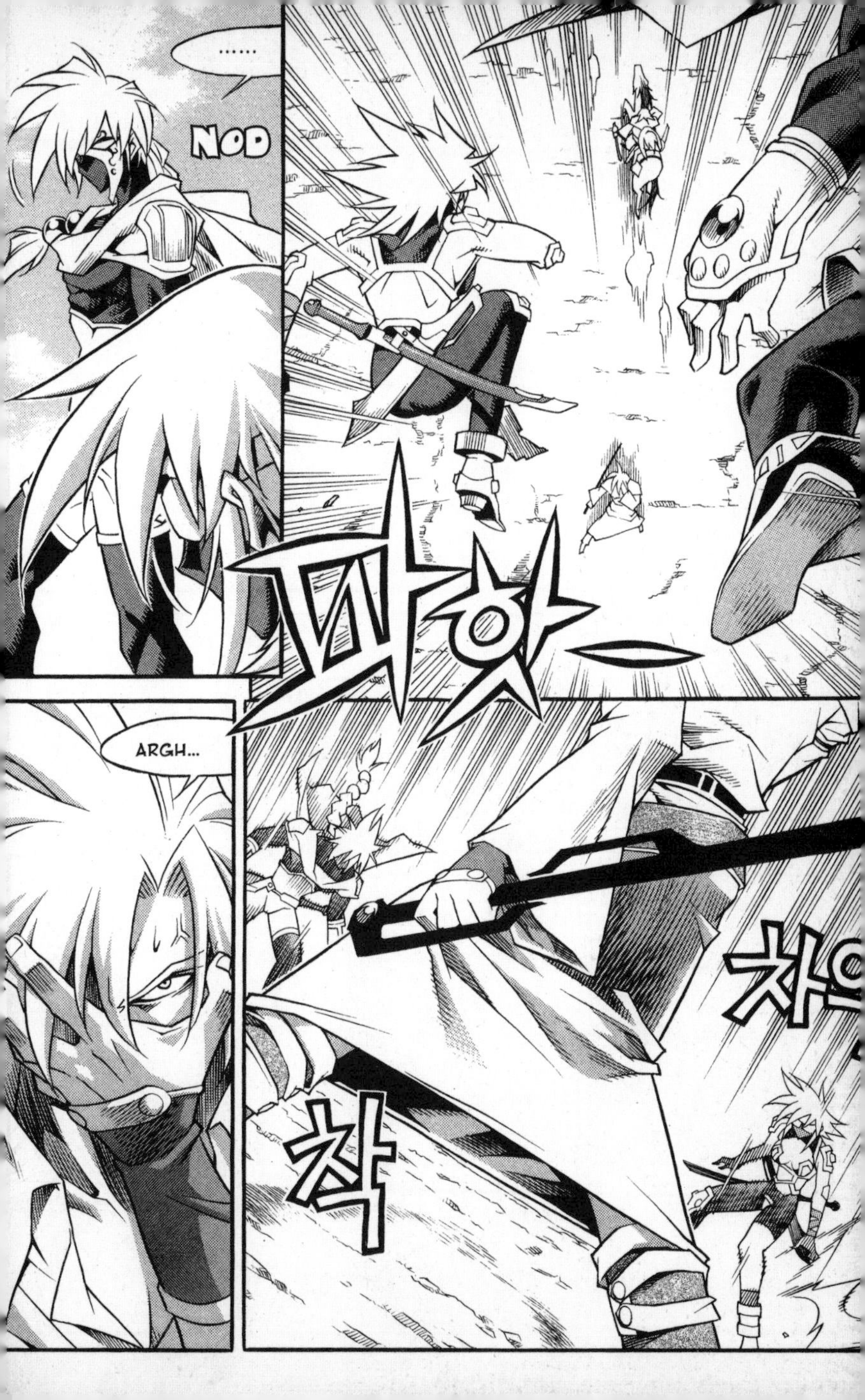

......
NOD
파앗—
ARGH...
차앗
착

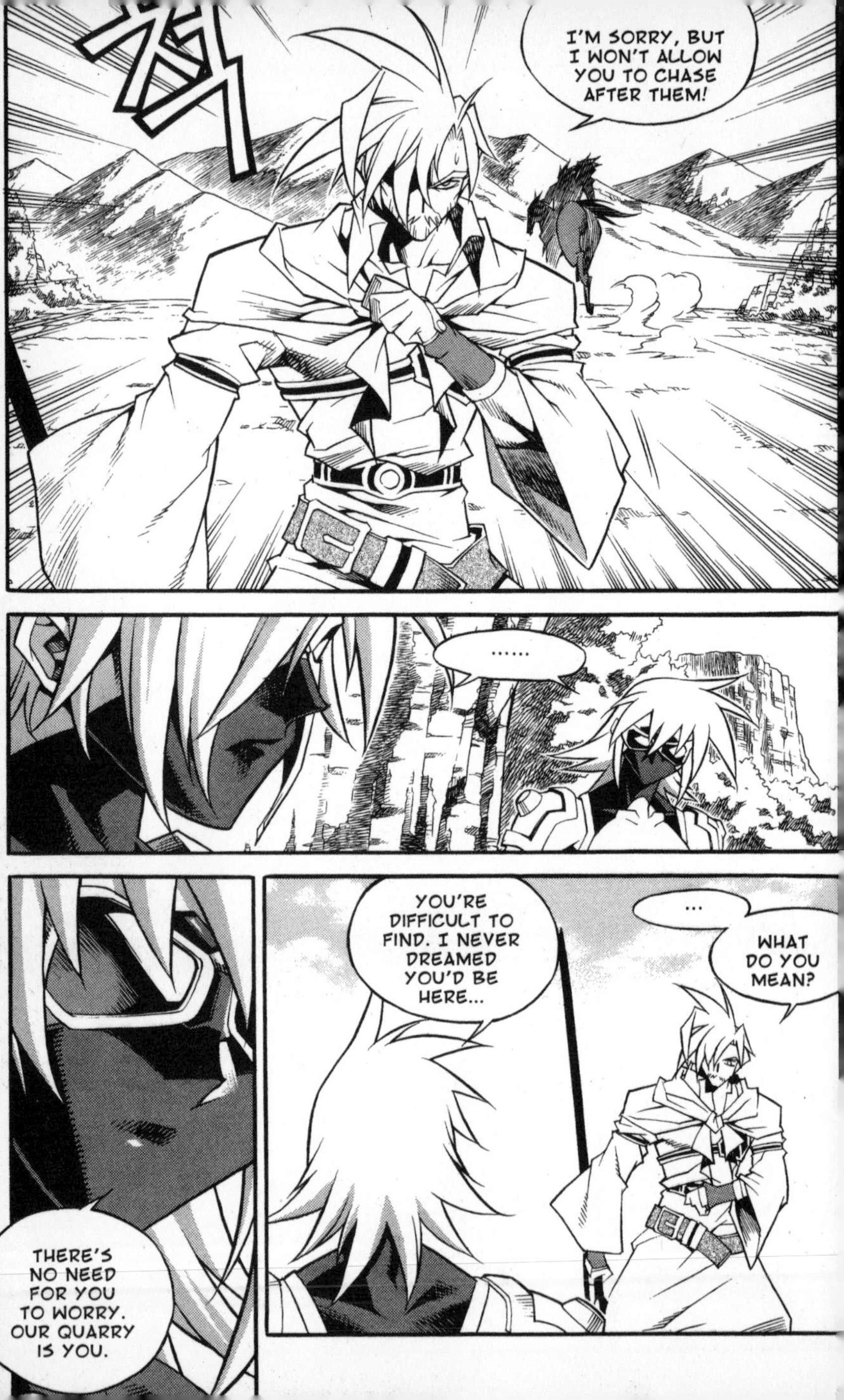
I'M SORRY, BUT I WON'T ALLOW YOU TO CHASE AFTER THEM!
......
YOU'RE DIFFICULT TO FIND. I NEVER DREAMED YOU'D BE HERE...
...
WHAT DO YOU MEAN?
THERE'S NO NEED FOR YOU TO WORRY. OUR QUARRY IS YOU.

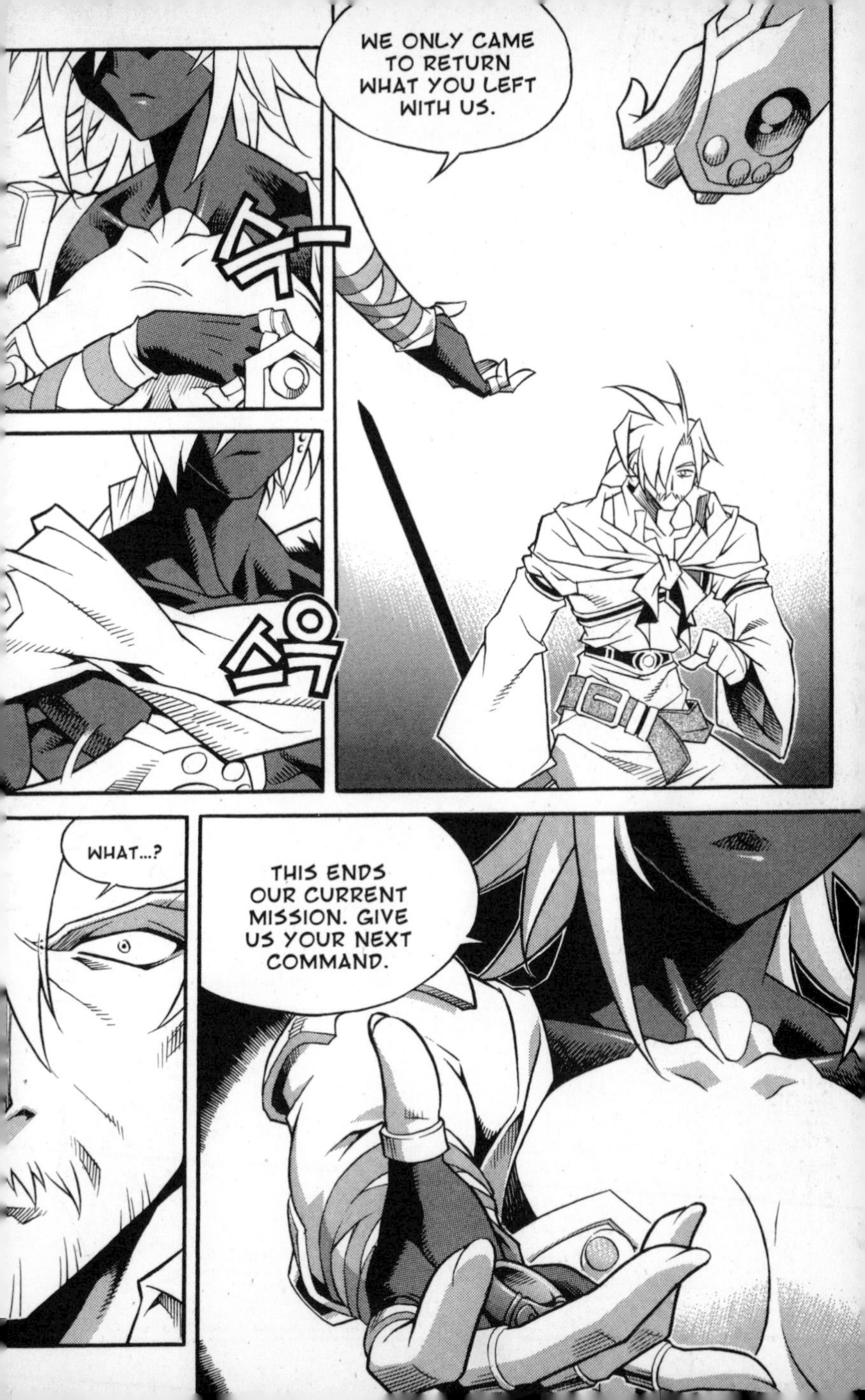
WE ONLY CAME TO RETURN WHAT YOU LEFT WITH US.
WHAT...?
THIS ENDS OUR CURRENT MISSION. GIVE US YOUR NEXT COMMAND.

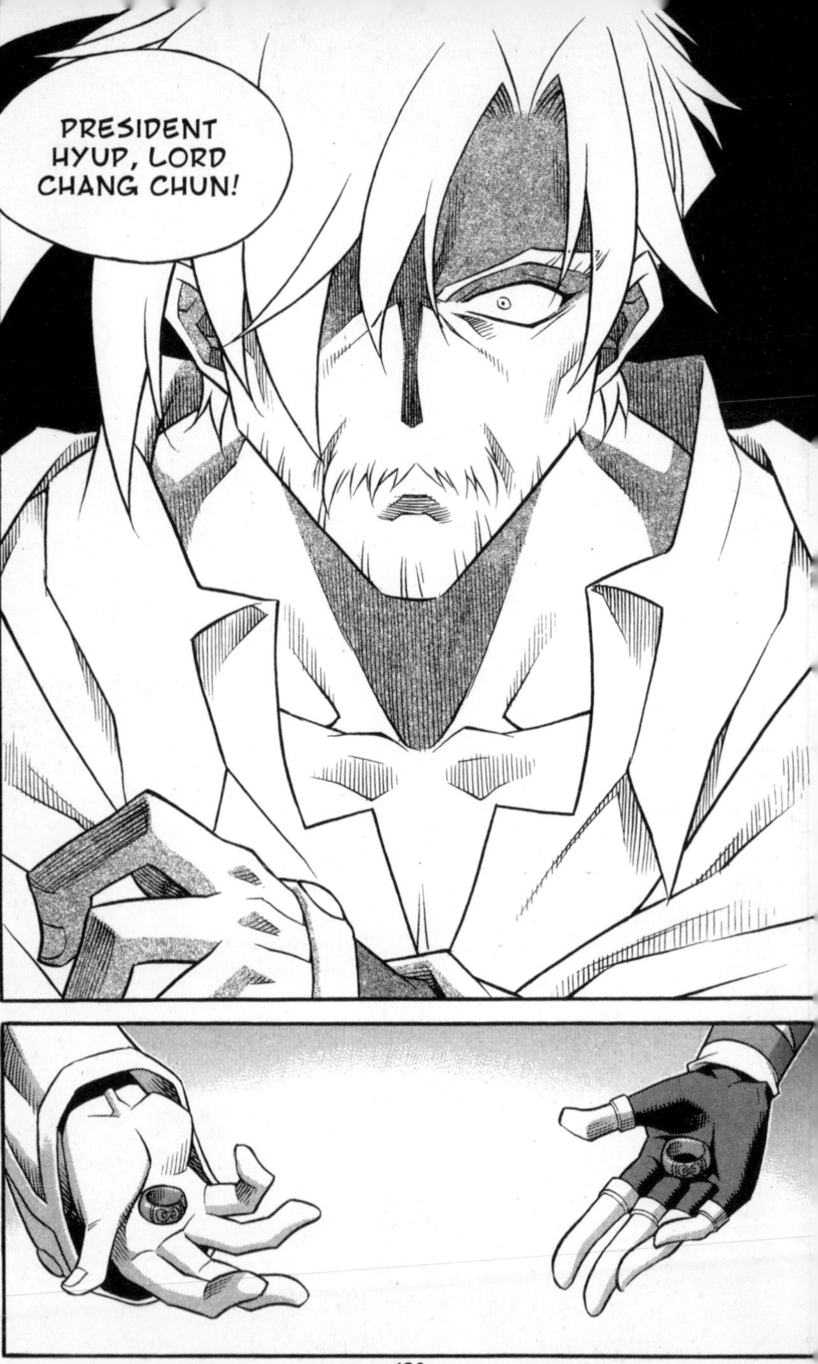
PRESIDENT HYUP, LORD CHANG CHUN!

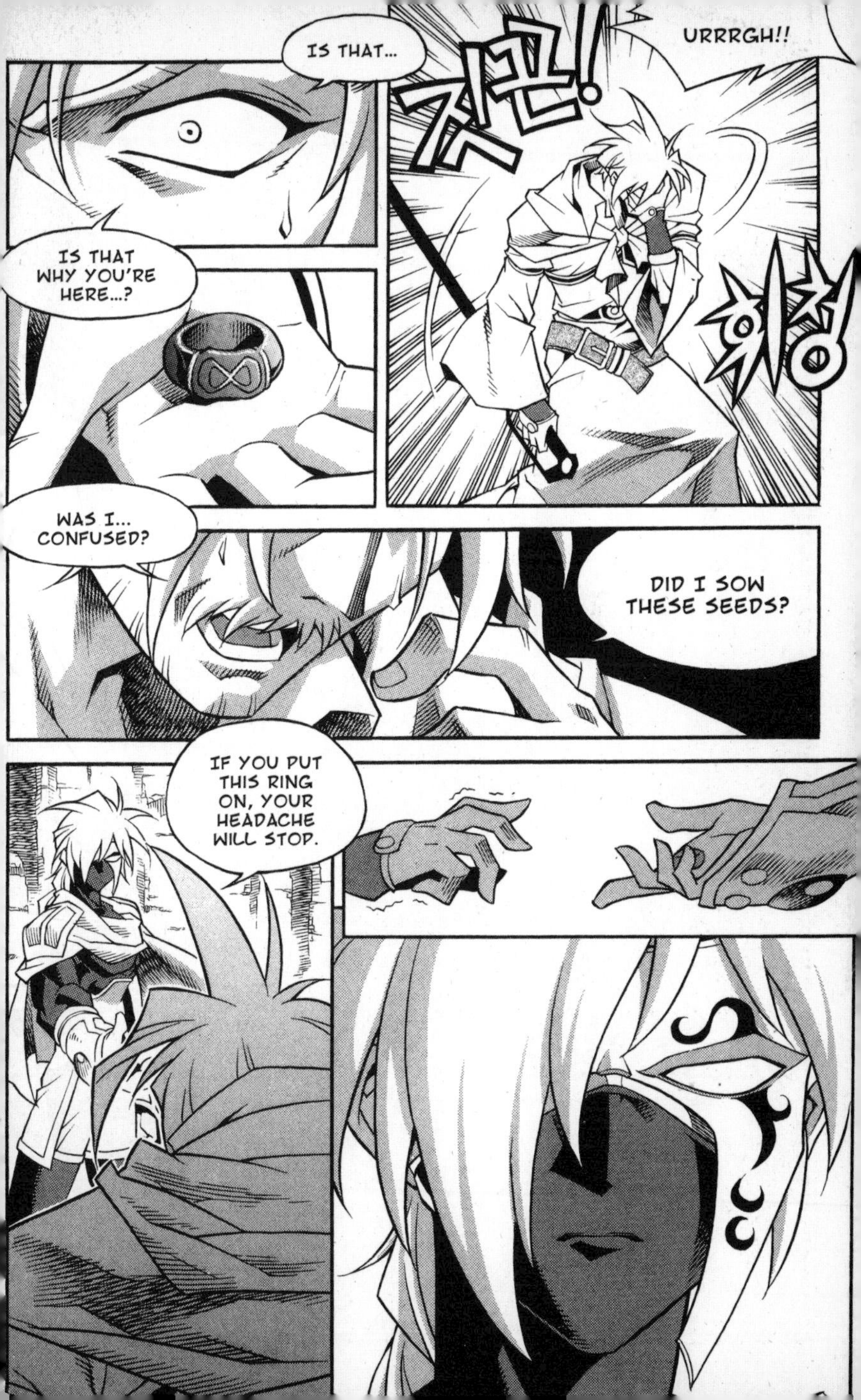
IS THAT...
지끈!
URRRGH!!
IS THAT WHY YOU'RE HERE...?
WAS I... CONFUSED?
DID I SOW THESE SEEDS?
IF YOU PUT THIS RING ON, YOUR HEADACHE WILL STOP.

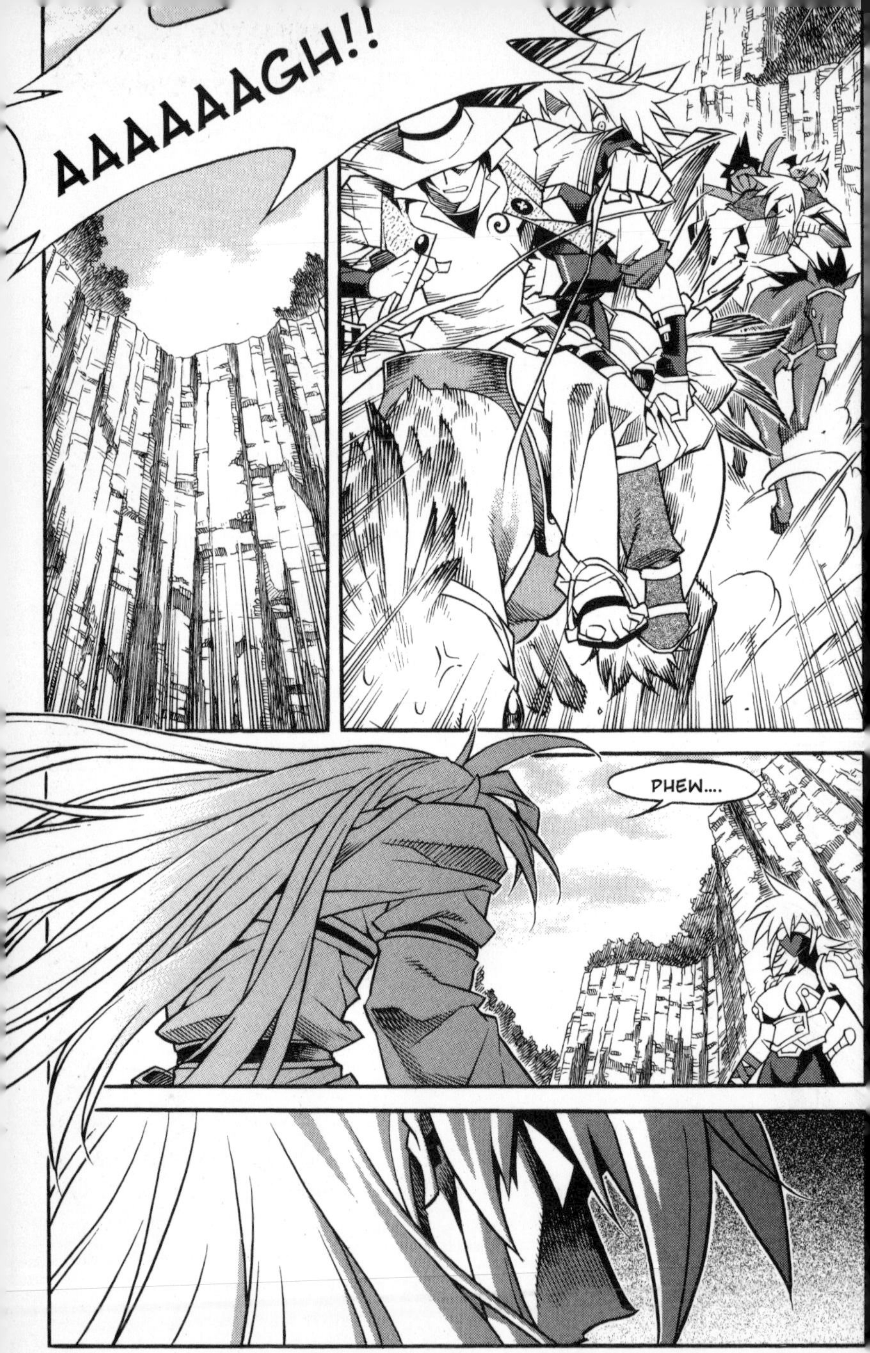
AAAAAAGH!!
PHEW....

Quest 95

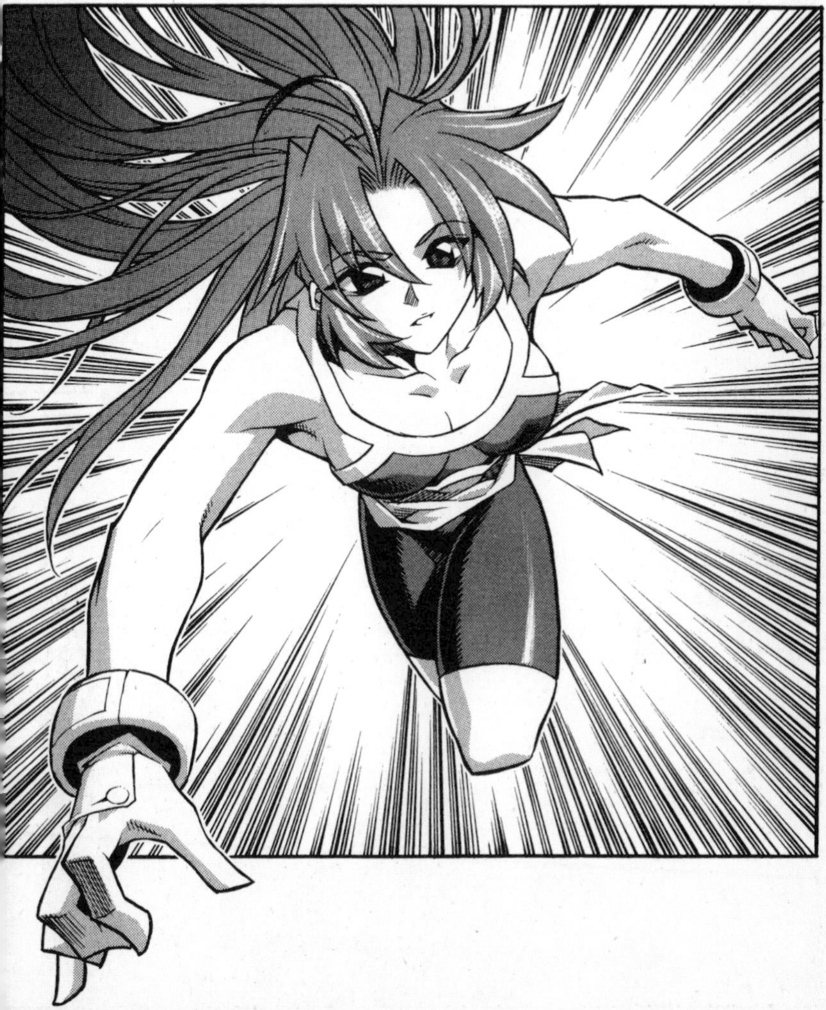

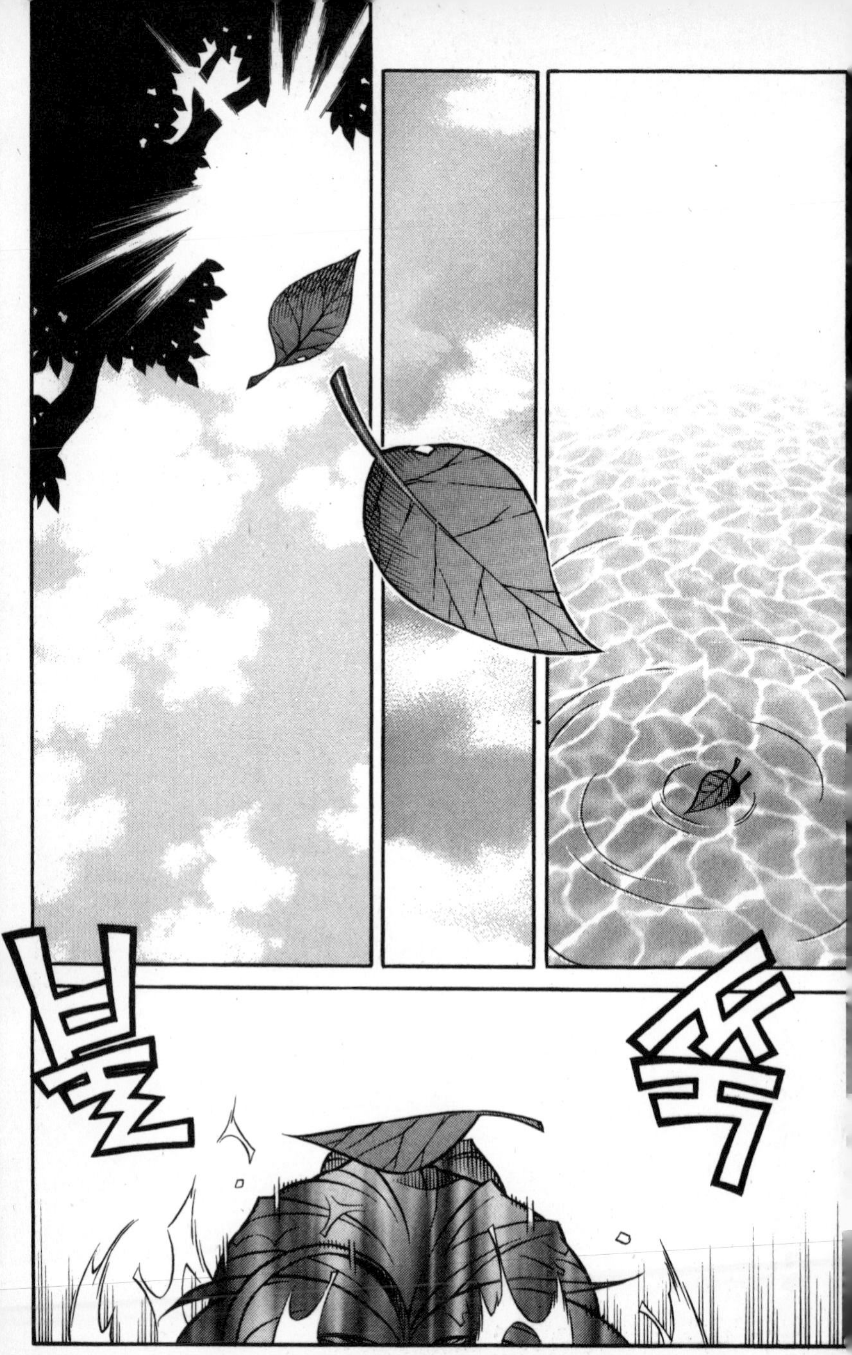

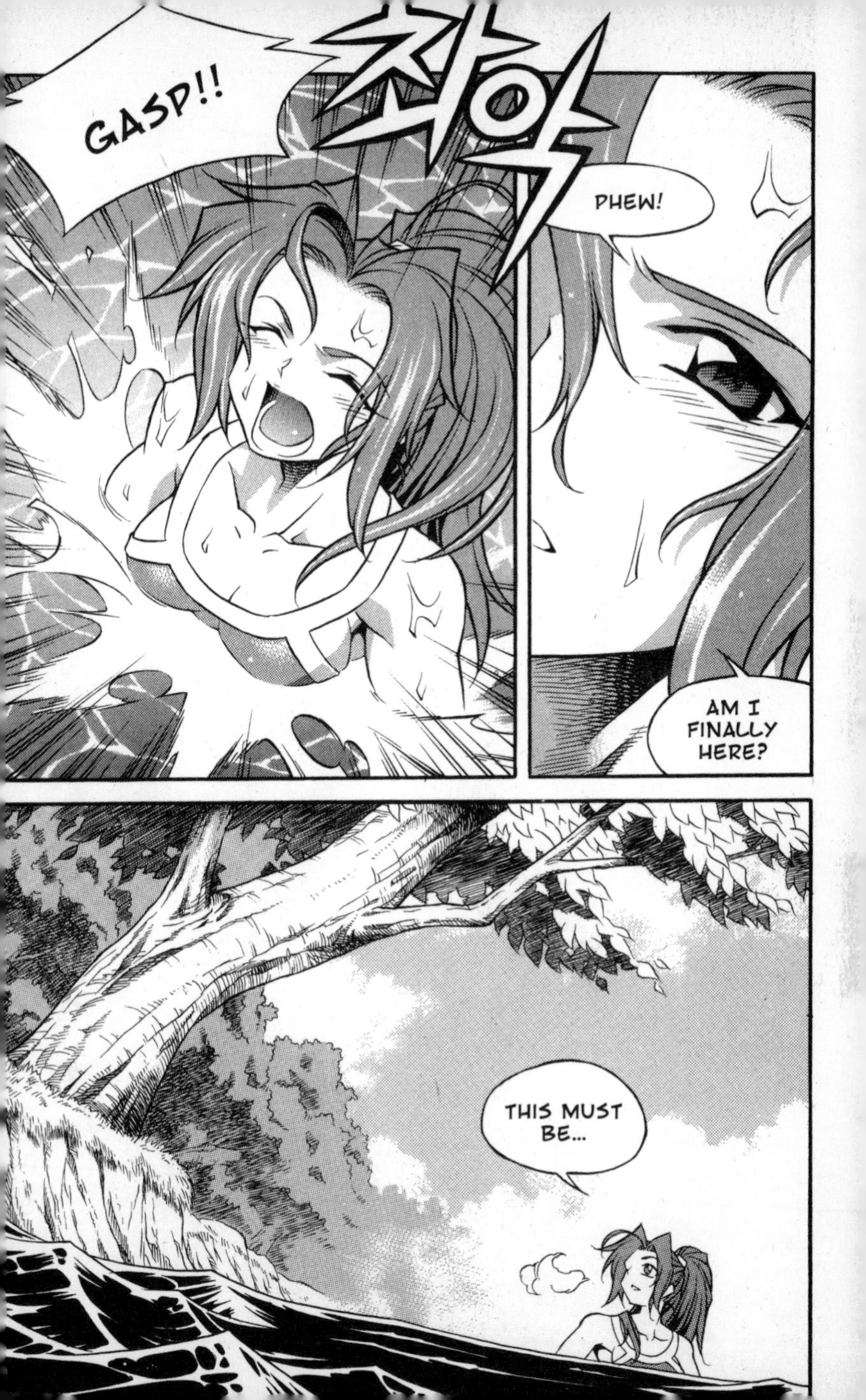
GASP!!
PHEW!
AM I FINALLY HERE?
THIS MUST BE...

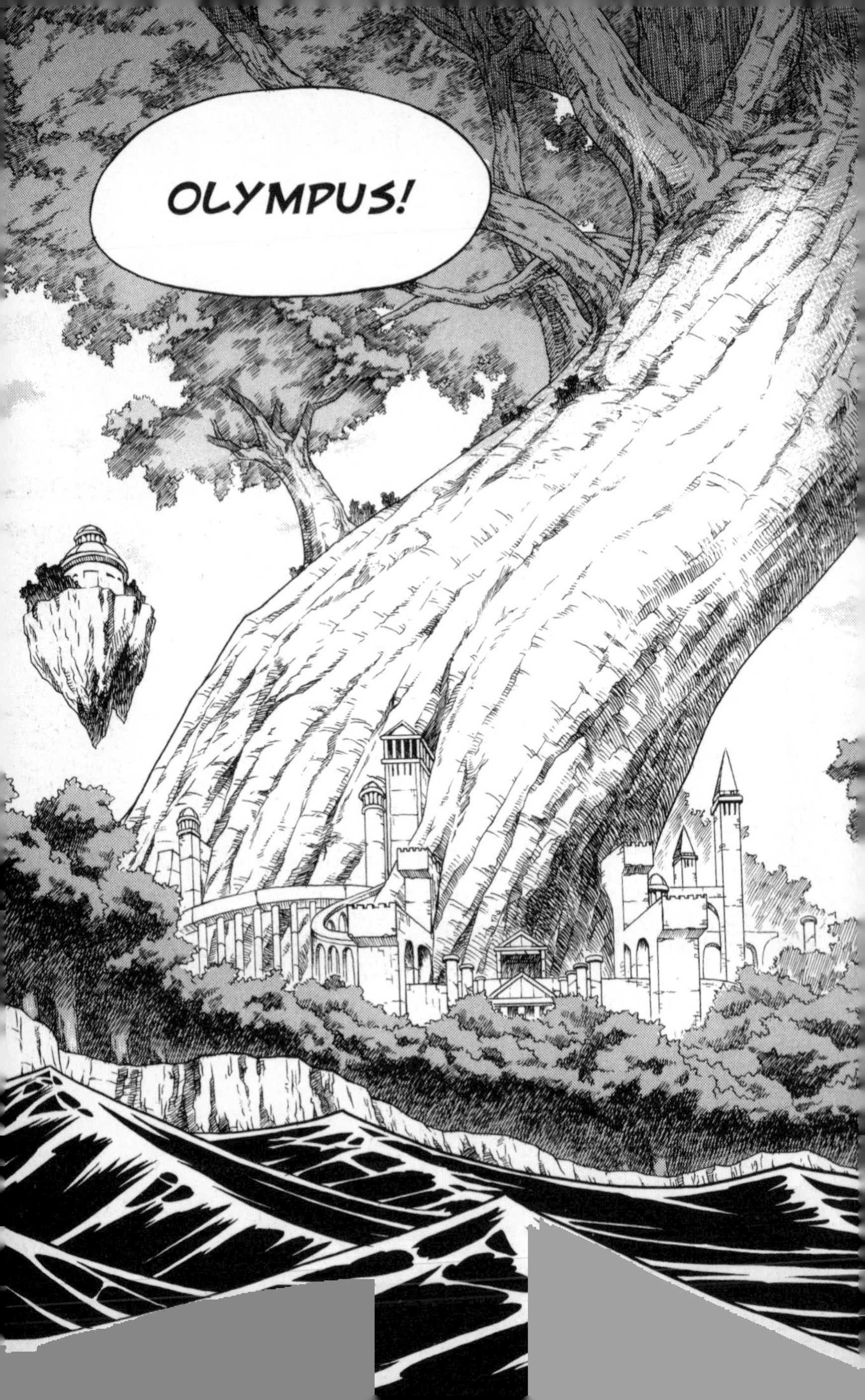
OLYMPUS!

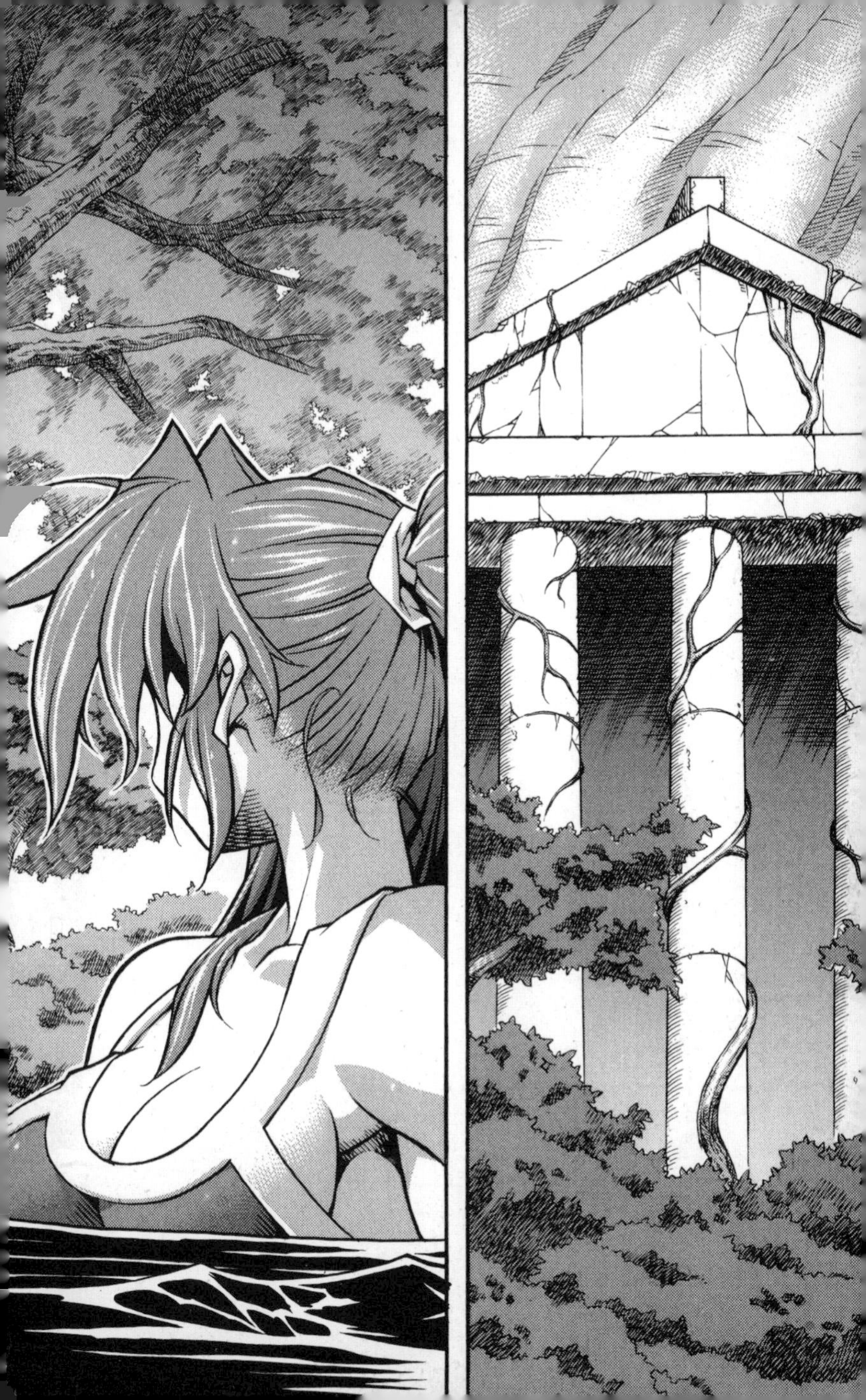

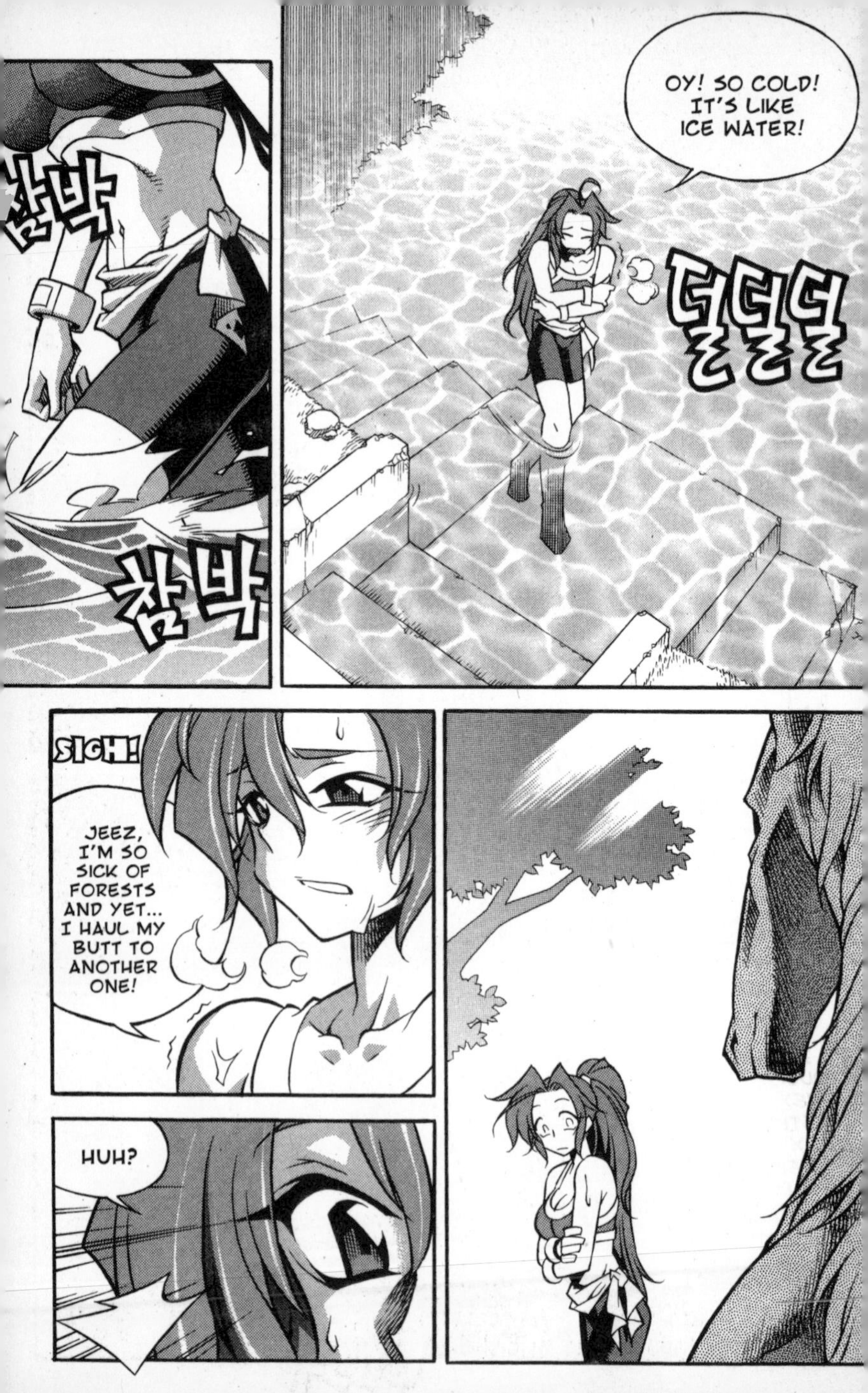
찰박
찰박
OY! SO COLD! IT'S LIKE ICE WATER!
덜덜덜
SIGH!
JEEZ, I'M SO SICK OF FORESTS AND YET... I HAUL MY BUTT TO ANOTHER ONE!
HUH?

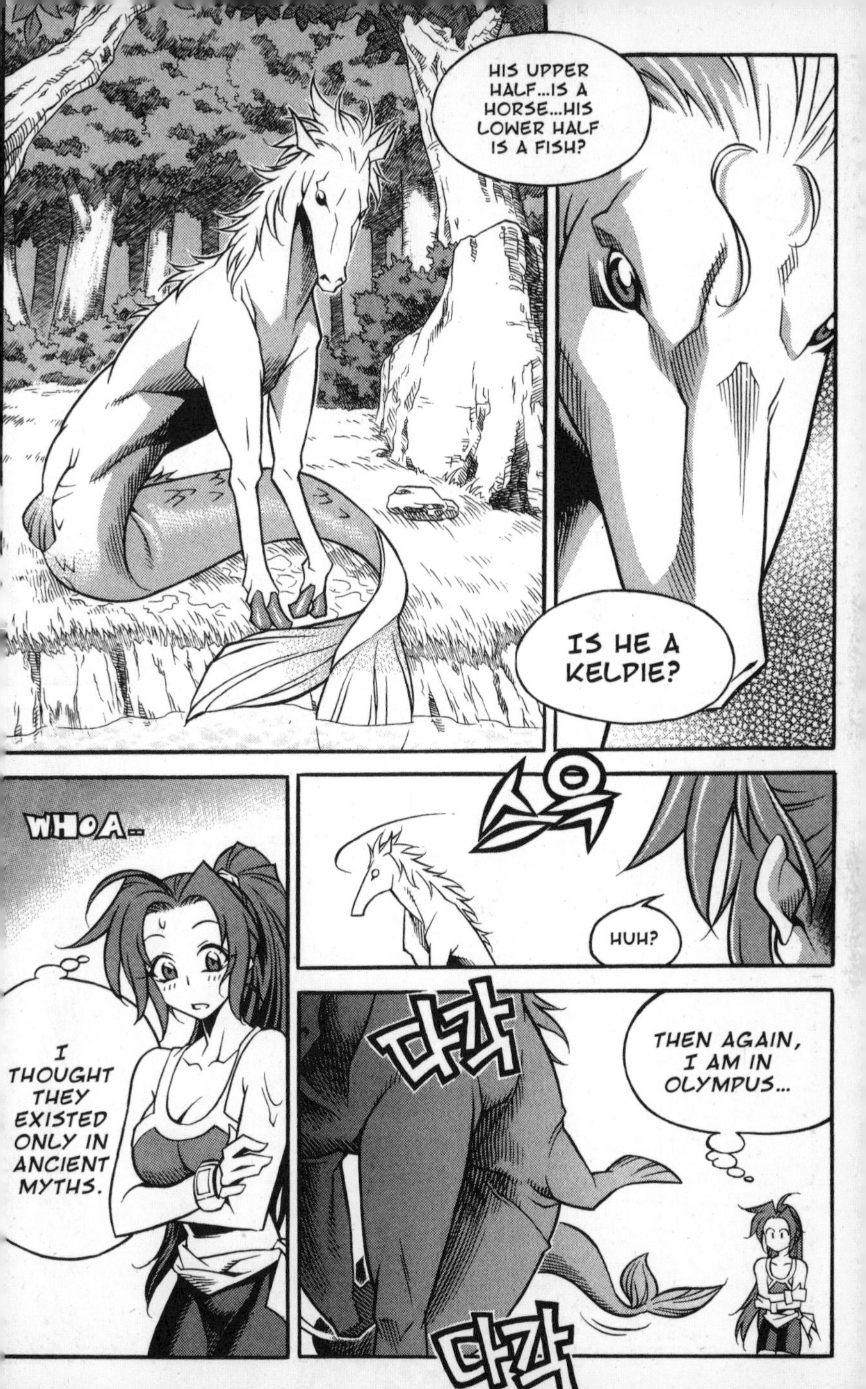
HIS UPPER HALF...IS A HORSE...HIS LOWER HALF IS A FISH?
IS HE A KELPIE?
WHOA..
I THOUGHT THEY EXISTED ONLY IN ANCIENT MYTHS.
스윽
HUH?
따각
THEN AGAIN, I AM IN OLYMPUS...
따각

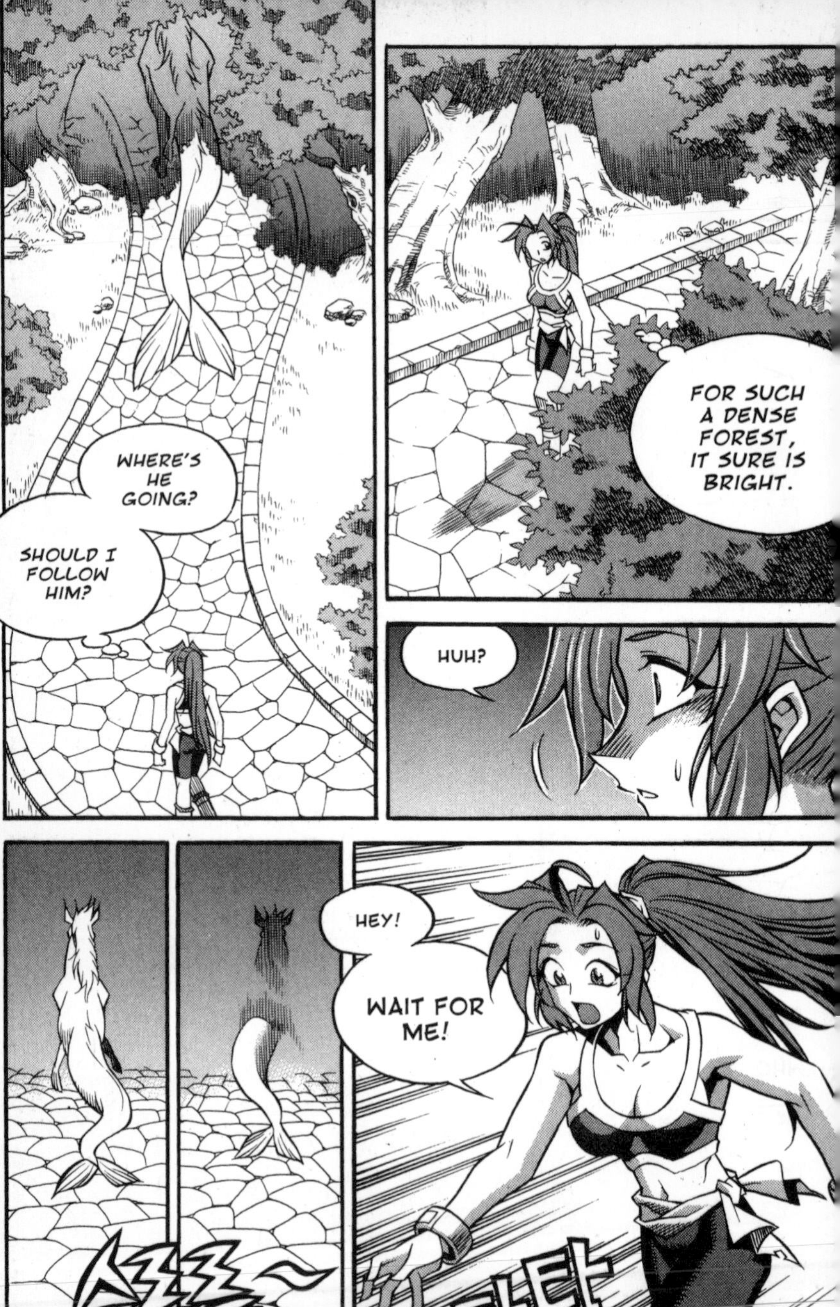
WHERE'S HE GOING?
SHOULD I FOLLOW HIM?
FOR SUCH A DENSE FOREST, IT SURE IS BRIGHT.
HUH?
HEY!
WAIT FOR ME!

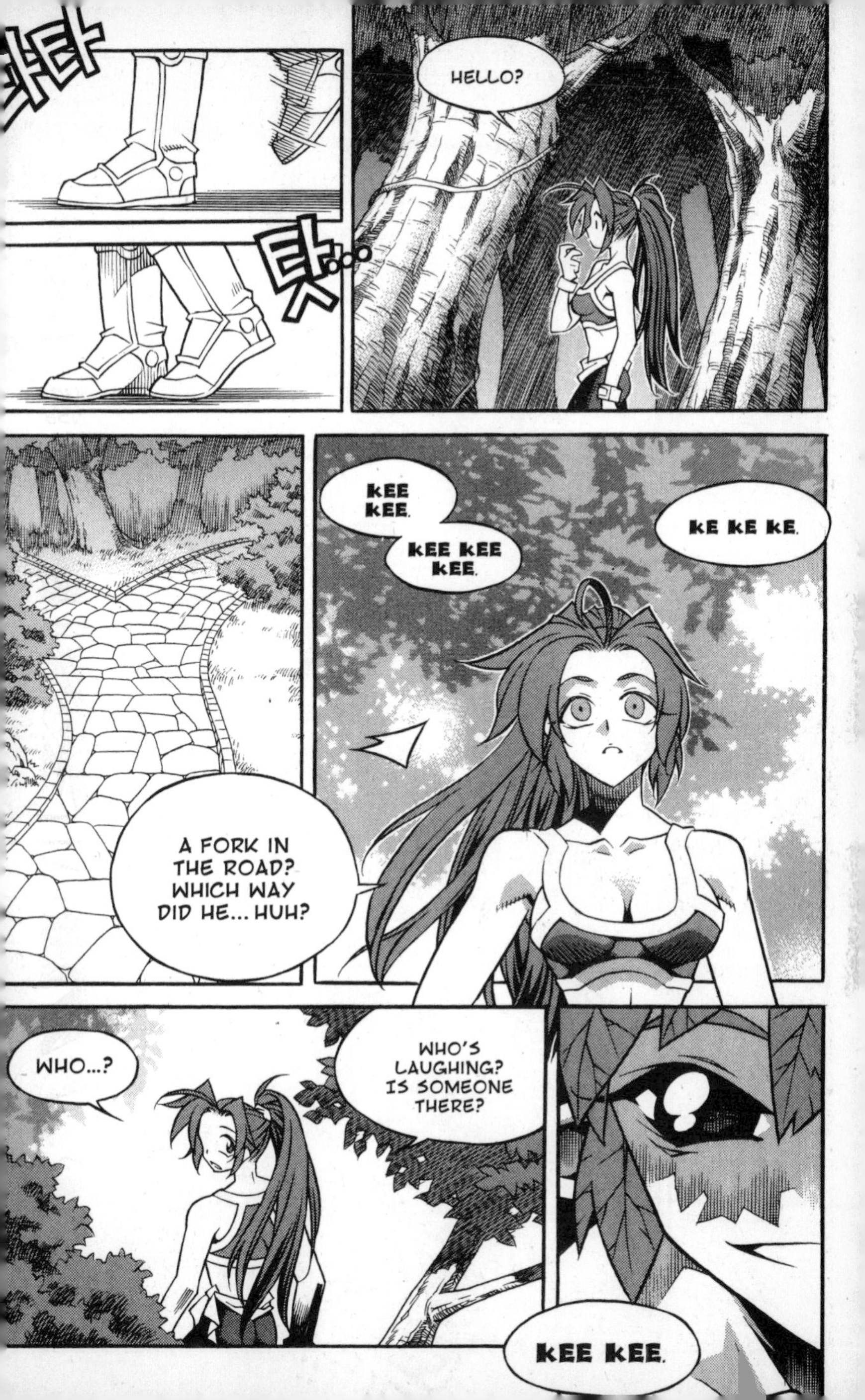
HELLO?
A FORK IN THE ROAD? WHICH WAY DID HE... HUH?
KEE KEE.
KEE KEE KEE.
KE KE KE.
WHO...?
WHO'S LAUGHING? IS SOMEONE THERE?
KEE KEE.

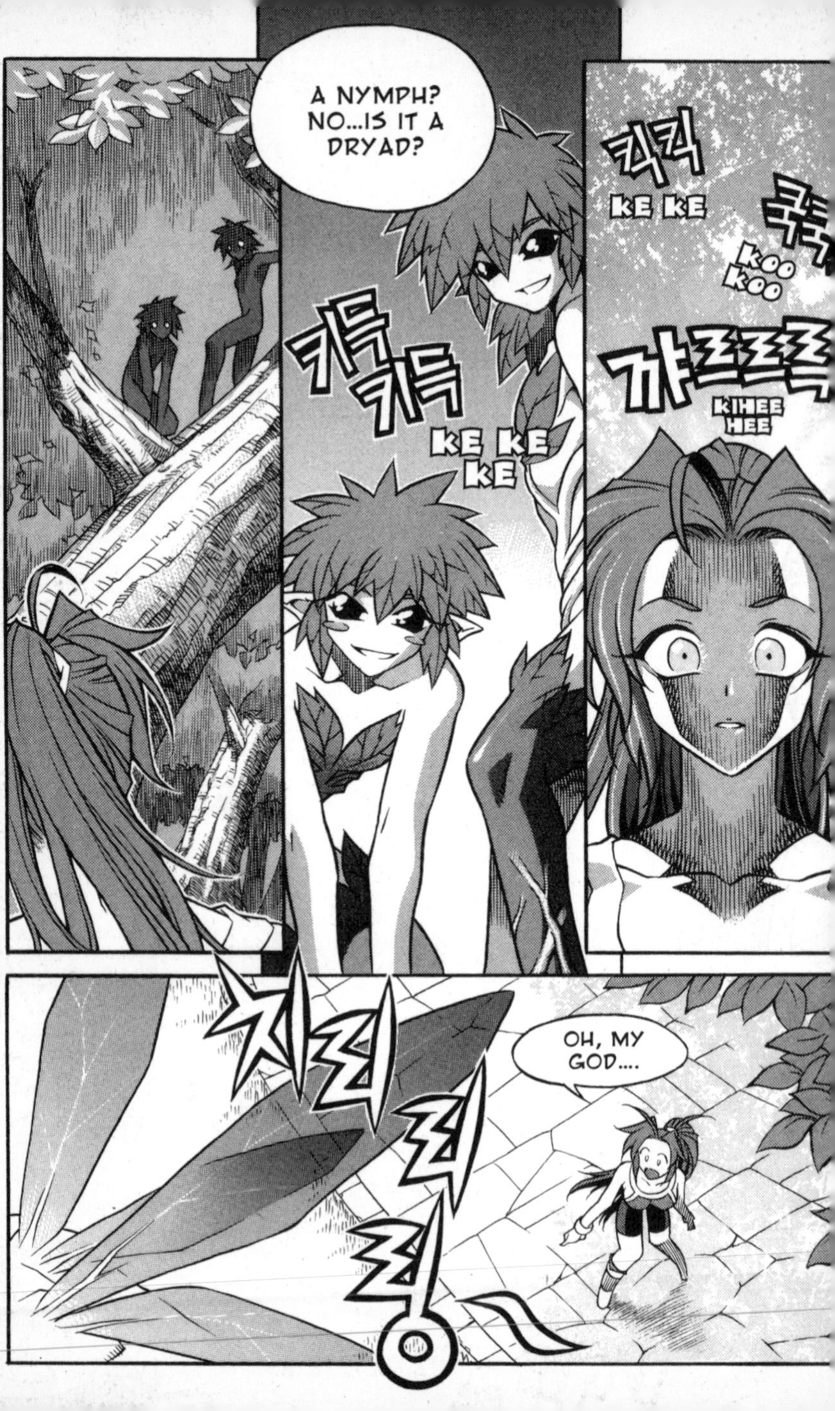

A NYMPH? NO...IS IT A DRYAD?
키득 키득
KE KE KE
KE KE
KOO KOO
KIHEE HEE
OH, MY GOD....

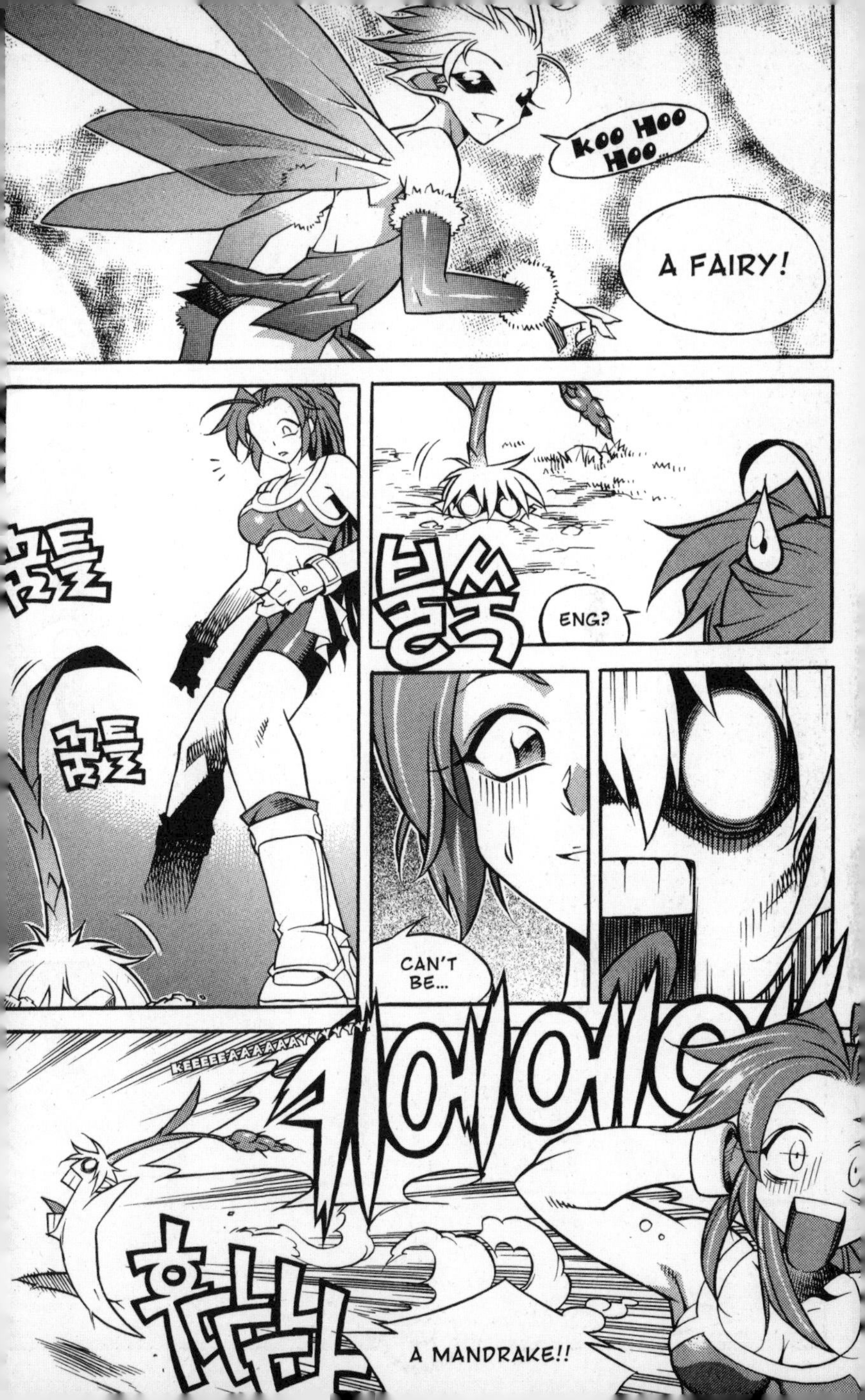
KOO HOO HOO...
A FAIRY!
ENG?
CAN'T BE...
KEEEEEEAAAAAAYYYYYY
A MANDRAKE!!

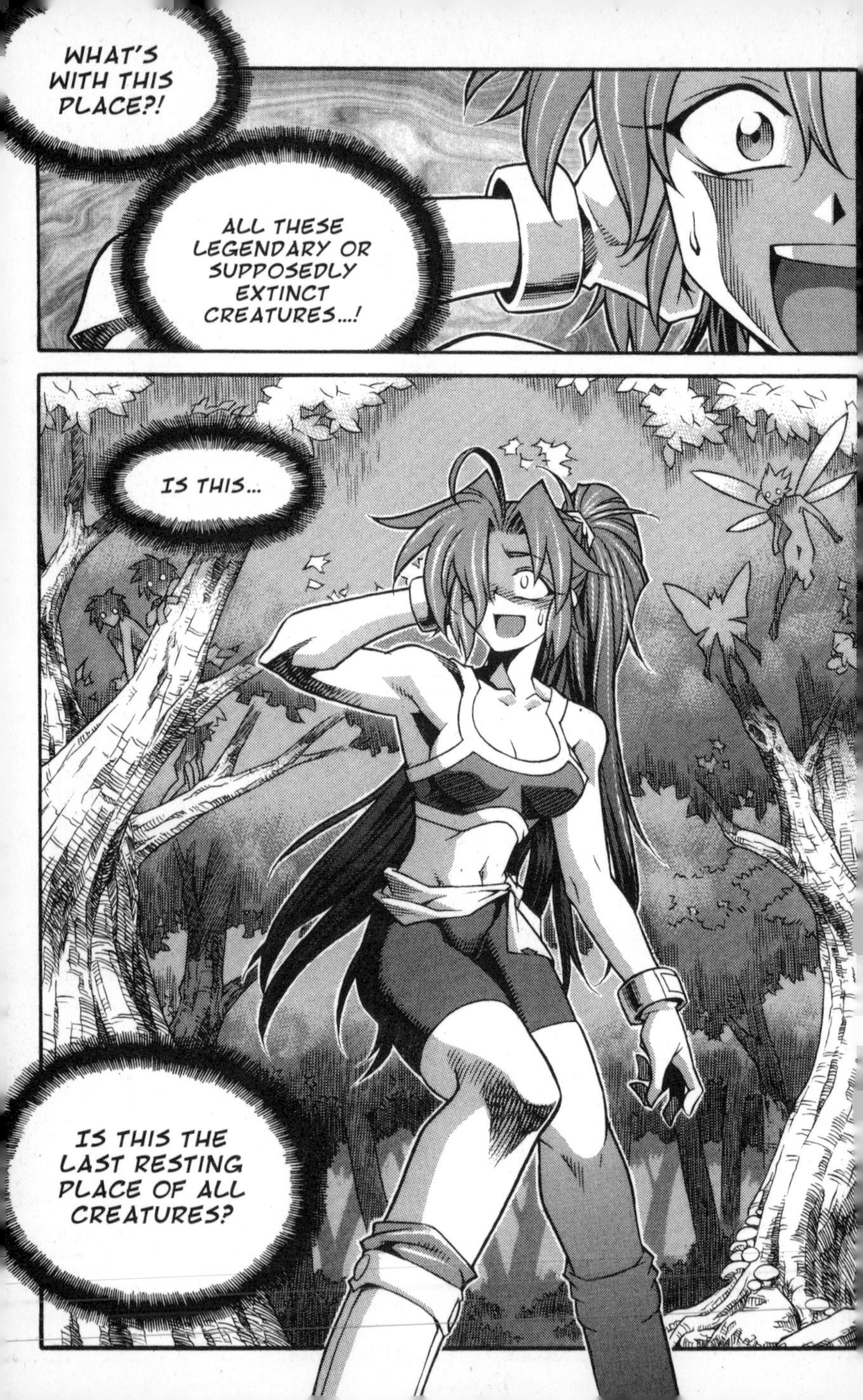
WHAT'S WITH THIS PLACE?!
ALL THESE LEGENDARY OR SUPPOSEDLY EXTINCT CREATURES...!
IS THIS...
IS THIS THE LAST RESTING PLACE OF ALL CREATURES?

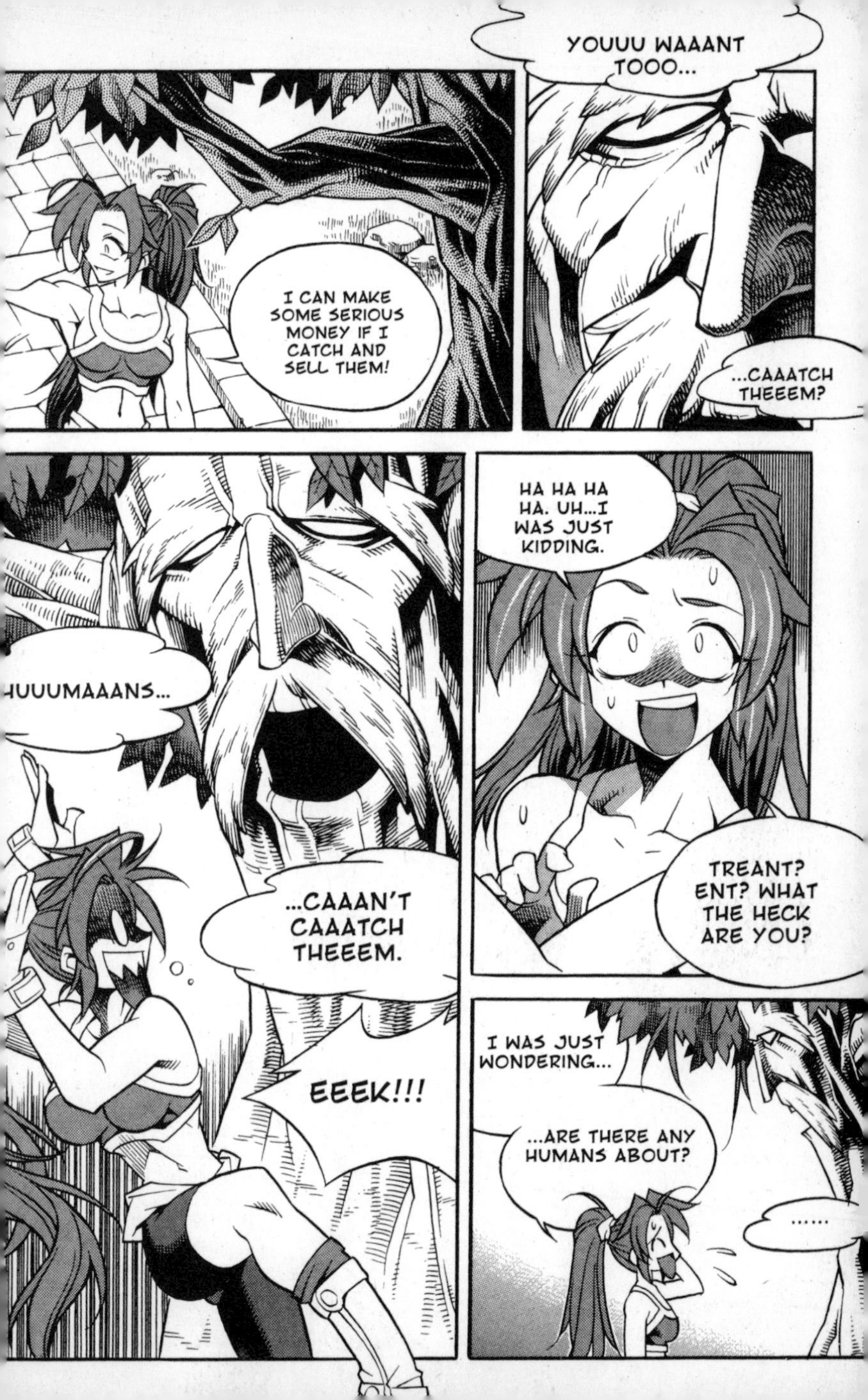
I CAN MAKE SOME SERIOUS MONEY IF I CATCH AND SELL THEM!
YOUUU WAAANT TOOO...
...CAAATCH THEEEM?
HA HA HA HA. UH...I WAS JUST KIDDING.
TREANT? ENT? WHAT THE HECK ARE YOU?
HUUUMAAANS...
...CAAAN'T CAAATCH THEEEM.
EEEK!!!
I WAS JUST WONDERING...
...ARE THERE ANY HUMANS ABOUT?
......

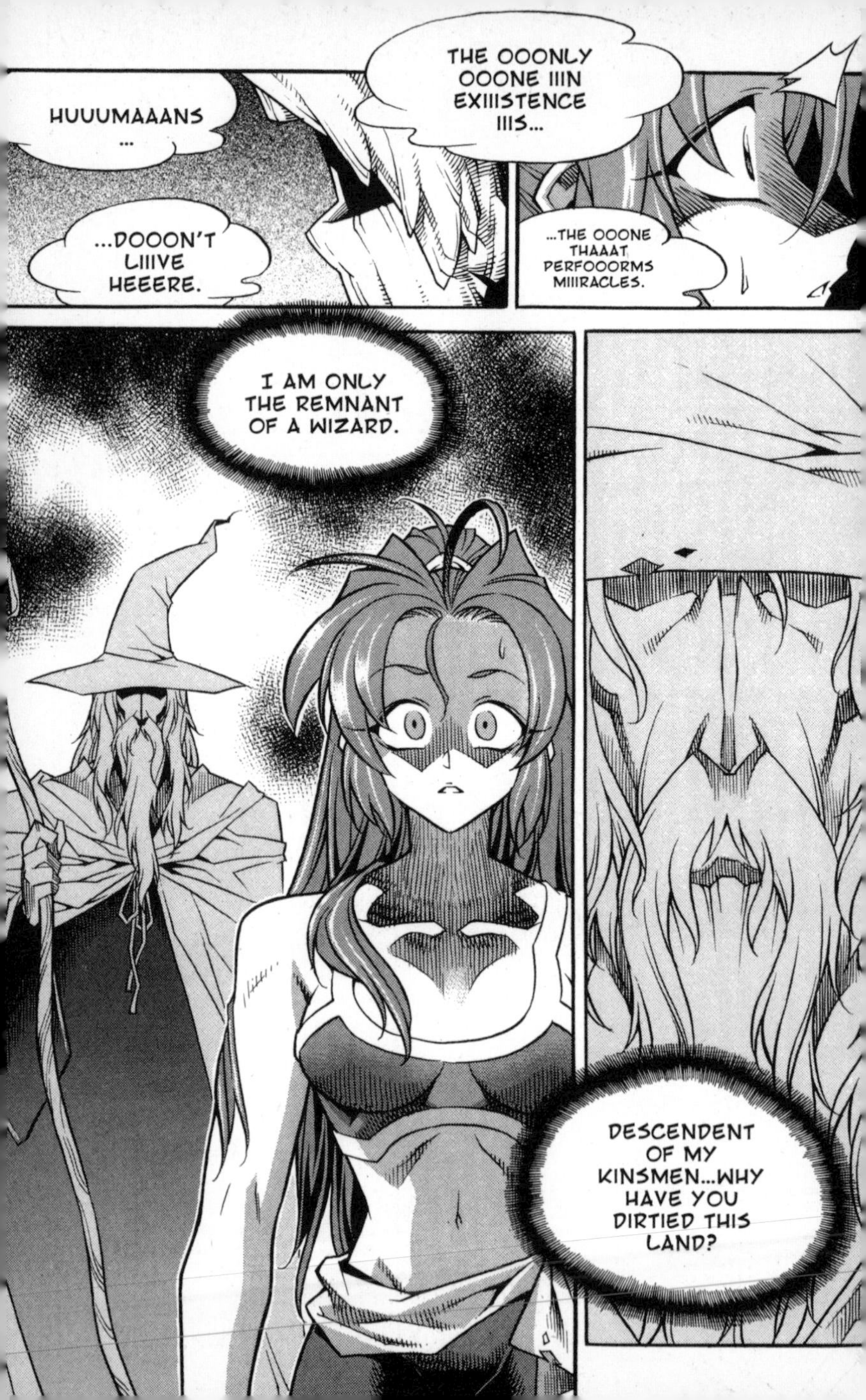

THE OOONLY OOONE IIIN EXIIISTENCE IIIS...
...THE OOONE THAAAT PERFOOORMS MIIIRACLES.
HUUUMAAANS ...
...DOOON'T LIIIVE HEEERE.
I AM ONLY THE REMNANT OF A WIZARD.
DESCENDENT OF MY KINSMEN...WHY HAVE YOU DIRTIED THIS LAND?

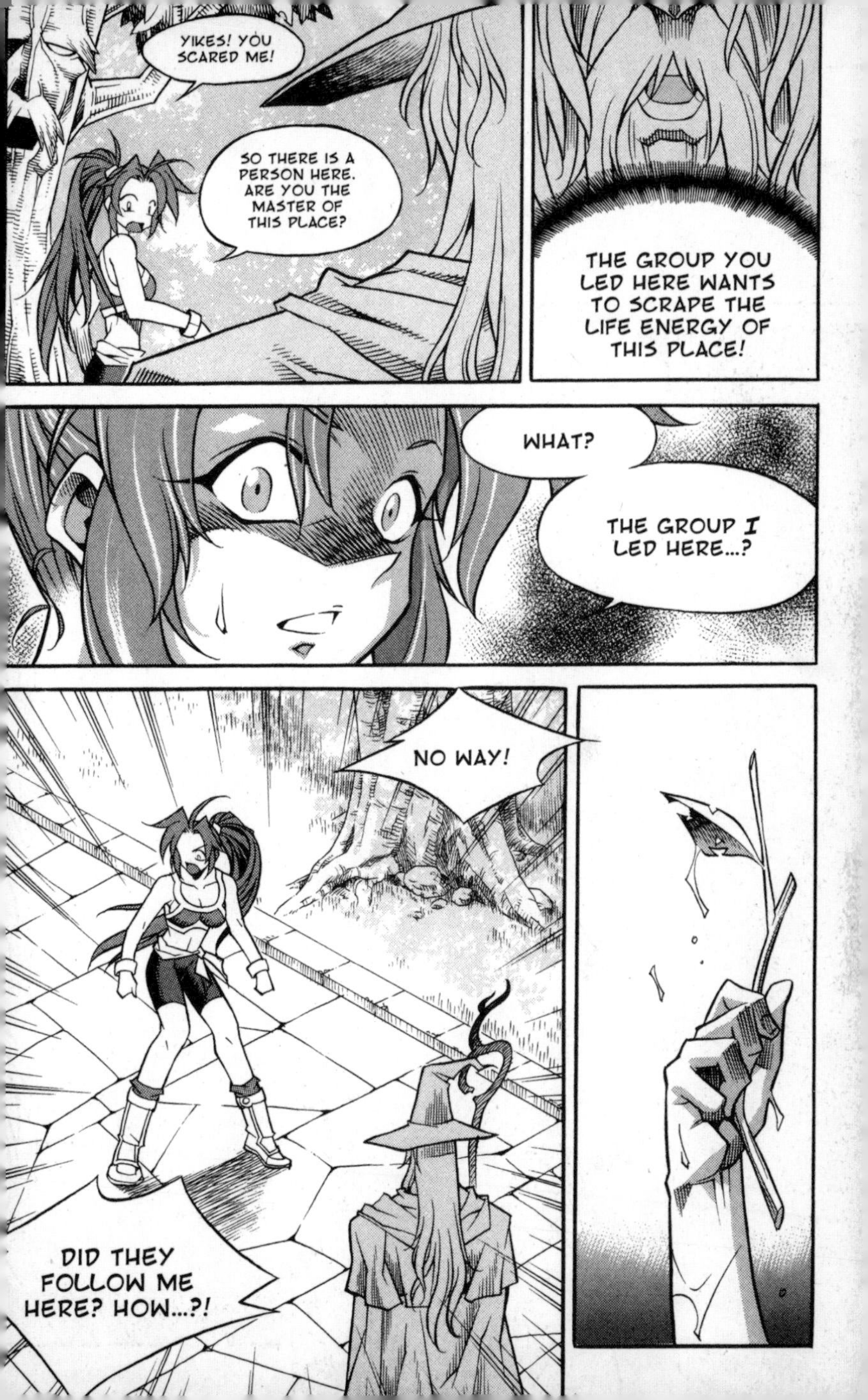
YIKES! YOU SCARED ME!
SO THERE IS A PERSON HERE. ARE YOU THE MASTER OF THIS PLACE?
THE GROUP YOU LED HERE WANTS TO SCRAPE THE LIFE ENERGY OF THIS PLACE!
WHAT?
THE GROUP I LED HERE...?
NO WAY!
DID THEY FOLLOW ME HERE? HOW...?!

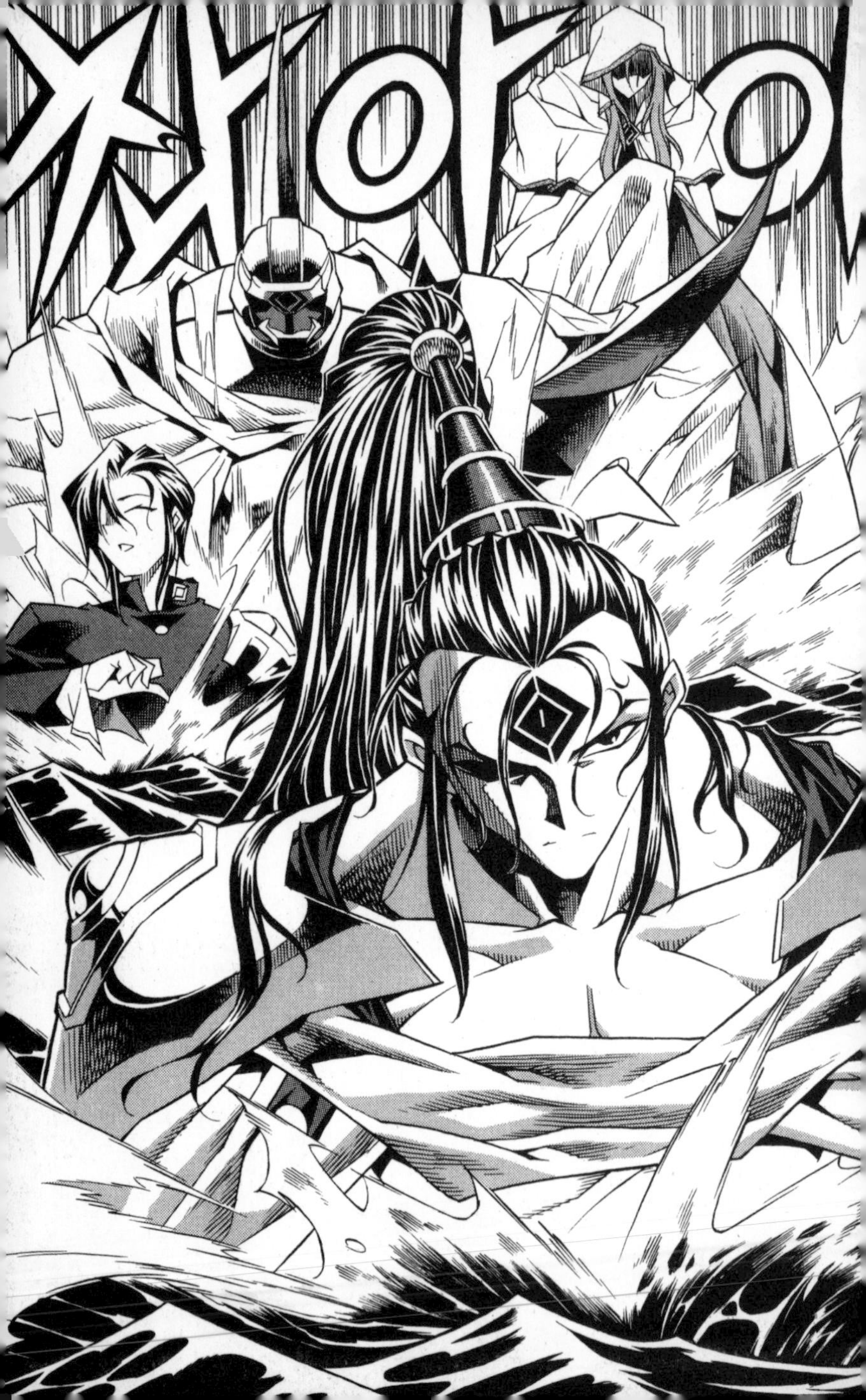

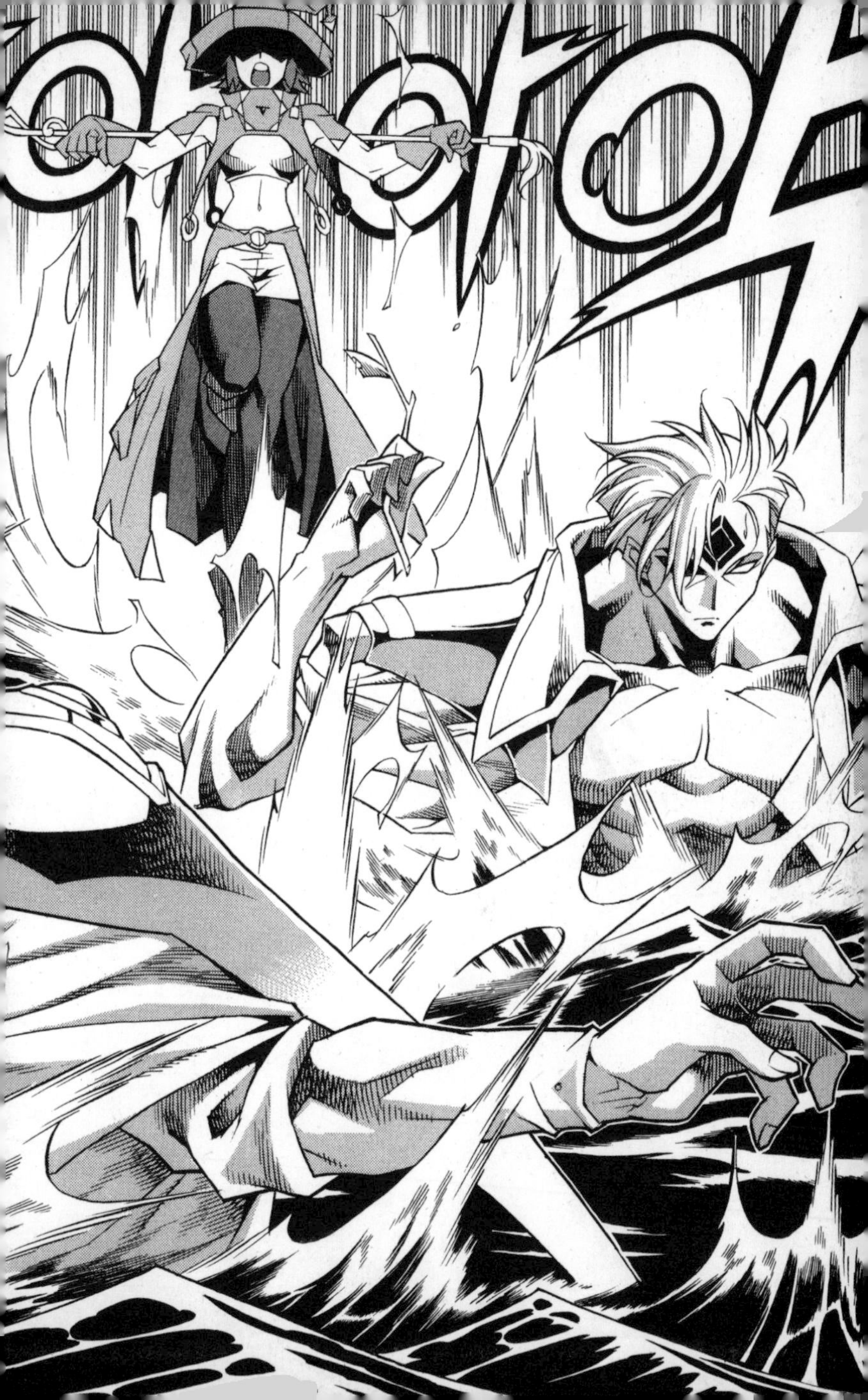

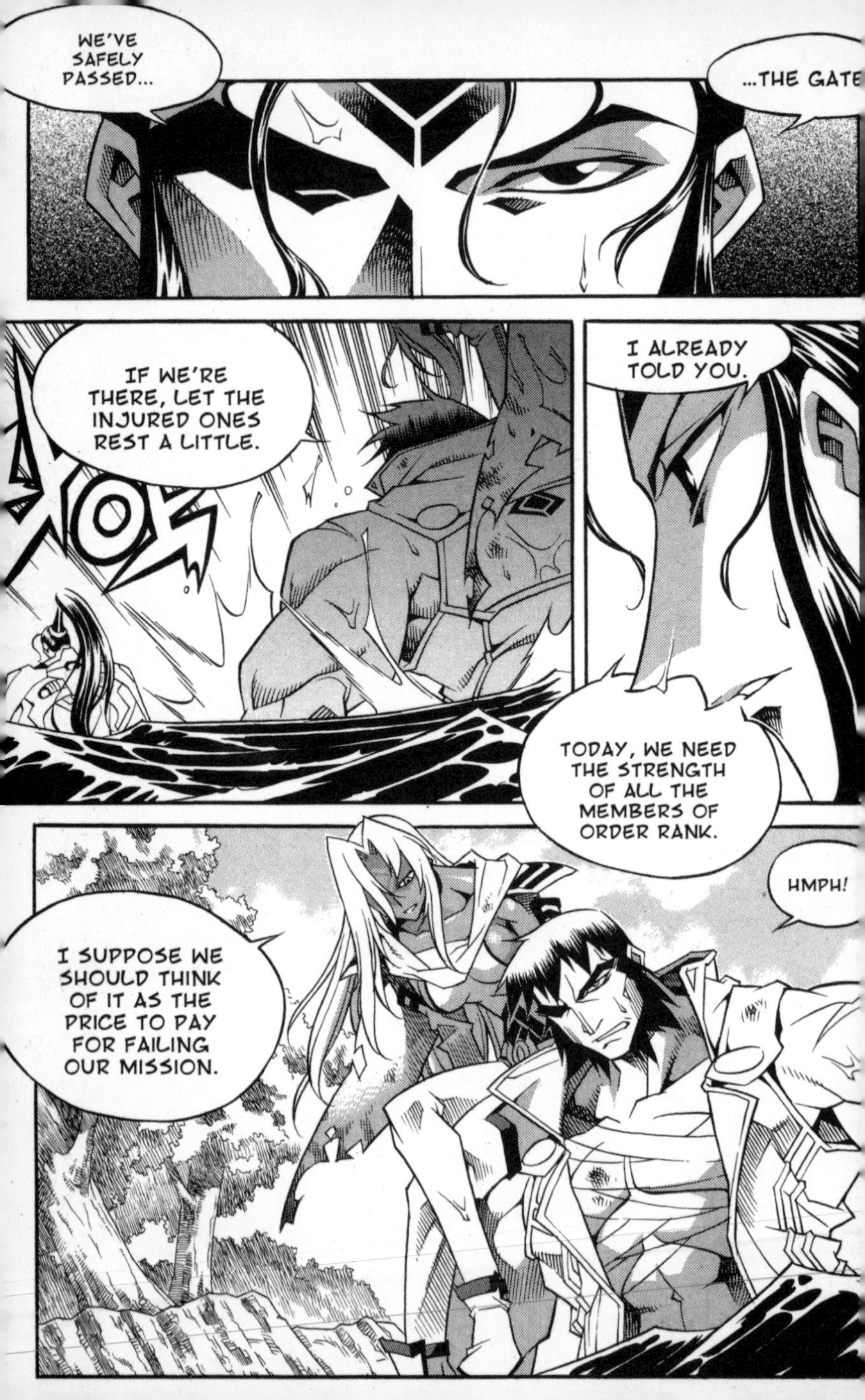
WE'VE SAFELY PASSED...
...THE GATE
IF WE'RE THERE, LET THE INJURED ONES REST A LITTLE.
I ALREADY TOLD YOU.
TODAY, WE NEED THE STRENGTH OF ALL THE MEMBERS OF ORDER RANK.
HMPH!
I SUPPOSE WE SHOULD THINK OF IT AS THE PRICE TO PAY FOR FAILING OUR MISSION.

Quest 96

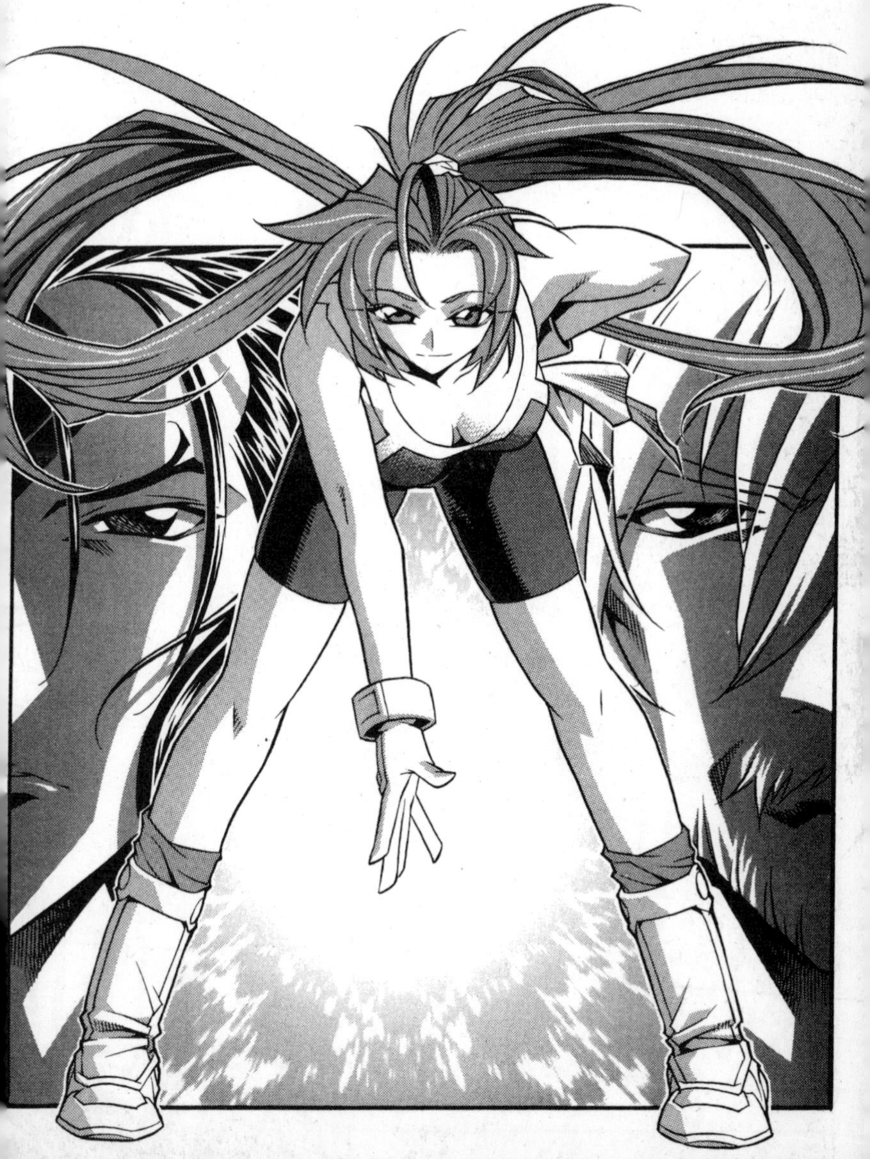

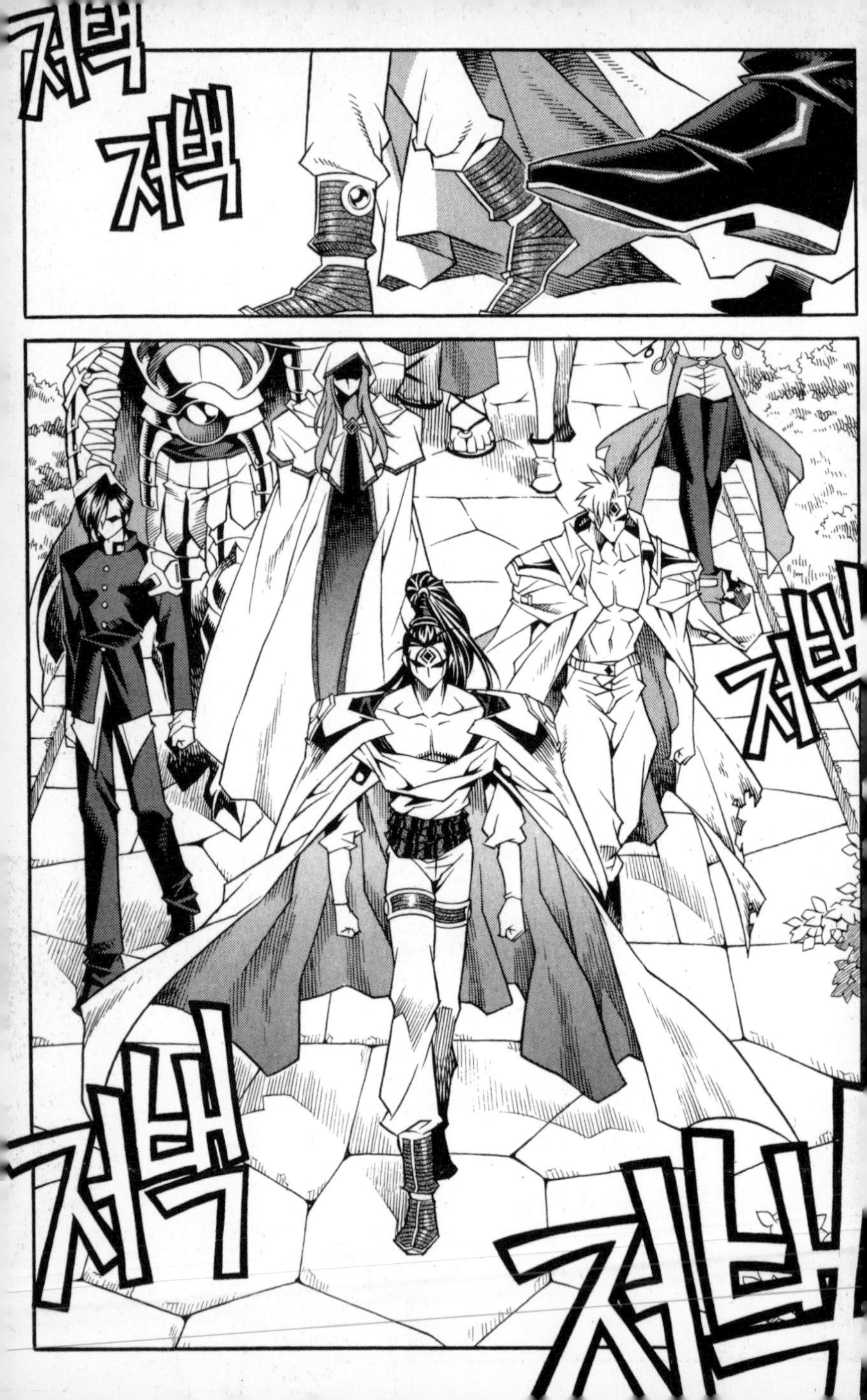
저벅
저벅
저벅

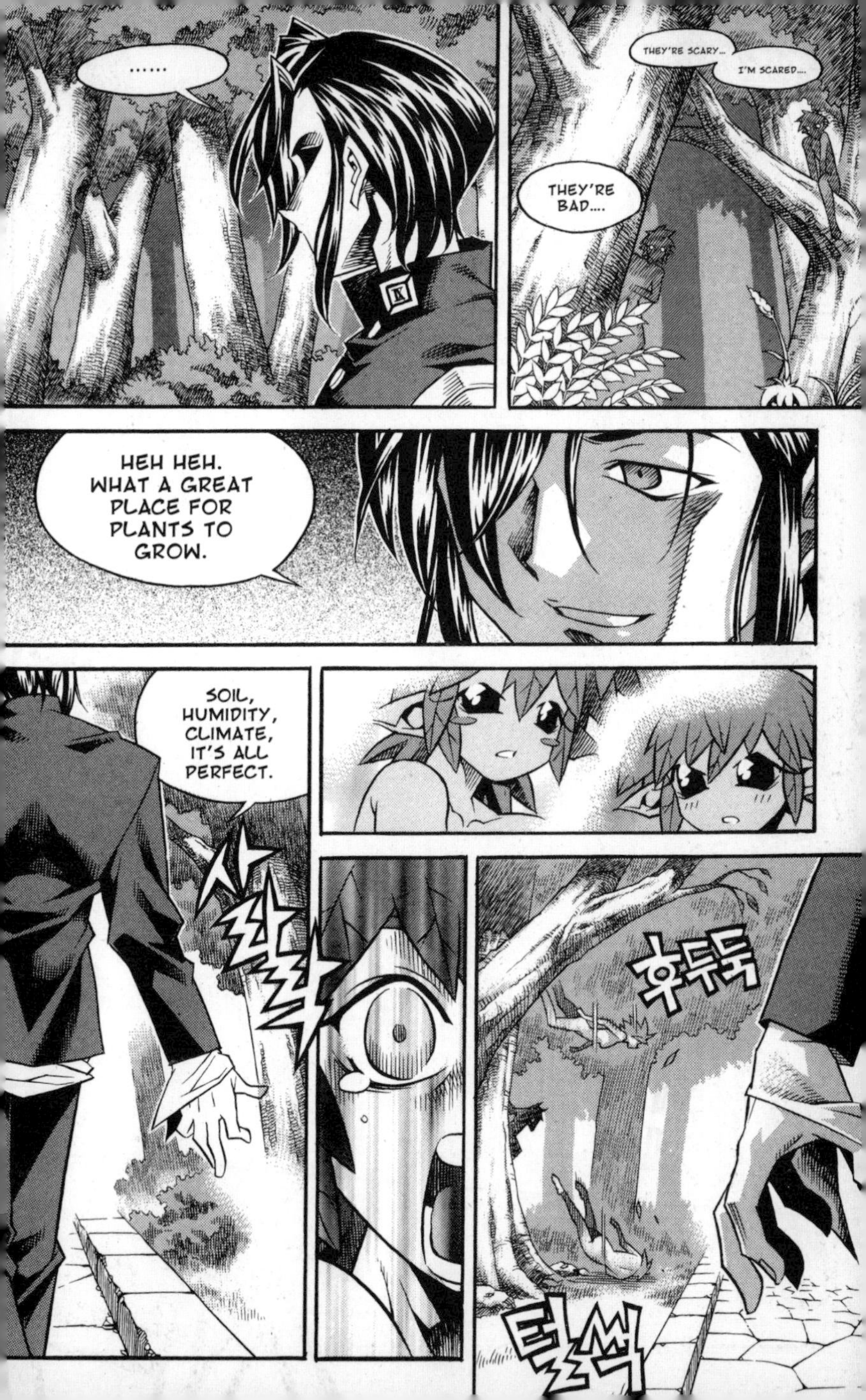
......
THEY'RE SCARY...
I'M SCARED....
THEY'RE BAD....
HEH HEH. WHAT A GREAT PLACE FOR PLANTS TO GROW.
SOIL, HUMIDITY, CLIMATE, IT'S ALL PERFECT.
후두둑
털썩

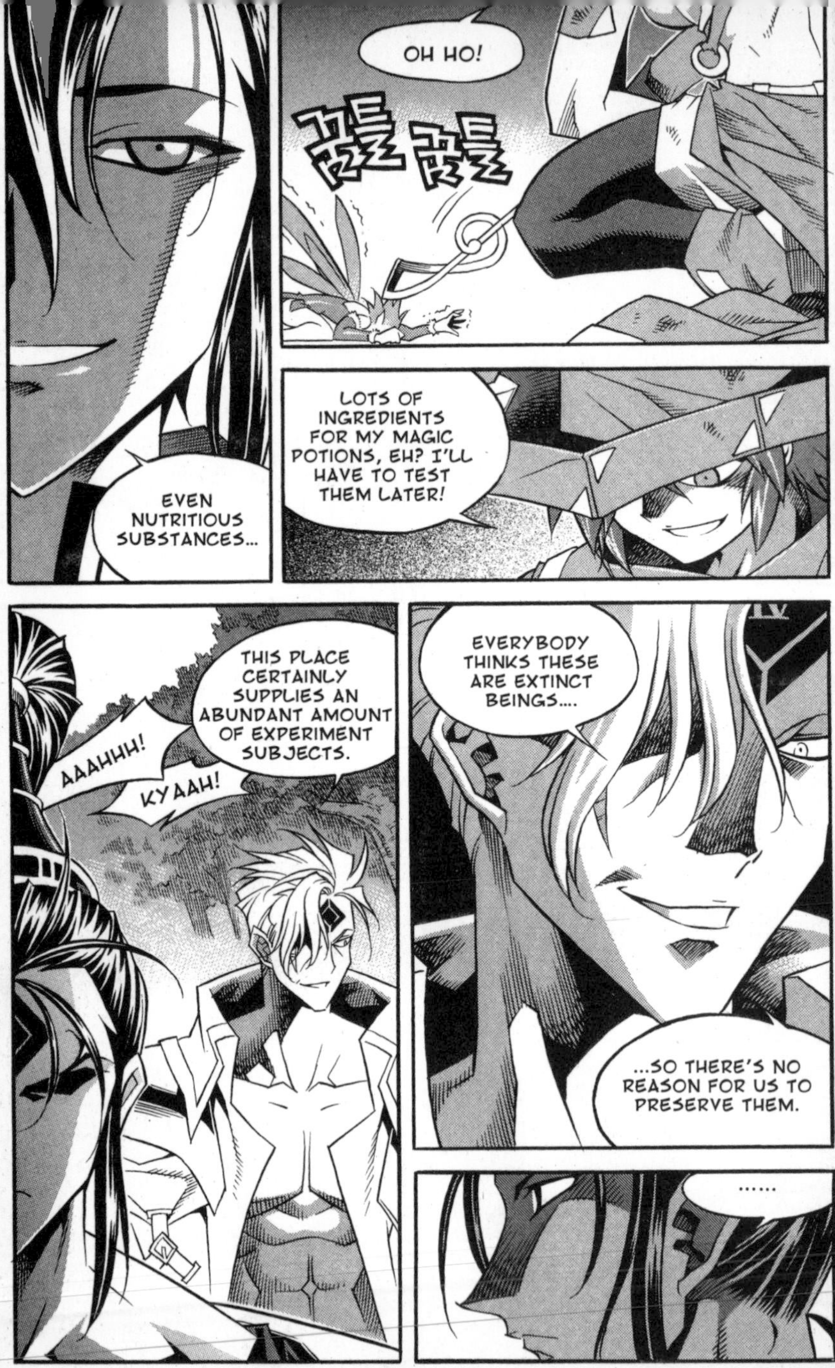
OH HO!
EVEN NUTRITIOUS SUBSTANCES...
LOTS OF INGREDIENTS FOR MY MAGIC POTIONS, EH? I'LL HAVE TO TEST THEM LATER!
THIS PLACE CERTAINLY SUPPLIES AN ABUNDANT AMOUNT OF EXPERIMENT SUBJECTS.
AAAHHH!
KYAAH!
EVERYBODY THINKS THESE ARE EXTINCT BEINGS....
...SO THERE'S NO REASON FOR US TO PRESERVE THEM.
......

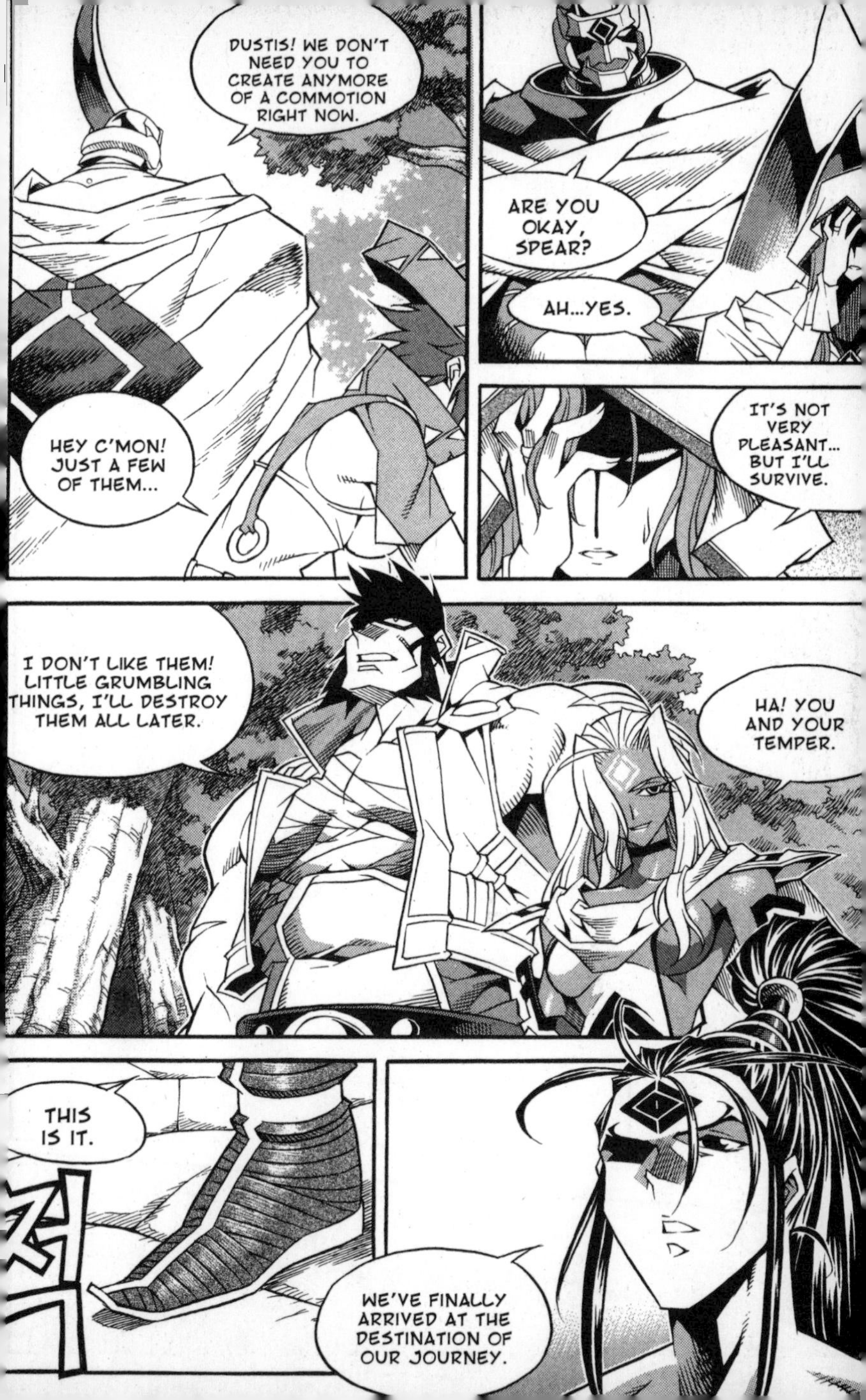
DUSTIS! WE DON'T NEED YOU TO CREATE ANYMORE OF A COMMOTION RIGHT NOW.
HEY C'MON! JUST A FEW OF THEM...
ARE YOU OKAY, SPEAR?
AH...YES.
IT'S NOT VERY PLEASANT... BUT I'LL SURVIVE.
I DON'T LIKE THEM! LITTLE GRUMBLING THINGS, I'LL DESTROY THEM ALL LATER.
HA! YOU AND YOUR TEMPER.
THIS IS IT.
WE'VE FINALLY ARRIVED AT THE DESTINATION OF OUR JOURNEY.

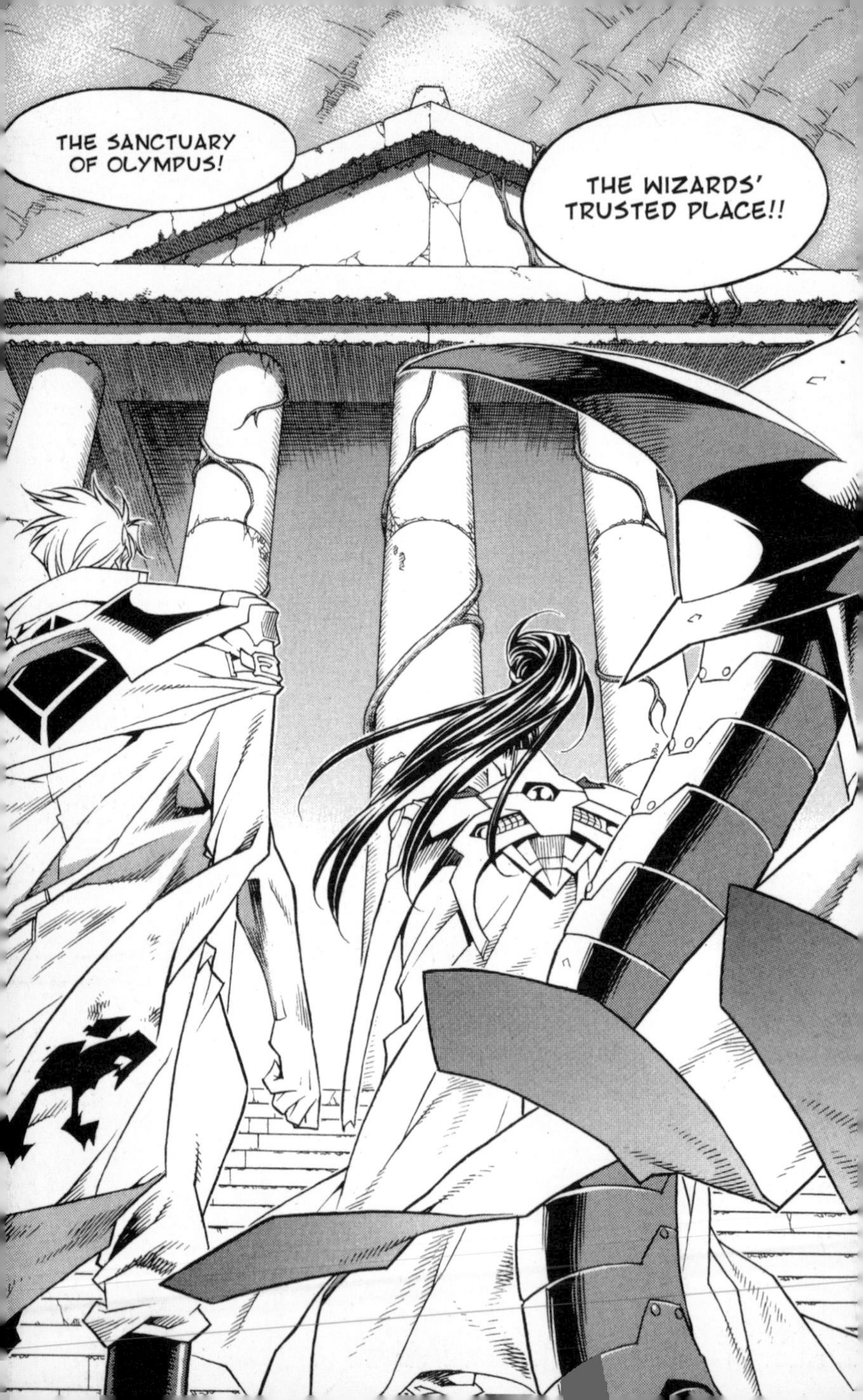
THE WIZARDS' TRUSTED PLACE!!
THE SANCTUARY OF OLYMPUS!

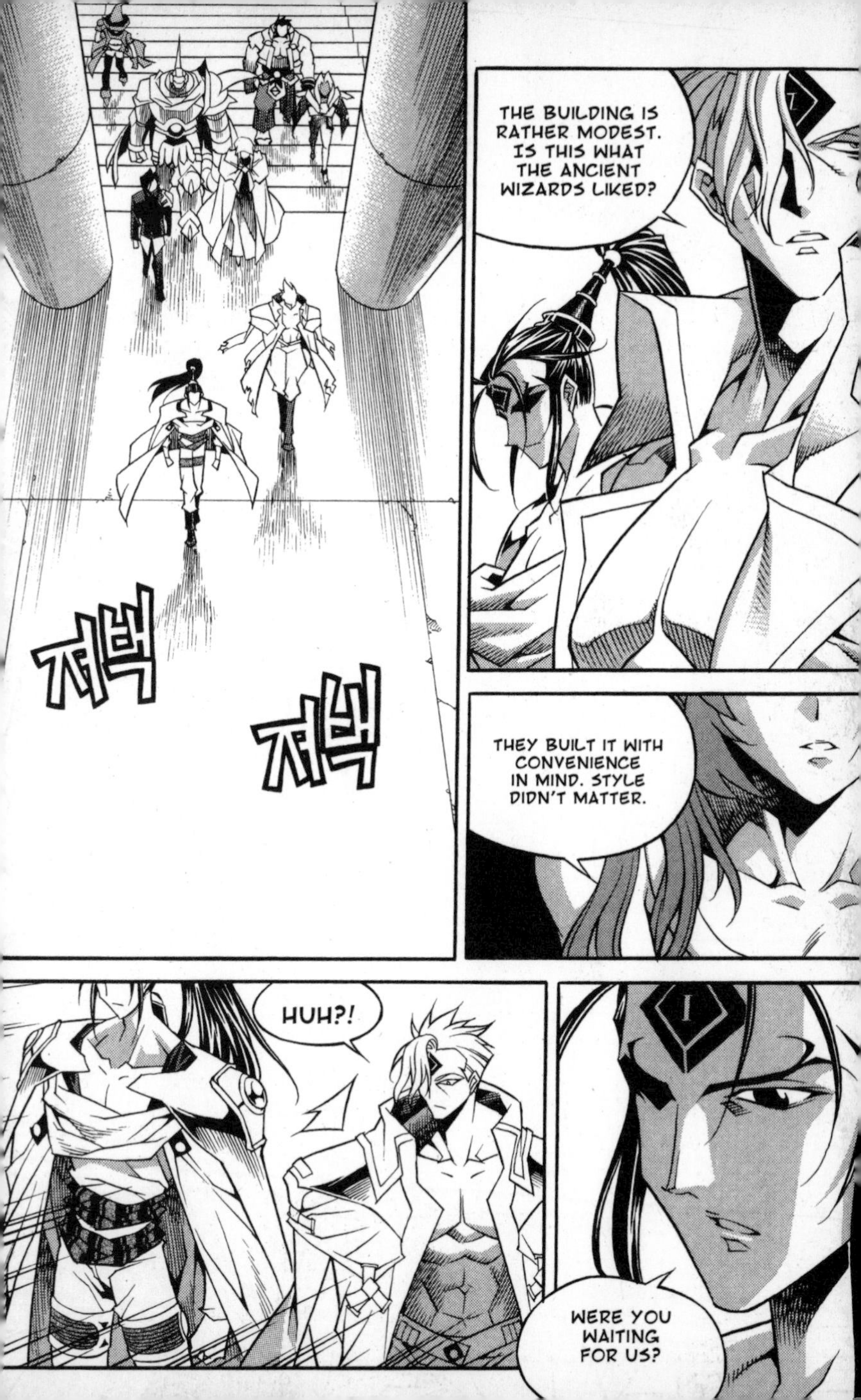
저벅
저벅
THE BUILDING IS RATHER MODEST. IS THIS WHAT THE ANCIENT WIZARDS LIKED?
THEY BUILT IT WITH CONVENIENCE IN MIND. STYLE DIDN'T MATTER.
HUH?!
WERE YOU WAITING FOR US?

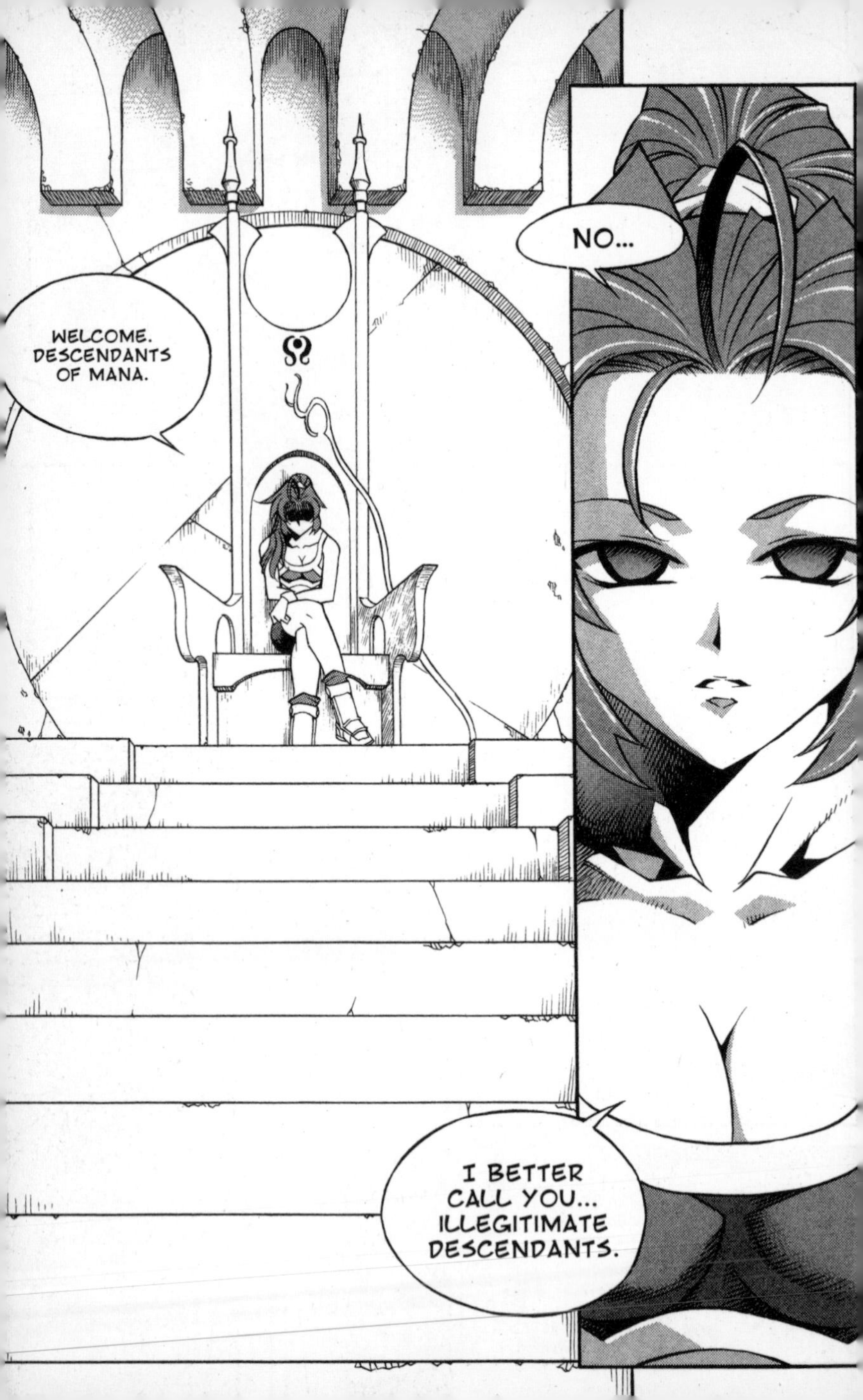
WELCOME. DESCENDANTS OF MANA.
NO...
I BETTER CALL YOU... ILLEGITIMATE DESCENDANTS.

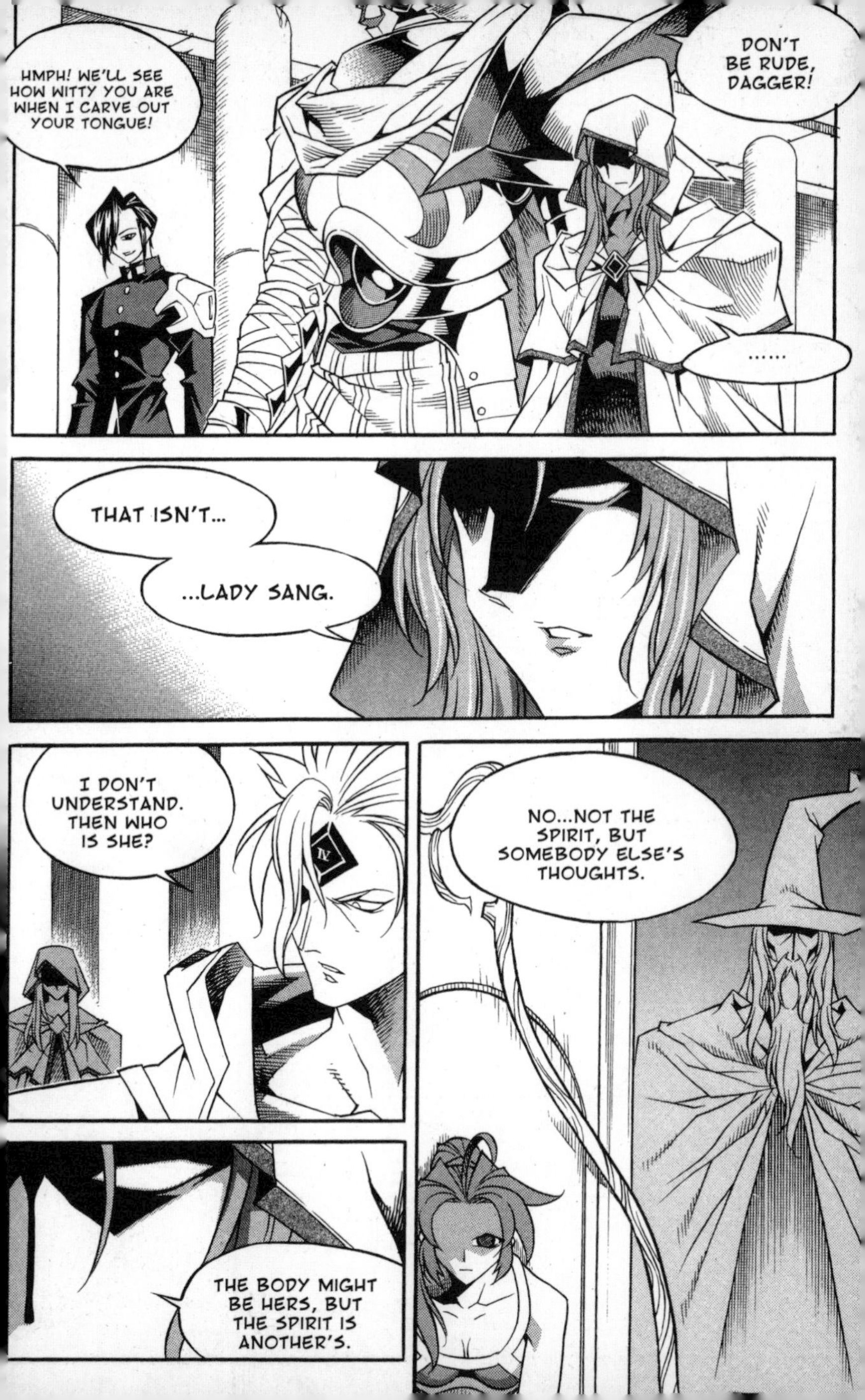
HMPH! WE'LL SEE HOW WITTY YOU ARE WHEN I CARVE OUT YOUR TONGUE!
DON'T BE RUDE, DAGGER!
......
THAT ISN'T...
...LADY SANG.
I DON'T UNDERSTAND. THEN WHO IS SHE?
NO...NOT THE SPIRIT, BUT SOMEBODY ELSE'S THOUGHTS.
THE BODY MIGHT BE HERS, BUT THE SPIRIT IS ANOTHER'S.

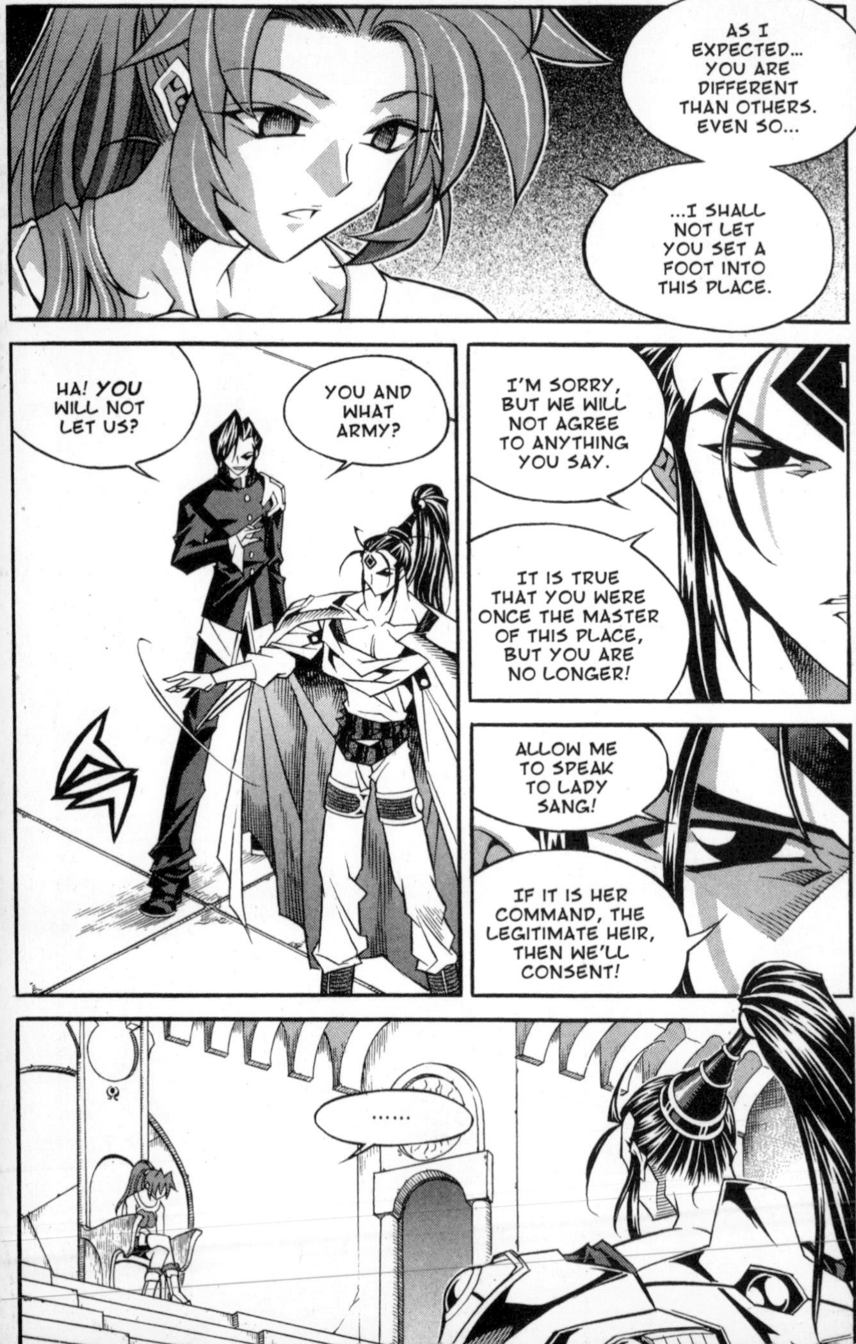
AS I EXPECTED... YOU ARE DIFFERENT THAN OTHERS. EVEN SO...
...I SHALL NOT LET YOU SET A FOOT INTO THIS PLACE.
HA! *YOU* WILL NOT LET US?
YOU AND WHAT ARMY?
I'M SORRY, BUT WE WILL NOT AGREE TO ANYTHING YOU SAY.
IT IS TRUE THAT YOU WERE ONCE THE MASTER OF THIS PLACE, BUT YOU ARE NO LONGER!
ALLOW ME TO SPEAK TO LADY SANG!
IF IT IS HER COMMAND, THE LEGITIMATE HEIR, THEN WE'LL CONSENT!
......

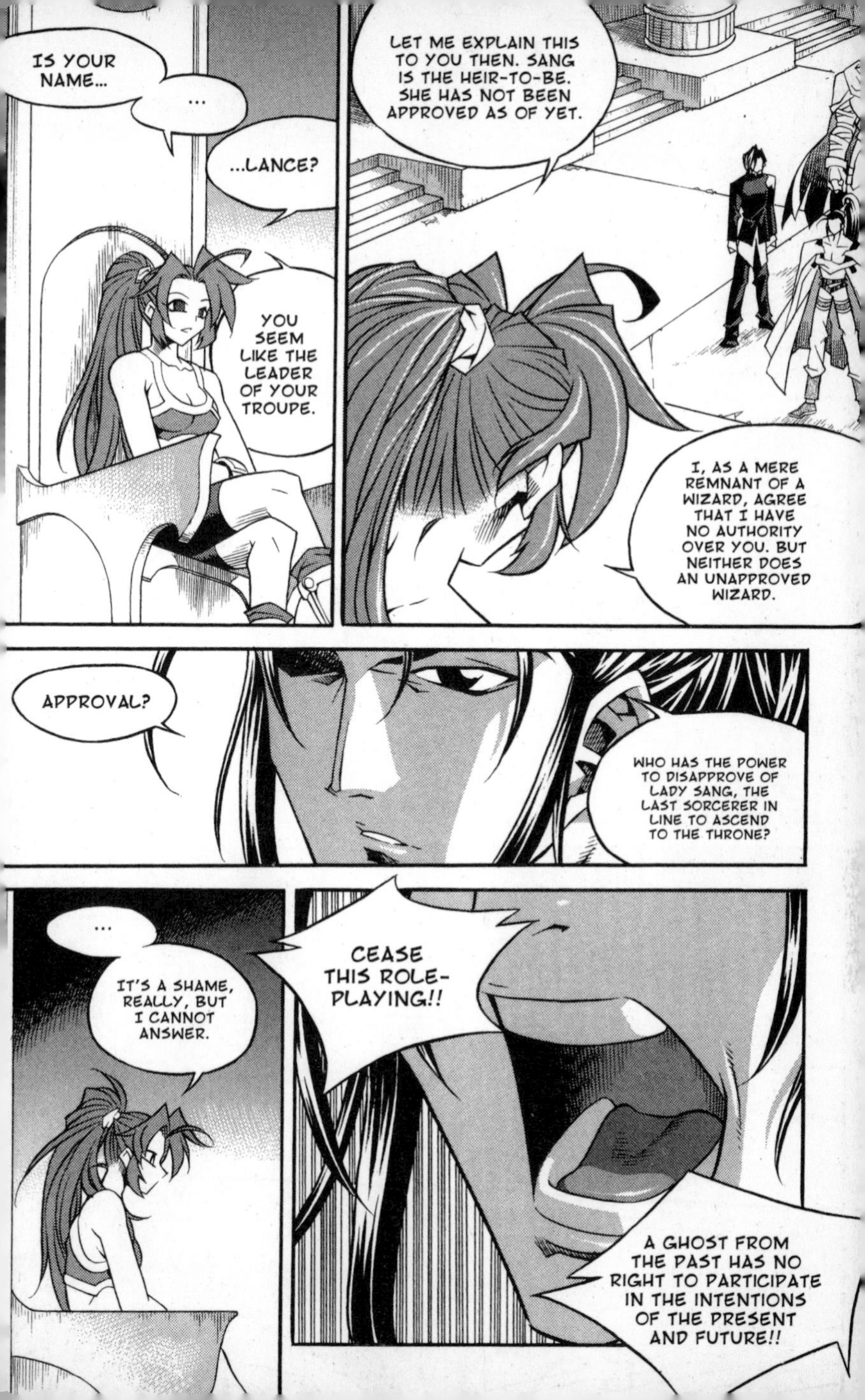
IS YOUR NAME...
...
...LANCE?
YOU SEEM LIKE THE LEADER OF YOUR TROUPE.
LET ME EXPLAIN THIS TO YOU THEN. SANG IS THE HEIR-TO-BE. SHE HAS NOT BEEN APPROVED AS OF YET.
I, AS A MERE REMNANT OF A WIZARD, AGREE THAT I HAVE NO AUTHORITY OVER YOU. BUT NEITHER DOES AN UNAPPROVED WIZARD.
APPROVAL?
WHO HAS THE POWER TO DISAPPROVE OF LADY SANG, THE LAST SORCERER IN LINE TO ASCEND TO THE THRONE?
...
IT'S A SHAME, REALLY, BUT I CANNOT ANSWER.
CEASE THIS ROLE-PLAYING!!
A GHOST FROM THE PAST HAS NO RIGHT TO PARTICIPATE IN THE INTENTIONS OF THE PRESENT AND FUTURE!!

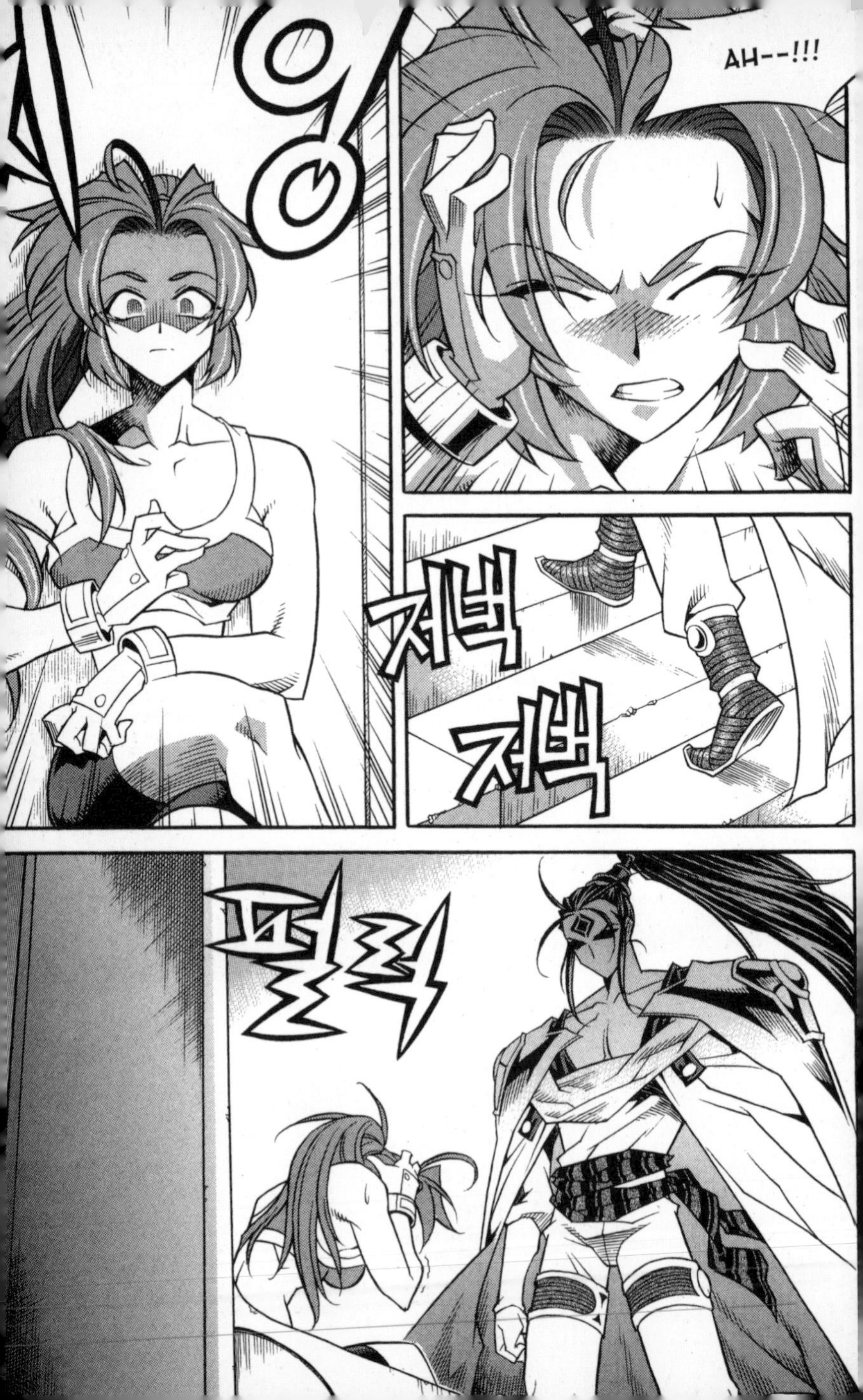
AH--!!!
저벅
저벅
펄럭

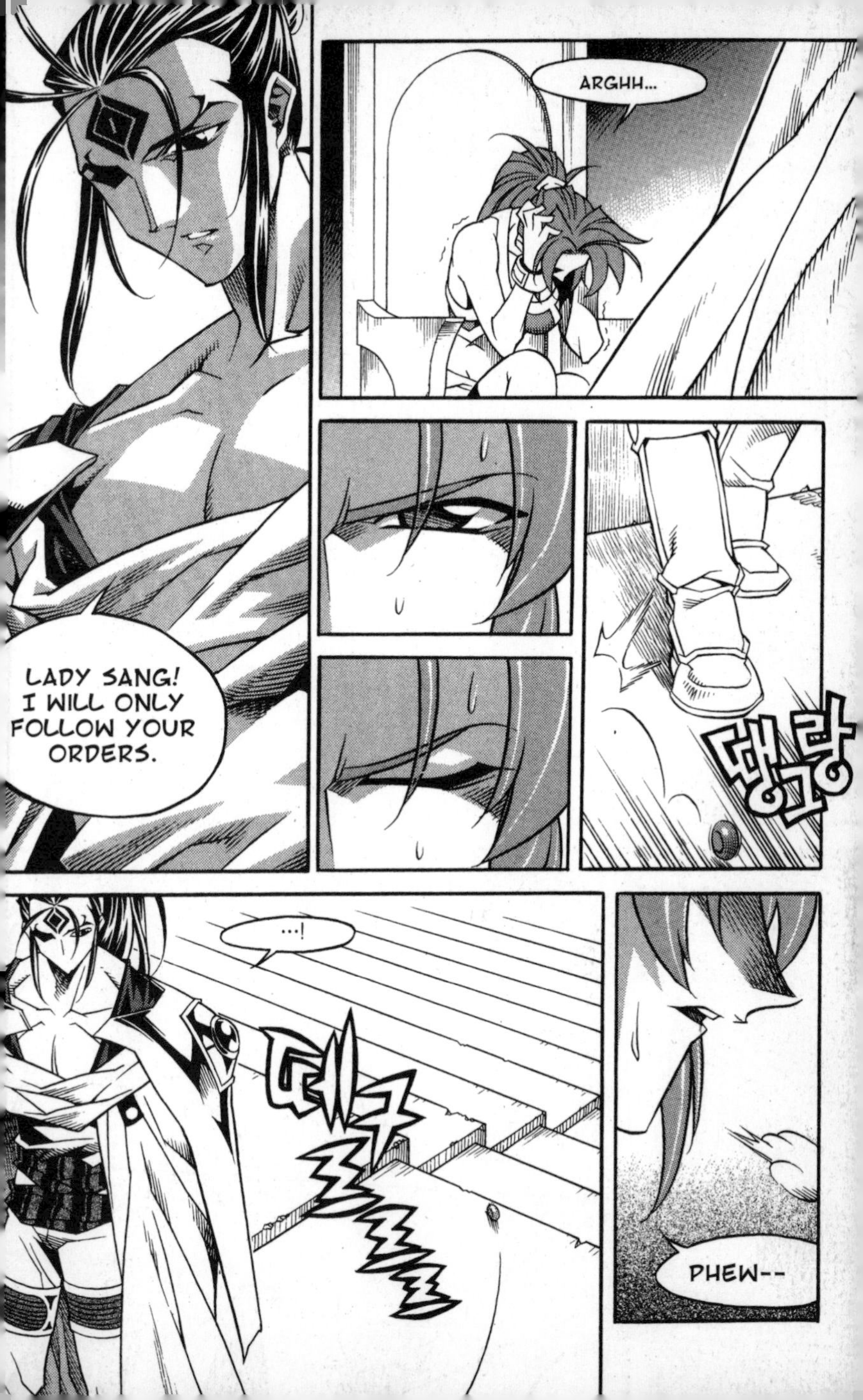
LADY SANG! I WILL ONLY FOLLOW YOUR ORDERS.
ARGHH...
댕그랑
...!
PHEW--

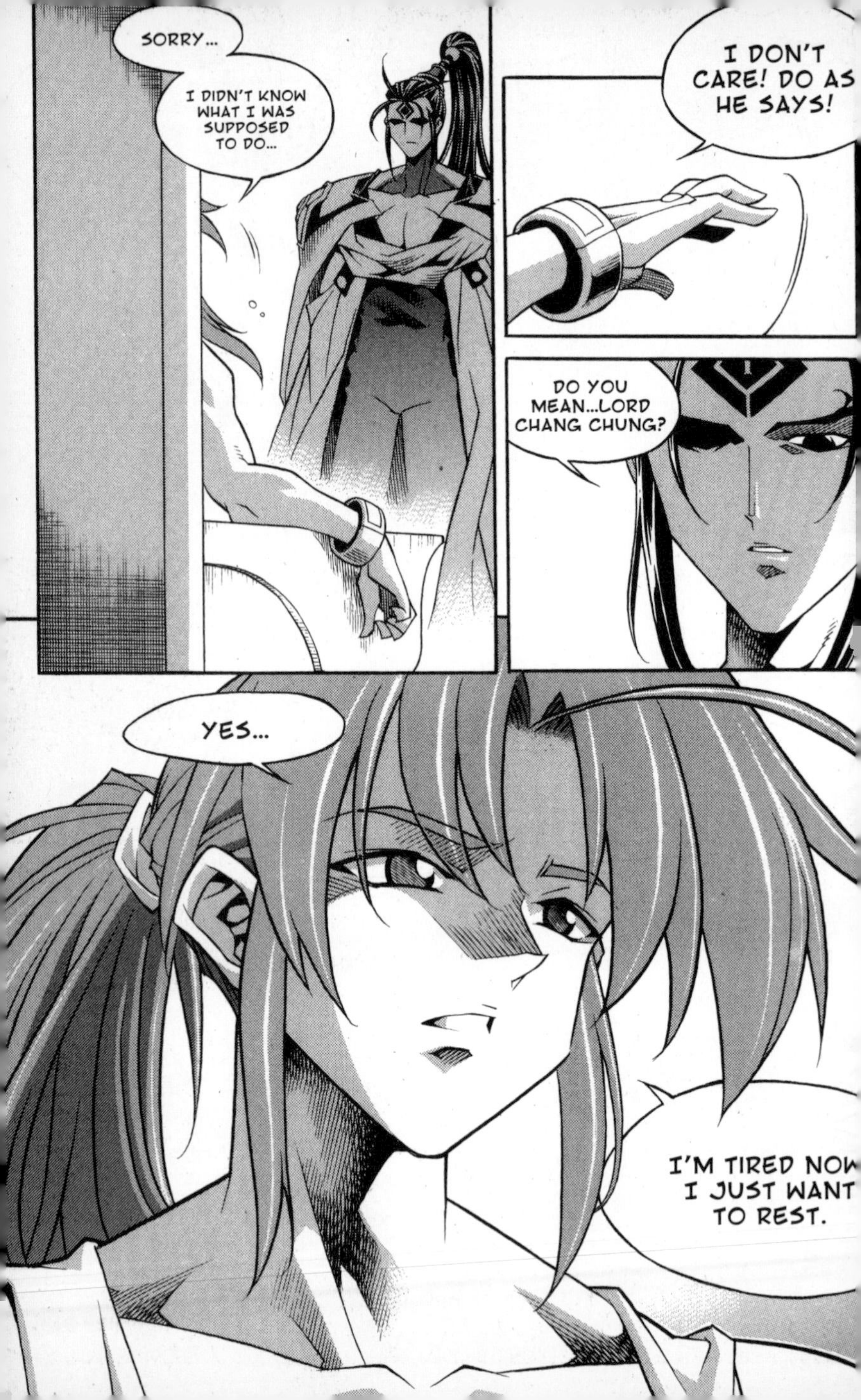
SORRY...
I DIDN'T KNOW WHAT I WAS SUPPOSED TO DO...
I DON'T CARE! DO AS HE SAYS!
DO YOU MEAN...LORD CHANG CHUNG?
YES...
I'M TIRED NOW
I JUST WANT TO REST.

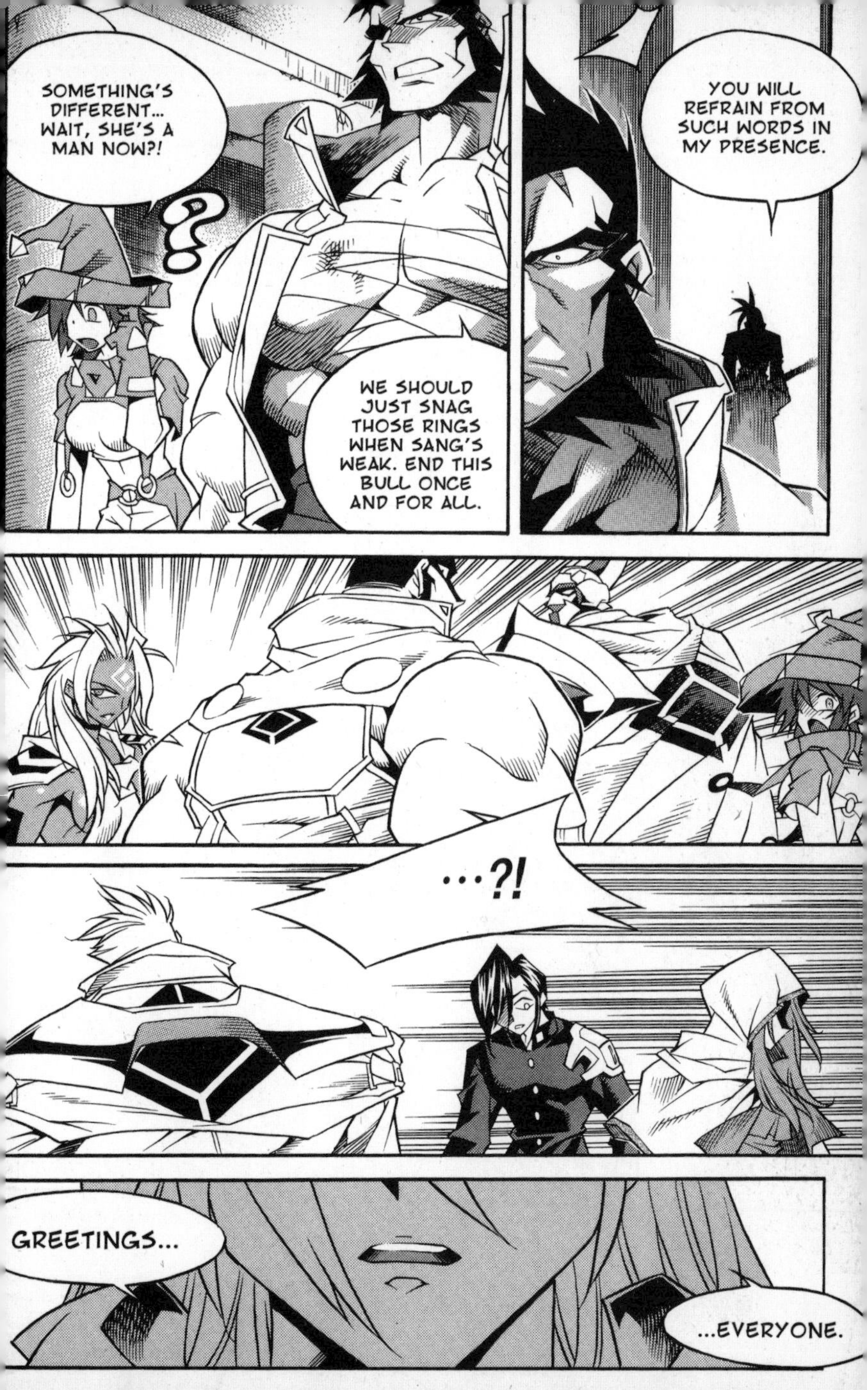
SOMETHING'S DIFFERENT... WAIT, SHE'S A MAN NOW?!
?
WE SHOULD JUST SNAG THOSE RINGS WHEN SANG'S WEAK. END THIS BULL ONCE AND FOR ALL.
YOU WILL REFRAIN FROM SUCH WORDS IN MY PRESENCE.
...?!
GREETINGS...
...EVERYONE.

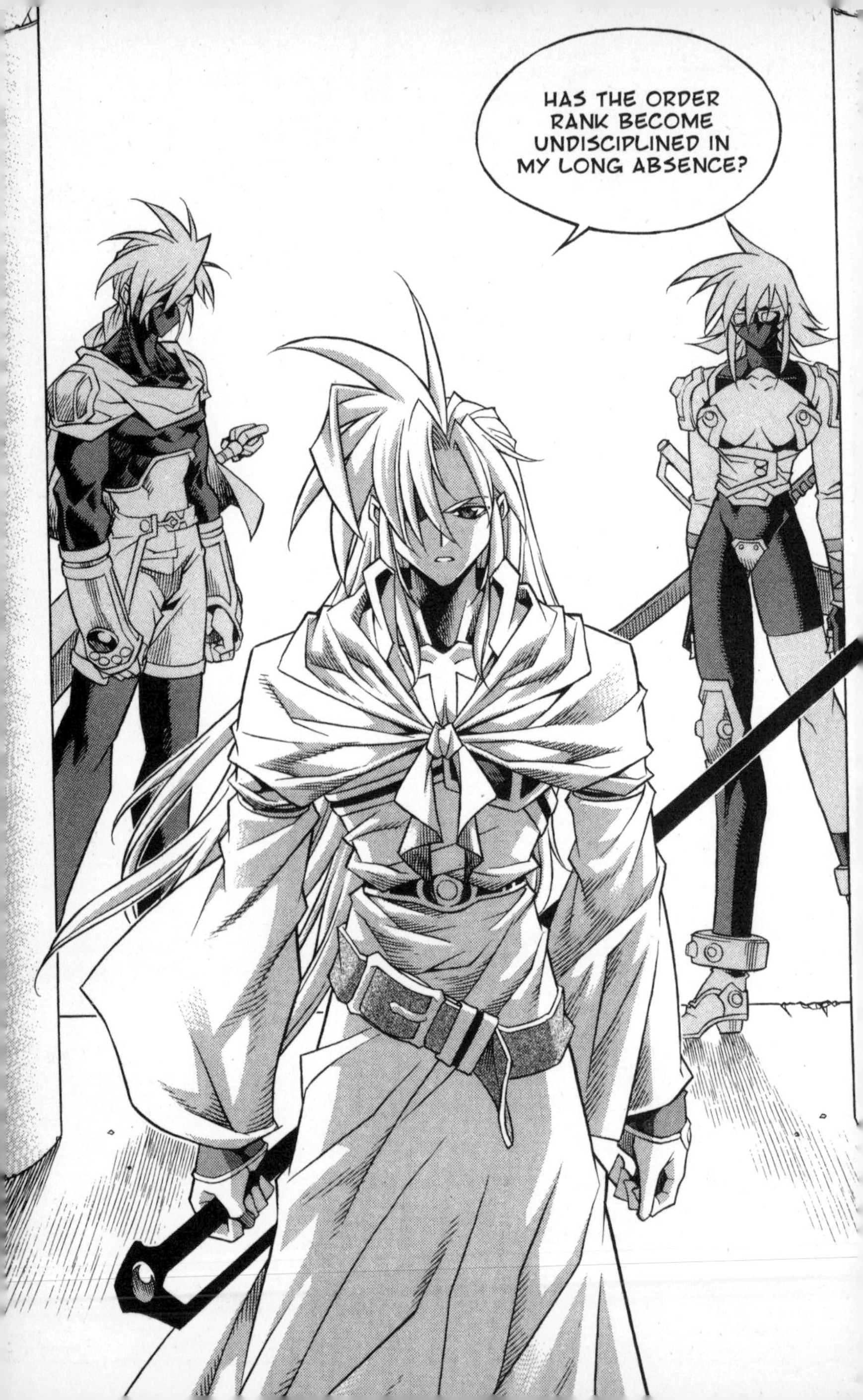
HAS THE ORDER RANK BECOME UNDISCIPLINED IN MY LONG ABSENCE?

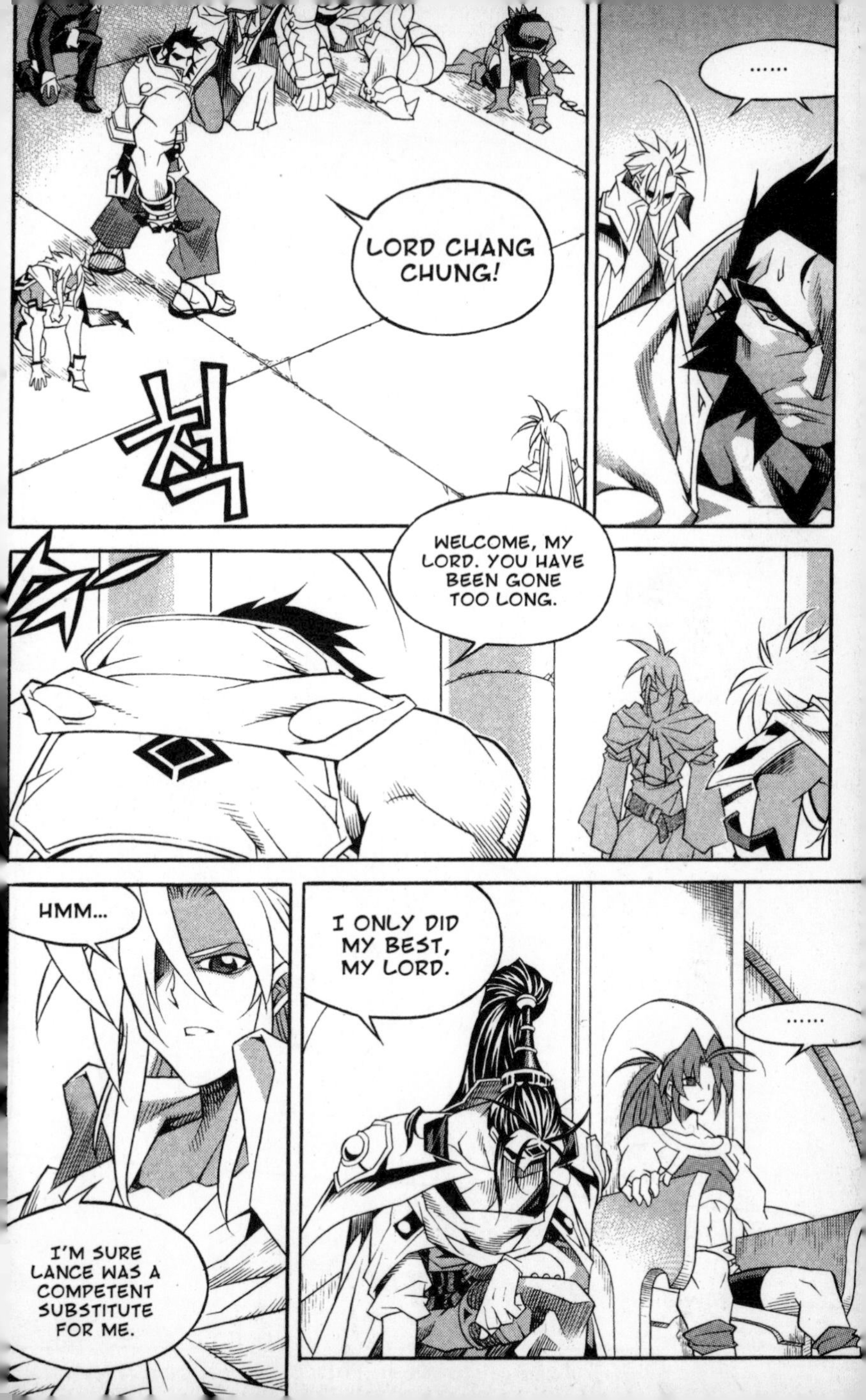
LORD CHANG CHUNG!
척
......
WELCOME, MY LORD. YOU HAVE BEEN GONE TOO LONG.
HMM...
I'M SURE LANCE WAS A COMPETENT SUBSTITUTE FOR ME.
I ONLY DID MY BEST, MY LORD.
......

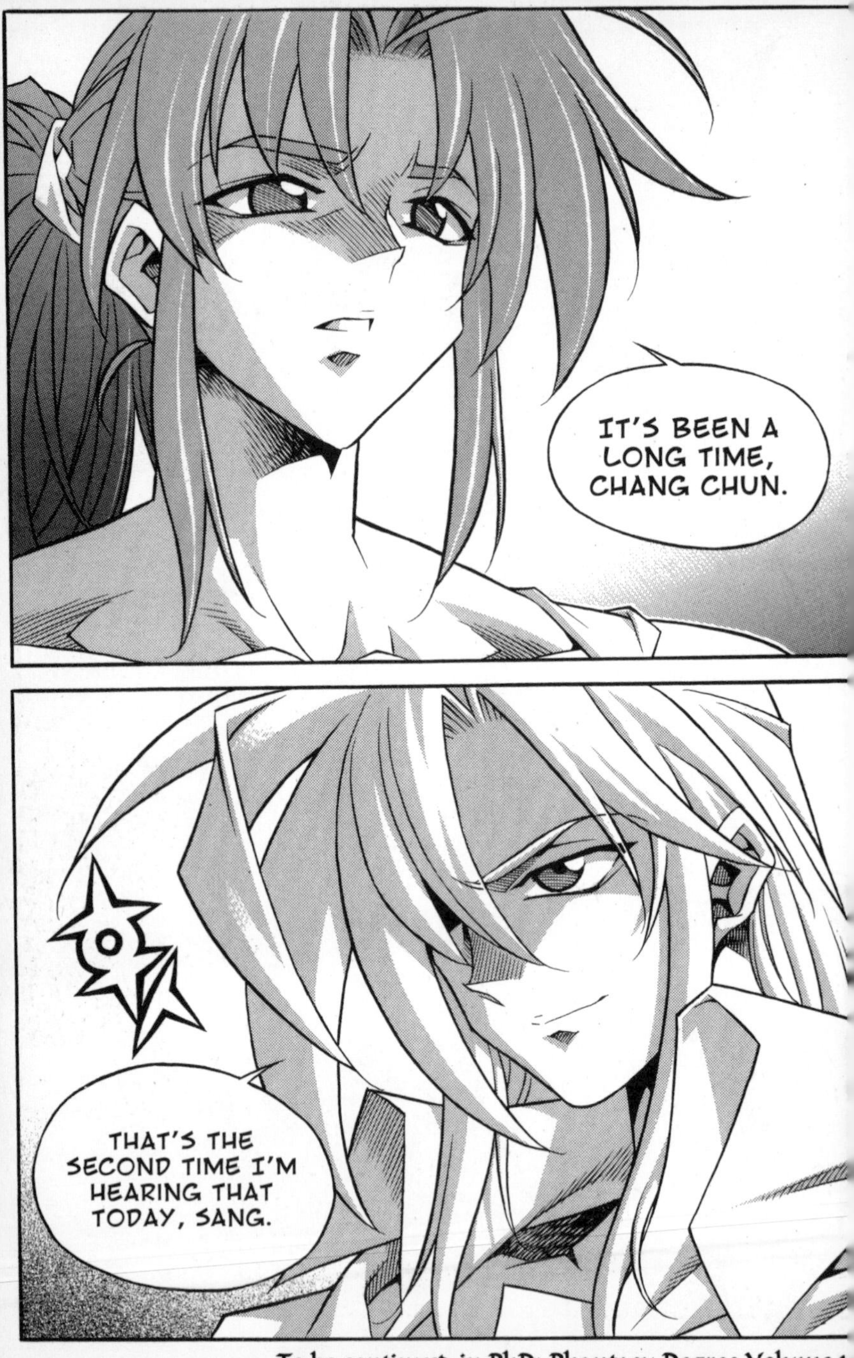
IT'S BEEN A LONG TIME, CHANG CHUN.
THAT'S THE SECOND TIME I'M HEARING THAT TODAY, SANG.

To be continued in PhD: Phantasy Degree Volume 1

THE MANGA ARTIST'S STUDIO

망가져 화실

놀고프다

I WANNA PLAY

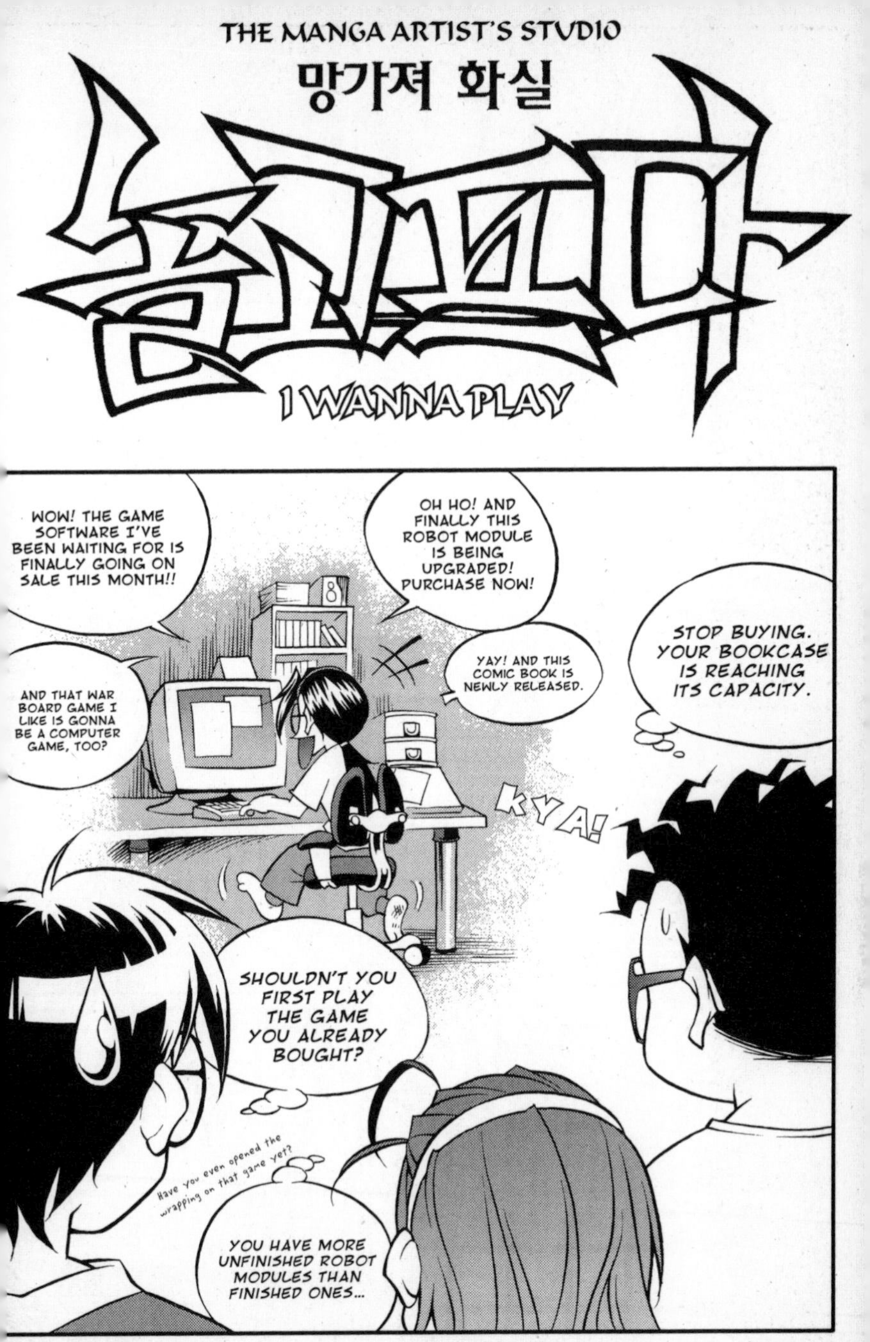
WOW! THE GAME SOFTWARE I'VE BEEN WAITING FOR IS FINALLY GOING ON SALE THIS MONTH!!
OH HO! AND FINALLY THIS ROBOT MODULE IS BEING UPGRADED! PURCHASE NOW!
AND THAT WAR BOARD GAME I LIKE IS GONNA BE A COMPUTER GAME, TOO?
YAY! AND THIS COMIC BOOK IS NEWLY RELEASED.
STOP BUYING. YOUR BOOKCASE IS REACHING ITS CAPACITY.
KYA!
SHOULDN'T YOU FIRST PLAY THE GAME YOU ALREADY BOUGHT?
Have you even opened the wrapping on that game yet?
YOU HAVE MORE UNFINISHED ROBOT MODULES THAN FINISHED ONES...

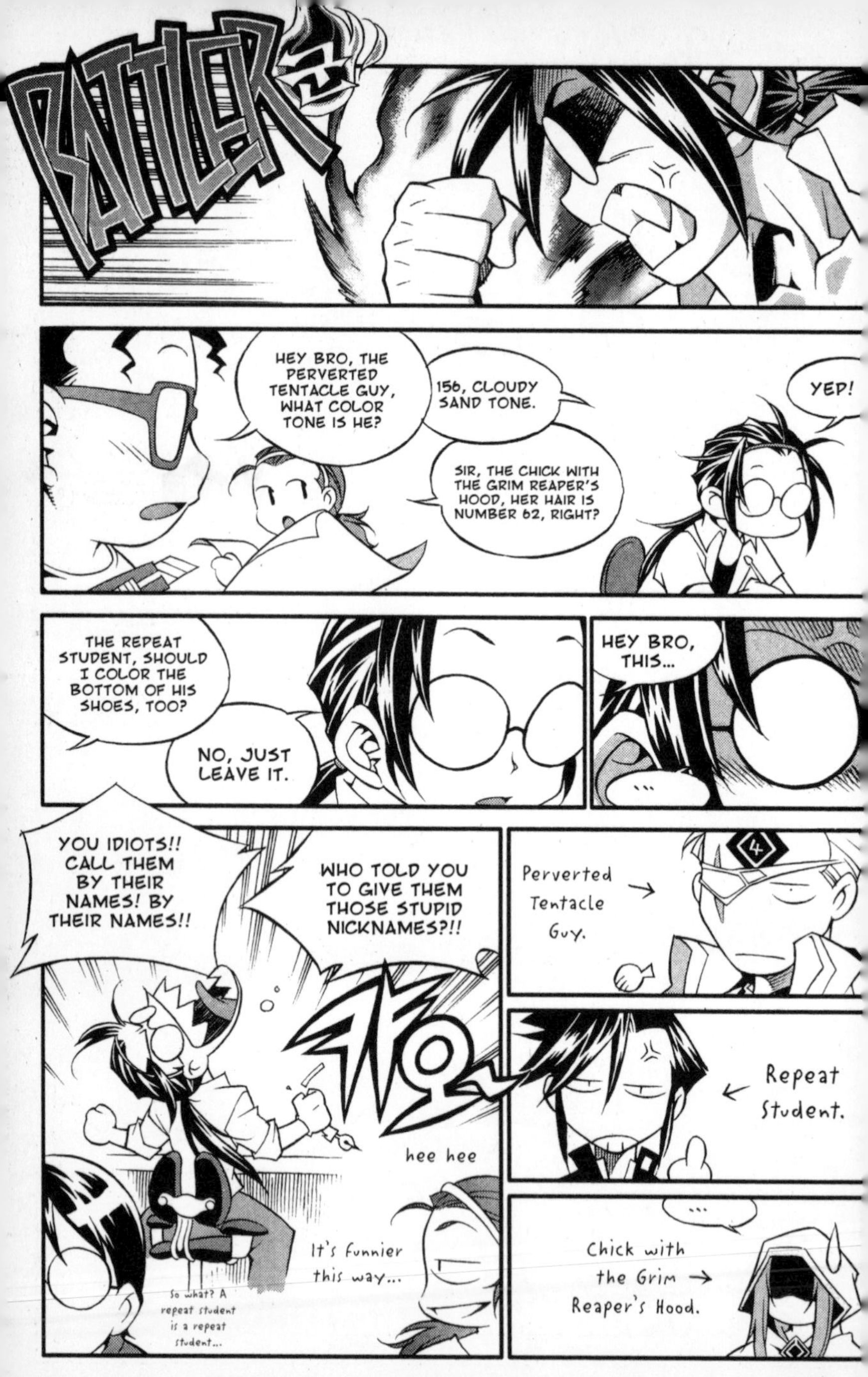
BATTLER
HEY BRO, THE PERVERTED TENTACLE GUY, WHAT COLOR TONE IS HE?
156, CLOUDY SAND TONE.
SIR, THE CHICK WITH THE GRIM REAPER'S HOOD, HER HAIR IS NUMBER 62, RIGHT?
YEP!
THE REPEAT STUDENT, SHOULD I COLOR THE BOTTOM OF HIS SHOES, TOO?
NO, JUST LEAVE IT.
HEY BRO, THIS...
...
YOU IDIOTS!! CALL THEM BY THEIR NAMES! BY THEIR NAMES!!
WHO TOLD YOU TO GIVE THEM THOSE STUPID NICKNAMES?!!
Perverted Tentacle Guy.
Repeat Student.
...
Chick with the Grim Reaper's Hood.
hee hee
It's funnier this way...
So what? A repeat student is a repeat student...

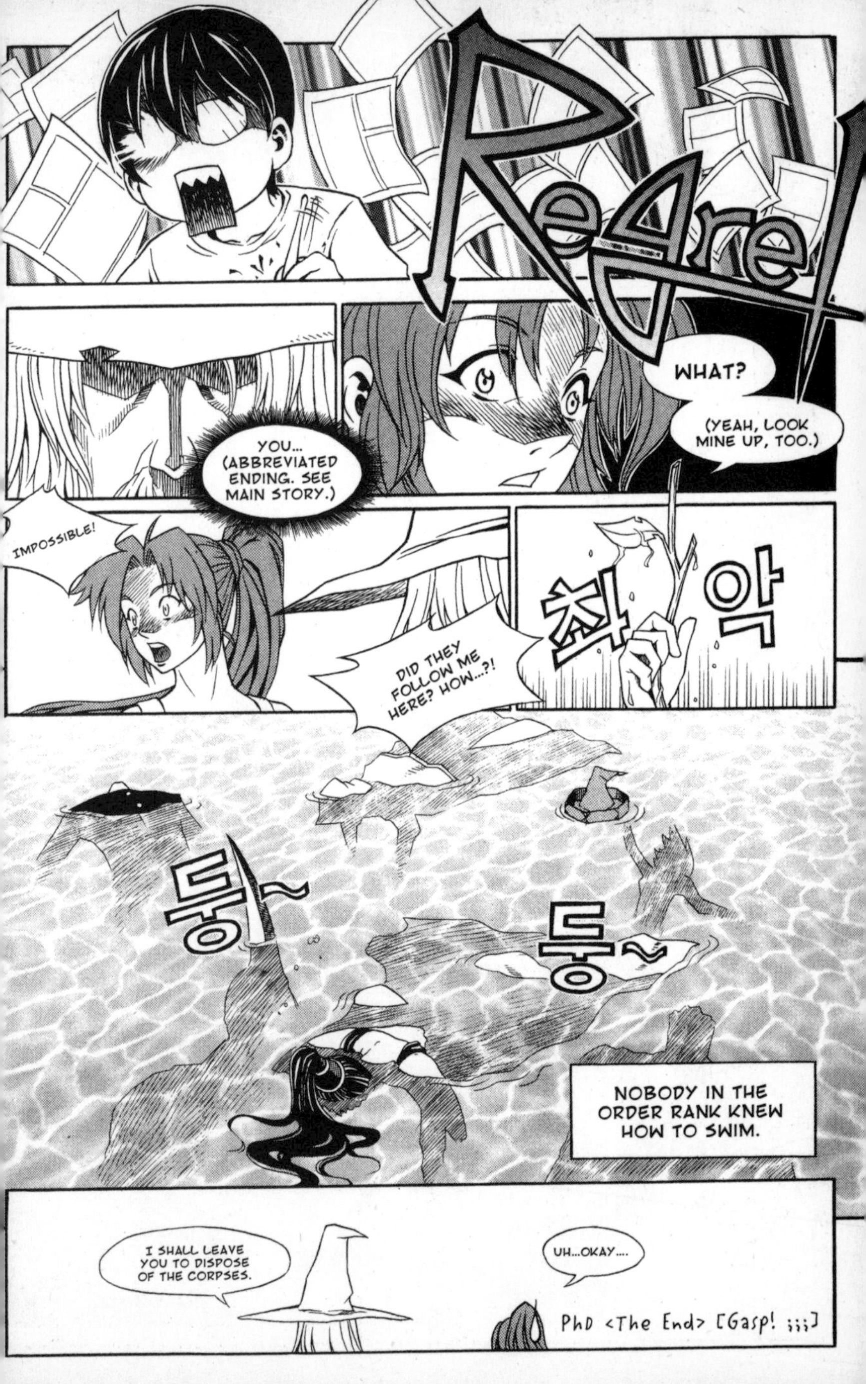
Regret
WHAT?
(YEAH, LOOK MINE UP, TOO.)
YOU... (ABBREVIATED ENDING. SEE MAIN STORY.)
IMPOSSIBLE!
DID THEY FOLLOW ME HERE? HOW...?!
최 악
둥~
둥~
NOBODY IN THE ORDER RANK KNEW HOW TO SWIM.
I SHALL LEAVE YOU TO DISPOSE OF THE CORPSES.
UH...OKAY....
PhD <The End> [Gasp! ;;;]

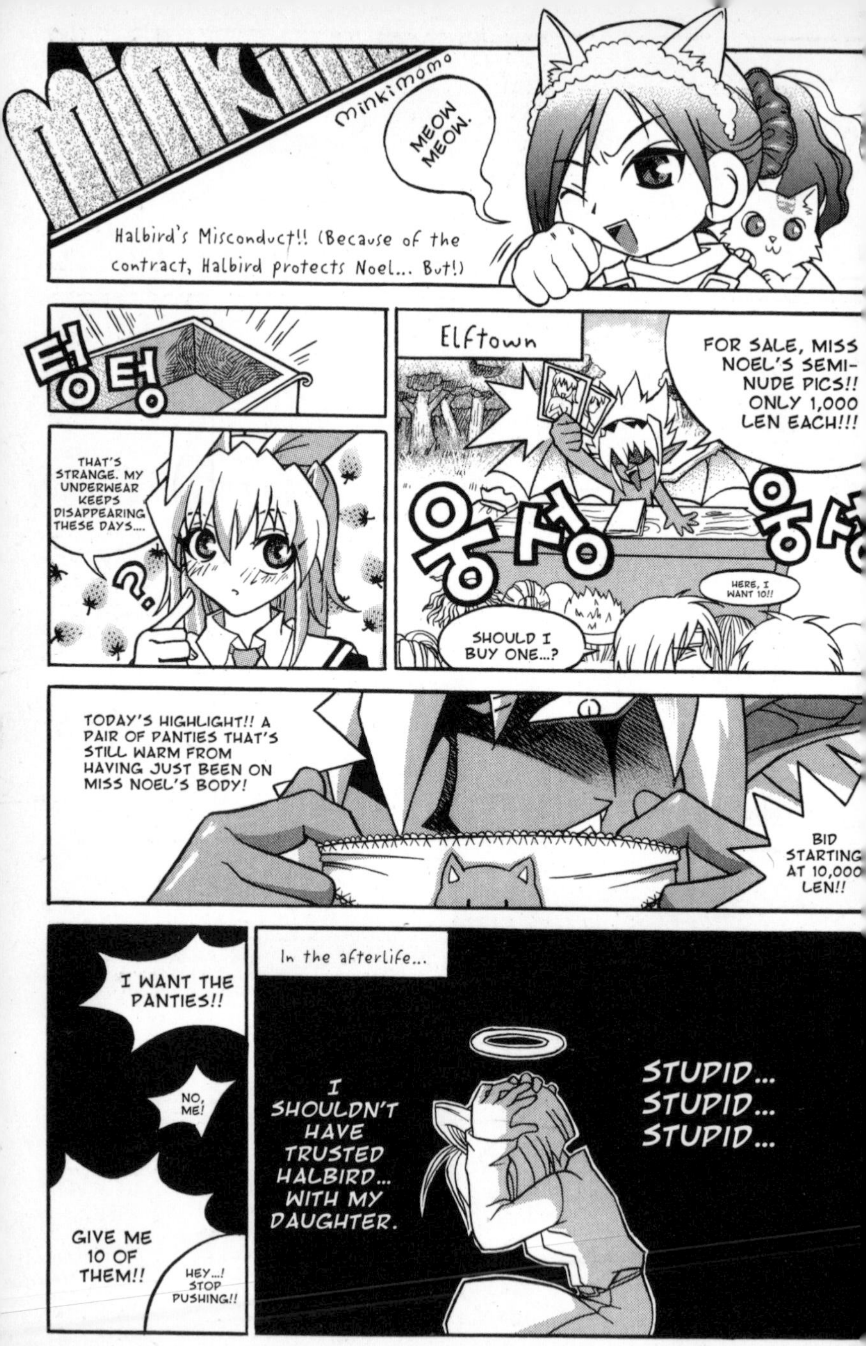
minkimomo
MEOW MEOW.
Halbird's Misconduct!! (Because of the contract, Halbird protects Noel... But!)
텅 텅
Elftown
FOR SALE, MISS NOEL'S SEMI-NUDE PICS!! ONLY 1,000 LEN EACH!!!
THAT'S STRANGE. MY UNDERWEAR KEEPS DISAPPEARING THESE DAYS....
?
웅성 웅성
HERE, I WANT 10!!
SHOULD I BUY ONE...?
TODAY'S HIGHLIGHT!! A PAIR OF PANTIES THAT'S STILL WARM FROM HAVING JUST BEEN ON MISS NOEL'S BODY!
BID STARTING AT 10,000 LEN!!
I WANT THE PANTIES!!
NO, ME!
GIVE ME 10 OF THEM!!
HEY...! STOP PUSHING!!
In the afterlife...
I SHOULDN'T HAVE TRUSTED HALBIRD... WITH MY DAUGHTER.
STUPID... STUPID... STUPID...

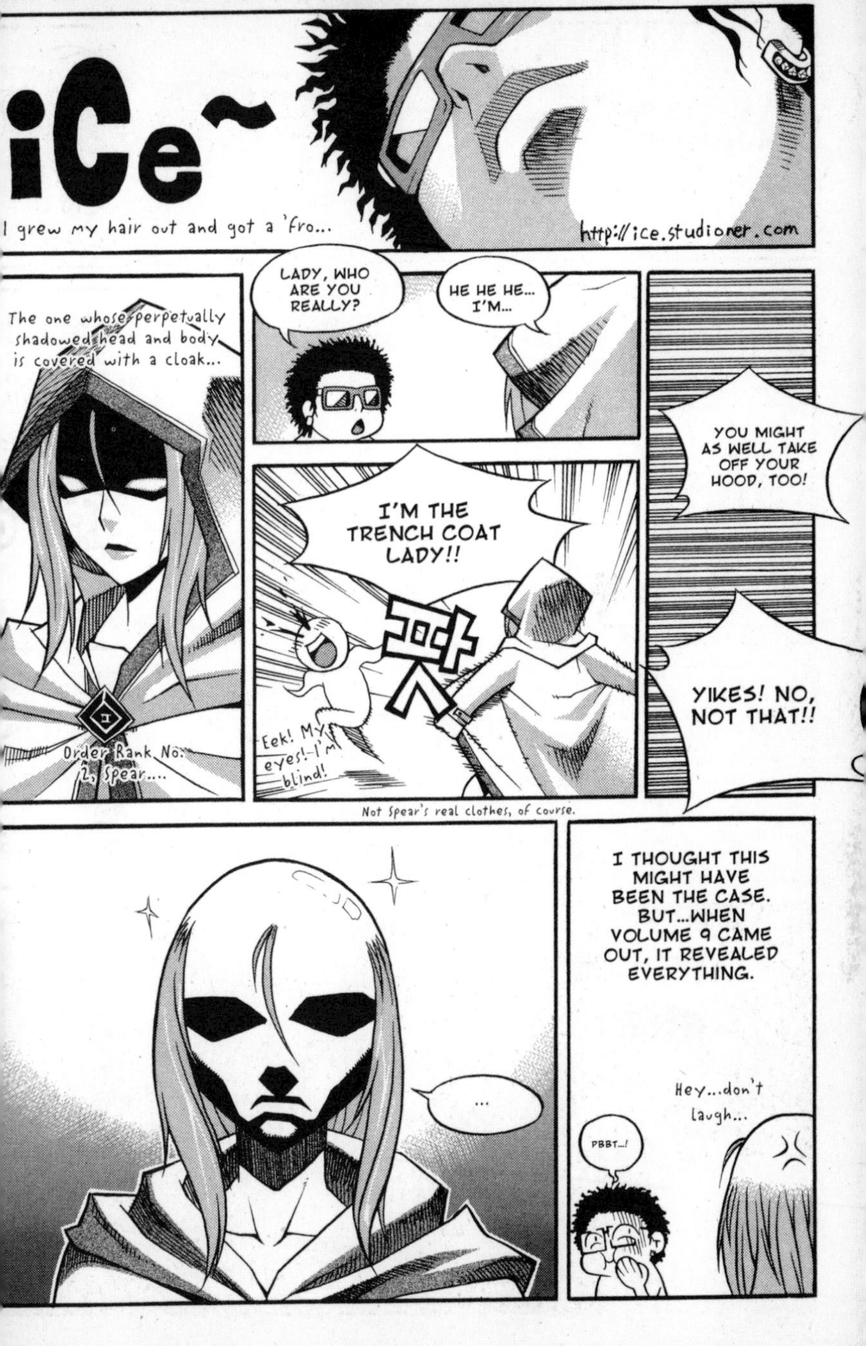
iCe~
I grew my hair out and got a 'fro...
http://ice.studioner.com
The one whose perpetually shadowed head and body is covered with a cloak...
Order Rank No. 2, Spear....
LADY, WHO ARE YOU REALLY?
HE HE HE... I'M...
I'M THE TRENCH COAT LADY!!
Eek! My eyes!-I'm blind!
YOU MIGHT AS WELL TAKE OFF YOUR HOOD, TOO!
YIKES! NO, NOT THAT!!
Not Spear's real clothes, of course.
...
I THOUGHT THIS MIGHT HAVE BEEN THE CASE. BUT...WHEN VOLUME 9 CAME OUT, IT REVEALED EVERYTHING.
PBBT...!
Hey...don't laugh...

In the next volume of...

PhD
PHANTASY DEGREE

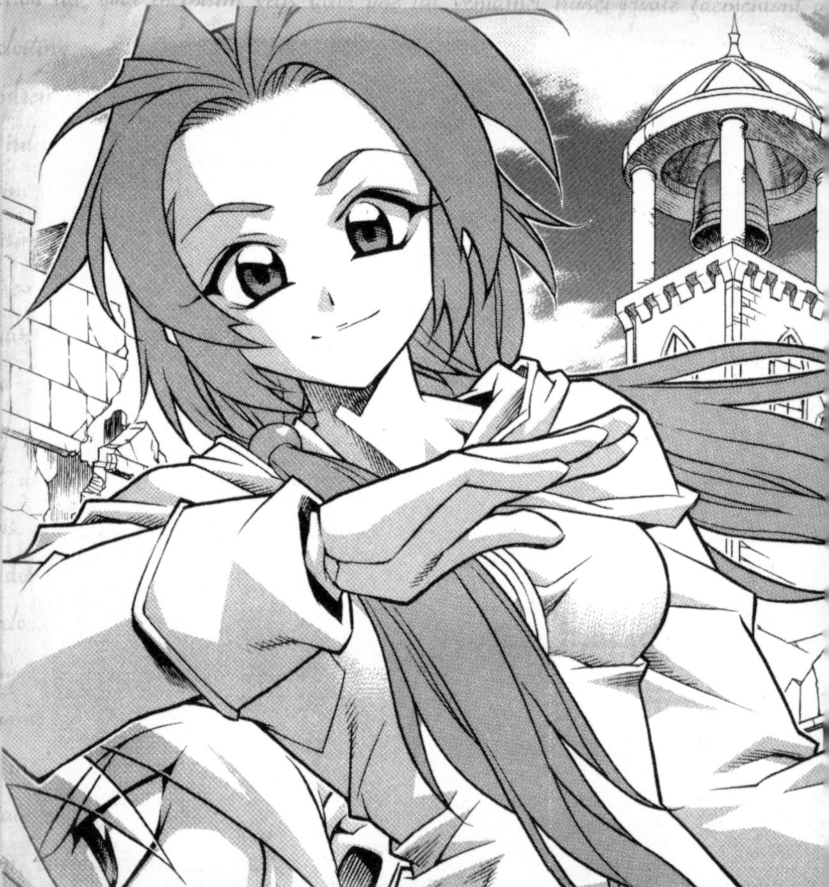

Available September 2007

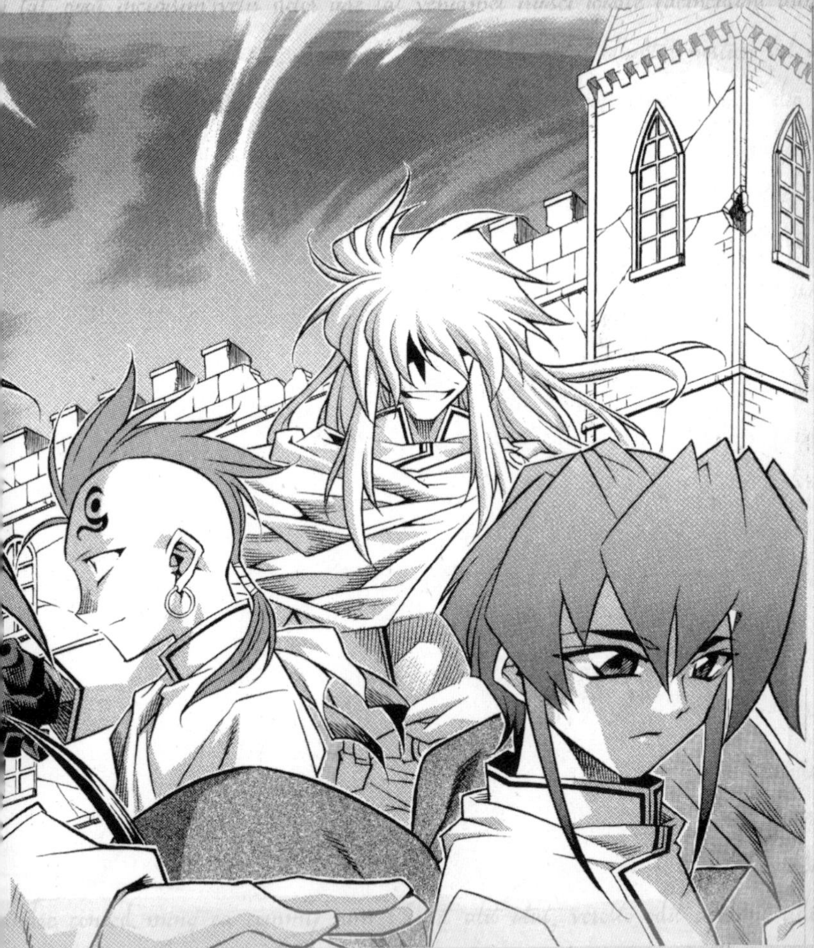

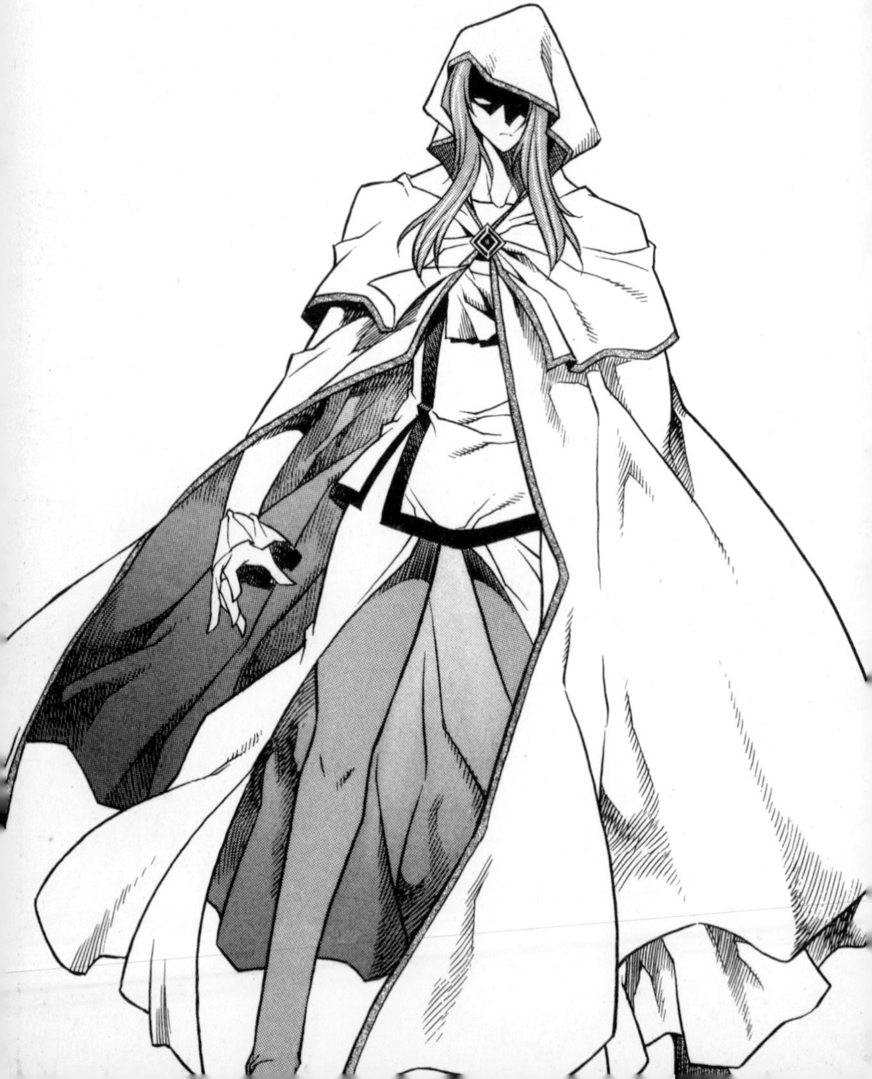

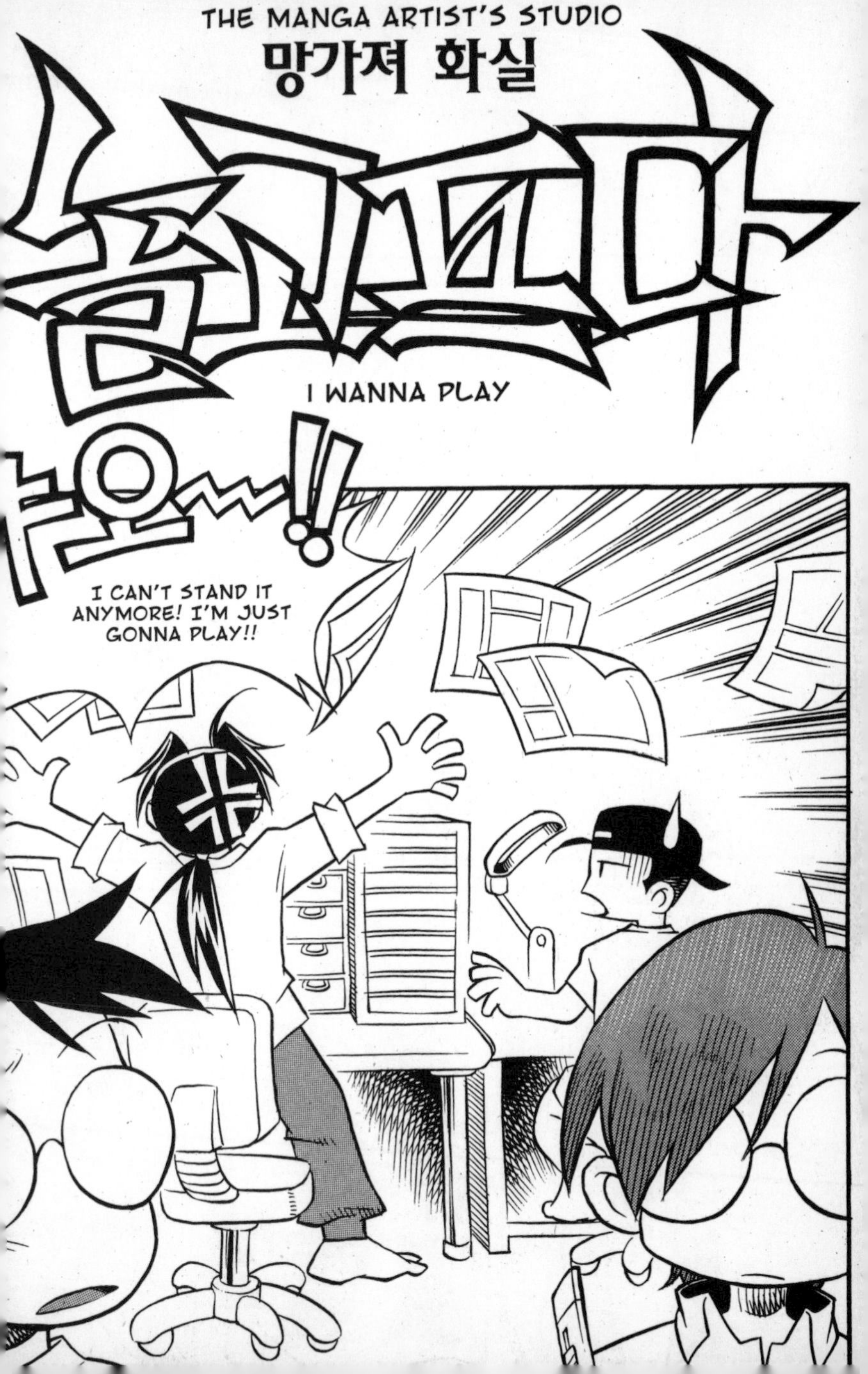
THE MANGA ARTIST'S STUDIO
망가져 화실
I WANNA PLAY
I CAN'T STAND IT ANYMORE! I'M JUST GONNA PLAY!!

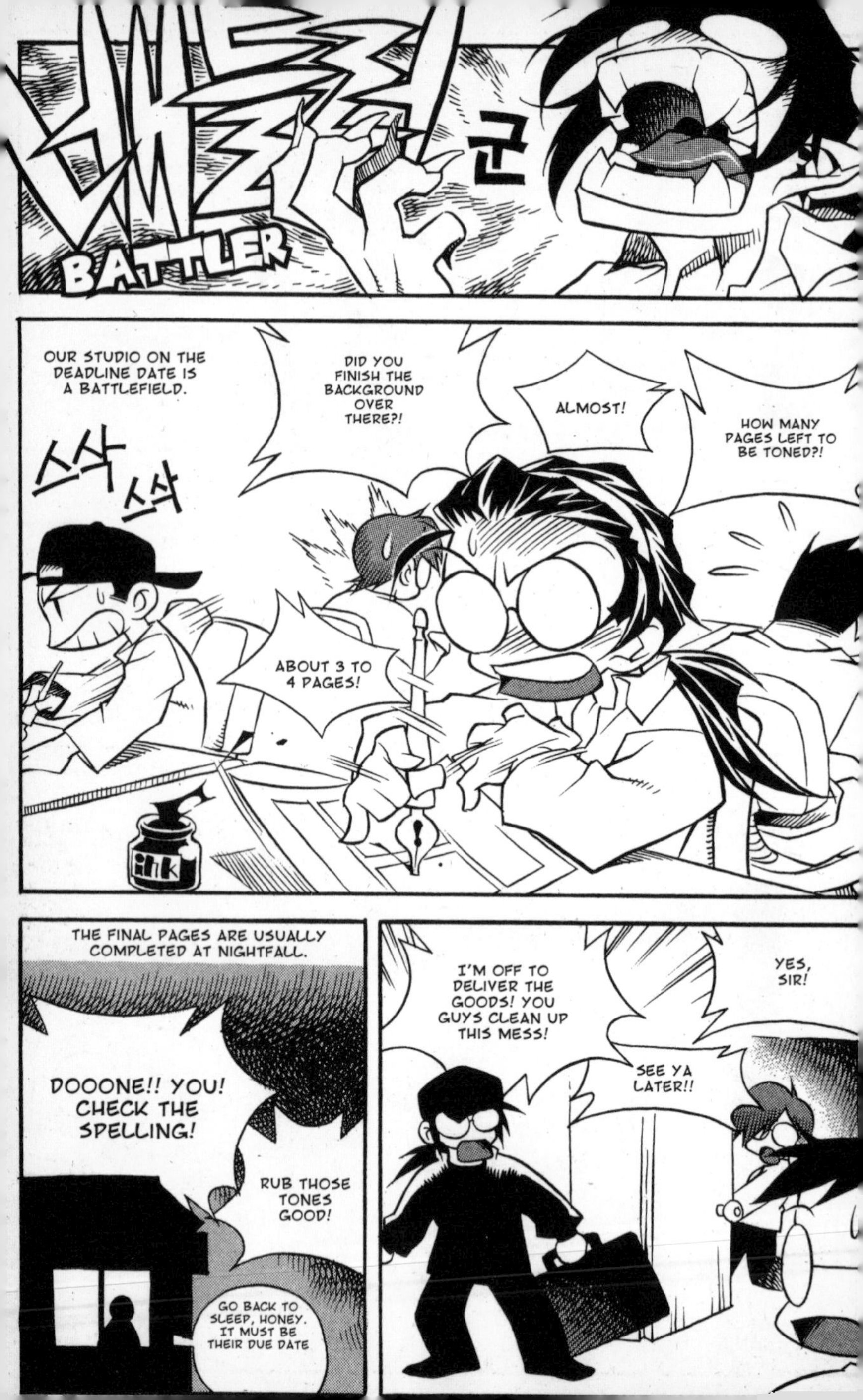

BATTLER
OUR STUDIO ON THE DEADLINE DATE IS A BATTLEFIELD.
DID YOU FINISH THE BACKGROUND OVER THERE?!
ALMOST!
HOW MANY PAGES LEFT TO BE TONED?!
스삭 스삭
ABOUT 3 TO 4 PAGES!
ink
THE FINAL PAGES ARE USUALLY COMPLETED AT NIGHTFALL.
DOOONE!! YOU! CHECK THE SPELLING!
RUB THOSE TONES GOOD!
GO BACK TO SLEEP, HONEY. IT MUST BE THEIR DUE DATE
I'M OFF TO DELIVER THE GOODS! YOU GUYS CLEAN UP THIS MESS!
YES, SIR!
SEE YA LATER!!

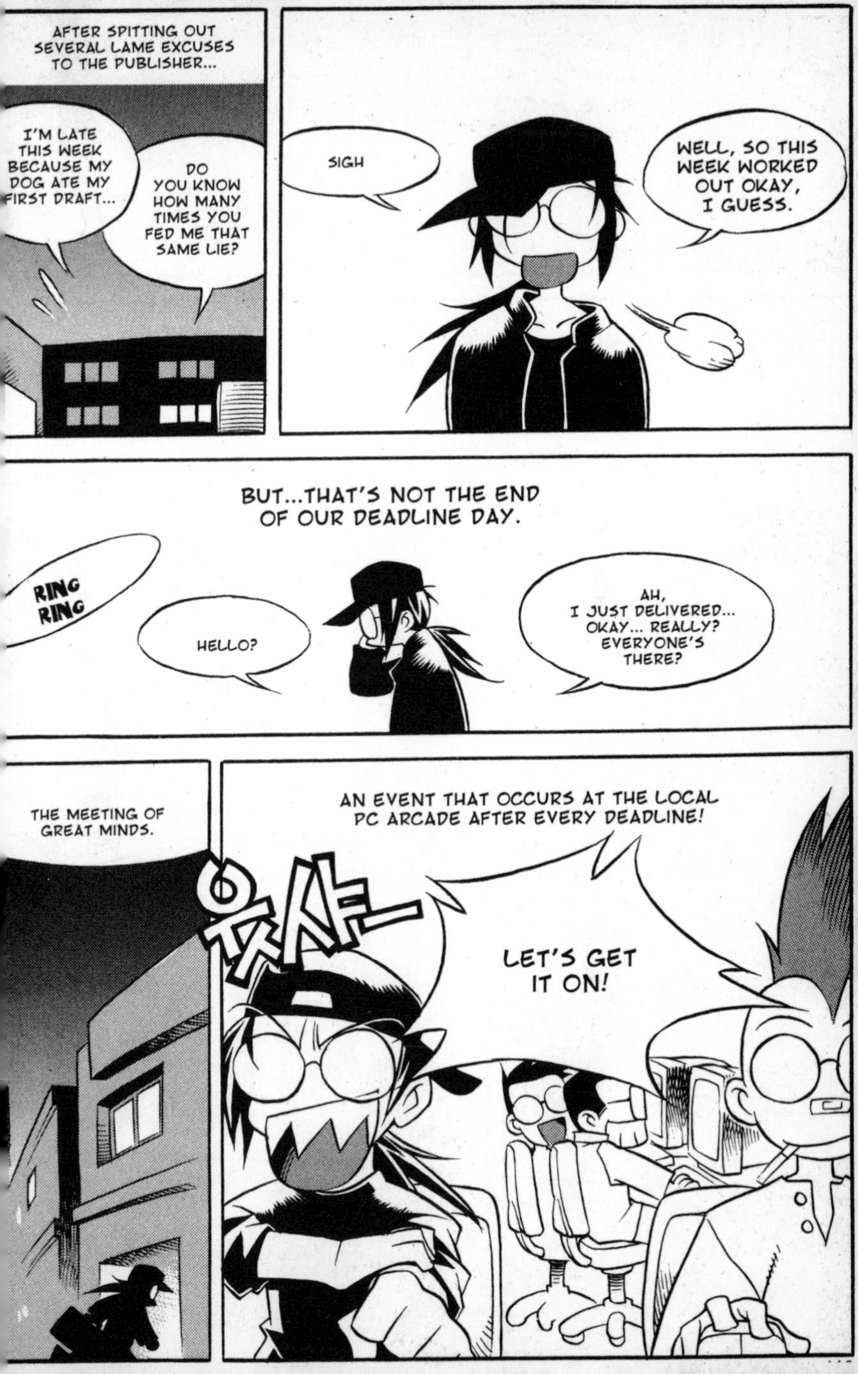
AFTER SPITTING OUT SEVERAL LAME EXCUSES TO THE PUBLISHER...
I'M LATE THIS WEEK BECAUSE MY DOG ATE MY FIRST DRAFT...
DO YOU KNOW HOW MANY TIMES YOU FED ME THAT SAME LIE?
SIGH
WELL, SO THIS WEEK WORKED OUT OKAY, I GUESS.
BUT...THAT'S NOT THE END OF OUR DEADLINE DAY.
RING RING
HELLO?
AH, I JUST DELIVERED... OKAY... REALLY? EVERYONE'S THERE?
THE MEETING OF GREAT MINDS.
AN EVENT THAT OCCURS AT THE LOCAL PC ARCADE AFTER EVERY DEADLINE!
LET'S GET IT ON!

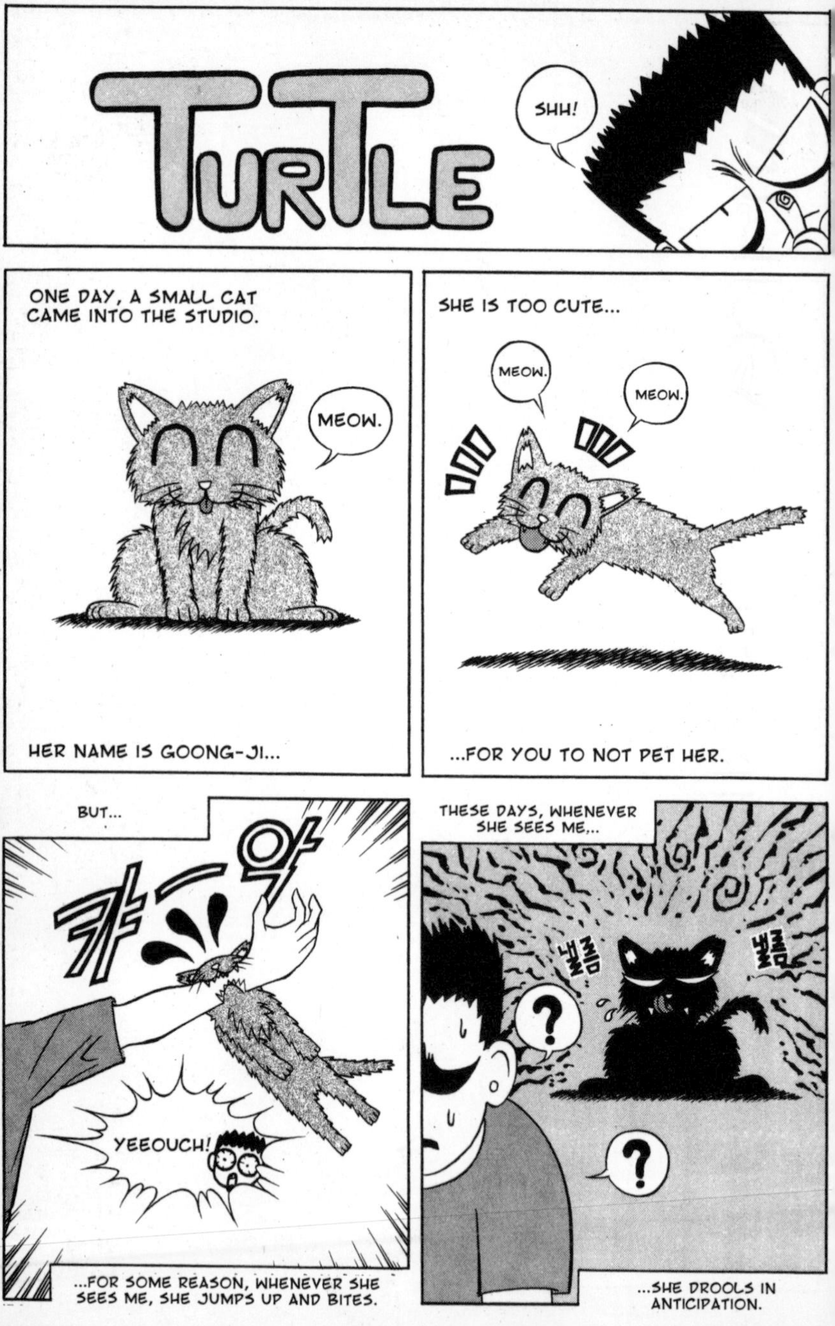

TURTLE
SHH!
ONE DAY, A SMALL CAT CAME INTO THE STUDIO.
MEOW.
HER NAME IS GOONG-JI...
SHE IS TOO CUTE...
MEOW.
MEOW.
...FOR YOU TO NOT PET HER.
BUT...
YEEOUCH!
...FOR SOME REASON, WHENEVER SHE SEES ME, SHE JUMPS UP AND BITES.
THESE DAYS, WHENEVER SHE SEES ME,...
?
?
...SHE DROOLS IN ANTICIPATION.

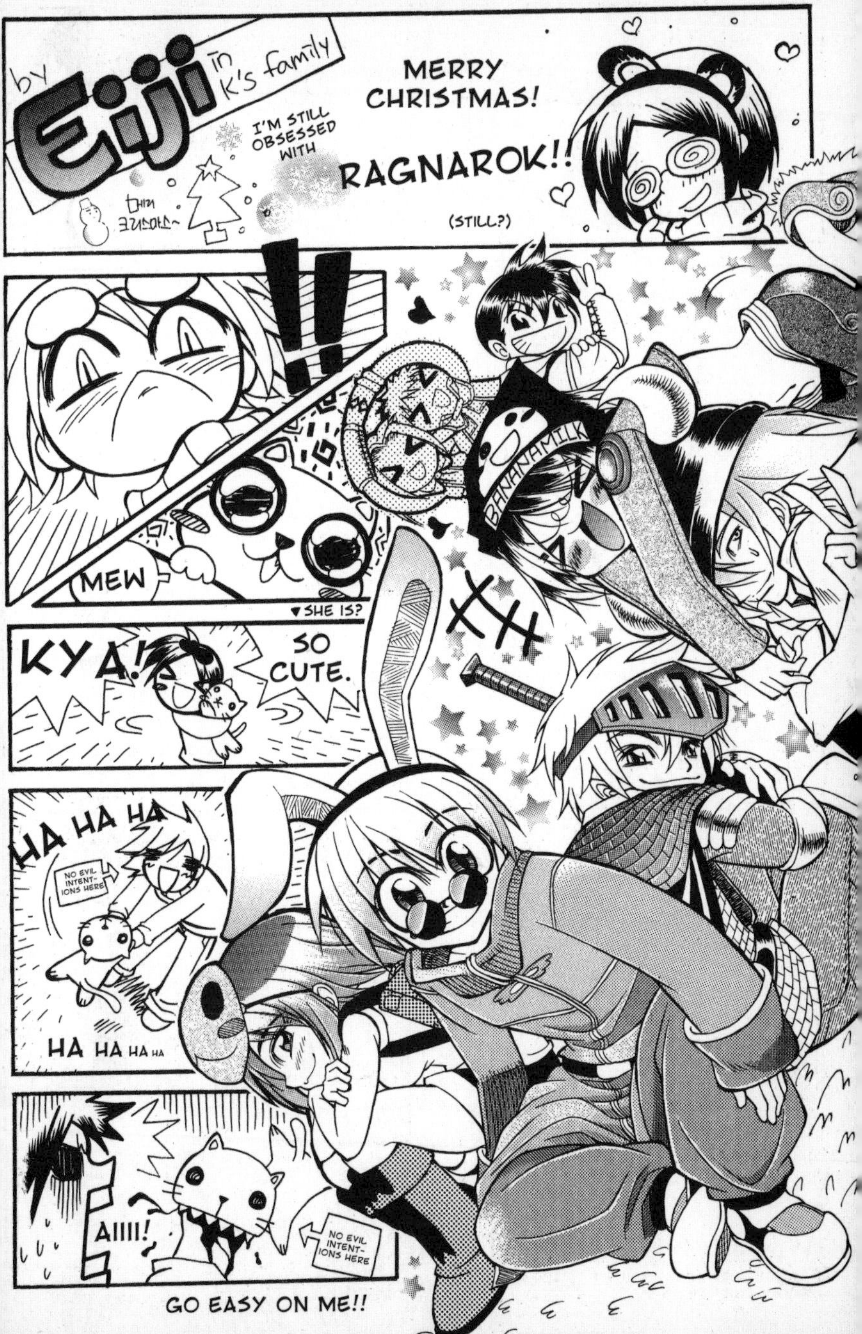
by Eiji in K's family
MERRY CHRISTMAS!
I'M STILL OBSESSED WITH
RAGNAROK!!
메리 크리스마스~
(STILL?)
!!
BANANAMILK
MEW
♥SHE IS?
KYA!
SO CUTE.
HA HA HA
NO EVIL INTENTIONS HERE
HA HA HA HA
AIIII!
NO EVIL INTENTIONS HERE
GO EASY ON ME!!

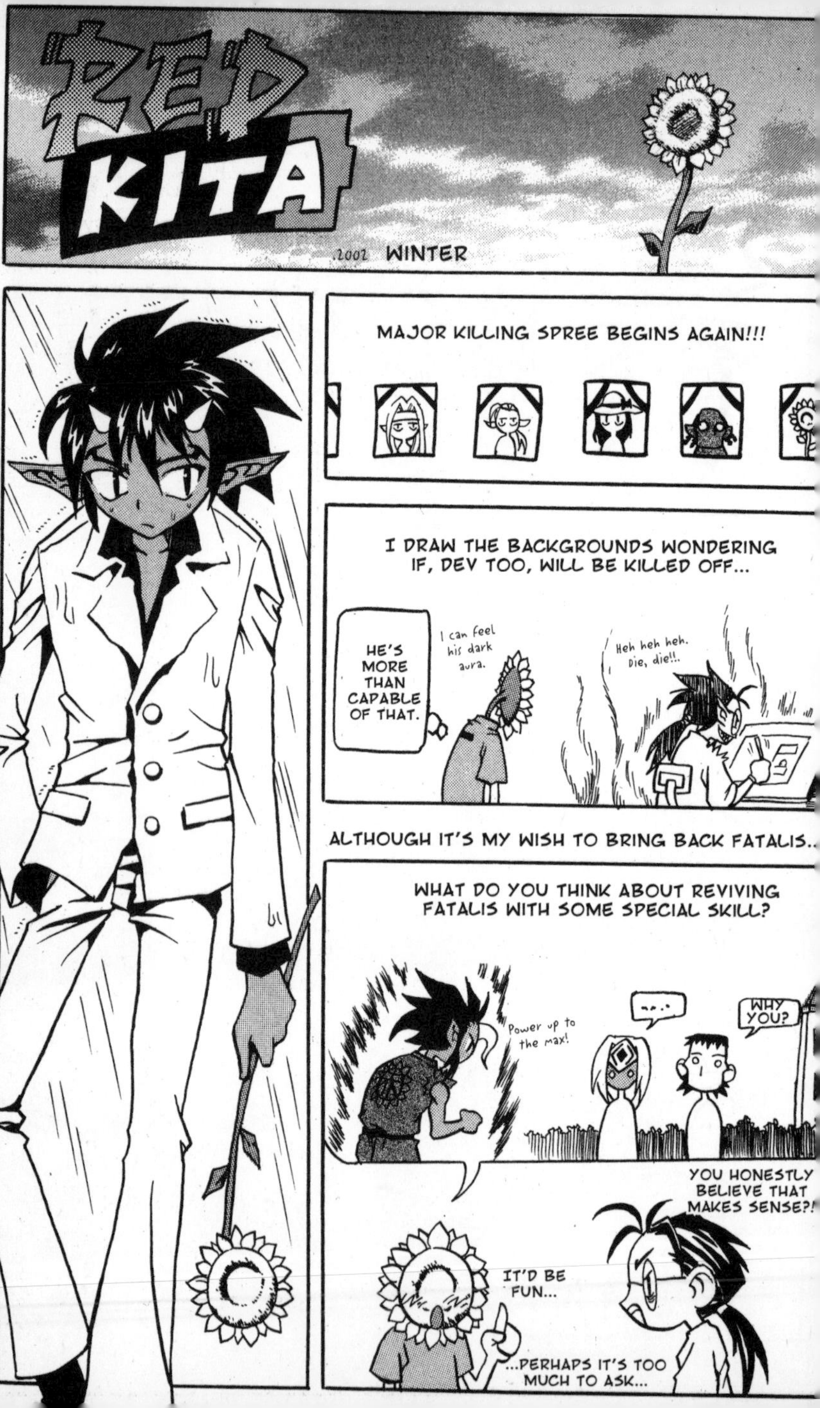
RED KITA
2002 WINTER
MAJOR KILLING SPREE BEGINS AGAIN!!!
I DRAW THE BACKGROUNDS WONDERING IF, DEV TOO, WILL BE KILLED OFF...
HE'S MORE THAN CAPABLE OF THAT.
I can feel his dark aura.
Heh heh heh. Die, die!!
ALTHOUGH IT'S MY WISH TO BRING BACK FATALIS...
WHAT DO YOU THINK ABOUT REVIVING FATALIS WITH SOME SPECIAL SKILL?
Power up to the max!
WHY YOU?
YOU HONESTLY BELIEVE THAT MAKES SENSE?!
IT'D BE FUN...
...PERHAPS IT'S TOO MUCH TO ASK...

THE MANGA ARTIST'S STUDIO

망가져 화실

I WANNA PLAY

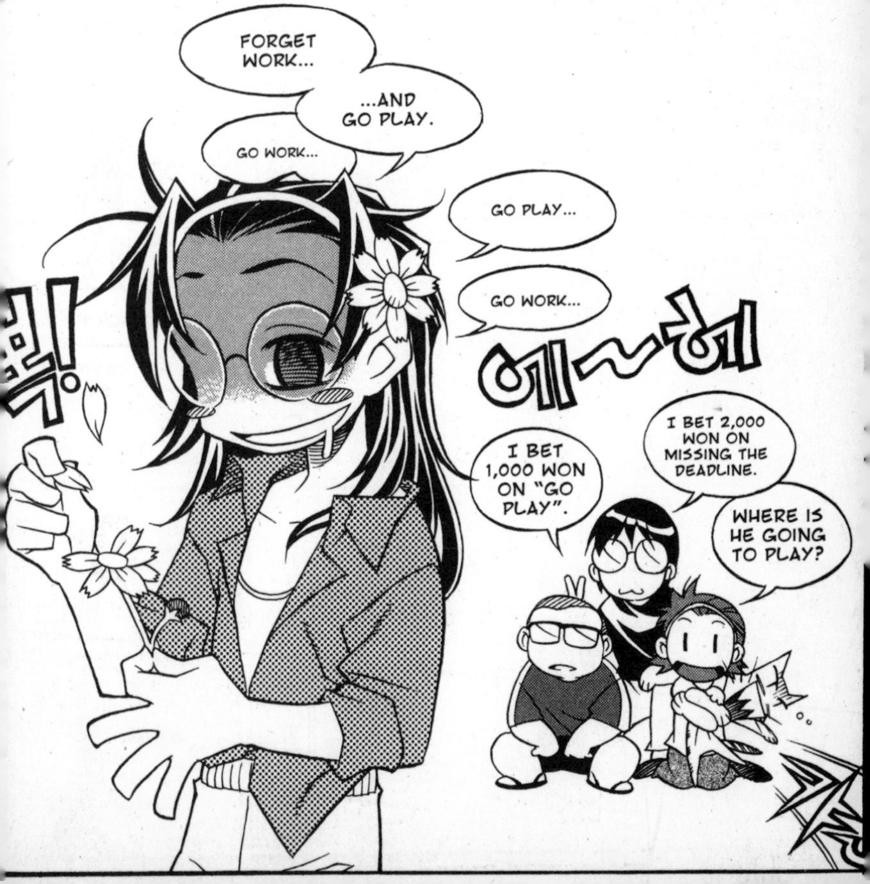
FORGET WORK...
...AND GO PLAY.
GO WORK...
GO PLAY...
GO WORK...
에~헤
I BET 1,000 WON ON "GO PLAY".
I BET 2,000 WON ON MISSING THE DEADLINE.
WHERE IS HE GOING TO PLAY?

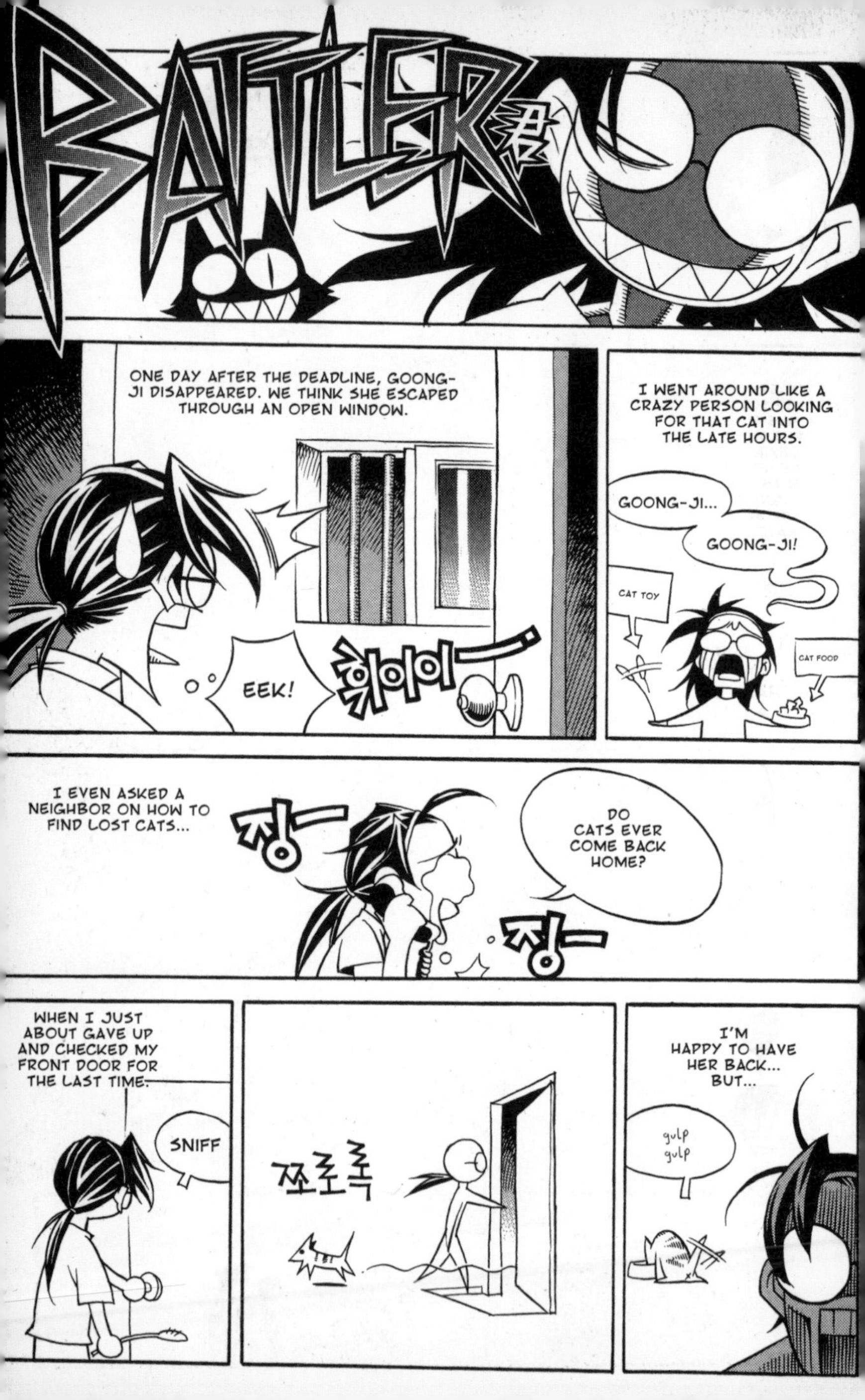
BATTLER君
ONE DAY AFTER THE DEADLINE, GOONG-JI DISAPPEARED. WE THINK SHE ESCAPED THROUGH AN OPEN WINDOW.
EEK!
휘이이—
I WENT AROUND LIKE A CRAZY PERSON LOOKING FOR THAT CAT INTO THE LATE HOURS.
GOONG-JI...
GOONG-JI!
CAT TOY
CAT FOOD
I EVEN ASKED A NEIGHBOR ON HOW TO FIND LOST CATS...
징—
DO CATS EVER COME BACK HOME?
징—
WHEN I JUST ABOUT GAVE UP AND CHECKED MY FRONT DOOR FOR THE LAST TIME.
SNIFF
쪼르륵
I'M HAPPY TO HAVE HER BACK... BUT...
gulp
gulp

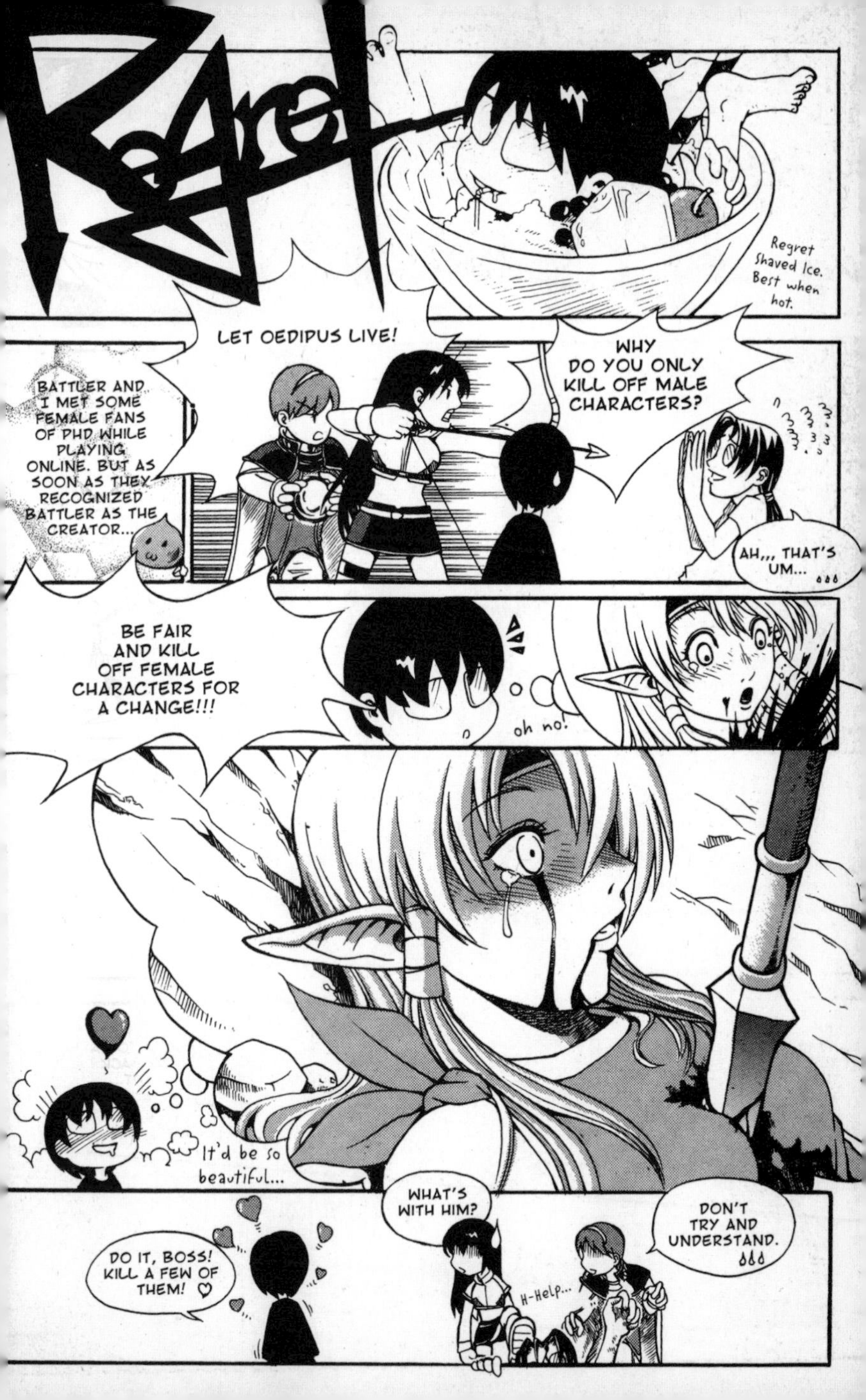
Regret
Regret Shaved Ice. Best when hot.
LET OEDIPUS LIVE!
BATTLER AND I MET SOME FEMALE FANS OF PHD WHILE PLAYING ONLINE. BUT AS SOON AS THEY RECOGNIZED BATTLER AS THE CREATOR...
WHY DO YOU ONLY KILL OFF MALE CHARACTERS?
AH,,, THAT'S UM...
BE FAIR AND KILL OFF FEMALE CHARACTERS FOR A CHANGE!!!
oh no!
It'd be so beautiful...
WHAT'S WITH HIM?
DON'T TRY AND UNDERSTAND.
DO IT, BOSS! KILL A FEW OF THEM!
H-Help...

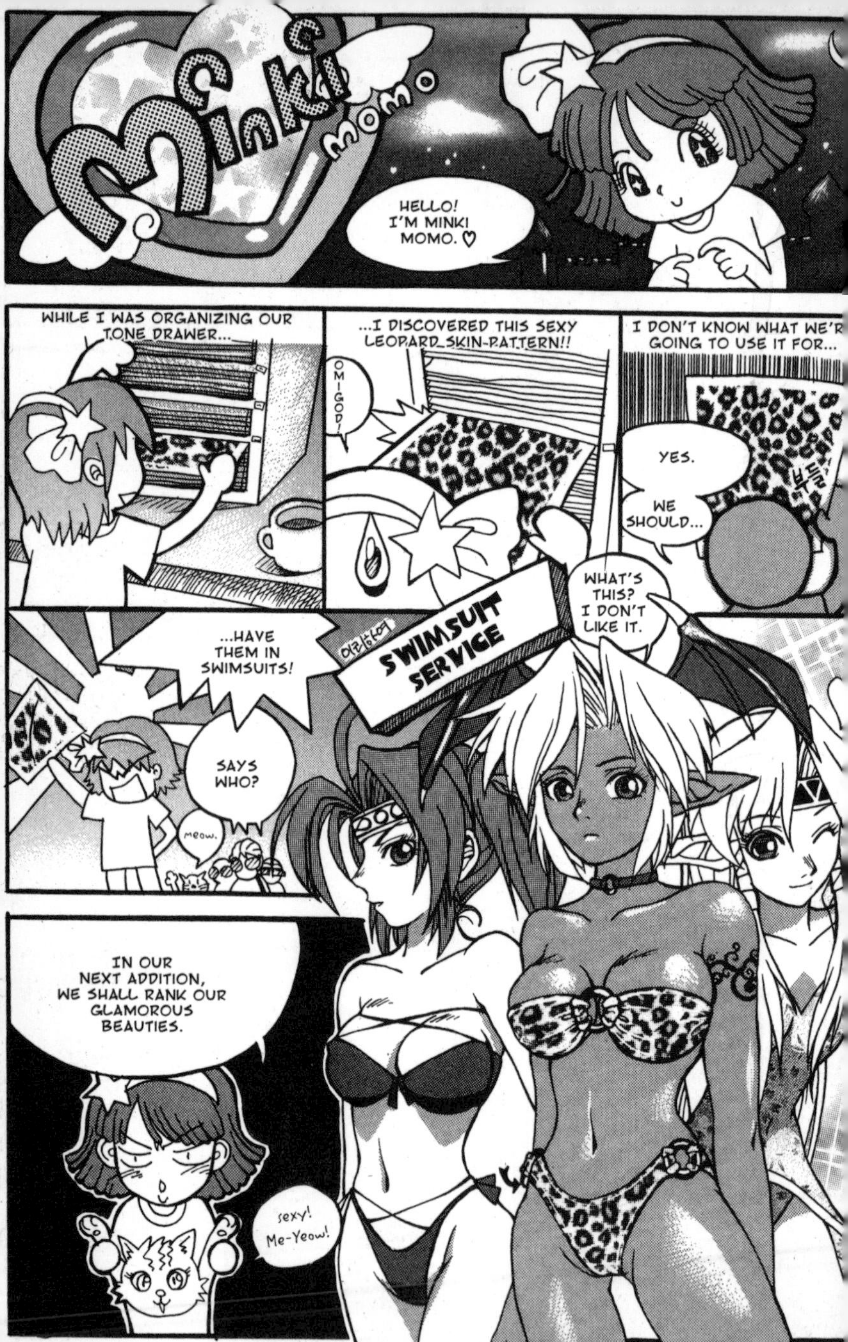

Minki momo
HELLO! I'M MINKI MOMO. ♡
WHILE I WAS ORGANIZING OUR TONE DRAWER...
...I DISCOVERED THIS SEXY LEOPARD-SKIN-PATTERN!!
OMIGOD!
I DON'T KNOW WHAT WE'R
GOING TO USE IT FOR...
YES.
WE SHOULD...
...HAVE THEM IN SWIMSUITS!
SWIMSUIT SERVICE
WHAT'S THIS? I DON'T LIKE IT.
SAYS WHO?
meow.
IN OUR NEXT ADDITION, WE SHALL RANK OUR GLAMOROUS BEAUTIES.
sexy! Me-Yeow!

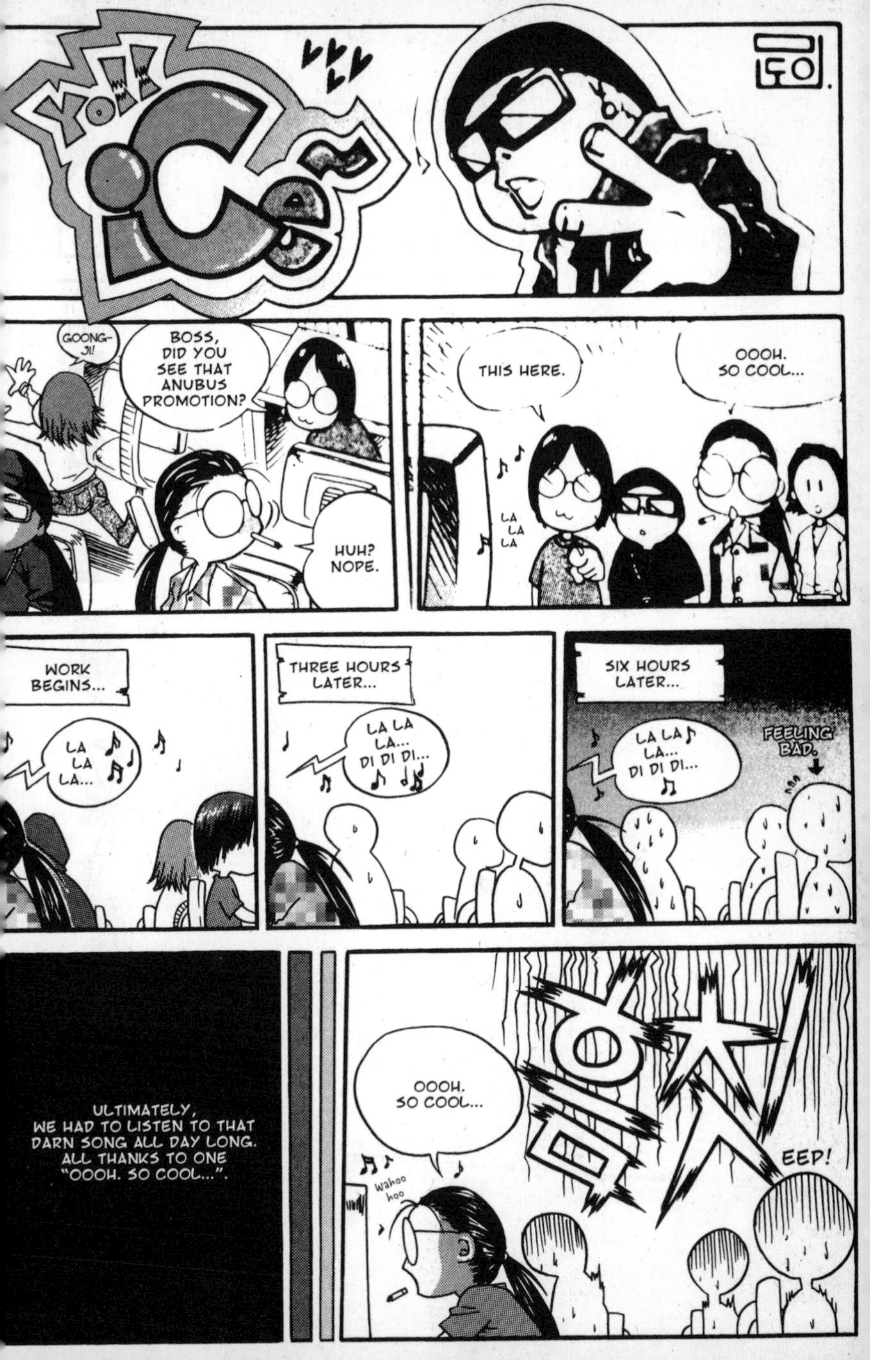

YO! ICE~
GOONG-JI!
BOSS, DID YOU SEE THAT ANUBUS PROMOTION?
HUH? NOPE.
THIS HERE.
LA LA LA
OOOH. SO COOL...
WORK BEGINS...
LA LA LA...
THREE HOURS LATER...
LA LA LA... DI DI DI...
SIX HOURS LATER...
LA LA LA... DI DI DI...
FEELING BAD.
ULTIMATELY, WE HAD TO LISTEN TO THAT DARN SONG ALL DAY LONG. ALL THANKS TO ONE "OOOH. SO COOL...".
OOOH. SO COOL...
Wahoo hoo
EEP!

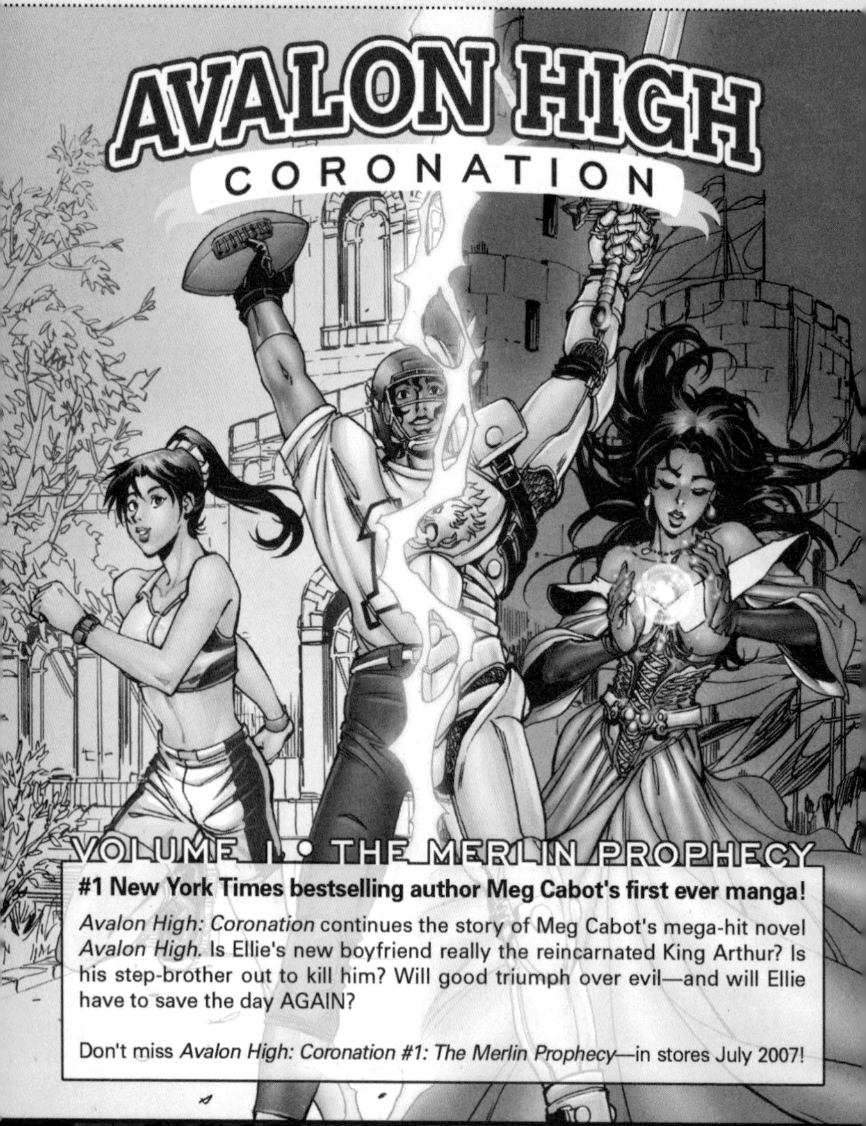
AVALON HIGH
CORONATION
VOLUME 1 • THE MERLIN PROPHECY
#1 New York Times bestselling author Meg Cabot's first ever manga!
Avalon High: Coronation continues the story of Meg Cabot's mega-hit novel Avalon High. Is Ellie's new boyfriend really the reincarnated King Arthur? Is his step-brother out to kill him? Will good triumph over evil—and will Ellie have to save the day AGAIN?
Don't miss Avalon High: Coronation #1: The Merlin Prophecy—in stores July 2007!

KING OF THORN

YUJI IWAHARA

ACTION

OT OLDER TEEN AGE 16+

WARNING: Virus outbreak!

Kasumi and her sister, Shizuku, are infected with the fatal Medusa virus. There is no cure, but Kasumi is selected to go into a cryogenic freezer until a cure is found. But when Kasumi awakens, she must struggle to survive in a treacherous world if she hopes to discover what happened to her sister.

From Yuji Iwahara, the creator of the popular *Chikyu Misaki* and *Koudelka*.

© YUJI IWAHARA

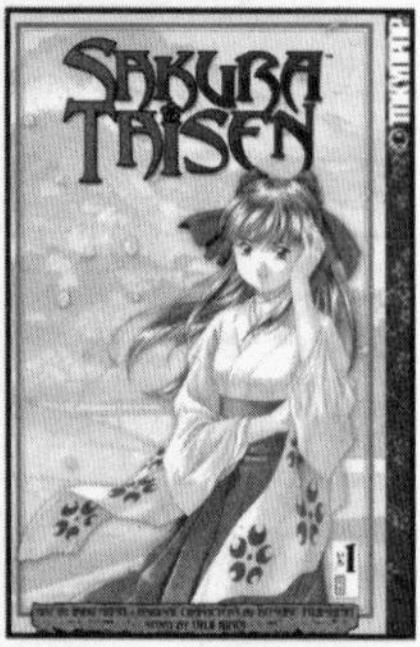
SAKURA TAISEN
TOKYOPOP

ACTION T TEEN AGE 13+

SAKURA TAISEN

BY OHJI HIROI, IKKU MASA AND KOSUKE FUJISHIMA

I really, really like this series. I'm a sucker for steampunk-type stories, and 1920s Japanese fashion, and throw in demon invaders, robot battles and references to Japanese popular theater? Sold! There's lots of fun tidbits for the clever reader to pick up in this series (all the characters have flower names, for one, and the fact that all the Floral Assault divisions are named after branches of the Takarazuka Review, Japan's sensational all-female theater troupe!), but the consistently stylish and clean art will appeal even to the most casual fan.

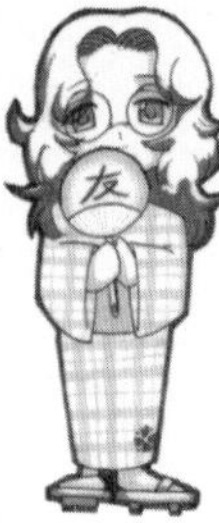

~Lillian Diaz-Przybyl, Editor

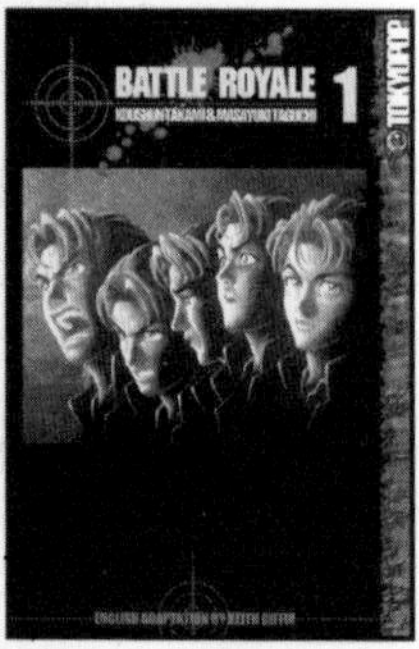
BATTLE ROYALE 1
TOKYOPOP

ACTION M MATURE AGES 18+

BATTLE ROYALE

BY KOUSHUN TAKAMI AND MASAYUKI TAGUCHI

As far as cautionary tales go, you couldn't get any timelier than *Battle Royale*. Telling the bleak story of a class of middle school students who are forced to fight each other to the death on national television, Koushun Takami and Masayuki Taguchi have created a dark satire that's sickening, yet undeniably exciting as well. And if we have that reaction reading it, it becomes alarmingly clear how the students could so easily be swayed into doing it.

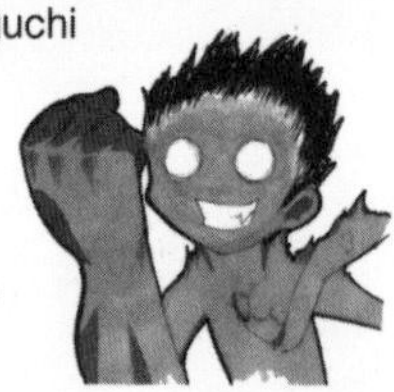

~Tim Beedle, Editor